Iran and the CIA

Iran and the CIA
The Fall of Mosaddeq Revisited

Darioush Bayandor

© Darioush Bayandor 2010

All rights reserved. No reproduction, copy or transmission of this publication may be made without written permission.

No portion of this publication may be reproduced, copied or transmitted save with written permission or in accordance with the provisions of the Copyright, Designs and Patents Act 1988, or under the terms of any licence permitting limited copying issued by the Copyright Licensing Agency, Saffron House, 6-10 Kirby Street, London EC1N 8TS.

Any person who does any unauthorized act in relation to this publication may be liable to criminal prosecution and civil claims for damages.

The author has asserted his right to be identified as the author of this work in accordance with the Copyright, Designs and Patents Act 1988.

First published 2010 by
PALGRAVE MACMILLAN

Palgrave Macmillan in the UK is an imprint of Macmillan Publishers Limited, registered in England, company number 785998, of Houndmills, Basingstoke, Hampshire RG21 6XS.

Palgrave Macmillan in the US is a division of St Martin's Press LLC, 175 Fifth Avenue, New York, NY 10010.

Palgrave Macmillan is the global academic imprint of the above companies and has companies and representatives throughout the world.

Palgrave® and Macmillan® are registered trademarks in the United States, the United Kingdom, Europe and other countries.

ISBN-13: 978–0–230–57927–9 hardback

This book is printed on paper suitable for recycling and made from fully managed and sustained forest sources. Logging, pulping and manufacturing processes are expected to conform to the environmental regulations of the country of origin.

A catalogue record for this book is available from the British Library.

A catalog record for this book is available from the Library of Congress.

10 9 8 7 6 5 4 3 2
19 18 17 16 15 14 13 12 11 10

Printed and bound in Great Britain by
CPI Antony Rowe, Chippenham and Eastbourne

*For my grandchildren Max, Tara, Angelika and Arthur;
hoping this book may serve them as a bridge to their roots*

History, unresolved, can be a heavy weight
　　　　　President Barack Obama

Contents

List of Illustrations	x
Acknowledgements	xii
Preface	xiv

Introduction	1
How the story evolved	3
How did a myth about the CIA role develop and prevail?	5
Why did the CIA files remain unclassified?	9

1 The Context	11
Foreign influence as a prime mover in Iranian politics	12
The *Tudeh* Party	13
The Azerbaijan Crisis, 1945–46	14
Shah Mohammad-Reza Pahlavi	16
The *Ulama* as a socio-political force	18
Ayatollah Seyyed Abol'qassem Kashani: the precursor of clerical activism	20
Razmara: prelude to the oil nationalization crisis	22

2 The Advent of Mosaddeq and the Oil Crisis	27
The rise of the National Front	27
The nomination of Mosaddeq	29
Doctor Mohammad Mosaddeq: a sketch	31
The initial British reaction to oil nationalization	33
The early American attitude to the oil dispute	35
Political line-ups in Tehran	39
Early conduct of the oil dispute	40
The British complaint to the Security Council	43
The Washington oil talks	44
The World Bank proposal	48
Early forebodings	50

3 Mosaddeq's Second Government, July 1952 to August 1953 — 52

The Qavam hiatus and the *Siy'e Tyr* popular uprising (21 July 1952) — 54
Rift among Mosaddeq supporters — 57
A wedge to break the oil log-jam: the Truman-Churchill joint offer — 59
Mosaddeq's reforms and the theory of legitimacy — 62
The British two-pronged strategy: subversion and engagement — 64
  The covert track — 65
  The engagement track — 68
Diplomatic relations with Britain are broken off — 69
Final attempts to resolve the oil dispute — 70
A day forgotten in the Iranian collective memory — 72

4 The Downslide — 74

The clash at the helm; the February 1953 jumble — 75
The Grand Ayatollah Boroujerdi: a retrospective sketch — 78
General Fazlollah Zahedi — 81
Internal conspiracies — 82
  The abduction of the police chief — 84
The link-up: TPAJAX and the internal cabal — 84
The summer of all dangers — 87
The taming of the Shah — 89
The failure of the TPAJAX *coup* — 94

5 The Downfall — 98

The gathering storm, 16–18 August 1953 — 99
The backlash: events leading to the fall of Mosaddeq on 19 August — 105
  Monitoring by the US Embassy — 110
  The final hours — 111
  The military factor in the fall of Mosaddeq — 113
  TPAJAX military planning and the role of Iranian officers — 115

6 The Anatomy of 19 August — 118

CIA station activism in Tehran, 16–19 August — 123
The role of Iranian agents — 125
Surprise in Washington — 131
Ambassador Henderson's last meeting with Mosaddeq — 133
The CIA money — 136

	An orphan British secret document	140
	Analysis of the British secret document	141
	A *coup d'état*, a popular uprising or something else?	144
7	**Where Did the Spark Come From?**	**147**
	The missing link: the Boroujerdi factor	150
8	**Summary and Conclusions**	**155**
	Power structure and internal dynamics in the early 1950s	155
	Mosaddeq's rule	158
	The handling of the oil crisis and stalemate	161
	External and internal conspiracies	162
	The TPAJAX *coup* and its aftermath	165
	The involvement of *ulama*	172
	The causes of Mosaddeq's defeat	173

Notes 176

Direct Sources of the Study 234

Index 238

List of Illustrations

1	Mohammad-Reza Pahlavi, Shah of Iran (1941–79)	17
2	Ayatollah Seyyed Abol'qassem Kashani	20
3	Ayatollah Kashani flanked by Seyyed Navvab-Safavi, the leader of *Fadā'iān Islam* terrorist group	22
4	Prime Minister Razmara, shortly before his assassination in March 1951	24
5	Doctor Mosaddeq's first Cabinet. General Fazlollah Zahedi as Minister of the Interior is second from the left	31
6	Mosaddeq's likeness on the cover of *TIME* Magazine, 4 June 1951	32
7	Mosaddeq being greeted by Ambassador Henry Grady (left) on arrival in New York, October 1951. Mosaddeq's son and personal physician Dr Qolam-Hossein Mosaddeq is looking on	38
8	Harriman's visit to Tehran in August 1951	42
9	Mosaddeq being helped by the UN Secretary-General Trygve Lie to his seat at the Security Council	44
10	Mosaddeq talking to Under-Secretary George McGhee	45
11	Mosaddeq being greeted at the White House by President Truman	47
12	Mosaddeq on the cover of *TIME* Magazine, 7 January 1952, designating him as 'Man of the Year' for 1951	52
13	Ahmad Qavam	55
14	Grand Ayatollah Seyyed Mohammad-Hossein Boroujerdi	79
15	General Fazlollah Zahedi as he emerged from his hideout on 19 August 1953	81
16	Court Minister Hossein Ala	83
17	Princess Ashraf Pahlavi, the Shah's twin-sister, April 1951	91
18	Brigadier-General Norman Schwarzkopf	92
19	Kermit (Kim) Roosevelt, as an oil executive in the 1960s	93
20	Under-Secretary of State (General) Walter Bedell Smith	97
21	The Shah and Queen Soraya arriving in Rome, 18 August, 1953	100

22	Crowds drag down Reza Shah's statue from Shah-Reza Square, 17 August, 1953	102
23	Interior Minister Dr Golam'hossein Sadiqi arriving at Mosaddeq's house in the early afternoon of 19 August as described in his memoirs	109
24	Mosaddeq waving from his car	112
25	General Zahedi and close associates shortly after Mosaddeq's downfall in 1953	113
26	Kim Roosevelt in his guise of the gentleman-spy in the late 1940s	123
27	Asadolloh Rashidian, successful businessman, in the early 1960s	126
28	A scene from a well-groomed *Tudeh* Party procession in Tehran, *c.* 1951	127
29	*Tudeh* boss Noreddin Kianouri in a pose in the early 1980s	129
30	Loy Henderson US Ambassador in Tehran 1951–55	134
31	A scene from the 19 August pro-Shah demonstrations in Tehran	139
32	A sparse group of pro-Shah demonstrators fraternizing with the military on 19 August while ordinary people applaud from the balconies of their houses	148

Acknowledgements

This project started off as an extension of academic debates and private discussions in inner Iranian circles. It was expanded to its current form thanks to encouragement from many friends and scholars who read the earlier drafts. My special thanks go to Professor Sharam Chubin, Director of Studies, Geneva Centre for Security Policy, and to Charlie Naas, the former State Department Director for Iran and Chargé d'Affaires in Tehran, for their encouragement and endorsing the publication of this book. Professor Houshang Nahavani, former rector, board- director and professor in Tehran and Paris, provided useful comments and encouragement. Professor Mark Gasiorowski, who should be regarded as the doyen of historians of this chapter of Iran's history, was kind enough to patiently read an early draft and make comments, maintaining, needless to say, his position as reflected in his extensive and valuable writings. I wish also to thank Professor Ervand Abrahamian of Baruch College (CUNY) who, in spite of reservations on certain points, recommended its publication. Karim Sadjadpour of Carnegie Endowment was most generous with his time, encouragement and support.

Ardeshir Zahedi, a key player in the events leading to the fall of Mosaddeq – later the Shah's foreign minister, ambassador to London and twice to Washington – was most generous with his time, granting me interviews and some photos from his personal collection for which I am most grateful. Farhad Shirzad of IBEX publishing house in Washington kindly authorized reproduction of some historical photos from the Zahedi memoirs he published in Persian in 2006; also helpful in this respect was Farrokh Derakhshani from the Agha Khan Foundation in Geneva. My thanks also go to Stephen Langlie who, as an eyewitness to the events of August 1953, shared his insights as well as a valuable photo from his personal collections. The Mosaddeq Foundation Library in Geneva enabled me to have ready access to invaluable material and sources, especially in the Persian language. I wish to address a warm word of thanks to its distinguished founder/director Professor Majid Bayat. The Harry S. Truman Presidential Library kindly authorized publication of a number of archive photos from Doctor Mosaddeq's trip to New York and Washington in October–November 1951. I am also indebted to Chelsea Millner of the Eisenhower Presidential Library for her help.

Friends and former colleagues Iraj Amini, Jamshid Anvar, Said Amirdivani, Bijan Dolatabadi, Dr Ahmad Minai, Parviz Mohajer, Ali Seirafi and Dr Ahmad Tehrani read the earlier drafts of this book and provided useful comments and much encouragement. Last but not least, Anandi Rasanayagam, a colleague from my UN days and himself author of a marvellous book on Afghanistan, and Jean Swoyer, a veteran of the American Foreign Service, provided valuable editorial advice having read selected chapters of the manuscript. I am indebted to them both.

Preface

This book is an attempt to canvass the 27-month-long premiership of Doctor Mohammad Mosaddeq in a dispassionate effort to shed further light on the events which led to his downfall on 19 August 1953. The event no doubt changed the destiny of Iran and may have had an impact on the broader scheme of things on the world scene. It surely created a political fault-line that has divided Iranians for several generations. For reasons elaborated in the Introduction, its searing effects have not been effaced. Further, judging by its frequent evocation in the media and the volume of academic and pseudo-academic publications, the subject has lost little of its political relevance or intellectual allure. Indeed, few episodes in Middle East contemporary history have been the subject of such an incisive probe. A first question, then, is why to rewrite that chapter of history?

Writing in 2003 for a scholarly work on the downfall of Mosaddeq, a renowned American historian, Professor William Roger Louis, started his chapter with a thoughtful caveat: The overthrow of the Mosaddeq government in August 1953, he wrote: 'is a subject that invites periodic reassessment... Greater distance and greater access to archive material encourage a more dispassionate view of a subject *still riddled with ideological assumptions*' (emphasis is mine).[1]

When in the winter of 2006 I began preparing the rudiments of the present volume, I was animated in part by the same conviction. As an avid student of Iran's contemporary history, I was broadly familiar with the literature on the Mosaddeq era. A perception of foul play causing his overthrow on 19 August 1953 had grown overwhelming, especially in the years following the publication in 1979 of a book authored by Kermit (Kim) Roosevelt, who by then was already reputed to have engineered the final blow against the Mosaddeq government.[2]

Spurred by his 'revelations', and no doubt by the demise of the imperial regime in Iran, a large volume of books, articles and treatises emerged in the following two and a half decades. Scholarship in the United States and Britain was based on extensive and meritorious research, including interviews with former CIA and SIS/MI6 agents involved in the *coup* plan in 1953. Memoirs published in Iran and elsewhere by the main protagonists or side-players have also enriched the literature. This impressive body of scholarship, however, had not, to my mind, escaped the ravages of ideologically-based assumptions. Nor, as was also noted by Professor Louis, have all Iran files been released in spite of the lapse of well over half a century.

In 2000, the leak of a secret CIA internal history to *The New York Times* produced the first authoritative account of the Agency's operations in Iran during 1953.[3] The document, written only a year after the event, was in great part concerned with the operation TPAJAX, a plot which culminated in a failed *coup* attempt against Mosaddeq in the late hours of 15 August 1953. The internal history's coverage of the events subsequent to that attempt – and their relation to activities carried out by the CIA Station in Tehran – is decidedly less limpid. The CIA internal history, in effect, remains inconclusive, even reticent, about the nexus between the action taken by CIA operatives in Tehran and the happenings that resulted in the collapse of the Mosaddeq government on 19 August. This is in spite of the fact that, perforce, the CIA document reflects debriefings by the field operatives, notably Kim Roosevelt. Yet an uninitiated reader could easily misconstrue the report as an endorsement of what Roosevelt later came to claim.

To my incredulous mind, something troubling was amiss. The narrative in Roosevelt's *Countercoup* had something of the unreal in its main thrust, not far from screen sagas where a hero single-handedly (or almost) manages to beat back incredible odds in a hostile environment. In this case, the American hero manages to turn around an initial setback and snatch victory from the jaws of defeat in less than 48 hours. On the flipside, the claim by Shah Mohammad Reza Pahlavi and his regime to the effect that the fall of Mosaddeq was the backwash of a spontaneous popular uprising (*Qīām'e Melli*) was hardly convincing.

What was the missing link in the conundrum that was the fall of Mosaddeq? That was the challenge I set out to explore. This book is the result of that endeavour. Substantive evidence and analyses on the main theme are laid out in Chapters 5, 6 and 7, while the first four chapters provide a schematic description of the background against which the dramatic events of August 1953 unfolded. The findings of the study are recapitulated in the Conclusions. The book is primarily based on the US archive documents, 1946–53, commonly abbreviated as FRUS, backed by the already tapped British Foreign Office material, covering the period up to the break-off of diplomatic relations between Iran and Britain in October 1952. The CIA internal history has been analysed and drawn on. A British top-secret report (dated 2 September 1953), which to this date, to the best of my knowledge, has gone unnoticed in history books of this episode, is printed in the State Department's declassified Iran files (FRUS 1952–1954, Volume X). Produced barely two weeks after the fall of Mosaddeq, the eight-page document is fully analysed in Chapter six. Other than material from governmental sources, memoirs and recollections of major protagonists – Mosaddeq, Kermit Roosevelt, and Ardeshir Zahedi – and some lesser actors like Qolam-Hossein Sadiqi, Mozaffar Baqa'ei, Norredin Kianouri, Christopher Woodhouse, Samuel Falle, and others – have also been thoroughly examined. As usually is the case with memoirs, they represent a personal baggage, a mix of facts, memory lapses or deliberate spins, leaving it to the historian to sift through facts and factoids. An effort to this effect has been made through cross-checking the information conveyed. Press coverage by *The New York Times* and *Time*, as well as titbits from the Iranian press and *Rouzshomari* (Iranian daily news archive), and also Persian language literature have been surveyed. Where conclusions are drawn from non-archival sources, they have invariably been cross-checked for corroborating evidence. The career paths, character traits and mannerisms of the main protagonists are sketched-out to the extent that these elements were believed to have influenced the events.

The narrative is backed up with extensive annotations in reference notes which provide peripheral information on the specific topics treated and the background against which the interplay of actors can better be understood. They should be considered as an adjunct to the narrative, kept separate only to maintain the flow of the main text yet essential for a better understanding of the period and the political context in which events unfolded.

When it comes to the Iranian protagonists of the drama, I have remained within the strict confines of evidence and archive. No one is condemned or vindicated. The primary task of the historian is to produce data and conduct probes; there are no verdicts, only findings. Those of this study, at any event, are unlikely to satisfy *unconditional* supporters of any of the national or religious figures of the time. Yet one single observation about Mosaddeq might be deemed in order.

Mosaddeq as a historical persona need not be idolized. He is justly remembered as the man who shed the shackles of the neo-colonialist hold over Iran's main source of livelihood, the oil industries. He is also in the vanguard of third-world awakening in the post-Second World War period. Yet Mosaddeq was not infallible; his strategic errors contributed to the ripening of cumulative factors which brought about his downfall. This reality should not prevent Iranians from proudly cherishing his memory and lauding his historical accomplishments.

A word about transliteration of Persian

The guideline in the *Chicago Manual*, Edition 14, has been flexibly applied to all Persian words, exception being made for diacriticals in proper names. Transliterations, in general, are based on the Persian pronunciation of the names of Arab origin (Mohammad rather than Muhammad; Hossein rather than Hussein); composite proper names have been separated by a hyphen (Mohammad-Hossein); while in cases of fusion of two elements in a single proper name, the apostrophe (') is used to separate the components (Abol'qassem, rather than Abol-Qassem; Abdol'hossein rather than Abdol-Hossein). The same punctuation mark, combined with the letter (e), is used for vocal liaisons between the words where applicable, (Khāterāt'e Avalīn Sepahbod'e Iran, rather than Khāterāt-i Avalīn Sepahbod-i Iran). Finally, ('ei) rather than (i) is used for endings of such names as Tabataba'ei or Baqa'ei.

Darioush Bayandor

Introduction

Well over half a century after the fall of the government of Dr Mohammad Mosaddeq on 19 August 1953, the topic has not ceased to stir interest among historians or arouse passion in Iranian circles. The event has been described by many in Iran and abroad as a CIA-inspired *coup* which extinguished national aspirations for democracy and economic emancipation; others have hailed the event as a popular uprising (*Qiām'e Melli*) that saved the country from chaos and a drift towards communism – 19 August 1953 thus remains a fault-line that divides Iranians. Yet none of the two assumptions, in absolute, stand the test of a vigorous probe. The present volume is an attempt in hindsight to embark on such a probe, exploring new angles with the help of data that, while in public domain, has not been fully tapped.

Why, despite cataclysmic events that followed the Islamic revolution (1978–79), has the overthrow of Mosaddeq not faded in collective memory? To what could this enduring quality be attributed? The answer may lie in the fact that two flawed, yet plausible assumptions link that historical episode to present-day events. These assumptions have become a part of the conventional wisdom on Iran and its relations with the United States. They have come to take on aspects of a credo or dogma.

The first assumption, to which we alluded above and shall dwell on at length in this book, maintains that the eviction of Mosaddeq on 19 August 1953 resulted from a premeditated *coup d'état* planned, financed and executed jointly by the CIA and the British Secret Intelligence Service (SIS/MI6) as an integral part and extension of a plan code-named TPAJAX. To the extent that in this assessment internal factors are unaccounted for, the fall of Mosaddeq has become disconnected from its indigenous context and historically distorted. The ownership of this event was, at least implicitly, claimed by, and became a laurel added

1

to galloons of the CIA and MI6. We shall shortly discuss factors that entrenched that belief in public consciousness; what needs to be stressed here is the fact that the attendant sense of exaltation and bravado was short-lived. Following the Islamic revolution, the triumphalism associated with Kermit Roosevelt's *Countercoup: The Struggle for the Control of Iran* gradually waned. The fall of Mosaddeq became a sore point and a burden for anyone to claim credit for.

Following the US Embassy hostage crisis (November 1979–January 1981), a second dogma emerged. The manifest hostility of the Islamic regime under Ayatollah Khomeini towards the United States was traced back and blamed on the American cabal in August 1953. The sense of guilt over the removal of Doctor Mosaddeq, stereotyped as 'the popular and democratically-elected prime minister of Iran', became a motive for self-deprecation and remorse. Yet, as will be seen in the main body of this study, the core group in the Islamic revolution was in effect of direct ideological lineage to the clerics who played a key part in Mosaddeq's downfall on 19 August 1953. By their own admission, it was not to Mosaddeq, but to his sworn enemies that leaders of the Islamic republic profess allegiance.[1] After the Islamic Revolution the most ferocious foes of Mosaddeq, namely Ayatollah Kashani and the *Fadā'iān Islam* leader, Navvab-Safavi, were idolized and became icons of the new order.

The fallacy, however, endured. Liberal opinion in America had long been critical of the privileged relationship between the United States and the Shah; it now had a platform to assail that geostrategic partnership as ill-conceived and myopic. These relations had developed over 25 years, spanning six administrations. Yet fingers were pointed at two landmarks: The *coup d'état* planned and executed by the Eisenhower administration and the *Nixon doctrine*, which had given the partnership its most extravagant expression.[2]

A range of academic works appeared in America, encompassing accounts of the overthrow, roots of the Islamic revolution or the failure of American policy in Iran. Invariably they were based on extensive research and contained a wealth of valuable information; but the flawed assumptions referred to above cast a shadow over most.[3] In some cases, reliance on recollections rather than on archives fostered falsehoods. In the less academic and sensational genre, the flawed assumptions were dramatized to a feverish pitch.[4] Uninformed opinion in Iran, the United States and elsewhere falls for factoids, flat-wrong data and interpretative accounts nourished by faulty premises in this latter category of publications. Stereotyping and simplification is equally prevalent in American media. A CBS/Historical Channel documentary entitled *Anatomy of a Coup: The CIA in Iran* is a case in point.[5] The logline of this widely diffused production reads: 'Documentary about how the stage for the 1979 Iranian revolution was set some thirty years before it happened. Recently discovered CIA documents reveal America's role in the military *coup* that ousted Iran's elected prime minister in favor of returning the Shah to power.' Irrespective of the merit or demerit of the production, the message it conveyed to its audiences typifies the fallacy of rooting the Islamic revolution in the fall of Mosaddeq.

In March 2000, in a conciliatory gesture to the Islamic Republic of Iran, Secretary Madeleine Albright acknowledged past American meddling in Iran saying: 'In 1953 the United States played a significant role in orchestrating the overthrow of Iran's popular Prime Minister, Mohammed Massadegh [sic]. The Eisenhower Administration believed its actions were justified for strategic reasons; but the *coup* was clearly a setback for Iran's political development. And it is easy to see now why many Iranians continue to resent this intervention by America in their internal affairs.'[6] Many informed Iranians, especially of older generation, surely do hold a grudge for that meddling, but few disagree that Secretary Albright sought to appease a regime which in its soul was an accomplice in the overthrow of Mosaddeq.

How the story evolved

In explaining factors that led to the actual downfall of Mosaddeq on 19 August 1953, this study ascribes a larger role to internal dynamics than is generally admitted in the current literature. To be sure, the focus on external covert action by Britain, later joined by the United States, is fully maintained just as the evolution of their open policies during the oil crisis is thoroughly examined. By March 1953, the Eisenhower administration had lost all hope of resolving the oil dispute with the Mosaddeq government. Against the backdrop of McCarthyism and the Korean War, the fear of a communist takeover of Iran had crept into the American psych and found a larger-than-life existence. This fear became the dominant factor in America's policy thinking under the Dallas brothers, John Foster and Allen, who as of 20 January 1953 were in charge of American overt and covert foreign conduct. The administration thus joined Britain in trying to oust Mosaddeq by underhanded means. He was to be replaced by a prime minister willing to crush the pro-Soviet leftist party, *Tudeh*, while resolving the oil dispute amicably. The plan, code-named TPAJAX, foresaw a propaganda campaign to be culminated in a military *coup*. In this plan, internal opposition forces, including Shiite high clerics were to play a pivotal role. The Shah's co-operation had been deemed all but indispensable.

The *internal opposition* was ominously real and willing to act as conditions grew ripe. The oil-less economy had strained the country's material and monetary resources and narrowed Mosaddeq's support base. The Shah and Mosaddeq were at loggerheads over their respective constitutional prerogatives. The pro-Soviet *Tudeh* Party was visibility getting stronger by day. A crescendo cacophony of anti-establishment noises, from leftist propaganda to an array of anarchist or irreverent tabloids, street demonstrations and daily mayhem, raised the spectre of chaos with the implied risk of regime change. Undaunted, Mosaddeq single-mindedly pursued a quixotic anti-colonial drive in parallel with sweeping internal reforms which budded dissension among interest groups. The politically active clerics were openly defying the government. Ayatollah Kashani was indeed the iconic figure of the opposition. The traditionally quietist and by far the more influential segment of the clerical establishment led by the Grand Ayatollah Boroujerdi in Qom also became alarmed. The purged senior military officers had formed another group of opposition activists. They were actively plotting to undermine the government. Some among them gravitated around General Fazlollah Zahedi, a former Mosaddeq cabinet minister who made no secret of his ambitions to replace him as prime minister.

The external and internal schemers, at a given juncture in summer of 1953, sought one another out and converged. The Shah, while at odds with his prime minister, was averse to cabalistic methods. He preferred normal parliamentary procedures as a means to dismiss the government. Faced with overwhelming Anglo-American pressures, he finally conceded. The TPAJAX *coup* plan was tried in the night of 15 to 16 August and failed. The Shah flew off in panic to Baghdad and Mosaddeq was in full control.

There is little discrepancy between the findings of this study and the current literature up to this point. Where things become fuzzy and disagreements surface is about the ensuing four days, which ended in a dramatic reversal of the situation and brought in its wake Mosaddeq's downfall. The conventional wisdom, as stated at the outset, is that CIA operatives, with the help of local MI6 agents, choreographed the move. This is in essence what Kermit Roosevelt, the CIA field manager of the TPAJAX, has claimed in his book *Countercoup*.

The present volume contests this account and maintains that Roosevelt cunningly twisted a near-fluke to his personal advantage. This travesty was made possible by the fact that during the intervening days, the CIA station in Tehran had not remained idle. It had provided certain support, encouragement and possibly guidance to General Zahedi's camp, which had remained defiant and willing to start an armed insurrection from a place outside the capital, a patently mid-term strategy. Thus, while preparing to leave the country, Roosevelt embarked on a flurry of activities, essentially support and backstopping, in cahoots with the Zahedi camp. Against such a background, it was not difficult to later attribute the end-result, namely the fall of Mosaddeq, to those activities, notwithstanding the reality that the Zahedi camp itself played only a marginal, if any, role in the ensuing events leading to the downfall. In *Countercoup* Roosevelt claimed that he specifically designated Wednesday 19 August as D-Day and went as far as claiming that contacts with military commanders in Esfahan and Kermanshah (respectively 400 and 600 kilometres from Tehran) were intended to get those garrisons to march to Tehran in the immediate term.[7] Chapters 5 and 6 of this volume are devoted to exposing all facets of this travesty.

How did a myth about the CIA role develop and prevail?

It has to be underscored that public perception of the CIA role long predates Roosevelt's account in the *Countercoup*. It is as such important to dwell on factors that went into the making of a CIA myth in Iran.

Rumours of the CIA involvement in the downfall of the Mosaddeq government did indeed spread on impact. In a lengthy commentary on 19 August, the Soviet Communist party mouthpiece, *Pravda*, had accused the United States of having engineered the earlier *coup* against Mosaddeq. *Pravda* had accurately implicated Brigadier General H. Norman Schwarzkopf, a one-time trainer of the Iranian Gendarmerie, as an American emissary carrying secret orders to Tehran.[8] This was before the news of the actual overthrow had reached Moscow. Radio Moscow was then quick to blame the fall of Mosaddeq on American plots. The *Tudeh* Party, which had been instrumental in foiling the TPAJAX putsch on 15 August, was now convinced that overthrow of Mosaddeq was a *coup de grâce* executed by Western intelligence services as part of a broader plan.

As early as 21 August the US Ambassador in Tehran, Loy Henderson, warned Washington of the 'widespread impression' that the US government had contributed with 'funds and technical assistance to overthrow of Mosadeq [sic]'. Henderson in effect refers to *Tudeh* and radio Moscow propaganda but also to public expressions of 'indebtedness' by associates of General Zahedi, the new prime minister, which are being 'given deeper meaning than intended'. Henderson reported that the Embassy was doing its utmost to remove that impression because, he went on presciently, 'It is not in [the] US interest over the long run to be given credit for internal political developments in Iran.'[9] In this dispatch, Henderson also referred to a trait in the Iranian political culture, according to which: 'Iranians [are] unable [to] believe [that] any important political development can take place in [the] country without foreigners being involved.' This valid observation must not be discounted as a factor in the formation of a deeply entrenched conviction among Iranians that the fall of Mosaddeq on 19 August resulted from the CIA intrigues and manipulations. The manner in which the oil dispute was eventually resolved must no doubt have reinforced the impression of American foul play. MajorAmerican oil companies indeed obtained the lion's share in a new oil consortium which was created to operate Iranian oil following the overthrow of Mosaddeq. The consortium had involved the participation of nearly all oil conglomerates in the production and marketing of the Iranian oil in a fifty-fifty revenue-sharing partnership with the state-owned National Iranian Oil Company (NIOC).

Over a year later, on 6 November 1954, an article appeared in *The Saturday Evening Post* as part of a series dubbed, 'The Mysterious Doings of the CIA.' The two journalists, Richard and Gladys Harkness, should have been credited for being among pioneers of investigative journalism in American media were it not for a strong probability that the CIA deliberately planted the articles as part of an Inside the Beltway promotional campaign.[10] The authors must have been tipped off by an insider, as their story roughly corresponded to the way the operation TPAJAX had evolved. However, as in all later accounts, the crucial link between this plan and the downfall on Wednesday 19 August had been botched. Many details were either fabricated or wrongly transmitted by the anonymous informer. Yet, coming as it did from an American source, the article was taken as gospel. A decade later Richard Cottam, in his acclaimed book *Nationalism in Iran*, reproduced the article *in extenso*, observing in passing that it had been widely read in Iran. Yet Cottam, himself an insider, vehemently criticized the article, not just for its inaccuracies but because it distorted what he then characterized as a '*spontaneous*' uprising.[11] It should be pointed out that Richard Cottam is arguably unique among American academics to have attributed the event to internal factors as opposed to CIA foul play. Much later in his academic career, however, Cottam made a turnabout and contradicted himself in a piece he published in a Quebec journal in 1980.[12]

Another signpost on the road to the CIA myth was *The Invisible Government*, also published in 1964 by two prominent journalists David Wise and Thomas .B. Ross.[13] The impact of this work on opinion in the United States was large. This was mainly because it covered the full breadth of the American intelligence gathering apparatus – the CIA being the centrepiece – and referred to other similar operations, including the *coup* against President Arbenz in Guatemala, stories related to the Bay of Pigs, Burma, Indonesia, Laos and Vietnam, and so on. The brief chapter on Iran (ibid., pp. 110–12) was again nothing but a rehashing of stories on the TPAJAX *coup*, which did not clarify its link with Mosaddeq's downfall on 19 August 1953. Iranian opposition activists abroad, however, took to this passage as yet another irrefutable proof.

The big landmark was yet to come. In 1979 Kermit Roosevelt created a sensation by publishing *Countercoup: The Struggle for the Control of Iran*. We just outlined the essence of what he had claimed in that book. The legend was now crystallized. Roosevelt had left the CIA in 1958 to become an oil executive with Gulf Oil. In the 1970s he was involved in corporate consultancies and was reputed to be on the Iranian government payroll as well as Northrop's. Given these sinecures, he was not about to burn his bridges with the Shah. For publication of his memoirs he is known to have tried, as of 1976, to obtain the Shah's clearance. According to the diaries of the ex-Court Minister, Asadollah Alam, the Shah reacted blandly to the news of Roosevelt's memoirs, leaving the matter to his Court Minister to handle. The latter however had a grimmer view of Roosevelt's chapters. Relevant entries in Alam's diaries are interesting, if only because they reveal a facet of the Shah's character.[14] The fall of the monarchy early in 1979 removed obstacles and scruples relating to publication of the book.

A main theme in our study is to demonstrate why Roosevelt's main claims in that book are disingenuous. In real life, Roosevelt managed to sell his story to the main protagonists. The Shah was reported to have told him 'I owe my throne to the Almighty God, my people, my army and you!'[15] Roosevelt was also received by Churchill. A frail Churchill in his sickbed – in an elated mood nevertheless – reportedly told him, 'If I have been a few years younger, I would have loved nothing better than to have served under your command in this great venture.'[16] President Eisenhower read Roosevelt's report while still in Denver, Colorado, and later personally awarded a medal to Roosevelt who by then had fully earned the lustre attached to his name. But when he sat to hear Roosevelt in person, the President was not impressed. According to his biographer, Stephen Ambrose, Eisenhower wrote in his diary on 8 October 1953, 'I listened to his [Roosevelt] detailed report and it seemed more like a dime novel than historical fact.'[17] Still, Roosevelt's debriefings then must have been less flamboyant than his *Countercoup* narrative, judging by the contents of the more sober and authoritative CIA internal history *Overthrow*, drafted in 1954. This document, to which we shall turn shortly, contains glaring contrasts with Roosevelt's tales in *Countercoup*. In the event, both the SIS/MI6 and CIA headquarters accepted Roosevelt's account with alacrity, overlooking certain ambiguities and inconsistencies which must have been apparent, given deficiencies both in the number and substance of messages which Roosevelt transmitted to Washington and London during the final four days. The SIS boss, Major-General Sinclair, did indeed ask Roosevelt to take him along to the Foreign Office debriefings so that he could show results to senior diplomats, who must have been reticent about spy action as a way to conduct foreign affairs.[18] The same mentality prevailed in CIA headquarters. The fledgeling operational wing of the CIA was striving to break loose from the straightjacket of the 1947 National Security Act; this law had accorded the agency a primarily intelligence coordination and analyses role, as opposed to a field operation role and, while this handicap was somewhat improved in 1952, interagency intelligence rivalries were intensified.[19] Both Woodhouse and Richard Helms – one of the longest serving CIA directors – are on record saying that the CIA deliberately leaked, even exaggerated its role in Iran in order to enhance its own stature in Washington.[20]

In June 2000 *The New York Times*, decided to release an internal CIA document leaked to it earlier by an unnamed official. Written in March 1954, the report and its annexes constitute a unique authoritative document emanating from official sources on the planning and execution of the plot to take out Mosaddeq's government. (See also Chapter 6, section 'An Orphan British Secret Document' in this volume). The author of the report, Donald Wilber, was the main drafter of TPAJAX, together with a British agent named Norman Darbyshire. The report is essentially a post-mortem drawn up from the then existing records, cable traffic and debriefings, notably by Kim Roosevelt, who other than directing the operation in Tehran was Wilber's superior in the CIA hierarchy.

While precise about the events leading to the failed *coup* attempt of 15–16 August, the Wilber account or '*Overthrow*' – as we shall henceforth refer to it – remains fuzzy about factors that led to the actual downfall. Nowhere in this report is there an explicit claim that the overthrow of Mosaddeq was a direct result of moves by the CIA station in Tehran between 16 and 19 August. These activities, however, were fully described and will be analysed in the main body of this volume. We will highlight doubts, if not disclaimers, expressed in *Overthrow* proper, about the nexus between CIA station activities and the fall of Mosaddeq. What merits further reflection here are the circumstances surrounding the release of this document.

Why did the CIA files remain unclassified?

During the 1990s, three successive CIA directors pledged to review and release the historically valuable material on Iran and on ten other widely known covert operations during the Cold War. Documents related to the overthrow of President Arbenz of Guatemala were declassified in 1997; yet in spite of litigations brought against the agency by various interested parties under the Freedom of Information Act, the CIA has doggedly refused to release the documents pertaining to the Mosaddeq episode.[21] In 1998, citing resource restrictions, the then CIA director, George Tenet, in effect postponed the release of documents promised by his predecessors. Other officials have cited deliberate destruction of Iran files in the early 1960s. Still others have claimed that the records were destroyed in a fire. For his part, the Information Review-Officer for the CIA's Directorate of Operations, William McNair, invoked high national security implications for the release.[22]

It was against the backdrop of such brouhaha that the Wilber report was leaked to *the New York Times*. Was this a deliberate act to put an end to ongoing squabbles? Was the leak in any way related to the Clinton administration's attempt – on the road to mending fences with the Islamic regime in Tehran – to take the skeletons out of the closet? No one could be sure.[23] What is even more curious is that the Iran files of 1953 do not figure among some 420,000 additional pages that the CIA declassified in 2007 and released to the National Archives and Records Administration (NARA).[24]

While in essence the CIA plot and its involvement in a failed *coup* attempt in 1953 is public knowledge, and officially acknowledged, it is hard to comprehend the CIA obstinacy in holding back the remaining archives, particularly during the eight-year Bush administration when US ties with the Islamic Republic of Iran were at a low ebb. One should resist the temptation to speculate on the CIA's inner reasons, although plausible hypotheses are not lacking. Britain's MI6 has been even less generous in releasing its archives; the fact that its key operatives such as Christopher Woodhouse and Samuel Falle have published their memoirs does not preclude emergence of hitherto untapped material. We all should look forward to full release of the relevant files by both intelligence agencies. For now, our study attempts to refute the more talked about fairy-tale aspects of this history and shed new light on its darker sides, but by no means do we pretend offering the last word.

1
The Context

The period between 1941 and the advent of Mosaddeq as Prime Minister in 1951 marked one of the third-world's early experiments with democracy. The Allied occupation of Iran in September 1941 ended the dictatorial reign of Reza Shah – the founder of the Pahlavi dynasty and the man credited with the rebirth of Iran as a viable nation-state. His 20-year rule had been rigorous and unrelenting. Amidst profound reforms and innovations, centrifugal tendencies in ethnic and tribal regions were crushed; the intelligentsia was silenced or co-opted, while clerics were assigned a lumpen status. For individuals belonging to these categories, the abdication of the monarch in September 1941 had meant deliverance. The eruption of liberties following his downfall spawned a full spectrum of political parties as well as a plethora of newspapers and tabloids. Politicians re-emerged from banishment and isolation; the gild-edged *hezār fāmīl* (1000 families[1])resurfaced from relative eclipse. Turncoats, muckrakers and other political fortune hunters found a free reign. The country had begun experimenting with democracy.[2]

However, the take-off point in 1941 was an oligarchic structure. The constitutional revolution in 1906–09 had endowed the nation with a legislative organ, *Majles Shorāy'e Melli* (National Consultative Assembly), short-named *Majles*. The country was, however, predominantly rural with a lopsided land tenure structure where the mosque, the Crown, the government and a tiny group of big landowners possessed close to half of the cultivating land.[3] The landed gentry, provincial dignitaries, local notables and clerics, in concert with top civilian and military provincial officials, were in a position to influence the elections. Once elected, the deputies regrouped along party lines or common socio-political background and outlook and worked through caucuses called *'fraktion'*. The Shah named prime ministers after the *Majles* had expressed a preference for a candidate through a straw poll. Between 1941 and the rise of Mosaddeq, 11 politicians formed 16 governments.[4]

Foreign influence as a prime mover in Iranian politics

Over this oligarchic structure, the British influence cast a large shadow, while on the opposite side of the spectrum the *Hezb'e Tudeh'e Iran* (the party of the masses) gravitated towards the Soviet Union and soon became its surrogate. These two poles of influence played a critical part in the events that were to unfold following Mosaddeq's assumption of premiership.

Throughout the nineteen century, the British and the Russian Empires had competed in Iran over strategic and commercial interests. Britain saw Iran as a buffer state to fend off Russian ambitions over India; while, inversely, the Russians saw the British hegemony in Persia as a potential threat to their empire. This rivalry was transformed into an alliance in the early twentieth century and by 1907, through an infamous accord, the two powers divided Iran into zones of influence.[5] Both powers intervened militarily in Iran as of 1911 and remained there through to the end of the Great War. The Bolshevik Revolution in 1917, however, changed the nature of Iran's relations with its northern neighbour. The attitude of the new Soviet rulers was contrary to the rapacious behaviour of Tsarist Russia. The new Soviet commissar for foreign affairs cancelled the Tsarist concessions and loans, and a treaty of friendship was signed in February 1921. An article in that treaty authorized the Soviet Union to enter Iran should a foreign power antagonistic to the USSR intervene there. This reflected the USSR's early-day fears of encirclement, but as a superpower a few decades later the Soviets held on to this provision as a Damocles sword.

The British focus thenceforth shifted to oil. In 1901, Mozafar'uddin Shah Qajar had granted to a British entrepreneurs, William Knox D'Arcy, a 60-year concession to extract oil in Iran's southern provinces. When D'Arcy struck oil in 1908, the British government acquired the majority shares of the Anglo-Persian Oil Company (renamed in 1935 Anglo-Iranian Oil Company, AIOC). As the First Lord of the Admiralty during the First War, Churchill had switched the royal navy fuel from coal to oil, something that imparted added strategic importance to Britain's interests in Iran. In 1932, Reza Shah Pahlavi made a losing gamble to cancel the D'Arcy concession. That roused British anger and in the shadow of gunboat diplomacy, a new oil accord was signed in 1933. As a partner to AIOC, Iran was now entitled to 4 shillings per ton of oil extracted as well as 20 per cent of dividends from AIOC's profits for a period of 60 years.

Britain assured her influence through a network of stealthy contacts with Southern tribes, corrupt officials, provincial magnates and right-wing politicians, at times referred to as anglophiles. A curious blend of reality and perception, British influence was seen as ubiquitous and had taken on a larger-than-life existence. Across the board, initiated Iranians believed in the implacable power of Britain to shape the events, even if most profoundly resented it. Both the Shah and Mosaddeq belonged to this latter category; with the difference, however, that Mosaddeq's attitude was one of open defiance whereas the Shah dissimulated his resentment and was at times acquiescent.

The phenomenon of 'Anglophiles' was also complex in its properties. It comprised a heterogeneous class of the elite who, with a mix of awe and admiration, or for reasons of personal expediency, hailed Britain's worldwide ascendancy. Many among them genuinely believed that the best interests of Iran lay in casting its lot in with Britain. The doyen of this breed of politicians was Seyyed Zia Tabataba'ei who back in 1921 had led a *coup d'état* and was briefly prime minister before being ousted by Reza Khan, the founder of the Pahlavi dynasty. After the latter's demise in 1941, and under Allied wartime occupation of Iran, Seyyed Zia had returned to the political limelight wearing the patriarchal mitre of the anglophile clan. In the early tumults of the oil crisis in 1951, Seyyed Zia was the British trump card to supplant Mosaddeq.

The *Tudeh* Party

The communist movement in Iran largely predates the establishment of the *Tudeh* Party in 1941.

Both the Democrat Party of Azerbaijan[6] and the *Edālat* (Justice) Party, dating to the First World War, are in a way the *Tudeh* precursors. Reza Shah had outlawed communist activism. Anyone who espoused communist ideology (*marām'e eshterāki*) was liable to arrest. A group of 53 intellectuals suspected of harbouring such a doctrine had been arrested and sentenced to prison terms.[7] Most joined *Tudeh* when it was created in October 1941. Membership comprised old communists, social democrats and a coterie of leftist intellectuals. The party avoided the *communist* label for a host of pragmatic as well as for ideological reasons, something that was not greeted with enthusiasm by the old cadres.[8] Yet the Party grew fast to become, by the mid-1940s, the largest political grouping in Iran. *Tudeh* established branches in all major cities and ran an array of newspapers, affiliated labour organizations as well as an ultra-secret military wing.[9] The party peaked in number of adherents and political fortune in 1946 when Prime Minister Ahmad Qavam added three *Tudeh* ministers to his cabinet. This was during the height of the Azerbaijan crisis.

The Azerbaijan Crisis, 1945–46

The episode known as the Azerbaijan Crisis marked the first major inter-Allied rift which ushered in the Cold War. The crisis was sparked by Soviet refusal to withdraw its forces from Iran at the expiration of an agreed deadline set at the outset of Iran's occupation by Allied forces.[10] In the meantime, under the complaisant watch of Soviet troops, two autonomous movements cropped up in Azerbaijan and Kurdistan. The insurrectional forces evicted the Tehran-appointed senior officials and overran the military garrisons in Tabriz, Rezā'ieh and Mahābād.

To mollify the Soviets, Prime Minister Qavam travelled to Moscow and offered Stalin an oil concession. Qavam's predecessor, Ebrahim Hakimi, had already involved the United Nations in defiance of British Foreign Secretary Bevin, who was keen to avoid confrontation between the wartime Allies: Bevin had proposed that the Azerbaijan crisis be tackled by a tripartite UK, USSR, USA commission, rather than the UN. Nor, contrary to widely held assumption, was the referral to the United Nations initially supported by the United States.[11] Yet a showdown between the wartime Allies was looming. In March US Secretary of State James Byrnes warned Stalin to withdraw his troops from Iran at once.[12] Stalin, unwilling to confront the West – and no doubt lured by Qavam's oil concession – decided to withdraw his forces, but not before securing from Qavam a pledge to pursue in earnest the autonomy talks with rebel authorities who barely disguised their intimate ties with the USSR.[13] In June 1946, Qavam signed an agreement with the head of the Azerbaijan insurrectional authority granting all but the totality of their demands.

A by-product of these occurrences was a revolt in the tribal and ethnic regions in southern Iran. This time, many observers, including the Qavam government itself, saw the British footprint.[14] With possible British encouragement, southern tribes, including *Qashqā'eis*, *Bakhtiārīs* and the *Boir'ahmadīs*, demanded the same autonomy rights that Qavam had granted to insurrectional authorities in the north. The assumption among British officials at working level was that the cessation of the Azerbaijan Crisis was a *fait accompli* and the Iranians should try to make the best of an inevitable situation. The British Ambassador in

Tehran, Sir John Le Rougetel, had no qualms about saying as much to US Ambassador George Allen in a late September conversation.[15] This perverse logic also pushed Britain to take its own precautionary measures to protect its economic interests. In the oil-rich province of Khuzestan, Britain attempted to curb the influence of the *Tudeh* Party among oil workers and shore up her own dominance.[16] Further, a union of Arab tribes in Khuzestan was making vague noises about secession of the oil-rich province. A few months earlier the exiled son of Sheikh Khaz'al, the former Arab semi-autonomous ruler of Mohammarah (renamed Khorramshahr in 1925), had attempted an expedition against the Khuzestan province.[17] There again, British complicity had been suspected. The scene was reminiscent of the 1907 Anglo-Russian arrangement to divide Iran into zones of influence, to which we alluded earlier. The country was on the verge of disintegration.[18]

Under Soviet pressure, Qavam agreed to hold parliamentary elections at a time when Azerbaijan was not under government control and tribes in the southern provinces were in rebellion.[19] He further contemplated a joint venture with the USSR to establish an air route monopoly to the Northern provinces. This would have tightened the Soviet embrace and sealed the Soviet sphere of influence in the northern part of Iran.

By October 1946, Qavam was, in the words of a US official, 'virtually a prisoner of his own policies of retreating before Soviet pressure and that Iran is daily losing what remains of its independence'.[20] Late in the game Qavam realized that his policies had taken Iran to the edge of the abyss. To retract he needed urgent military and financial support from the United States, which he requested through Ambassador George Allen but which was not forthcoming.[21]

The Shah had followed the events of the previous several months with a mix of anguish and resignation. He had strongly resented the prime minister's policy of appeasement towards the Russians, but had remained mainly acquiescent. By mid-October, however, the Shah was ready to emerge from his reserve. With possible encouragement from Ambassador Allen[22] and army support, he contemplated a dramatic dismissal of Qavam, taking advantage of the parliamentary interregnum. Details of this episode are chronicled in the US Department of State archives. On 17 October, the Shah confronted Qavam and forced his hand to make a swift policy shift by dropping the three *Tudeh* ministers in his cabinet.[23] The Shah also demanded that Qavam's left-leaning and fiercely anti-Pahlavi deputy Mozafar Firouz be removed.[24]

Once the policy shift was made Qavam, with the active encouragement of Ambassador Allen who also lobbied Washington, took a firm stand vis-à-vis the Soviets.[25] He used the upcoming fifteenth *Majles* elections as an alibi to dispatch troops to Azerbaijan, something that the Shah had urged incessantly.[26] In a shrewd move, Qavam informed the Security Council of the evolving situation and of the implied Soviet threat to reintervene.

Shortly thereafter government troops secured Azerbaijan and Kurdistan. Stalin did not react. The insurrectional leaders fled to the USSR, while the provincial capital Tabriz was liberated by its population before the arrival of Teheran forces.[27] Tribal and possibly religious leaders in Zanjan and Azerbaijan had helped.[28]

A cunning Qavam took full credit for his 'under-handed moves' and left the impression that all preceding events had indeed been scripted by him in advance. Many believed him, and to this day some historians praise him for his astute handling of the Azerbaijan Crisis. In political milieus in Tehran matters were perceived differently. Qavam's political fortunes declined and his party soon unravelled. Barely a year later he was voted out of office after the *Majles* also turned down the oil concession he had offered to Stalin.[29]

The *Tudeh* leaders had colluded openly with the Azerbaijan and Kurdish insurrections. They paid a heavy cost in terms of party adherence and prestige. A period of retrospection and purges followed. Before recovering from this setback, the *Tudeh* found itself in another morass. In February 1949 the Shah survived an assassination attempt in which *Tudeh* was implicated. Its leadership had prior knowledge of the attempt but had not, in all likelihood, instigated it.[30] This did not prevent Prime Minister Mohammad Sa'ed from officially implicating and banning the party. Its leaders either fled or were arrested.

Those who had written off the *Tudeh* Party, however, were in for disappointment. Barely a year later, under the premiership of General Ali Razmara – some believe with his complicity – *Tudeh* staged a spectacular jailbreak; all arrested leaders escaped. The Party regrouped through several front organizations and newspapers. Its return to the limelight was helped by the liberal policies of Mosaddeq when the latter became prime minister late in April 1951. By the end of Mosaddeq's tenure in 1953, *Tudeh* may have had an estimated 100,000 card-holders and three times as many sympathizers.

Shah Mohammad-Reza Pahlavi

The oligarchic structure of the polity in Iran, while tied to the monarchy, was inherently unreceptive to a strong monarch. Reza Shah had shaken

Figure 1 Mohammad-Reza Pahlavi, Shah of Iran (1941–79). Photo © AP, 2007

up that structure. Having alienated much of the conservative elite, Shiite clerics as well as the intelligentsia, Reza Shah had left his successor with few assured loyalties outside the armed forces. Mohammad-Reza's debut as the Shah was, as such, tottery and insecure (Figure 1). The Shah's psyche was a product of tumults that had placed him on the throne in September 1941, at the age of 22. He knew that the British, who had engineered his father's abdication, were tepid at best towards him; they came close to discarding him as heir to the throne in view of his perceived pro-axis sympathies. A cable from Eden to the British Minister in Tehran, Sir Reader Bullard, dated 19 September 1941, reflects the British unwillingness to accept the ascension of Mohammad-Reza to the throne.[31] This background nourished the Shah's fears and suspicions of Britain. Upon accession to the throne, Mohammad-Reza tried to assuage internal foes and appease the Allied powers which had occupied Iran.[32] In the ensuing 12 years, he struggled to remain afloat, overcoming a myriad of adversities. To avoid British shenanigans, the Shah was complaisant towards anglophile politicians, even known British agents.[33] Yet he strived to keep the British influence at bay by discrete support of personalities known for political integrity or loyalty to his person. On at least two occasions during this period he offered Mosaddeq the premiership.[34] Yet his sense of insecurity made him chary when faced with strong or popular prime ministers.

He favoured American entry into Iran's political arena as a counterweight to both Britain and Russia. The Shah also had a deplorable, if as yet suppressed, propensity to hold the reins of power in his hands. The army and foreign affairs were the domains of his predilection. During the earlier years of his reign when he had not yet cemented his grip on power, he used cunning methods to collect information or undercut his prime ministers. He sent private emissaries to British or American Embassies to feel them out on crucial issues and was attentive to their views, although not always acquiescent.[35] He kept a network of contacts with deputies, veteran politicians, and tribal chieftains as well as traditional high clerics. Yet his manipulative moves during this episode should not be overstated in either scope or effectiveness. He was fiercely patriotic and capable of cold calculation in what he perceived as the high interests of the Crown and the nation, two notions which he juxtaposed and frequently confounded. His political realism was often misconstrued as indecision or timidity, qualities which he did not nonetheless lack.

The Azerbaijan episode had boosted the Shah's standing as well as army morale. Another wave of sympathy came after a failed assassination attempt in February 1949. The Shah took advantage by having the constitution amended to increase his prerogatives. He was henceforth empowered to dissolve the parliament and fill half of the senate's seats by appointment. Perennial constitutional debates on the nature and extent of the Crown's powers did not, however, wane. The National Front, led by Mosaddeq, in fact challenged the validity of the Constituent Assembly and its amendments. Once in power Mosaddeq moved aciduously to curb the Shah's authority. The tug of war between the two became a factor in Mosaddeq's fall and the Shah's subsequent autocratic rule.

The *Ulama* as a socio-political force

The rise of the *Ulama*, or Shiite clerics, as a major social force in Iranian society can be traced to the declining phase of the *Safavid* dynasty (1502–1736) when their influence in the Court reached its vertex. The Sunnite-Shiite rifts had been one among several factors that led to Afghan revolt and subsequent downfall of the *Safavid* Empire.[36] By the late eighteenth century the influence of the *Ulama* had decisively grown when, in the internecine Shiite theological clashes, the *Usoulīs* gained ascendancy over the *Akhbārīs*. This latter school believed that Shiite Moslems could rely on the *Akhbār* (reporting), namely the accounts given of the discourse, the behaviour and the human qualities of the Prophet and the 12 Imams, without needing the *Ulama* to act as intermediaries or interpret the Islamic canon.[37] *Usoulīs*, on the other hand, believed in *Ijtīhad* or religious edict by ranking clerics (*mojtahīd* or ayatollah).

By the mid-nineteenth century a solid alliance between the traditional urban middle class, mainly bazaar merchants, and the *Ulama* had been forged. The *bazaaris* saw to the pecuniary needs of clerics through religious taxes (*Khoms*), while *Ulama* defended the interests of the bazaar merchants and guilds against the arbitrariness of *Qājār* monarchs and their henchmen. The *Ulama* also wielded economic power through exploitation of the *Vaqf* (or property endowment by the pious rich to religious charities). Many clerics also benefited from the court prebends and sinecures. Further, through a network of mosques, neighbourhood vigilantes, mob honchos and the like, they could field throngs of zealots into the streets on religious processions or occasionally for non-religious motives. The tradition of *bast* (taking sanctuary in an inviolable locale) and, less frequently, exodus to other Shiite poles was resorted to as a means of pressuring the central authority.

The history of the past 150 years of Iran is rife with instances when the *Ulama* displayed their potency as a social force capable of influencing political events. In 1891–92 for instance, the *Ulama* threw their weight behind the *bazaar* against arbitrary economic decisions by the Court. The best known among these episodes is the 'tobacco boycott movement' which forced the Qājār monarch, Nasser'uddin Shah, to rescind a tobacco concession he had granted to a British subject.[38]

The triggering events of Iran's Constitutional Revolution (1905–09) could also be attributed to complicity of *bazaaris* and clerics. Both *bast* (in the shrine of Shah-Abdol'azim in Rey, near Tehran) and exodus to the holy city of Qom were resorted to. *Ulama* protested the mistreatment of bazaar merchants by *Qājār* officialdom. When the intelligentsia joined the protests, the movement became irreversible. An ailing Shah yielded to popular demands, initially confined to the establishment of *'edālat-khāneh'* (a house of justice). Later, when under the impulse of intellectuals a fundamental law, modelled after the Belgian Constitution, was adopted, the traditional clerics rejected it as un-Islamic.[39] Throngs of rabble were massed in major cities to protest the drift towards secularism. This notwithstanding, an alliance of convenience, joining secular intellectuals, enlightened clerics, tribal chieftains and provincial warlords allowed the constitutional movement to take hold.

Another landmark in which clerics played a decisive role occurred in 1925. The *Ulama* vigorously opposed a bill by Prime Minister Reza Khan (the future founder of the Pahlavi dynasty) to end the age-old monarchy and replace it with a secular republic modelled after that newly founded in Turkey. Alarmed by that prospect, crowds formed a procession from the main mosque to the parliament building while bazaar guilds declared a strike.[40] Reza Khan had the bill withdrawn and made a successful bid to form a new dynasty to replace the discredited *Qājārs*. We will later highlight the paramount relevance of this episode to the events that led to the fall of Mosaddeq in August 1953.

Ayatollah Seyyed Abol'qassem Kashani: the precursor of clerical activism

The Constituent Assembly that had been called to formalize the formation of a new dynasty included a cleric who was to play a key role in the oil nationalization movement a quarter of a century later. He also became a main instrument of its undoing. His name was Seyyed Abol'qasem Kashani (Figure 2). Kashani had fought the British in Mesopotamia during 1920 where his father, a senior cleric, had been killed in disturbances the year earlier.[41] The San Remo conference and the Sèvres Treaty had effectively passed control of the Shiite shrine cities of Najaf and Kerbela from Ottomans into non-Moslem hands, namely Britain, which obtained a mandate over Mesopotamia. For Kashani that added insult to injury. A *Fatwa* (a religious ruling) had been issued around June 1920 by a *Marja* (source of religious emulation in the Shiite creed), Ayatollah Mohammad-Taqi Shirzi, according to which Moslems could not be ruled by non-Moslems. This led to the Shiite uprising in which Sunnites also participated. The episode had left an irredeemable grudge against Britain in Kashani. His opposition to the Turkish model of secular republicanism and his later pro-German sympathies – which cost him arrest and banishment by the British occupying force in the early 1940s – could all be traced back to events in Mesopotamia.

During the 1940s Kashani had waged a two-track struggle. One was against the Anglo-Iranian Oil Company's (AIOC) grip over Iran's oil resources. The second track was activism and support for Islamic militancy, of which he became the lightning-rod and the spiritual leader.

Figure 2 Ayatollah Seyyed Abol'qassem Kashani

His support-base and *modus operandi* reflected the classical bazaar-cleric alliance. At his call bazaar merchants and guilds, the procession headmen (*jelo'dār*) and neighbourhood honchos (*jāhel'e mahal*) organized strikes and fielded crowds into streets.[42] Earlier in the decade, Kashani had been elected to the thirteenth *majles* through the same devices, but had been unable to serve due to his banishment by Britain. He was part of an Allied sweep of suspected German sympathizers of whom General Fazlulah Zahedi, the future leader of the anti-Mosaddeq campaign and his eventual successor, also formed part. As Crown Prince in 1941, Mohammad-Reza himself had been counted among the group, something that nearly cost him the throne, as we just alluded to.

In 1946, Kashani was arrested and banished, this time by Prime Minister Qavam, for fomenting religious unrest. The climate in the country was jittery at the height of the Azerbaijan Crisis and in the wake of the assassination of a secular intellectual, Ahmad Kasravi, by the newly formed terrorist group *Fadā'iān Islam*. The latter was known to have links with Kashani and other radical clerics, including the then middle-ranking cleric, Rouhollah Khomeini.[43] *Fadā'iān Islam* had just been formed by a radical seminary student by the name of Seyyed Mojtaba Navvab Safavi (*nom de guerre*). This aroused dismay in Grand Ayatollah Boroujerdi, the Shiite world's undisputed leader, whose attitude and impact on the events in 1953 in Iran is one of the central themes of this study, treated in several chapters.[44]

Less than three years later, Kashani was to be arrested yet again and exiled, this time in connection with the assassination attempt against the Shah in February 1949. The would-be assassin, Nasser Fakhrara'ei, carried a press card issued by *Parcham'e Islam* (*Banner of Islam*), a newspaper run by Kashani's son-in-law, Faqihi Shirazi, and clearly his mouthpiece. As mentioned before, the *Tudeh* Party was also implicated and officially banned.[45]

Before this incident, Ayatollah Kashani, with the active support of the more radical clerics in Qom, was involved in a passionate campaign against the newly born state of Israel.[46] In Tehran, the Jewish Agency delegates were lobbying the government to grant recognition to Israel. Some authors have attributed Kashani's banishment to the cabinet deliberations for a *de facto* recognition of Israel and insinuate that Prime Minister Sa'ed may have been bribed for this purpose through an unnamed American intermediary.[47]

Be that as it may, by the time of his departure to Beirut in exile, a kindred spirit bound the activist clerics, featuring Kashani and a coterie of middle- to low-ranking radical mullah's on the one hand, and the *Fadā'iān Islam* on the other. This was in spite of differences in their approach to politics.[48] Their *modus operandi* and ideological baggage were not identical but there was commonality in the ultimate goal: creation of an all-encompassing Islamic state to run the affairs of the *ummah*. Kashani was primarily a political figure who acted within the established political context. For him, the struggle against Western influence – British imperialism in particular – had priority. Khomeini

Figure 3 Ayatollah Kashani flanked by Seyyed Navvab-Safavi, the leader of *Fadā'iān Islam* terrorist group

and the *Fadā'iān* believed in the ascendancy of religion and strongly held that politics must be subordinated to Islamic rules. This led to a temporary split in 1951–52 when Khomeini criticized Kashani for having accepted the Speakership of the *Majles* and *Fadā'iān* threatened to kill him.[49] Kashani for his part is reported to have said that '*Agha Rouholah*' (i.e., Khomeini) was not cut out to be in politics.[50] Apart from this year-long hiatus, an ideological lineage linked the postwar clerical militancy to the Islamic Revolution (1978–79). After success of the Islamic Revolution in 1979, the by-then-defunct Ayatollah Kashani became an iconic and venerated figure among the revolutionaries. Some of his close associates and immediate family tried to cleanse his legacy – forging letters in the process – that would distance Kashani from the anti-Mosaddeq cabal in 1953 and his direct involvement in the latter's downfall.[51] Cleansing efforts, however, were not pursued when it became clear that Ayatollah Khomeini himself made no bones about his anti-Mosaddeq sentiments.

But back in the late-1940s Islamic radicalism was still a fringe movement and Kashani was revered as a spiritual force buttressing an essentially nationalistic and anti-colonial drive. When he was allowed to return in June 1950, he was met by delirious welcoming throngs of supporters.[52] Mosaddeq in person was at the airport to welcome him. In the feverish political climate of the time, marked by popular opposition to the 'Supplemental Oil Agreement', the hour of the charismatic Ayatollah had ineluctably arrived. He immediately sided with Mosaddeq who, together with his National Front associates, had made a triumphal return to the *Majles* a few months earlier.[53]

Razmara: prelude to the oil nationalization crisis

The return of Kashani to Tehran had coincided with the premiership of General Ali Razmara. A Saint-Cyrien, erudite former chief of the army general staff, Razmara had a reputation for hard work and probity. Mosaddeq and his associates, notably Kashani, viewed him as subservient to Britain and believed his appointment had been imposed on the Shah in order to obtain the ratification of the unpopular Supplemental Oil Agreement (SOA) in the *Majles*. The previous legislative session of the *Majles* had indeed mandated the government to obtain from Britain equitable revenue-sharing terms for Iran but the resulting 'Supplemental Oil Agreement', negotiated by the Sa'ed government with the Anglo-Iranian Oil Company (AIOC), fell far short of public expectations.[54]

Against the backdrop of drought and severe economic recession Iran badly needed an immediate infusion of funds, for which the Truman administration was considering some tentative and patently insufficient remedies.[55] Britain had proposed a series of reforms to the Shah, including redistribution of Crown lands among the peasants but her recipe for Iran's short-term ills was the ratification of the Supplemental Oil Agreement (SOA).[56] To be sure, the SOA increased Iran's oil receipts but did not address some simple and perfectly legitimate demands by Iran, such as the right of Iran to look into AIOC accounts, greater Iranian participation in the management, broader Iranization of the workforce etc. Many in the *Majles* expected a fifty-fifty revenue-sharing scheme in line with the Standard Oil of New Jersey/Creole contract in Venezuela. The Shah was anxious to get funding for the seven-year development programme and was pressing the United States to increase its military aid to Iran as the oil revenues en block were earmarked for the seven-year programme. Both top economists in Iran and US officials in Washington had urged the Shah to reach an oil settlement with Britain to ensure the flow of the badly needed funds.[57] The Nationalist deputies in the *Majles* were not of the same mind. Some of these deputies had staged a filibuster to block the SOA ratification during the waning days of the previous legislative term when the bill might have obtained a majority.

By the end of 1949, British officials at the working level were ready to bend to a non-interventionist injunction by foreign secretary Bevin and pressure the Shah to name a *'strong'* personality as prime minister to force the hand of the recalcitrant *Majles* and obtain the ratification of the SOA.[58] The American Embassy in Tehran had a similar analysis of the socio-economic ills that beset the country and the need for a strong personality to deal with them. Bevin and Acheson discussed Iran's urgent needs during the London ministerial meeting in May 1950 where, among other things, the need for early ratification of the SOA was stressed, in spite of reservations that some in the US administration held about its revenue sharing equity.[59] While both powers stressed the need for strong leadership, neither appears to have gone as far as recommending General Razmara. On the contrary the State Department specifically instructed the embassy in Tehran not to be pinned down to a given candidate in order to maintain its freedom.⁶⁰ General Razmara, however, was perceived by most observers as the personality with the requisite profile, an impression that may have been reinforced by individuals on the US embassy staff in Tehran. On his own initiative, the Deputy Chief of Mission, Gerald Dooher, lobbied for General Razmara. By late May the Shah had decided to name him prime minister although, paradoxically, he was unsure of British support.⁶¹ Over the years the British Embassy had projected a negative image of Razmara, no doubt preferring his anglophile military rival General Hassan Arfa', just as their candidate for the post of prime minister was the veteran anglophile politician Seyyed Zia Tabataba'ei. To ease British misgivings, Razmara had lobbied the embassy while the Shah assured them that once appointed prime minister, Razmara would have no say in military affairs.⁶² By early June the British Embassy was ready to endorse Razmara's nomination.

The nationalist opposition's assessment about the rise of Razmara to the premiership, to which we alluded earlier, and assertions made in published literature about Anglo-American pressures on the Shah to name Razmara in June 1950 should thus be nuanced in the light of the above clarifications. While the involvement of the two powers was partly true, the depiction of Razmara by his *Majles* foes as 'subservient' to foreign interests was unjustified and politically motivated.

When the new prime minister requested the *Majles* to approve or reject the Supplemental Oil Agreement, he was upbraided by opposition deputies and billed a traitor. By year-end the image of Razmara as the strong prime minister had faded and the US Embassy had mixed feelings about his durability. Both the Shah and Razmara, and indeed ambassador Grady, were disappointed with the level of US aid to Iran. At one point in November 1950, US policies in Iran earned the Shah's harsh and uncharacteristically public criticism, which angered Washington.⁶³ The volume of US aid, including the proposed $25 million loan by EXIMBANK, was manifestly disproportionate to Iran's dire needs. This further alienated the *Majles* and prompted Razmara to adopt a more neutral stance in the raging Cold War by improving ties with the Soviet Union. In November, Iran

Figure 4 Prime Minister Razmara, shortly before his assassination in March 1951

signed a trade agreement with the Soviet Union. More significantly, in a gesture to the USSR, Razmara cancelled both the BBC and VOA relay stations.[64]

Washington was concerned about the deterioration of its position in Iran and suspected that Tehran's flirtations with the USSR were calculated to play one major power against the other to gain concessions.[65] This did not prevent the administration from increasing pressure on Britain to become more forthcoming on the oil negotiations that Razmara was discreetly conducting with the AIOC representative in Tehran. Under-Secretary McGhee, whom we will meet in the next chapter, warned Britain of the upcoming ARAMCO concession with the Saudi government which was also based on equal profit sharing.[66] American pressure may have been one of the two main factors that in February 1951 induced the AIOC to quietly agree to a fifty-fifty deal with Iran (for more details on this topic see the first section in Chapter 2).

In December, the *Tudeh* staged a spectacular jailbreak allowing the party leaders implicated in the assassination attempt against the Shah to escape. Coming as it did on the heels of improved ties with the USSR, the jailbreak fed rumour-mongering in Tehran's political circles. To this day some older Iranians are convinced that Razmara had a hand in the jailbreak and may have been somehow involved in the assassination attempt against the Shah.[67]

On 7 March 1951, Razmara was assassinated by a *Fadā'iān Islam* zealot. Kashani and a few other opposition deputies and politicians openly defended the crime and lauded the assassin as a hero and patriot.[68] A year into Mosaddeq's tenure as prime minister, the *Majles* approved a bill to exculpate Razmara's killer, just as in 1946 the assassin of Ahmad Kasravi had been allowed to walk free only to recidivate three years later, killing the Court Minister Abol'hossein Hazhir. Later, when Mosaddeq became prime minister, he was given notice by *Fadā'iān* to introduce *shari'a* or face the consequences. Mosaddeq paid no heed, but had to take extra precautions to avoid assassination. His closest associate and foreign minister, Dr Hossein Fatemi, was later the target of an assassination attempt from which he escaped with serious wounds.

The assassination of Razmara caused some trepidation in London and Washington. Only a few months earlier they had urged the Shah to select a strong personality for the post of prime minister and had chided his preference for insipid old-guard politicians. Now, in March 1951, the two powers categorically advised the Shah to opt for someone whom he could fully trust and work with. The choice of Hossein Ala to replace

Razmara is likely to have been the result of this *démarche*.[69] The fifty-fifty revenue sharing offer by the AIOC was repeated to Ala, but by then the tidal wave of nationalist fervour had swept the country, as will be seen in the next chapter. The offer was by then too little too late. This in essence was what Ala told both Sir Francis Shepherd and Henry Grady.

2
The Advent of Mosaddeq and the Oil Crisis

This chapter will follow the rise of Mosaddeq to power in late April 1951 and his handling of the crisis during the first nine months of his premiership. Early British reaction to oil nationalization as well as the initial American attitude towards Iran and its nationalist movement will be followed by a brief description of the political climate and the early signs of vulnerability forecasting the events of August 1953. Special attention will be given to different phases of the oil negotiations, first in Tehran, brokered by Averell Harriman, and later in Washington where Mosaddeq resided for almost a month and met top American leaders. The chapter also covers the British referral of the oil dispute to the UN Security Council where the aged and ailing prime minister defended Iran's case.

The rise of the National Front

The National Front was officially formed in November 1949, composed of Mosaddeq and 19 other personalities who had staged a sit-in at the Shah's palace in mid-October. The protest was to draw attention to election irregularities by the government. Contrary to affirmations made by some US scholars, the protest was not directed against the Shah, not at least in appearance.[1] Hazhir, the Court Minister received the group with courtesy but the *démarche* remained inconclusive. The Constituent Assembly had just granted the Shah the prerogative to dissolve the parliament, but he chose not to do so on the grounds that the full composition of the *Majles* was not yet known. Hazhir himself was assassinated shortly thereafter by a *Fadā'iān* zealot as we just alluded to. The conjunction of events made some of the sit-in participants potential suspects. In the ensuing witch-hunt some were briefly detained. Figuring among detainees was Hossein Makki, who later played a pivotal role in the oil nationalization campaign and became one of the historical figures of the National Front. Upon their release from detention, a Charter for the movement was drawn up and approved by the group of 20, who thus became the founders of the National Front. Reforms in electoral law, press law and regulation of martial law were the three objectives incorporated in the Charter. Paradoxically, the nationalization of oil industries was not mentioned in the original Charter.

The assassination of Hazhir prompted prime minister Sa'ed to annul the polling results in the Tehran electoral district thus ceding to the earlier demand by Mosaddeq and his comrades.[2] Helped by the newly appointed chief of police, General Fazlullah Zahedi, free elections could then be held in which Mosaddeq received the highest number of votes cast. Seven other National Front members, including Ayatollah Kashani who was still in exile in Lebanon, were also elected from Tehran and the provinces.

While the oil issue had not been included in the National Front Charter, it became the Front's rallying cry soon after the sixteenth legislative session commenced its work in February 1950. Mosaddeq and his associates vehemently criticized a Supplemental Oil Agreement (SOA) as it will be recalled from the previous chapter. Mosaddeq now chaired a *Majles* Sub-Committee on Oil and managed to block its ratification. A first attempt in late November 1950 by Mosaddeq and his supporters to present a bill for the nationalization of oil industries failed to rally enough support in the *Majles*. However, the idea was gaining currency among the public and in some political circles, something that strengthen the hands of Prime Minister Razmara in his discreet talks with George Northcroft, the AIOC representative in Tehran. In December Razmara withdrew the SOA from consideration by the *Majles*; he had already served notice to Northcroft that the new oil contract should be aligned with the ARAMCO deal in Saudi Arabia, which was then in the final phases of conclusion.

It did not take the AIOC and Britain long to realize that their intransigence only fuelled nationalistic sentiments to their detriment. On 10 February 1951, they agreed to Razmara's proposal for a fifty-fifty split, with a caveat, however, that the Iranian part of the AIOC operations would thenceforth be detached from the rest of the company operations.[3] This in essence meant that Iran could no longer benefit from the company's profits in other Middle-Eastern operations. For reasons that remain obscure, Razmara did not get around to publicly announcing the breakthrough. It is not clear who in his immediate entourage was aware of the offer or whether the delay was in any way related to a more in-depth consideration of the offer. Different explanations provided subsequently about Razmara's reticence are all speculative. Before putting his hand into the fire in the *Majles*, some argued, Razmara would have wanted to ensure that the wily old lion, namely Britain, had not lured him into a scheme no better than the despised SOA. Others have suggested that he might have been preparing the ground to receive a new mandate from the parliament to renew negotiations with the AIOC, following which he could announce the break-through as a personal triumph.[4] Be that as it may, his assassination on 7 March 1951 triggered off an irreversible process which rendered the British concession stillborn. By then the national fervour for restoration of Iran's full control over the oil industry had reached boiling point.

On 15 March, a week after Razmara's assassination, the *Majles* overwhelmingly approved the Nationalization Act. The same bill had not found enough sponsors in the previous November to be placed on the *Majles* agenda for consideration, let alone approval.[5] Razmara's killing became a deciding event in Iran's march forward. Ayatollah Kashani and a few cantankerous deputies openly hailed the act and billed the perpetrator a national hero as we have noted; this fanned the climate of intimidation and cowed the reluctant deputies. But the passage of the Nationalization Act above all inspired genuine pride. The nation was in effervescent mood as jubilant crowds roamed the streets of Tehran and the provinces in a seething climate of national exaltation. Mosaddeq's day had finally arrived. As mentioned in an earlier passage, the successor to Razmara, Hossein Ala, was caught up in the whirlwind and had to bow out. The immediate reason brought up for his resignation was a new bill which Mosaddeq proposed on 26 April for the *implementation* of the Nationalization Act. Ala protested that he had had not been consulted.

The nomination of Mosaddeq

Events that led to Mosaddeq's assumption of power in late April 1951 are chronicled in numerous books and articles in several languages. They are not the focus of this study. Suffice it to say that provoked by Jamal Emami, a *Majles* deputy close to the Shah, Mosaddeq accepted the nomination with the proviso that the parliament ratified beforehand a bill for the implementation of the Nationalization Act. The bill called for the expropriation of the AIOC installations and assets.

Some Iranian chroniclers have postulated that the Shah played a subtle role in propelling Mosaddeq to premiership, while thwarting British pressures to name the anglophile veteran politician Seyyed Zia Tabataba'ei by the same stroke. This assumption is deduced from an earlier offer made by the Shah to Mosaddeq to become prime minister a few days before the assassination of General Razmara. The intermediary who had conveyed that offer was none other than Jamal Emami, the same deputy who provoked Mosaddeq into accepting the nomination for premiership in the 26 April session of the *Majles*. Both Mosaddeq and his son Dr Qolam-Hossein Mosaddeq have confirmed the Shah's offer as well as the identity of the intermediary in their respective memoirs.[6] Yet stretching this to suggest that the Shah outplayed Britain by willingly pushing Mosaddeq to the centre stage is somewhat farfetched. The Shah's motive in offering the premiership to Mosaddeq while Razmara was still in office is hard to fathom and any explanation would be speculative. The Shah was averse to strong personalities if he could avoid them. He did not hesitate to play off politicians one against the other, but the temperamentally insecure Shah preferred more malleable personalities as prime minister. More to the point, the Shah appears to have had misgivings about oil nationalization and its security implications, something that he shared with Ambassador Grady barely a week after Mosaddeq's appointment.[7] He was anxious to see the quick infusion of funds into the government coffers that only an agreement with AIOC could generate; this desire must have been whetted after Britain repeated the fifty-fifty offer to the government of Ala.

The nationalization, on the other hand, entailed a long drawn out struggle, with the potential risk of military conflict with Britain, then still a superpower. Even before the accession of Mosaddeq to power, Britain had made it a point to show off its naval prowess in the waters of the Persian Gulf, something that raised concerns in Washington.[8] In other words, while the Shah had seemingly attempted some two months earlier to replace Razmara with Mosaddeq, now in late April he had misgivings about a heavyweight prime minister who championed the perilous course of oil nationalization. As will be seen in coming pages, the Shah's concerns over the security implications of the Nationalization Act were not unfounded. Yet it is also fair to observe that in spite of those reservations, the Shah preferred Mosaddeq to the British candidate Seyyed Zia, another heavyweight who, other than having the backing of Britain, had an axe to grind against the Pahlavis.[9] Added to the Shah's innate mistrust of Britain it is therefore plausible that he may have stalled Zia's nomination till the *Majles* turned to Mosaddeq.

Figure 5 Doctor Mosaddeq's first Cabinet. General Fazlollah Zahedi as Minister of the Interior is second from the left. Courtesy of IBEX publishers, ©IBEX

Doctor Mohammad Mosaddeq: a sketch

Mosaddeq was born to *Qājār* landed gentry in 1882. He had served as provincial governor in Fars and Azerbaijan, and had held the finance and foreign affairs portfolios in different governments under the *Qājār* dynasty in the early 1920s. It was as a parliamentarian, however, that Mosaddeq was in his element. He had been elected to two successive legislative sessions in the 1920s (the fifth and the sixth *Majles*) and was elected deputy in the fourteenth and sixteenth legislative sessions during the reign of Mohammad-Reza Shah in the 1940s.

Throughout his political career, which spanned half a century, Mosaddeq had defended constitutionality as the quintessential quality of governance. For him, the *Majles* incarnated the will of the nation, which should run supreme. The power went with accountability and as the monarch was held by the Constitution to be '*not accountable*', it followed that powers bestowed on him in the constitution were *nominal*. Mosaddeq had opposed Reza Khan's accession to the throne on that same ostensible ground, arguing that his leadership talents would go to waste were he to be named king.

Mosaddeq (Figure 6) was incorruptible and fiercely nationalistic. He advocated a policy described as 'negative balance' towards the great

Figure 6 Mosaddeq's likeness on the cover of *TIME* Magazine, 4 June 1951. Portrait by Ernest T. Baker, reproduced by permission of *TIME* Magazine. ©Time Magazine, 2008

powers, meaning in effect that none should be privileged. Contrary to a widely held view at the time in the West, he was neither xenophobic nor harboured a *hatred* for Britain, still less for its citizenry.[10]

He had opposed their overarching influence and strongly resented the exploitation of Iran's natural resources. He openly criticized Britain for what he saw as the underhanded and contemptuous methods used to influence the course of events in Iran. This was at odds with Britain's self-image as a benevolent power bent on uplifting Iran despite itself. British diplomats in Tehran and his other detractors stigmatized Mosaddeq. They depicted him as a demagogue, even a lunatic given to 'prolixity' and 'impervious to argument'.[11] These hypes were unhelpful at best as the crisis deepened.

Yet Mosaddeq was also a product of an archaic political and managerial culture. His years of schooling in France and Switzerland had not fully eradicated certain traits common in *Qājār* officialdom. In oil negotiations he received foreign interlocutors alone and often reacted instantly to long and meticulously prepared proposals without benefit of expert advice. He was authoritative, distrustful, inflexible and secretive, qualities that had not escaped his foreign interlocutors.[12] He was emotional and, while profusely courteous, was capable of abusive language which he could heap on allies and adversaries alike.[13] Mosaddeq's poor health no doubt compounded these foibles.[14]

The initial British reaction to oil nationalization

The news of Mosaddeq's appointment in late April, coming back-to-back with the adoption by the *Majles* of the ordinance for implementation of the Nationalization Act, confronted the British cabinet with stark choices. It will be recalled that the Nationalization Act per se had already been approved by the *Majles* on 20 March. In between, Sir Francis Shepherd had done his level best to have the Shah appoint the Anglophile veteran politician Seyyed Zia, but was circumvented in circumstances that we tried earlier to unravel. Negotiation with Mosaddeq was the logical course of action, but the reporting and analyses from the British Embassy in Tehran cast doubt over Mosaddeq's willingness, even ability to engage in a serious dialogue.[15] Both Mosaddeq's temperament and the emotional climate that reigned in Iran were seen as impediments to a successful outcome.

The cabinet was also divided over the issue of 'intervention', the nature and scope of which had yet to be defined. A move contemplating the seizure of the southern oil fields posed nearly insurmountable logistical challenges. An invasion, moreover, could trigger a Soviet military reaction in line with the 1921 treaty of friendship between the USSR and Iran which was explained earlier. The United States was, in particular, concerned that a British military move could set off a chain of events leading to an overall war at a time when the Truman administration weighed its options against a Red China in the Korean theatre.[16]

However, once the immediate shockwaves were absorbed, Britain petitioned the International Court of Justice (ICJ) and proposed arbitration. This measure did not foreclose other options. Iran, on the other hand, argued that the Anglo-Iranian Oil Company (AIOC) and not Britain was the party to the dispute and hence the ICJ, created by UN Charter to deal with inter-state disputes, was not competent to adjudicate. The Nationalization Act required the government to seize the assets of an oil company, not of a state; and the fact that Britain was the majority share-holder in AIOC could not, in Iran's view, alter the company's non-state character.

When Mosaddeq rejected the ICJ arbitration on these grounds, Britain began to raise her tone. In an *aide-mémoire* dated 19 May, Britain threatened that failure to negotiate or any unilateral act will entail 'most serious consequences'.[17] This threat accompanied military gestures. Britain deployed three brigades of airborne troops to *Shaiba* base in Iraq, paratrooper were on standby in Cyprus, and naval vessels were dispatched to adjacent waters off Abadan in the Persian Gulf. To avert logistical problems inherent in a wider military move, the scope of a possible 'intervention' was narrowed. The operation, code-named *Buccaneer*, was now aimed at occupying Abadan, the main operation centre of the AIOC and location of the world's largest refinery.[18] This, the British officials argued, drastically reduced the chances of a major Soviet offensive in the north. The Russians would at worse occupy some northern provinces in a pattern resembling the sinister arrangements foreseen in the 1907 Anglo-Russian treaty. Clearly, resort to brute force was now the preferred recipe for the British Foreign Secretary Herbert Morrison, his defence colleague Emanuel (Manny) Shinwell, and a few others in the Labour cabinet who managed to bring a reluctant Atlee and other ministers in line. In a June cabinet decision 'the use of force' was authorized 'if necessary'.[19] They both argued that over and above economic losses, a diplomatic defeat in the face-off with Mosaddeq would deal an insufferable blow to British prestige and its position in the Middle East as a whole.

The Truman administration was not of the same mind. The Department of State took a serious view of British military deployments. On 16 May, Assistant-Secretary of State McGhee repeated to the British Embassy in Washington that the United States saw grave dangers in, and could not contemplate support for, any military action by Britain.[20] Acheson, for his part, told Ambassador Sir Olivier Franks that 'a substantial difference [was] developing between our views on the permissible use of force in Iran'.[21] Truman followed up with a letter to Attlee on 31 May calling for restraint. The possibility of military intervention was serious enough for Acheson to ask Averell Harriman to invite Ambassador Frank to his home on 4 July 1951 so that Acheson could warn him against a military intervention in Iran.[22] Under sustained American pressure, the Atlee government reluctantly desisted in late July, although the military option was not taken off the table. Attlee personally vetoed the plan on *realpolitik* grounds, knowing Britain would not be supported by Washington and that military action would not end the oil crisis.²³ This was in line with and comforted Atlee's own non-interventionist leaning but it is reasonable to assume that had it not been for the American opposition, Britain might have resorted to force, with unfathomable consequences which may well have included a premature and humiliating end to the oil nationalization movement. The Anglo-French *Operation Musketeer* in the Suez Canal in October 1956, though a Tory venture, is a parallel which attests to this British impulse during those declining years of the empire.

In the event, short of a military solution, a sequence of direct or US-mediated talks failed to produce results. A debate at the UN Security Council and litigation by the International Court of Justice followed. These events will be covered briefly in as much as they left an imprint on policies and perceptions both within and outside Iran. What needs to be highlighted here is a parallel measure which Britain took to thwart Mosaddeq's attempt to sell Iranian oil on the international market. By summer 1951, a boycott of Iranian oil sales had been decreed and was being enforced by the British Admiralty. The AIOC officially served notice in September that any transaction in Iran's oil products by oil companies was deemed unlawful and liable to judiciary pursuit by the AIOC.²⁴ The major oil companies soon joined the boycott, which was being observed at three levels: oil sales, tanker transport and hiring of technical personnel needed by Iran to replace the AIOC British technicians. Complicity among the oil companies also resulted in a decision to ratchet up production in other Middle-Eastern oil fields which, coupled with an already existing oil glut, rendered the Iranian oil all but unmarketable. This factor by itself was sufficient to make the boycott work, in spite of occasional escapades by lesser oil company tankers. Finally, to close the circle, Britain also began plotting covert action to subvert the Mosaddeq government, a policy that was pursued by Tories when they came to power in October of the same year and came to be known as *Operation Boot*. We will explore this topic in the forthcoming chapters.

The early American attitude to the oil dispute

If Americans were instrumental in fending off British military designs, their attitude towards Iran and the oil dispute was otherwise shaped by complex and contrasting tendencies. Foremost was anxiety about Iran being drawn into the communist fold. Policy documents approved by President Truman in this period highlight this fear. Because of its key strategic position, its petroleum resources and different vulnerabilities, 'Iran must be regarded as a continuing objective of Soviet expansion', one such document read.²⁵ Opposition to British interventionism was in part predicated on this concern. Acheson, in particular, viewed a British military intervention as a licence for the Soviet Union to re-enter the north of Iran and reclaim the oil concession it had obtained in 1946 from Qavam, then lost in the ensuing political peripety, (see 'Azerbaijan Crisis' in Chapter 1). Acheson did not exclude an invitation by Mosaddeq to the USSR to intervene in order to force Britain to withdraw.²⁶

Equally central to American thinking was the imperative of maintaining strong ties with Britain, America's staunchest ally as well as the country that had the highest number of troops in the Korean theatre next only to the United States and South Korea. The State Department, on the other hand, was aware that a lopsided policy in favour of Britain could alienate Iran to the possible advantage of the USSR. The communist scare drove top American diplomats to pressure Britain for concessions to Iran's nationalistic aspirations. The Foreign Office under Morrison viewed American *démarches* with a galling sense of betrayal, a sentiment no doubt mirrored by the United Kingdom's astute ambassador, Sir Olivier Franks. For Washington, the balancing act was not always easy. In a subtle rebuff to Acheson and McGhee, the National Security Council moved to balance what must have appeared to some in the administration as a skewed pro-Iranian view by the State Department. In its 16 May meeting, chaired by Truman, the NSC ruled that: 'The United States should indeed give vigorous support to the British in reaching an equitable settlement [with Iran].' A synthesis emerged in a public statement in May 1951 by the State Department proclaiming that the United States was friends with both parties; it had expressed to the British 'the need for greater Iranian control over its petroleum resources' while pointing out to Iran 'the serious effects of unilateral cancellation of a contract'. The statement ended by expressing the hope that, through negotiations, the interests of both parties could be realized.²⁷ By early July, the United States was considering a mediation role; this led to Averell Harriman's mission to Tehran, discussed in subsequent chapters.

In its approach to the oil dispute, the US government had to also factor in the economic interests of American oil firms, both as rivals of the AIOC but also as its accomplices. This was yet another element that influenced the American attitude in the oil dispute. Both in Venezuela and Saudi Arabia, American oil conglomerates were operating on a fifty-fifty profit-sharing arrangement; exceeding this threshold was deemed to be detrimental to American oil concerns. Here was a 'red line' that the American officialdom could not ignore.²⁸ Mosaddeq was aware of this constraint yet remained adamant in refusing any fifty-fifty profit-sharing arrangement.²⁹ As referred to earlier, the US oil conglomerates soon acted to ramp up the oil output to offset the halt in Iran's production. To facilitate their task, the Truman administration went out of its way to grant immunity from prosecution under the anti-trust law to American oil companies.³⁰ Furthermore the United States had attempted, by its own admission, to dissuade American oil companies from business discussions with Iran while efforts to bring about a UK-Iran settlement continued.³¹ The American oil companies rallied to the British embargo fearing a similar fate if they shirked solidarity with the AIOC.

To complicate the picture further, traces of American aversion to colonialism occasionally crept up in the behaviour of the lower echelon American officials, distorting the real policy thinking in Washington. The impression had been formed by some sympathetic American diplomats in Tehran such as the fiercely anti-British Gerald Dooher, who as will be recalled from the previous chapter lobbied for Razmara's premiership while ensuring that the embassy staff remained in contact with nationalist leaders.³² The image of benevolent Uncle Sam was particularly reinforced by Henry Grady (Figure 7), who was appointed ambassador in Tehran in June 1950 from his post in Athens, coinciding with the appointment of Razmara as prime minister. Henry Grady had the distinction of having been the first American ambassador to India; he reputedly fell out with the Department which he regarded as biased towards Britain.³³ Another sympathetic voice was the Assistant-Secretary of State for South Asia, Near-East and North Africa, George McGhee, who had played a key role in warding off British military intervention in May. A scion of the Texas oil industries³⁴ and himself an Anglophile, McGhee was paradoxically a vocal advocate of fair play in resolving the oil dispute with Iran. In his talks with British officials in London and with the UK ambassador in Washington, McGhee invariably pressed his interlocutors to be more forthcoming towards Iran even if the latter's demands followed an upward curve. In September 1950, well before Mosaddeq became prime minister, McGhee had pressed the Foreign Office to match the ARAMCO fifty-fifty model with Iran, something that might have influenced the British offer to Razmara as we saw earlier. When in March 1951 the *Majles* adopted the Nationalization Act with a crushing majority, McGhee was relentless in urging his British interlocutors to acquiescence, in some form or another, to *the principle of nationalization*, while maintaining the fifty-fifty profit-sharing cap.³⁵

Figure 7 Mosaddeq being greeted by the former US Ambassador to Tehran, Henry Grady (left), on his arrival in the United States, October 1951. Mosaddeq's son and personal physician Dr Qolam-Hossein Mosaddeq is looking on. Photo, the US Department of State, courtesy of the Harry S. Truman Library

British officials appear to have understood him as saying that Britain should accept nationalization 'without compensation'.[36] All this did not endear McGhee, or for that matter Henry Grady, to London. Their sympathies for Iran's national aspirations led to British gripes which were communicated to Washington later during the year.[37]

The nationalist leaders in Tehran were vaguely aware of these tendencies, presumably through US diplomats in Tehran.[38] Later in October 1951, McGhee held marathon talks with Mosaddeq in Washington which, although inconclusive, earned him profuse praise from the Iranian prime minister.

The above complex policy texture with its contrasts and ambiguities was the root of some misunderstandings and missteps on the part of Mosaddeq. To ensure continued American sympathy and support, Mosaddeq tended to overplay the *Tudeh* card as scarecrow. The latitude he accorded to the banned *Tudeh* party to reorganize itself and display its political muscles in street rallies was only in part driven by his bent for democratic values; it equally stemmed from a desire to lead Americans to believe that he was the bulwark, indeed the only alternative to communism in Iran.[39] This double-edged sword worked for a time, but ultimately turned against him. Furthermore, Mosaddeq supporters and the nationalist press tended to overrate – at least in earlier days – the perceived anti-colonial strains in the American attitude at the expense of more earthly factors.[40]

During his trip to Washington, however, Mosaddeq appears to have been disillusioned, especially with the attitude of the State Department which he thought tilted towards Britain. By then the bilateral and the US-mediated oil talks in Tehran had been tried and failed. On his return from Washington in November, Mosaddeq publicly attributed the departure of Henry Grady, as well as the reassignment of McGhee as ambassador to Turkey, to malice against Iran, which he thought prevailed in the State Department (see 'The Washington Oil Talks' below).[41]

Political line-ups in Tehran

Back in Iran, the *Tudeh* Party was denouncing Mosaddeq as an American lackey and lambasted his oil nationalization as a ploy that allowed the American oil companies to participate in plundering Iran's riches.[42] At the opposite end of the spectrum, the *Fa'dāiān Islam* – defying Kashani – enjoined Mosaddeq to meticulously follow the *shari'a* or face their curse.[43] This was not a hollow threat: Mosaddeq had to take extra precautions, including working from his relatively modest house to avoid exposure. Less than a year later, Mosaddeq's close associate and firebrand Foreign-Minister Hossein Fatemi was victim of an assassination attempt by a *Fa'dāiān* zealot. Fatemi survived this attack; most *Fa'dāiān* leaders were arrested and remained in prison until the end of Mosaddeq's rule. The pro-British politician Seyyed Zia who, it will be recalled, failed in his bid for premiership at the time of Mosaddeq's nomination, was now currying favour with the *Fa'dāiān* in his contacts with the British diplomats in Tehran as a useful political tool to undermined Mosaddeq.[44] The group, as will be discussed in Chapter 4, became a part of the anti-Mosaddeq cabal.

The internal political scene during the first year of Mosaddeq's government, while agitated, was otherwise marked by a certain degree of cohesiveness among the main political poles, including the Shiite clerical hierarchy in Qom. If some lesser figures deserted the National Front,

Mosaddeq's main allies, namely the charismatic Kashani, the popular *Majles* deputy Hossein Makki as well as the enigmatic and plucky Mozafar Baqa'ei remained loyal.[45] All three were elected to seventeenth session of the *Majles*.

The Shah had supported Mosaddeq and his oil policy in spite of the misgivings and reservations we discussed earlier.[46] Initially he was sceptical about the Mosaddeq government's durability. Shortly thereafter the Shah realized that the nationalization of oil was irreversible and Mosaddeq too popular to be replaced. This realization underpinned the Shah's attitude towards his prime minister until nearly the end, disrupted only by spasmodic temptations that were often inspired by foreign diplomats or his immediate family and entourage.[47] One such episode followed the collapse of the oil talks with Lord Stokes, discussed in the next section. When in September 1951 Mosaddeq decided to end the contracts of British employees of the AIOC, the British cabinet bristled. Atlee attempted to elicit the support of Truman, not just for opposing Mosaddeq's move but also to join Britain in pressuring the Shah to remove Mosaddeq.[48] The United States agreed to help with the first request, but refused to make common cause with Britain to remove Mosaddeq. Undeterred, Ambassador Shepherd was formally instructed to see the Shah, using intimidation and persuasion tactics to persuade him to dismiss Mosaddeq. Dire consequences were evoked if Mosaddeq remained in power; conversely, Britain promised the Shah to reward Mosaddeq's successor with better terms than those proposed by Stoke. The Shah was in a quandary as he agreed the situation called for action, but was equally aware of his inability to confront a nation united behind Mosaddeq. He chose to ignore the British political strategy.[49]

Early conduct of the oil dispute

As alluded to earlier, British official were dubious about Mosaddeq's willingness or ability to engage in a meaningful give and take on the oil dispute. Mosaddeq believed any negotiations should conform to the terms of the Nationalization Act, a point that imparted his position a measure of rigidity. In June he rebuffed a renewed offer of a fifty-fifty split that an AIOC emissary, Basil Jackson, presented to him.[50] With all the hue and cry that the oil nationalization had caused, he could hardly be expected to settle now for a solution which had been offered to his immediate predecessors, Razmara and Ala.

Later Mosaddeq chose to ignore a preliminary *restraining order* issued on 5 July 1951 by the International Court of Justice (ICJ), which, as mentioned before, was petitioned by Britain to adjudicate on the substance of the dispute. The restraining order was procedural in nature. It enjoined Iran to refrain from any action that would change the status quo pending an opinion by the Court on the merit of the case. Legal arguments presented by either side on the substance of the dispute were complex but in a nutshell could be stated as follows: Britain argued that both Iran and Britain had, in time, accepted the compulsory jurisdiction of the ICJ with respect to international and bilateral agreements and that Britain, by virtue of its 'diplomatic protection rights' vis-à-vis the AIOC, was a party to the oil dispute. Iran, on the other hand, disputed the jurisdiction of the ICJ, arguing that it had not recognized the ICJ jurisdiction on matters arising essentially from its national sovereignty and that at any rate Iran's acceptance of the court's jurisdiction was not retroactive, that is, did not cover international accords signed prior to the date of acceptance of the court's compulsory jurisdiction. Finally, and more to the point, Iran argued that the ICJ had no jurisdiction in disputes between a state and a private company.[51]

With military option now on the backburner, Truman interceded with Mosaddeq for a negotiated solution. In a letter addressed to the Iranian prime minister on 8 July, Truman strongly urged Mosaddeq to accept the ICJ injunction and proposed to send Averell Harriman, a close friend and advisor, for mediation. Mosaddeq flatly rejected the president's appeal to obey the court order, but welcomed the offer of American mediation.[52] Foreign Secretary Morrison was reluctant about the US mediation role, but went along in view of firm American support for the ICJ restraining order.[53] Harriman (Figure 8) arrived in Tehran on 15 July amidst violent *Tudeh* demonstrations protesting his arrival.

Mosaddeq made it clear to the American mediation team that dialogue with Britain was contingent upon recognition by the latter of the reality of oil nationalization, a position Attlee himself had argued for since mid-May.[54] The Labour government had already hinted its acquiescence in the nationalization 'in some form' during the Jackson mission earlier but now in early August, through Harriman's midwifery, Britain formally recognized 'the principle of oil nationalization in Iran' on its own as well as on the AIOC's behalf. The formula was something of a compromise to the extent that Iran wished, but could not obtain, recognition by Britain of the terms of the Nationalization Act; this would have implied British acquiescence to Iranian control over the full gamut of

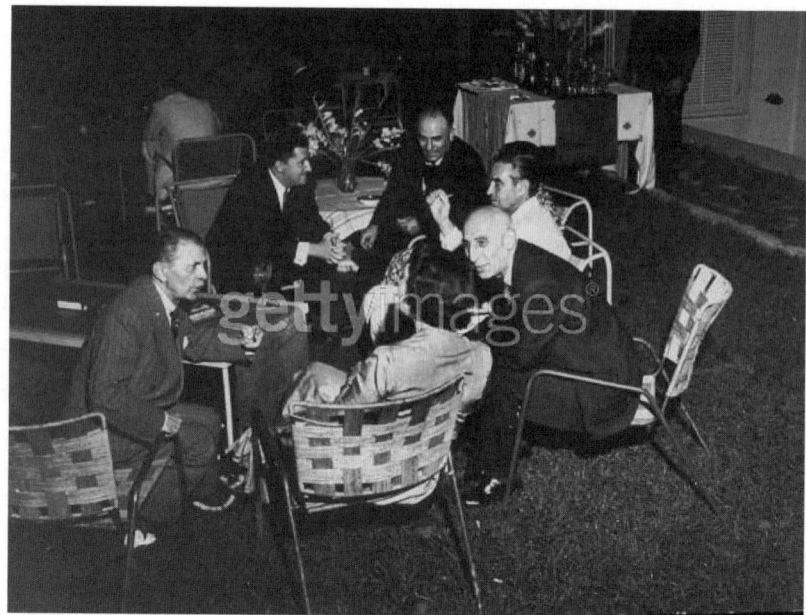

Figure 8 Harriman's visit to Tehran in August 1951. Seated from left to right are Hossien Ala, the Court Minister, Col. Vernon Walters, Mosaddeq's son Dr Qolam-Hossein Mosaddeq, Averell Harriman, Prime Minister Mosaddeq and Mrs Harriman (Marie Norton Whitney). In a private chat in 1985, Vernon Walters, then the US ambassador to the UN, confided tongue-in-cheek to this author that, in spite of all appearances, Mosaddeq was not insensitive to feminine charm judging by the attention he paid to Mrs Harriman. ©Time-Life-Getty, 2009

activities, namely exploration, extraction and exploitation. The British cabinet decision, however, provided the needed impetus to get substantive talks underway. The Lord Privy Seal, Richard Stokes, was dispatched to Tehran in early August.

Talks over a three-week period under Harriman's aegis proved barren. Stokes's proposal was little more than a convoluted form of equal revenue sharing which allowed Britain to maintain its control over operational aspects. It contained the following points: Transfer of all AIOC assets in Iran to the Iranian government's possession against 'compensation'. A 'purchasing company' would buy the bulk of Iranian oil at a discount price, leaving a smaller percentage of the produce to be directly marketed by Iran. The rate of the discount to the purchasing company had been calculated to keep Iran's profit share to 50 per cent. In addition, the creation of an executive firm, responsible for all operational aspects in Iran, had been mooted. Though placed under nominal Iranian supervision, practical arrangements would make this subsidiary a disguised arm of the AIOC. Mosaddeq was not going to let himself be pinned down to the discussion of practical issues as long as the British proposals did not square with the terms of the Nationalization Act. In rejecting Stokes's proposal Iran underscored its objection to the creation both of a purchasing and an executive arm, and to the proposed profit-sharing scheme through discounts as well as to the terms for determination of the amount of the 'compensation'.

By the end of August, a dejected Stokes returned to London. While agreeing with British stereotyping of Mosaddeq as an eccentric demagogue, Stokes was not unsympathetic to a fairer share of profits for Iran beyond the generally admitted 50 per cent. In London he shared this view with Attlee, much to the dismay of the AIOC chairman Sir William Fraser.[55]

The British complaint to the Security Council

When the British employees of the AIOC refused to work under the appointed Iranian management, the government ordered their departure. The decision met vigorous objection, not just by Britain but also from Washington.[56] Interpreting the expulsion order as a breach of the ICJ's restraining order, Britain complained to the UN Security Council in October 1951. It will be recalled that a month earlier in September an oil boycott had been declared by AIOC with Royal Navy backing. The oil dispute had reached an impasse.

At the Security Council (Figure 9) Mosaddeq aired Iran's grievances, clearly out-playing Sir Goldwyn Jeff who represented Britain.[57] He denied the competence both of the International Court of Justice and that of the Security Council on the grounds that the dispute arose from Iran's sovereign right to nationalize a private firm. Amongst a host of other points, Mosaddeq contested the validity of the 1933 seeding accord with the AIOC, pointing out that it had been signed under duress and that the *Majles* which ratified it lacked legitimacy in view of the fact that, under Reza Shah's dictatorial rule, deputies were not genuine representatives of the people.[58] In spite of the US support for the jurisdiction of the Security Council, voiced by Ambassador Warren Austin, the British draft resolution failed to obtain sufficient votes. Upon a motion by France, the Security Council deferred a decision until the

Figure 9 Mosaddeq being helped by the UN Secretary-General Trygve Lie to his seat at the Security Council. In the background from left to right are Doctor Hossein Fatemi, an unknown official, Dr Mozaffar Baqa'ie (wearing spectacles) and Dr Qolam-Hossein Mosaddeq; standing against the wall is Dr Mehdi Vakil, who represented Iran at the UN with distinction in the 1960s. Photo, the US State Department, courtesy of the Truman Library®

ICJ awarded its substantive verdict. This was meant to be a face-saving draw for the parties, but in actual fact it was a victory for Mosaddeq who had thus blunted the formidable intimidation device Britain had resorted to.

The Washington oil talks

While the Security Council was discussing Iran, Tories won the elections in Britain and Churchill became prime minister. By then the British financial situation had reached a point where the Chancellor of the Exchequer Richard Butler announced in the Commons that Britain was on the verge of bankruptcy. The Tories had over the past few months chided Atlee for being too soft towards Iran. Now back in power in the wake of the failure of direct talks and a lacklustre performance at the UN

Security Council, they pinned their hopes on undermining Mosaddeq and bringing about his fall through a range of economic and political pressures. One prerequisite of this approach was to see to it that Mosaddeq returned from his trip to Washington empty-handed. This objective underpinned the British attitude during the period of consultations that took place during Mosaddeq's sojourn in Washington that lasted a full month to 20 November.

Mosaddeq met twice with President Truman and with Dean Acheson who appointed Under-Secretary George McGhee to pursue the talks. McGhee had already contacted Mosaddeq while he was still in New York (Figure 10). He now attempted to resume oil talks from where it had been left by Harriman some two months earlier. For that purpose, regular consultations with the Foreign Office were taking place. During the tripartite meeting of foreign minister's in Paris in November 1951, Acheson was in close consultation with Antony Eden. Based on these contacts, McGhee prepared a compromise proposal

Figure 10 Mosaddeq talking to Under-Secretary George McGhee. Photo, the US State Department photo, courtesy of the Truman Library®

that he thought would be sellable to Mosaddeq. When on 4 November Acheson shared it with Eden, he summarily rejected it.[59] In an analysis of the British attitude, Acheson wrote: 'The cardinal purpose of Brit policy is not to prevent Iran from going Commie; the cardinal point is to preserve what they believe to be the last remaining bulwark of Brit solvency; that is their overseas investment and property position.' Acheson went on to quote a British interlocutor who had remarked to him that if the American appraisal of Iran risking to go communist is correct, 'the choice before you [America] is whether Iran goes commie or Brit goes bankrupt.' Clearly the British expected the United States to consider the former a lesser evil. Finally Acheson concluded that the main purpose of Britain was to leave the United States without any bargaining material until Mosaddeq left Washington.

As for Mosaddeq, he had accepted the principle of payment of 'compensation' but rejected the notion of *future losses* as a factor in calculation of the compensation amount. He adamantly rejected any British role in the management and was no longer keen to keep the British technicians for the day-to-day running of operations in Abadan and elsewhere. He would, however, accept nationals from more neutral countries, notably the Dutch, to undertake the 'management' as a subsidiary to the NIOC. He was prepared to allocate a substantial portion of oil revenues against reparations to AIOC. Further, to cater to British strategic concerns, Mosaddeq agreed to sell Iran's oil to Britain as 'bulk purchaser' with a reasonable discount (in lieu of profit sharing), provided that Iran was given a free hand to sell a determined percentage of its oil products to other customers at the going market rate, including with discounts if needed. Finally, Mosaddeq was keen on a fair price that could be periodically adjusted to keep up with market trends.

On 9 November McGhee informed Mosaddeq that the gap in the position of the parties was too wide to allow hope for an agreement while Mosaddeq was in Washington (Figure 11). Prime Minister Mosaddeq took note. Before leaving Washington, he wrote a letter to Truman asking for a loan to help Iran meet a serious budget deficit pending a settlement of the oil dispute. An interim response was given on 15 November in which Truman confined himself to stating that Mosaddeq's request would receive careful consideration 'in accordance with our well-known desire to assist the people of Iran'.

It is interesting to note a sudden shift in Acheson's attitude towards Mosaddeq while he was still in Europe, which may be attributed to

Figure 11 Mosaddeq being greeted at the White House by President Truman. Photo, the US State Department, courtesy of the Truman Library®

Eden's influence. In a strange about-turn he cabled Washington on 16 November, instructing the State Department to make it clear (presumably to Mosaddeq) that 'any aid by the United States was given to the Shah and [the] Iranian people'. He went on to say that US concern 'was for the Shah and [the] Iranian people and not for Mosadeq [sic]'.[60] The State Department assured London that no response in the immediate term, if at all, would be given to Mosaddeq's loan request. This was predicated on an assumption that any policy that could help keep Mosaddeq afloat would produce a bad impression in the United Kingdom as Ambassador Gifford had advised the department.[61] In the same vein, they declined a request from Mosaddeq for a letter of assurance about the Mutual Security Program (MSP) to Iran.[62] Eden had thus succeeded on two counts. Firstly, to stonewall progress in the oil talks while Mosaddeq was in Washington and, secondly, to withhold all American aid that could enhance Mosaddeq's position back home.

Why Acheson bought into this attitude is hard to determine. Britain at that stage had intensified its efforts at undermining Mosaddeq in Tehran and was optimistic about their ability to have him removed. Eden presumably convinced Acheson that those chances were real. Ironically, the State Department and Acheson personally had, only a short while back, complained about British inaction and had gone out of their way to bring them into line in order to arrive at a settlement while Mosaddeq was in Washington. Cable traffic and memoranda related to this period reflect tense moments in the exchanges between Acheson and Eden.[63] In his otherwise meticulously written memoirs, Acheson has shed no light on his about-face while confirming the British rigidity.[64] The apparent shift in Acheson's attitude may have been the reason why on his return to Tehran, Mosaddeq bitterly complained about the attitude of the State Department even if a few weeks earlier he had profusely praised US policies, adding that on his return he would inform the Iranian people of the goodwill shown by the United States.[65]

The World Bank proposal

Before leaving Washington, Mosaddeq met World Bank Vice-President Robert Garner, seemingly to discuss a loan. As a UN-affiliated institution to which both Britain and Iran were parties, the World Bank (IBRD) was well-placed to play a role in defusing the crisis. Contrary to common perceptions, the initiative for the meeting and the Bank's subsequent involvement did not come from the US administration; if anything, American official had some misgivings about IBRD entering into the intricate world of the oil business. The Bank was nevertheless encouraged to pursue its efforts, especially as Britain appeared favourable to the approach.[66] In the course of November to December 1951, World Bank officials toured Iran and Britain and tried hard to strike a bargain. The World Bank proposed a two-year transitional arrangement – renewable on request by both parties – in which the Bank would independently operate the Iranian oil on a non-profit basis through a subsidiary group. This outfit would produce and sell Iranian oil at bulk to the AIOC at a discount price, with a ten per cent free allotment of the products to Iran for direct sale in the free market. The Bank would retain a portion of the sale proceeds as deposit for eventual settlement of the compensation and credit the balance to the Iranian and the UK treasuries on an equal basis. A key point in the IBRD proposal was the caveat according to which the transitional arrangements were 'without prejudice' to the positions of either side.

Scrutiny of the World Bank package reveals little substantive difference with proposals presented to Iran in Washington.[67] Mosaddeq was particularly concerned about the IBRD's pricing structure that foresaw bulk sale to AIOC at a larger discount rate than Iran was prepared to concede. The United States in contrast considered the amount of discount to be too low to make Iranian oil competitive. Furthermore, according to the proposal, Iran could market no more than 10 per cent of the oil products independently. Even for this volume, Iran had no pricing leverage and was required to sell it without a discount; a constraint which, in view of the then existing glut, rendered the sale impractical.

The World Bank proposal, nevertheless, offered Mosaddeq a badly needed breathing space to attain economic solvency and consolidate his hold on power; he appears to have favoured the approach initially yet – in the politically charged climate of the time – he ended up rebuffing the World Bank.[68] In an *ad hominem* remark on 20 March 1952, addressing the nation on the *Norouz* eve he said, 'I could not accept this shameful stain on my honour or on yours.'[69]

It must be emphasized here that for Mosaddeq and his associates, oil nationalization was not merely a move to secure the economic interests of the nation. It had strong anti-imperialistic properties, a dimension that arguably carried equal weight. If the history of foreign dominance in much of Iran's recent past fully justified the weight accorded to this dimension, the attitude nevertheless lacked realism and was oblivious of the intricacies of the oil market.

By the last quarter of 1951, increases in oil production in Iraq, Kuwait and Saudi Arabia had indeed eliminated the need for Iranian oil.[70] Mosaddeq's oil advisors were not sufficiently alive to this reality and might not have possessed an in-depth knowledge of the market intricacies, as Averell Harriman observed in one of his reports to Washington.[71] Mosaddeq's high-flying goal of breaking the log-jam on his own terms thus clashed with market realities just as it fretted the Tory's sense of grandeur. Not only did Churchill consider Mosaddeq's nationalization 'disastrous to a country like ours', but he toyed with the idea of retracting the acceptance of the principle of oil nationalization which the Atlee's labour government had conceded.[72] Further elaboration on this point is given under the heading 'A wedge to break the oil log-jam' in Chapter 3).

Early forebodings

On his return from the United States, Mosaddeq set out to organize elections for a new *Majles*. Reform of electoral law was one of his priorities but the task had remained unfulfilled. Once embarked on the elections, he could not overcome the influence of tribal chieftains, big landowners and provincial notables who traditionally determined – often with the government complicity – the outcome of elections in almost all electoral districts, with the notable exception of the Capital. Only the most stringent opposition from the central government could affect this trend. The fledgling democracy in Iran was too feeble to resist dominant oligarchic pressures.

A fervent constitutionalist, in earlier years Mosaddeq had acknowledged this reality by whispering that illiterate masses – which comprised close to 90 per cent of the population – should be disenfranchised.[73] Now, in an unprecedented move, Mosaddeq suspended the seventeenth *Majles* elections after only 79 of 136 seats had been filled. The National Front candidates had won 30 seats. Mutable old-guard politicians had won the bulk of the remaining seats. Diehard Mosaddeq opponents formed a minority that grew to 27 deputies over the following 12 months.

A lame *Majles* started its session in late April 1952, but Mosaddeq had clearly lost a crucial test in his quest to consolidate democracy. The stalemate in the oil dispute was taxing. To buy time Mosaddeq needed American financial aid but, as described earlier, the United States wanted to assess Mosaddeq's survival chances and was in no hurry to come to his rescue unless the country became visibly prone to fall to communists. The new American ambassador, the stoic Loy Henderson, unlike his predecessor Henry Grady, was less inclined to seek to bail Mosaddeq out without concrete concessions on the oil issue. The amounts of aid considered by the United States were at any rate paltry compared to the real needs.[74] Grady had requested a loan for $100 million from EXIMPBAK before Mosaddeq came to power. Truman agreed to 25 million only, but the loan could not be paid out due to the onerous conditions attached to it. Mosaddeq's own request to Truman for a loan of $10 million a month was not followed up. Henderson willingly followed the State Department's approach to the effect that aid should be linked to an oil concession by Mosaddeq. Henderson in fact had a negative view of Mosaddeq from the outset and seemed to be leaning towards the British position. After the severance of diplomatic relations with Britain in October 1952, he acted as if he represented the United Kingdom as well. His zeal earned him praise from Eden; something that did not escape the vigilance of Mosaddeq who in his memoirs later pointedly cites Eden's profuse praise of Henderson.[75] The above notwithstanding, Mosaddeq held on to the illusion of American largess for still some time to come.

3
Mosaddeq's Second Government, July 1952 to August 1953

In spite of the oil impasse and other domestic difficulties, 1951 was Mosaddeq's *annus mirabilis*. He had nationalized oil, extricated Iran from the grip of British hegemony, and demonstrated that a weak nation could stand up for its rights even when faced with a superpower. By year-end, he had been picked by *Time Magazine* as 'Man of the Year' for 1951 (Figure 12). However, the road ahead was treacherous; the first test appeared soon after the new *Majles* began its work.

By this time the State Department viewed Mosaddeq with scepticism, wondering if an oil deal would be possible as long as he remained in power.[1] As of the second quarter of 1952, Henderson had discretely joined the British chargé George Middleton in lobbying the Shah for the removal of Mosaddeq.[2] The Shah was particularly concerned about the government's untenable financial situation and its difficulty in meeting its payment obligations, including the salaries of government workers.[3] The government had indeed begun to chip in on monetary reserves, sold government bonds (*qarzeh'e melli*) and resorted to printing banknotes.[4]

Figure 12 Mosaddeq on the cover of *TIME* Magazine, 7 January 1952, designating him as 'Man of the Year' for 1951. Reproduced by permission of *TIME* Magazine. ©Time Magazine, 2008

With the onset of the new legislative period – where prime ministers formalistically resigned to be reappointed – the Shah began toying with the idea of replacing Mosaddeq, no doubt goaded by his immediate entourage. The Court Minister Ala, aware of the Shah's indecision, tried to multiply sources of pressure, resorting notably to Henderson.[5] Yet, indecision as a character-trait in the Shah rarely impaired his political realism. He opined that if the upcoming ICJ verdict favoured Mosaddeq, his dismissal would backfire. Secondly, before embarking on such a perilous course, the Shah wanted to know whether the Americans were prepared to provide immediate financial relief to a new prime minister. A replacement government, he argued with Henderson, would not be able to quickly settle the oil dispute without losing credibility and a solution to the dispute must at any rate be within the purview of the Nationalization Act.[6]

Given this attitude and the US Embassy reservations about Seyyed Zia,[7] the British officials discretely fell back on supporting Ahmad Qavam, careful to dissimulate this support lest he be branded a stooge. Qavam had directly lobbied British officials – and no doubt the Americans – to enlist support for his premiership.[8] The Americans, in Henderson's words, had no particular favourite but the American Ambassador had informally met Qavam and had been 'favourably impressed'.[9]

At The Hague, Mosaddeq pleaded Iran's case, helped by the renowned Belgian jurist Professor Henri Rolin. On his return on 24 June, he told the Shah that he was optimistic about the ICJ verdict which should allow Iran 'to sell its oil freely'.[10] In a passionate plea, he urged the Shah to continue the struggle by supporting him. Respecting a parliamentary tradition, he then submitted his resignation in early July.

The stage appeared to be set to replace Mosaddeq with Qavam. The two embassies, the Court Minister Ala, the Queen Mother and the Shah's twin-sister Ashraf, as well as top conservative politicians had all pressed the Shah for this nomination; they now held their breath in a countdown to Mosaddeq's imminent fall. Contrary to all expectations, the Shah opted for the reappointment of Mosaddeq and threw his weight behind him to ensure parliamentary support. According to parliamentary practice in those days, before a prime minister could officially be named by the Shah, an inclination vote from the *Majles* and the Senate was needed. The Shah discretely intervened to obtain such support for Mosaddeq. He sent Deputy-Court Minister Ahmad Houman to convey his preference for the reappointment of Mosaddeq to a senate caucus opposed to the outgoing prime minister. The same message was conveyed through the Speaker, Hassan Emami (*Emam Jum'ah*), to pro-Shah *Majles* deputies. Mosaddeq obtained 53 favourable votes in the *Majles* (out of 79). In the Senate, he received 14 yes votes (out of 30 seats) with the rest of the senators either absent or abstaining.[11] The

Shah's sense of realism had once again prevailed. Middleton, Henderson and Ala were disappointed. The Queen Mother and the Shah's twin-sister Princes Ashraf, who had urged the Shah to dismiss Mosaddeq, were reportedly incensed by the Shah's perceived 'weakness'. In a post-mortem the British chargé, Middleton, and Ambassador Henderson lamented the fact that their governments had failed to provide the Shah firm assurances of financial backing or pledge greater flexibility in the oil dispute in order to obtain the Shah's consent to replace Mosaddeq.[12]

The Qavam hiatus and the *Siy'e Tyr* popular uprising (21 July 1952)

It was against the backdrop of such events that shortly thereafter the first serious rift between the Shah and his prime minister occurred. When he presented his new cabinet to the Shah in mid-July, Mosaddeq had proposed himself as Minister of War, a move intended to supplant the Shah's control over the Army. The deep-seated discord on the interpretation of the constitution had burst onto the surface.

The constitution in effect accorded supreme command of the armed forces to the Shah, as indeed also the prerogative to appoint or dismiss ministers. For Mosaddeq, those titles and prerogatives were *nominal* and the Shah's functions ceremonial in nature. This interpretation rested on an article of the constitution according to which ministers, irrespective of the Shah's orders, were accountable to parliament. The constitution had indeed exonerated the Shah of any *accountability*, a provision that led to a degree of semantic confusion. Many confused the term 'accountability' with *responsibility* for which the same word, namely *'mas'ouliat'*, is used in the Persian language.[13] The Shah's supporters argued that non-accountability arose from the monarch's exalted above-the-fray status and should not deprive him from exercising his constitutional prerogatives. This did not resonate well with liberals, who believed that authority goes with accountability. Nor was the jurisprudence on the Shah's authority strictly uniform. In 1924, the *Majles* had passed legislation to give the title of Supreme Commander of the Armed Forces to Reza Khan, then prime minister. On the other hand, during the long interregnum between the third and the fourth legislative periods of the *Majles*, coinciding mainly with the First World War, Ahmad Shah – or his regent on his behalf – had appointed and dismissed 11 prime ministers in 14 cabinet reshuffles thus establishing ample precedence for the Shah to exercise the contested authority at least during parliamentary interregna.[14] More to the point, in 1949 a constitutional assembly had empowered the Shah to appoint half of the senators as well as dissolving the parliament.

In the political climate of the time, however, real power trumped constitutional exegesis. The Shah's power-base was the army, to which he intended to cling. In the face of the discord over control of the armed forces Mosaddeq offered to resign. This time the Shah accepted his resignation. Under pressure and against his better judgement, the Shah appointed Ahmad Qavam (Figure 13) after the *Majles* expressed an inclination for his appointment. The National Front deputies had boycotted the straw vote.[15]

An octogenarian, Qavam had served as prime minister four times in the previous quarter of the century, notably during the Azerbaijan Crisis (see that section in Chapter 1). He had a reputation for ruse and for audacity in politics. He had fallen out with the Shah partly because of his strong character and haughty manner. In a gesture of displeasure in 1948, the Shah had rescinded Qavam's honorary title of *Jenāb'e Ashraf*.[16] Now in July 1952, it was with the same pompous title that the Shah addressed Qavam when he issued the royal *Farmān* appointing him prime minister. Qavam had solicited and was being discreetly backed by the British Embassy in Tehran; he had pledged to rule with an iron fist and break the oil log-jam, arresting Kashani or any other politician standing in his way, irrespective of parliamentary immunities.[17] Upon appointment, in a move regarded as dim-witted and ill-advised, Qavam issued a bellicose declaration in which he announced 'a drastic change of course' and draconian measures against agitators.

This was the low-point in Qavam's long political career and his final salvo. In a rare convergence of heterogeneous political formations, the *Tudeh* militants joined bazaar, shop-keepers, intelligentsia and other Mosaddeq supporters who had heeded a call for a general strike and rally on 21 July 1952 (30 tyr, 1331 in Persian calendar) issued by Ayatollah Kashani. The

Figure 13 Ahmad Qavam. Photo by Dmitri Kessel/Time & Life Pictures. ©Getty Images, 2009

crowds defied the martial law in a bloody showdown with security forces. Several dozens were killed and scores more were wounded. In panic the Shah ordered the army to back down.[18] By evening, Qavam had been ousted and Mosaddeq made a triumphal return. The Shah's premonitions had been vindicated.[19] The US and British Embassies in Tehran nevertheless described him as 'the weakling' for not having backed Qavam in the face of a popular uprising.[20] Others consider Qavam the victim of his own arrogance and failure to gauge the prevailing public mood.

As if this was not enough, the next day the International Court of Justice delivered its verdict. In a landmark nine to five decision, the ICJ opined that the oil dispute was not within its jurisdiction thus endorsing the Iranian position. The British judge, Sir Arnold McNair, was among the nine who voted against the court's jurisdiction thus refuting the British position. The court lifted the temporary injunction which it had issued a year earlier and which called on the parties to maintain the status quo pending the court's substantive award.[21]

The two events constituted a watershed. Mosaddeq had emerged stronger politically and was vindicated on the international scene. He had won his bid to sideline the Shah and assume control of the army. His political opponents were humbled and intimidated. The *Tudeh* Party, which up to that point had opposed Mosaddeq, now shifted its stance and espoused the slogan of 'united anti-imperialist front'.

On the negative side of the ledger, however, disconcerting handicaps loomed. The treasury was all but empty. Mosaddeq was becoming disillusioned with America's bona fide. At his meeting with Henderson on 28 July, Mosaddeq bitterly complained that in the face of the dire financial situation facing his government – and serious danger of communism – the United States had turned its back but had offered funds to Qavam's government. For the first time, Mosaddeq accused the United States of opposing an oil deal fair to Iran lest the interests of US oil companies elsewhere be compromised.[22] He had finally understood that as a result of production boosts elsewhere, Iranian oil was no longer needed or, lacking means of distribution, not sellable in significant quantities.[23] This realization led Mosaddeq to entertain the notion of an 'oil-less economy for Iran'.[24] The notion was serious enough for Mosaddeq to obtain advisory assistance from the United Nations in November.[25] To attain this goal the government needed a free hand to carry out sweeping reforms. The *Majles* composition and the less pliant Senate could hardly be relied on to allow the prime minister a smooth ride.

Rift among Mosaddeq supporters

Mosaddeq, riding on the crest of his victories, obtained emergency powers from the parliament to legislate for a six-month period, during which his proposed bills would be allowed a trial run. Many deputies, including some of his supporters, were reticent. In retrospect, the period that followed the seismic events of July 1952 proved precursory; they set the stage for the August 1953 debacle.

The first clear signs of fissure within the ranks of the National Front appeared in the immediate aftermath of the 21 July uprising. Simmering resentments fed by personal rivalries, hubris and turf wars compounded disagreements over substantive issues; they yielded discord and eventual enmity. The most significant was the rift between Mosaddeq and Ayatollah Kashani. The latter had become the *Majles* speaker despite Mosaddeq's reticence.[26] From this platform Kashani began to chart a separate course. Even before Qavam's ephemeral reappearance on the scene in July, Kashani had hinted to the Shah through Court Minister Hussein Ala that he would not be averse to replacing Mosaddeq with a suitable candidate. Kashani on that occasion reportedly mentioned the name of Senator Javad Bushehri.[27]

Over the previous two years, Kashani had galvanized the bazaar and traditional middle class in support of Mosaddeq. The culminating point was the *Siy'e Tyr* uprising, which brought the triumphal return of Mosaddeq in its wake. Even if the popular rally had little to do with Kashani's own political stature, his call was undeniably the rallying cry. Kashani therefore considered the prime minister indebted to him and expected reciprocation. He demanded a voice – if not a vetting prerogative – in cabinet appointments.[28] He had meddled in *the Majles* elections and intervened at different levels to slot his cronies into public positions.[29] Two of his sons, apart from himself, ran for the seventeenth *majles*.[30] Mosaddeq was secular at heart, polished and infinitely less Byzantine; he showed little patience for the prelate's unruly behaviour and often reacted to his intrusive letters in terse and dismissive language.[31]

Breaches of deontology aside, as the *Majles* speaker, Kashani was legitimately jealous of the prerogatives of the legislative branch. Mosaddeq's emergency powers were, in effect, at the expense of the legislators. This put the two magnates on a collision course. Some vocal deputies in the opposition had cogently argued that the transfer of their prerogative to the executive branch had been sanctioned neither by the constitution nor the electorate. Later in the year, when at the expiration of the six-month trial run Mosaddeq asked for renewal of his emergency powers, the rift between the two burst into the open. The alliance of convenience had gradually transformed into a vicious enmity. The National Front became irreparably fractured. But Mosaddeq's drive to obtain emergency powers produced other important defections. Chief among them were Hossein Makki and Dr Mozaffar Baqa'ei.[32] Both had entered the political arena under the wing of Qavam when the latter formed a political party in 1946 to consolidate his power. A self-made man with no college education, next only to Mosaddeq, Makki was the most popular National Front politician.[33] He was arguably the closest and most endeared to him.[34] During the fifteenth session of *the Majles* (1947–48), from which Mosaddeq had been excluded, Makki kept him up to date with the *Majles* back-fence talks and rap sessions and occasionally deputized for him by making his views known to *Majles* deputies.[35] In the waning days of the fifteenth *Majles*, Makki had staged a filibuster to block voting on the unpopular Supplemental Oil Agreement. He was on Mosaddeq's side during the October 1949 sit-in at the royal palace and hence a founding member of the National Front, which, as we explained earlier, came into existence shortly thereafter.[36]

Makki's finest hour came when, in June 1951, he led the government team to Abadan to seize the AIOC facilities and assets in line with the Nationalization Act. The effective seizure of the company was an ostentatious act of national self-assertion that instantly made Makki a folk hero. Makki maintained contacts with the Shah and possibly worked to broker harmonious relationship between the government and the Crown. He later claimed that this was out of a genuine concern to shield Mosaddeq against missteps he was being led into by his left-leaning advisors.[37] Makki's detractors accused him of opportunism, inflated ego and a disguised inferiority complex.[38] Be that as it may, Makki's open opposition to Mosaddeq did not become publicly known until early 1953. Makki lost in political lustre and prestige but Mosaddeq lost a key ally.

The third dissenter among the heavyweights was Dr Mozaffar Baqa'ei. His career path in politics was somewhat similar to Makki, but the two men differed in significant ways. Baqa'ei had his own socialist-leaning political party, *Zahmatkeshān* (the toilers). He, nonetheless, was fiercely anti-*Tudeh*. He had a solid constituency in his home province of Kerman which had procured him a seat in three consecutive legislative periods. From this platform, he had lambasted the proponents of the Supplemental Oil Agreement and projected himself as a staunch nationalist and Mosaddeq supporter. Despite his French training and academic credentials, he fraternized with radical clerics and was close to Ayatollah Kashani; he also maintained contacts with the palace. His wheeling and dealings, daredevil character, caustic rhetoric and effrontery made of Baqa'ei something of a political boss who inspired more fear than respect. Baqa'ei was the first among the top Mosaddeq advisors to break ranks.[39] Like Makki, he had accumulated considerable political capital as a key figure in the rise of the National Front. Both Makki and he must have realized that in splitting with the patriarch they risked losing much of that capital. From this vantage point, it is fair to say that parting ways with Mosaddeq took a certain political courage. Baqa'ei was particularly vilified by his opponents who accused him of accepting bribes from the CIA, other than charges of conspiracy to abduct and murder the Police Chief, a crime for which he was indicted by the Mosaddeq government but which he vehemently denies. Whatever the truth of these accusations, Baqa'ei was also a man of certain convictions for which he stood up in crucial junctures, often at his own peril.[40]

It is equally undeniable that the fissure in the ranks of the National Front encouraged those in Britain who advocated subversion rather than engagement. The split within the NF ranks was invoked by Eden to dampen American enthusiasm to work in earnest with Mosaddeq in the immediate aftermath of the 21 July uprising and the latter's return to power.[41]

A wedge to break the oil log-jam: the Truman-Churchill joint offer

Following his triumphs on both internal and international fronts, Mosaddeq decided to take a shot at the oil log-jam through direct talks with Britain. During the latter part of July, he held a number of meetings with the British Chargé Middleton. He appeared favourable to a British bid to submit the 'compensation' issue to a binding ICJ arbitration.[42] For the first time, Mosaddeq had bypassed the American Embassy in making what both Middleton and Henderson viewed as a positive signal.

The immediate American reflex was to seize upon this opening and built around it. A new American proposal, developed with input from Henderson, foresaw financial and other incentives to Iran; this was designed to meet immediate cash flow needs if the dispute over the compensation could be referred to ICJ. Longer-term arrangements for the production and sale of Iran's oil could then be worked out through additional talks. The United States had earmarked $10 million in grant, which was to be added to the cash receipts from the sale of ready-to-market oil products in storage facilities.

When Acheson submitted this proposal for British approval, the Foreign Office was initially lukewarm. To blunt the American zeal Eden argued in effect that Mosaddeq was no barrier against communism, if anything he was now beholden to the *Tudeh* and more amenable to their demands. Furthermore, because of dissensions within the National Front, Mosaddeq was more vulnerable. The army, Eden went on, was loyal to the throne and seemed willing to intervene. Then, in a surprising departure from Britain's earlier recognition of the Nationalization Act, Eden stated: 'we agree to arbitration if the terms of reference were sufficiently wide to permit the introduction during arbitration of the question of the validity of the Persian Nationalization Act and its compatibility with the AIOC concession.' Overall the British reaction, while ambivalent, revealed a leaning toward a military *coup*.[43] It will be recalled that similar arguments by Eden the previous November had resulted in a sudden change of attitude by Acheson towards Mosaddeq. Conditions now were different; Mosaddeq's ostentatious return to power must have served as a sobering lesson, rendering American officials less prone to British temptations.

Mosaddeq rightly regarded the issue of 'validity of the nationalization' as *Res adjudicate*. Acheson was of the same mind. No successor to Mosaddeq, Acheson retorted, could agree with the British about-turn.[44] This time it was Eden who soon realigned his position with Acheson, something that must have been helped by Middleton's reporting in mid-August when signs of a new flexibility in Mosaddeq's attitude had emerged. The British Chargé in effect considered that Mosaddeq might be amenable to a new language on the ICJ terms of reference for determining the compensation amount. The formula which he thought may appeal to Mosaddeq had been couched in a somewhat ambiguous language that lent itself to different interpretations; it became the core element of a joint proposal by Churchill and Truman which was submitted to Mosaddeq on 27 August. The full terms of reference paragraph read:

> There shall be submitted to the ICJ the question of compensation in respect of nationalization of the enterprise of the AIOC in Iran, having regard to claims and counterclaims of both parties and the juridical position of parties prior to 20 March 1951.

The joint proposal called for negotiations between Iran and AIOC aimed at 'making arrangements for the flow of oil from Iran to world markets'.

Further, if Iran agreed to the above, the AIOC would undertake to sell some two million tons of stored oil products at a price to be agreed on.[45] Britain would relax export and currency restrictions and finally, the United States would make an immediate grant of $10 million to help with budgetary problems.

When Henderson and Middleton presented the proposal to Mosaddeq on 27 August, he instantly and vociferously rejected it. In an ill-tempered tone, Mosaddeq warned the two that the publication of the proposal would raise public anger and consternation. Mosaddeq did not ask for a delay for consideration of the proposal. He called the package a snare designed to *reopen the issue of the validity of the Nationalization Act*. He further dismissed the American offer of $10 million, pointing out that Iran did not need alms. Instead, he insisted on payment by Britain of £50 million sterling – an amount which the AIOC had entered in its ledger as receivable by Iran in case the Supplemental Oil Agreement should have been ratified by Iran. This, the British officials considered as water over the dam. The two diplomats pleaded in vain that the joint proposal had been formulated in good faith and by no means intended to compromise the Nationalization Act.[46]

The package, to be sure, was far from perfect. Its acceptability hinged on the outcome of the foreseen negotiations aiming to determine the structure and modalities for the flow of the oil to world markets. The proposal needed to be, and no doubt could have been, amended in a business-like setting helped by legal experts. Still, its hasty rejection by Mosaddeq without benefit of sound legal advice and a correct understanding of its sense and implications is puzzling at best. Contrary to the interpretation given by Mosaddeq, the proposed terms of reference *could not* call into question the validity of the Nationalization Act *per se* as the object of the referral, namely *determination of the amount of compensation*, was in itself tantamount to tacit confirmation by the parties of the validity of the Nationalization Act. In other words the proposed arbitration would have lost its *raison d'être* if the act of nationalization was to be called into question. The summary rejection of the package by Mosaddeq reinforced the negative image London wished to convey to Washington to convince the Americans that no solution to the oil dispute was possible while he was in power.

This is not to say that Britain was acting without ulterior motives.[47] The Tory government no doubt hoped to exploit the issue of validity of the nationalization act as a means to obtain compensation for *future losses*.[48] For their part, Iranians dreaded a court verdict that would saddle Iran with an onerous debt. The terms of reference allowed enough leeway for each side to argue its case. While each side could present *claims and counterclaims*, nothing indicated that such claims by either side would be retained by the court. Iran had a legitimate case and legal claims of her own. Nor could reference to *'juridical positions of parties prior to 1951'* in the terms of reference override the Labour government's formal recognition of the principle of nationalization.

Mosaddeq belatedly submitted a confused and inscrutable counter-proposal which was given only cursory consideration by Britain and the United States. Both governments, however, re-emphasized the fact that Iran had misunderstood the joint Truman-Churchill proposal of late August.[49]

All was not lost, however, as the Truman administration, in its waning days in office, tried yet again to break the log-jam. Talks were carried over to the new Eisenhower administration, which took over the White House as of 20 January 1953. A revised, and as it turned out an ultimate, proposal was submitted to Mosaddeq on 20 February. We shall return to this episode shortly. Meanwhile Mosaddeq was grappling with a host of internal problems.

Mosaddeq's reforms and the theory of legitimacy

More worldly and disabused, Mosaddeq set out to reform the state apparatus, hoping to prepare the nation for a protracted struggle under his leadership. These reforms targeted the army, the judiciary and the royal household as well as land tenure among scores of other fields.[50] An important objective was to eliminate the budget deficit and achieve trade balance. This was an arduous task in which Mosaddeq and his ministers remarkably succeeded.[51] Reforms also aimed to remedy social ills and, among other things, attenuate inequalities in the status of women.[52] They were in most part well conceived. The share of farmers from crop yield was increased by 15 per cent and village councils were set up.

It is worthwhile to dwell briefly on these reforms in view of their relevance to the subject matter of this study. By targeting vested interests, these reforms perilously enlarged the ranks of the internal opposition. Admittedly, there was a facet to these reforms that lent itself to legitimate criticism and dissension. Through them, Mosaddeq set out to firm-up his grip on the state apparatus. He deemed this control essential for the nationalistic enterprise he had embarked on. By mid-August 1953, Mosaddeq had rid himself of both houses of parliament and was legislating in their place, he had suspended the Supreme Court,[53] curtailed the authority of the Shah, taken the army under his wing, launched the Societal (National) Security Act to cow his opponents and, in short, held all levers of power in his hands. As a staunch constitutionalist, he also brought upon himself the onus of self-contradiction. On the road to an elusive success, legitimacy trumped legality and institutions were tampered with.

The Senate, having become a hub of conservative opposition to Mosaddeq, was tossed out by a juridical sleight of hand.[54] Regarding the *Majles*, his home ground, Mosaddeq planned profound reforms. He proposed an increase in the *Majles* seats from 136 to 172. This was seen by the opposition as a ploy to incapacitate the already crippled *Majles*, in as much as the proposed seat numbers could prevent a quorum if the bill could be applied retroactively.[55] The bid to increase seats was finally approved after the government added a form of words to specify its non-retroactivity. The dissolution of the *Majles* had to wait until the next summer and more compelling reasons, but the episode widened the fracture in the ranks of the National Front.[56]

Mosaddeq's reform of the army took several facets. The first step was to downsize the armed forces, reducing its budget by 15 per cent. He then set out to replace the old guard with younger officers in key army posts. Many army generals and senior officers were prematurely retired. The army chief of staff, an old-timer and confidant of the Shah, General Morteza Yazdanpanah, who had refused to sign the retirement orders decreed by the prime minister, was replaced with a more neutral figure, General Mahmoud Baharmast. By October 1952, the Society of Retired Army-Officers had turned into a hotbed of opposition and conspiracy against Mosaddeq. After the crisis in February 1953 (see 'The Gathering of the Storm' in Chapter 5), Mosaddeq opted for a lesser known but more trusted officer, Brigadier-General Taqi Riahi. A polytechnician, General Riahi belonged to the engineering corps of the army and, though respected, was not known for his combat experience or skills, a fact that had not escaped the attention of TPAJAX planners.[57] Other trusted officers were also given command posts in several brigade-level garrisons around Tehran. The enigmatic Brigadier-General Mahmoud Afshartous, a diehard Mosaddeq supporter, was appointed chief of the National Police while Colonel Hassan-Ali Ashrafi was assigned to the key post of the martial law administrator.[58]

Other than purging the army of the Shah's loyalists, Mosaddeq reduced the budget of the royal household, reclaimed the Crown lands, closed down the private offices of the Shah's siblings, and had the Queen Mother and the Shah's twin–sister, Princess Ashraf, banished to Europe.

The two were known for their anti-Mosaddeq intrigues. He forbade the army top brass to see or report to the Shah. In the same vein, he discouraged foreign diplomats from frequenting the royal palace and ended up replacing the Shah's loyal Court Minister Hossein Ala with one of his own relatives, whom the Shah distrusted.[59] However, in order to reassure the Shah of his *bona fides*, Mosaddeq volunteered a hand-written inscription on the back of the Koran, pledging he would never betray the constitution and would never seek a regime change or accept the position of president of the republic.[60]

The British two-pronged strategy: subversion and engagement

The literature on the subject is rich in spite of the fact that archives of SIS/MI6 have not been declassified. A wealth of primary material emanates from the Foreign Office archives kept in the Public Record Office, mainly minutes prepared by a hybrid British officer, an academic cum diplomat-spy, by the name of Robin Zaehner. In a seminal work in 1982, supplemented by subsequent essays, the American historian, William Roger Louis, has extensively canvassed British archives, notably minutes of cabinet meetings, contributing a wealth of insights into the British decision-making processes during the early part of the oil crisis.[61] As he noted, the fact that Zaehner was appointed by the Foreign Office – doing what ordinarily is performed by MI6 officers – has, to a large extent, revealed the contents of secret British activities through the declassified Foreign Office archives, which extend roughly to the time of the rupture of diplomatic relations in October 1952. Archive files 'FO 371' and 'FO 248' have thus sourced several studies on British subversive activities in Tehran.

A note of caution is in order, however. Other than being a prodigious linguist and accomplished intelligence officer – having had extensive wartime experience in Iran and a mastery of the Persian language – Zaehner was also a man of psychedelic lifestyle, wont to nocturnal opium parties where long-tongued Iranian notables, Anglophone or not, would pontificate about politics and personalities. Ernest Perron was the Shah's contact with foreign embassies. He was particularly close to Zaehner, having known and befriended him from the latter's war-time service in Iran. Their Swiss roots added to other common traits. While a man of unimpeachable loyalty to the Shah, Perron's well-known foppish temperament made him prone to tattling. Much court gossip found its way into the minutes prepared by the British Embassy staff, notably, if not uniquely, by Zaehner; their contents were prone to be confused with the official policy line. This psychedelic climate of intelligence gathering fostered falsehood leading London to believe that in one way or the other Mosaddeq could be trashed. The embassy minutes bore the signature of their authors. Here a distinction must be made with the declassified archive material from the Department of State where reports to Washington are invariably signed by the chief of mission and often reflect formal talks with state personalities. Needless to say, this note of caution is not meant to reflect on the often informative and professional reporting by British officers.

This caveat aside, a top secret British document declassified, perhaps inadvertently, by the State Department may have gone totally unnoticed by authors and historians; it is dealt with separately in the penultimate section of Chapter 6 of this book. Other sources for British intelligence in this period notably include the published memoirs of such protagonists as Christopher Montague Woodhouse, the MI6 station chief in Tehran (August 1951–October 1952), who took over Zaehner's functions as of mid-1952 and continued to play a key part in British covert operations even after the severance of relations in October 1952. Sam Falle, at the time a junior MI6 officer in the Tehran embassy who rose to ambassadorial rank and a knighthood in his later career, has also included his recollection of service in Iran in his memoirs published in 1996.[62] British Chargé George Humphrey Middleton has also recounted his recollections in the Harvard Oral History project.[63] Drawing on the above sources as well as the Department of State archives, we will follow the evolution of British policy in Iran during Mosaddeq's rule along two parallel tracks: *Subversion*, through various subterfuges, and *diplomacy*, in the broad sense of the term that includes pressure and coercive measures to create leverage for dialogue and engagement.

The covert track

It will be recalled from an earlier chapter that British knee-jerk reaction to the Nationalization Act was to resort to force. Under sustained American pressure, *Operation Buccaneer*, aiming to seize Abadan, was shelved but interventionism as an approach did not die down. From the early days of the Mosaddeq government, covert action came to be seen by British officialdom as an adjunct to other means of pressure such as sanctions, naval blockades, oil-market manipulations, and recourse to relevant international bodies. Subversion had indeed been rationalized by veteran Persia-hands such as Doctor Ann (Nancy) Lambton in a curious analysis based on socio-psychological factors which were being attributed to Iranian society and the body politic.[64] Doctor Lambton had served as a press attaché at the British Legation in Tehran during the war and was at the time professor of Persian in the School of Oriental Studies, with connections in the Foreign Office and other high places. The Foreign Office deferred to her judgement. Her paternalistic conclusion was that Mosaddeq – considered neurotic – could not be removed by normal parliamentary means in the highly charged climate that reigned in Iran. It followed that the more level-headed 'patriotic' politicians, who could not openly oppose Mosaddeq without being stigmatized, must be helped to power through covert means. Curiously, planners in Whitehall saw the interests of Iran better served by politicians well disposed towards Britain (see the passage on Anglophiles in the first section of Chapter 1). They were convinced of Britons' intrinsic virtue while unrelenting about the character-flaws of the Iranians. This lowly view of Iran had gained currency among British officials partly as a result of the opinion conveyed by the British Ambassador in Tehran, Sir Francis Shepherd, an old-school diplomat with an unvarnished contempt for Iran, who was once described by Acheson as an 'unimaginable disciple of the *whiff of grapeshot*'.[65] He openly railed about the fact that Iran had never been *colonized thus remained unstraightened 'at the hands of a virile and civilized nation.'*[66] Engrossed in a colonial mindset, he failed to gauge and mirror to London the magnitude of nationalistic fervour that rendered the archaic ways of the past inoperable. His mainly specious analyses and assumptions underpinned a subversion plan which was launched as early as May 1951. As mentioned above Robin Zaehner was appointed by Foreign Secretary Morrison in May. His specific mandate was to subvert Mosaddeq's government and have him replaced by someone amenable to British interests.[67]

For the attainment of this objective Britain no doubt counted on her well-entrenched influence and a network of discrete contacts. Initially, as already dwelled on in this study, the veteran anglophile politician, Seyyed Zia Tabataba'ei was earmarked as an alternative to Mosaddeq. While the Iran brains-trust in London invariably touted moral qualities and rectitude in Iran's Anglophile politicians, no one in London was overly dismayed when Seyyed Zia made it known to Shepherd in September 1951 that he expected *'to be helped with some fairly generous payment'*.[68] Nor were British planners averse to bribing Iranians as a method of promoting their political objectives as will be seen in Chapters 4 and 5.

A modest journalist turned rich politician, Seyyed Zia had already in 1921 been helped to power in *a coup d'état* and was briefly prime minister before being ousted by Reza Khan, the founder of the Pahlavi dynasty. After the fall of Reza Shah in 1941, Zia had returned to Iran from his exile in Palestine, created a political party and continued to publish a newspaper. He was a deputy and majority leader in the fourteenth session of the *Majles*. Fiercely anti-communist he was ready to consort with clerics, even with *Fadāiān Islam*, for reasons of political expediency. His reputation as a British stooge had discredited him beyond redemption by the time of the oil nationalization. Early British attempts to replace Mosaddeq with Seyyed Zia again reveal a certain disconnect on the part of British officialdom with the realities then afoot in Iran.

When this realization finally came, Britain pinned its hopes on Qavam, who was not known for his pro-British sympathies yet deemed robust enough to stem the nationalistic tide. Qavam had discretely lobbied with the British (and no doubt with the Americans), seeking to reassure them. One of his emissaries, Abbas Eskandari, had assured Zaehner (and possibly British Chargé George Middleton) that Qavam wished to work closely with the British and would preserve their legitimate interest in Persia without jeopardizing Persia's political and economic independence.[69] A Conservative MP, Julian Amery, was sent unofficially to Paris in March 1952 to meet with Qavam. They later also met in London.[70] Qavam may have also been in contact with the MI6 agent Samuel Falle, who advocated British support for his premiership. Qavam had reportedly told him that should he become prime minister he would establish a dictatorship, arresting Mosaddeq and Kashani and others, and arrive at a reasonable arrangement on the oil issue.[71] When he was finally voted into office to replace Mosaddeq on 17 July 1952, his first act was to issue a stern declaration announcing a drastic change of course. He ordered the arrest of a number of personalities, notably Ayatollah Kashani. The BBC is said to have prematurely announced the arrest order on 20 July, something that alerted crowds which prevented it being carried out.[72] The Qavam gambit, as was seen earlier, ended in failure. Several months of scheming came to a nought.

A disillusioned Zaehner returned to Oxford convinced that clandestine work to undermine Mosaddeq was useless. During his stay in Tehran he had, however, set up an efficient network of British undercover operatives run by the Rashidian brothers. The latter would play a significant role in British efforts to unseat Mosaddeq in the coming months.[73] Zaehner's responsibilities were transferred to MI6, which was then headed in Tehran by Woodhouse. Not long after, Mosaddeq severed diplomatic relations with Britain. The rupture in October 1952, as we will come to shortly, followed the announcement of a plot against the government in which some opposition figures, including the Rashidian brothers, were briefly detained (for an elaboration see later in this chapter). See in Chapter 4 'The Link-Up' and Chapter 6 'An Orphan British Secret Document' for more on this subject.

The engagement track

It should be underscored that the British covert track during much of this period was essentially a sideshow that ran parallel, but in the shadow of the diplomatic activities, combining open coercive measures and engagement. Within the Foreign Office senior officials, notably Deputy Undersecretary Sir Roger Makins and his successor Pierson Dixon, favoured diplomacy. As a matter of principle, these top civil servants in the Foreign Office were loath to let MI6's foolhardy sleuths conduct Britain's foreign policy. The Foreign Office under Eden, more than his predecessor Morrison, strived to present a common front with the United States with a reasonable measure of success, despite differences on several key points. Americans exhibited a quasi-pathological fear that Iran could fall into the communist camp. Britain showed little anxiety on that score. Neither would Britain admit, as Americans often assumed, that Mosaddeq was a bulwark against communism. A corollary of these assumptions was the British opposition to any financial aid to Mosaddeq as long as he remained intransigent on the oil dispute. The United States tended to placate Mosaddeq each time he appeared invincible in internal showdowns. This led to some tension in the relations between the two allies, including at the highest level,[74] but invariably Britain succeeded in preventing any meaningful US help to Mosaddeq.[75] Britain in turn retreated, in time, from her earlier supercilious attitude where nothing short of AIOC pre-eminence was being conceded. Notwithstanding her diplomatic setback in Iran, Britain remained willing to engage in serious talks with the outgoing Truman administration agreeing to far-reaching concessions that we will expand on shortly. Dixon himself conducted these talks with the State Department's Director of Policy Planning, Paul Nitz.

While hope for a negotiated settlement existed, Britain thus privileged the engagement track yet, judging by the recollections of Woodhouse, it is safe to assume that subversion activities continued uninterrupted during the final weeks of the Truman administration when these consultations were taking place in London. Woodhouse and Sam Falle visited Washington in November and December 1952, and among aother things raised the possibility of a joint covert operation to overthrow Mosaddeq. It is difficult to judge whether such initiatives were co-ordinated with and sanctioned by the Foreign Office. Contacts and exchange of information and views between the two allied intelligence agencies must have been a matter of routine and it may be excessive to accord a seminal importance to Woodhouse's mission as do some scholars.[76] It is more likely that the idea of a joint plot was a MI6 shot-in-the dark without official British sanction. It received, at any event, a non-committal hearing in the CIA headquarters in Washington and by Woodhouse's own admission was cold-shouldered in the State Department.[77] A few months down the road in February 1953, Dixon reportedly stopped the covert track altogether to give diplomacy a chance to succeed. This was at a time when, with full American backing, Britain made a final oil settlement proposal to Mosaddeq.[78]

It was only after Mosaddeq withdrew from oil talks in March 1953 that Britain revived *Operation Boot* – as British anti-Mosaddeq activities were by then codenamed – and reverted full blast to covert means. By then the new American administration was fully on board. These developments will be covered in some detail in the coming chapters. For now, we follow the march of events during the second half of 1952 chronologically.

Diplomatic relations with Britain are broken off

As autumn set in, the earlier optimism about the oil dispute faded. Mosaddeq insisted that compensation to AIOC be calculated according to the same criteria which had been applied to companies nationalized in Britain itself. He agreed to arbitration if the award could be based on such criteria and, furthermore, if Britain agreed to pay immediately to Iran an amount of £50 million in back payments. Britain denied that such payment was due.[79]

On 22 October 1952, Mosaddeq broke off diplomatic relations with Britain. The rupturewas not, however, a surprise to either the United States or Britain. Nor was it an *ad hominem* reaction to an alleged foiled plot in mid-October, in which the Rashidian brothers among others had been implicated.[80] Mosaddeq had indeed been mulling over the idea of the break with Britain for some time and had warned Henderson, as early as late-August, that some such move was inevitable unless Britain changed its negative attitude.[81] The vision of an economy without oil required austerity measures, exposing the government to malicious attacks by opponents and making it prone to British subversion.[82] This at any rate was the explanation Mosaddeq gave to Henderson when he apprised him of his decision.[83] The opposition labelled the move as a demagogic act designed to galvanize street crowds. The rupture, as will be further elaborated on, did not hamper the Anglo-American efforts to settle the oil dispute.

Final attempts to resolve the oil dispute

Records show that the Truman administration, now in its waning days in office, made a determined effort to salvage the oil talks. It is equally noteworthy that Britain did not at any point in this period try to skirt these efforts or circumvent the Truman administration, and refrained from taking advantage of its lame-duck status.[84] The two governments in fact worked closely to bridge the gap in their respective positions and come closer to meeting Iran's concerns. By the end of 1952 Britain was ready to share responsibility for the flow of Iranian oil with American companies and consider cutbacks in production in Kuwait to make the proposition workable. Britain agreed to the purchase by American oil companies of some 10 million tons of Iranian oil annually, to be matched by a 10 million ton off-take by the AIOC as part of the arrangement for the flow of Iranian oil to the international markets; Britain dropped her objection to direct sale by Iran in oil markets. To help Mosaddeq's cash flow problems, it was agreed that the US Defence Materials Procurement Agency (DMPA) would purchase oil from the Iranian government to the tune of $133 million, of which about $100 million was to go to the Iranian treasury with immediate effect while the balance would be kept in an escrow account for eventual settlement of compensation. All this was contingent on Mosaddeq accepting to refer settlement of the compensation amount to the ICJ or another impartial arbitration.[85] Britain remained adamant on this latter point, hoping that through such arbitration the amount would be fixed in a way to include *future losses*.

Mosaddeq had all along insisted, somewhat paradoxically, that the determination of the compensation amount by the ICJ should be modelled after settlements that the British government itself had reached with various nationalized concerns notably in the British Coal Industry Nationalization Act (BCINA). Mosaddeq assumed – without having thoroughly investigated the cases – that these settlements were based only on the value of assets of the nationalized entity. Henderson, however, had pointed out to him on 26 December that *lost profits resulting from the nationalization act* had indeed been a factor in determination of compensation to the BCINA.[86]

When, on 15 January, with only five days remaining to the end of the Truman presidency, a new joint proposal was presented to Mosaddeq, he raised immediate objections to various passages, including the terms of reference of the ICJ. The proposed terms of reference had incorporated Mosaddeq's own suggestion that the settlement be based on the UK law applying to British nationalized industries. To Henderson's surprise, Mosaddeq later also objected to the use of the British Coal Industry Nationalization Act as a prototype for determination of the amount of settlement. Clearly, Mosaddeq had by then realized that his earlier insistence on application of British jurisprudence had been ill advised. The wording of the terms of reference, however, was deliberately ambiguous. It referred to redressing the NIOC for *'loss of its enterprise as a result of Nationalization Act'*. Mosaddeq correctly interpreted the wording to imply consideration by the ICJ of future losses. This and other instantaneous objections by Mosaddeq sent the drafters back to the drawing board.

It took another month of intense Anglo-American bargaining before a new – and as it turned out – final settlement proposal could be submitted to Iran. The bargaining process had not been interrupted by the change of hands in Washington. When Eisenhower moved to the White House, he was equally determined to find a satisfactory negotiated settlement of the oil dispute. The Dulles brothers, more than their predecessors, believed that the loss of Iran was a matter of time. All had to be done to gain time for the new administration to develop contingencies if *'Iran were to be lost to the free world'*.

A new oil proposal, which was submitted to Mosaddeq on 20 February, reflected relatively minor concessions by Britain. It was not, as some authors have suggested, a joint Anglo-American proposal. In fact, the Americans had deliberately avoided such linkage. Instead, the United States gave their blessing and endorsement to the proposal 'as fair and final'.

Mosaddeq's objections to the terms of reference had not been fully addressed and the language still left the impression that the arbitration body could take into account the future losses of the AIOC as a result of nationalization. But like previous versions, the terms of reference took account also of Iran's 'counterclaims' against the AIOC, which were substantial and could potentially balance the company's claim for future losses.

A day forgotten in the Iranian collective memory

The submission of the new oil proposal had coincided with a new bout in the long-running showdown between Mosaddeq and the Shah, culminating in the *noh'e esfand* crisis. We will turn to this important episode shortly. Suffice it to say here that the outcome of the showdown convinced the Dulles brothers that the Shah was finished as a political force and the United States should try to keep Mosaddeq afloat to avoid a communist takeover.[87] As in previous cases, Eden managed to sooth American anxieties when he met his American opposite number shortly thereafter.[88] Their joint communiqué reiterated US support for the British proposal of 20 February as *'reasonable and fair'*.[89] On the face of it, the joint communiqué had skirted tactical differences between the two allies in order to give added weight to the oil proposal. Mosaddeq's take was different. He took it as yet another mark of collusion between the two allies. On 9 March, Mosaddeq called Henderson to announce that he was putting an end to oil negotiations as the British inflexibility sanctioned by the United States rendered further talks pointless. In explaining his reasons, Mosaddeq referred to Eden's position that Britain stood by its 20 February proposal.

The abrupt end of the dialogue by Iran was no doubt linked to anxieties over the issue of compensation. Although Britain was no longer demanding participation in the management of Iran's oil industry or monopoly rights on purchasing or distribution of Iranian oil, Mosaddeq remained apprehensive. He remarked to Henderson that Britain insisted that Iran give the International Court a licence *'to put Iran under bondage for at least twenty years'*.[90] The fixation with the wily British – so much a part of Iranian political lore – now fed uncertainties and oozed out stress and fear. Mosaddeq also knew that his opponents in the *Majles*, who feigned being against even the principle of compensation, would be relentless in lambasting the government.

Still, many in his entourage, and certainly the technocrats at the National Iranian Oil Company (NIOC), were favourable to that oil proposal.[91] Mosaddeq himself was reportedly well-disposed initially and had ordered preparations for the signing of the accord. Yet, fired up by two of his advisors, he drifted back to the logic of distrust; *'You see? They had again planned to set us up'*, remarked Mosaddeq to the NIOC chairman Mortezaqoli Bayat, who he had summoned to issue the marching orders, cancelling the signing of the oil agreement. As a young aide to the NIOC Chairman, Fuad Rouhani – the future secretary-general of OPEC when the organization was first formed in

1960 – had accompanied Bayat to the prime minister's quarters. He later recited, not without the zest of bitterness, this historical anecdote in his well-researched biography of Mosaddeq. Entering the prime minister's quarters, he wrote, they bumped into the two Mosaddeq advisors, whom Rouhani chose not to identify by name in his book.[92]

The Mosaddeq decision to withdraw from the oil talks had a major impact on Eisenhower administration strategic thinking and should be regarded as a watershed. In the ensuing weeks, as we shall shortly dwell on, the administration succumbed to the temptation of removing Mosaddeq through coverts means. The change of humour in Washington was apparent when the National Security Council met on 11 March only hours after news of the break-off had flashed. The NSC decided that no oil purchase or financial aid to Iran were to be contemplated beyond *'technical assistance on a modest scale.'* Eisenhower made a sombre assessment of the United States acting unilaterally in Iran (i.e. divorced from Britain) saying he had 'very real doubts' that such an approach could succeed. He went on to say that such a deal (with Mosaddeq) may not be worth the paper on which it is written.[93]

The Monday 9 March 1953, passes incognito in Iran's political calendar. Yet the decision Mosaddeq took on that day to break off the oil talks was portentous in its historical ramifications. Had he not given in to vague and shapeless fears or vain nationalistic pride, the course of Iran's contemporary history may well have been different.

4
The Downslide

Splits in the ranks of the National Front and the rift with the Shah pushed Mosaddeq further to lean on the left wing of the National Front. They were composed principally of French- and German-trained lawyers, and engineers mainly from the elitist Iran party. Formed in the 1940s, the party blended nationalistic aspirations with a brand of socialism. Secular and moderate in its outlook, the party lacked mass appeal. The more radical figures in Mosaddeq's inner circle included Dr Ali Shayegan, a former deputy-minister in Qavam's government in 1946, as well as a journalist-cum-politician named Dr Hossein Fatemi. Serving as foreign minister in the last leg of Mosaddeq's tenure, the latter was the most republican among Mosaddeq's close associates. Fatemi projected the image of an *eminence grise*, which he probably was when it came to repressive aspects of the government's conduct.[1]

These politicians did not share the anti-Tudeh fervour of Mosaddeq's erstwhile right-wing NF allies.[2] As the United States became more entrenched in a policy of non-assistance to Iran, Mosaddeq and his associates began to look on the socialist camp as potential oil customers. By the same token, as the *Tudeh* Party shed its ideological inhibitions and finally sided with Mosaddeq, it was embraced with no recriminations. Mosaddeq continued to use *Tudeh* as a scarecrow to enhance his own appeal to the new American administration. The *Tudeh* rallies on the Mayday and the commemoration of the 21 July uprising of the previous year were resounding triumphs and must have indeed scared great many observers. *The New York Times* correspondent, Kennett Love, refers to these demonstrations as a signpost that alarmed Mosaddeq's opponents.[3]

One voice in Mosaddeq's circle of remaining allies was constant in warning him against appeasing *Tudeh*. Khalil Maleki, the socialist leader of the *Nīroy'e sevvom* (The Third Force) Party and himself a former high *Tudeh* official, was alive to negative repercussions of flirtation with *Tudeh*, both on the domestic and foreign fronts. He was equally critical of tergiversations on oil issue and on other matters where the less-discerning Mosaddeq advisors would lead him astray or acquiesced to his excesses.[4] On one such occasion, giving vent to his frustrations, Maleki caustically remarked to Mosaddeq, *'Where you are heading is to hell, but we shall follow you even there!'* This was during bickering in July 1953 over Mosaddeq's decision to dissolve the *Majles* through a referendum. Maleki's remark proved prophetic.

The clash at the helm; the February 1953 jumble

The showdown between the Shah and his prime minister, which culminated in the *noh'e esfand* (28 February) turmoil, is widely chronicled in the existing literature. Both the protagonists and many actors on the sidelines have given their respective versions of these events.[5] Reports from the American Ambassador in Tehran, Loy Henderson, provide valuable insights. But overall, contradictory accounts have not been fully reconciled; some nooks and crannies are yet to be brought into the light.

It was in a cabalistic climate in February 1953 that mutual mistrust between the Shah and Mosaddeq took on crisis proportions. The prime minister saw the Court as a hub of conspiracy. A revolt by a Bakhtiāri chieftain had just erupted. He suspected the Shah of being involved.[6] Other intrigues may have been afoot or trumped up. General Zahedi had been ordered detained a few days earlier.[7]

On 19 February, the day before Henderson handed him the amended version of the oil proposal, Mosaddeq demanded to meet a confidant of the Shah, through whom he sent word that he intended to resign shortly and publicly blame the Shah for his decision! A disturbed Shah sent Court Minister Hussein Ala to persuade Mosaddeq to retract. The prime minister remained adamant, accusing the Shah of inciting the Bakhtiāri insurgency. He then complained about the Shah's distribution of the Crown lands among peasants, presumably believing they should be transferred to the government.[8] He was equally critical of revenues accrued to the Crown from the Imam Reza Shrine Foundation in Mashad. Ala assured him that the Shah wished him to remain prime minister at least to the end of the oil dispute, and explained how Mosaddeq was misplacing the blame for Bakhatiāri insurgency.[9] When, finally, Ala relayed the Shah's desire to leave the country temporarily, Mosaddeq initially objected.

There is indeed no doubt that it was the Shah who had first raised the idea of departure abroad. This became the core issue of the crisis. The Shah cited as his reason medical matters related to sterility in the royal couple.[10] Some Mosaddeq critics, however, have postulated that he had deliberately stirred up a crisis to force the Shah to leave. Kazem Hassibi, from Mosaddeq's inner circle and his principal oil advisor, has an entry in his (unpublished) diary on 20 February. According to him, when Mosaddeq informed the inner group that he intended to resign on 24 February, Fatemi retorted, 'why shouldn't we rather force the Shah to depart?'[11] The hypothesis of Mosaddeq's scheming is, however, rather farfetched.

Mosaddeq ended up nodding to the Shah's travel plans.[12] The two decided to keep the trip secret given the possibilities of agitation. They agreed that the Shah would travel by road to Iraq for pilgrimage to holy shrines, and then proceed to Spain from where a state invitation had been discretely solicited.[13] The royal couple would then proceed to Switzerland for two months of skiing and medical checks.

The travel plan now scheduled for Saturday 28 February 1953 (*noh'e esfand* 1331 in the Iranian calendar) was, however, leaked. The Court's chamberlain, Hormoz Pirnia, no doubt fearful that the royal couple's departure may be definitive, tipped off two implacable enemies of Mosaddeq, both his own family relatives.[14] The first was Ahmad Qavam, the disgraced ex-prime minister. The second leak went to the Zahedi family. The General having been detained just a few days earlier, the call went to his son Ardeshir Zahedi. Pirnia had just set off the political sirens.

Qavam called Ayatollah Behbahani, the pro-Shah Shiite prelate of Tehran with close ties to Grand Ayatollah Boroujerdi in Qom. Ardeshir Zahedi on his part called Ayatollah Kashani as well as the *Majles* opposition heavyweights, Makki and Baqa'ei.[15] It is possible that Court Minister Ala may have also informed some key religious figures, as Queen Soraya later recalled in her memoirs.[16]

Unlike Behbahani who was alarmed by the news of the Shah's impending departure, Kashani saw in the event an opportunity to avenge Mosaddeq. As the Speaker of the *Majles*, he addressed a letter to the Shah and dispatched a parliamentary delegation (the *Majles* Bureau) urging him to desist; he promised resounding parliamentary support for the Shah if things came to a head. But the Shah could not be swayed.

On his part, Behbahani called the Grand Shiite *Marja*, Ayatollah Boroujerdi in Qom, who appears to have instructed him to intercede with the Shah as well as with Mosaddeq to prevent the departure.

Contact with, and intervention by, Boroujerdi is asserted by the Zahedi camp and tacitly confirmed by Mosaddeq himself. Ardeshir Zahedi recalls in his memoirs that initially, he was assigned to travel overnight to Qom and deliver a letter that had been prepared to the Grand Ayatollah; this plan changed, due probably to the imminence of the event.[17] According to him: 'He [Boroujerdi] was of the opinion that action must be taken to prevent the Shah from leaving.' In his memoirs, Mosaddeq also confirms a call from Behbahani enquiring about the Shah's departure. Surprised, Mosaddeq had responded that the decision had been taken by the Shah.[18] Behbahani subsequently called on the Shah, telling him bluntly that if he left the country, he might never be able to return.[19]

Both Behbahani and Kashani were quick in rallying a crowd of a few thousand from downtown neighbourhoods and athletic clubs;[20] they were joined by retired army officers and some alerted supporters of the Shah. Mosaddeq, who had a farewell lunch appointment with the Shah, was at the Winter Palace, a stone's throw from Mosaddeq's own residence. There he received a message from Henderson for an urgent meeting.

On his way out of the palace, Mosaddeq noted a hostile crowd in front of the main gate. He was helped by the Shah's personal driver and officers of the Imperial Guard to find his way out through a backdoor and reach his residence in time to receive Henderson at 13:30.[21]

In his report of the event to Washington, Henderson confirms that the news of the departure having been the talk of the town since the previous evening, he felt free to call on Mosaddeq and urge him to prevent the Shah's departure.[22] Mosaddeq's own take, in retrospect, is somewhat different. He was convinced that on that day there had been a plot to assassinate him in front of the Palace main gate. He implicitly implicates the US Ambassador in the plot, writing in his memoirs that the ambassador's request for an urgent meeting was puzzling at best as, 'he had nothing important to say.'[23]

Later in the afternoon, Mosaddeq's residence came under mob assault and a few people killed and some wounded in the mayhem.[24] Mosaddeq had to flee through a neighbour's wall and took sanctuary in *Majles*. He was persuaded later to return home, after the deputies pledged that the outstanding issues between the Shah and the prime minister would be settled through a parliamentary committee.[25]

Was there any plot afoot to eliminate Mosaddeq as he has insinuated? If Mosaddeq's bad vibes about Henderson were clearly preposterous, the same could not be said of the Rashidian brothers, the *Fadā'iān Islam* remnants, or other Kashani supporters. It is, however, unlikely that Mosaddeq's foes could have rallied quickly enough for an attempt on his life. In greater likelihood, Kashani had intended to deal a blow to the prime minister's prestige and induce him to resign.

Ayatollah Behbahani, on the other hand, had no axe to grind with Mosaddeq and his involvement must have been out of a genuine sense of alarm, shared by him and by his hierarchical superior, Boroujerdi in Qom, over the consequences of the monarch's departure. Yet by making common cause with Mosaddeq's opponents, a crucial threshold had been crossed: this was the realignment of the quietist Shiite leadership with the politicized clerics.

In retrospect, the 28 February collision was a prelude – some believe a dry run – to events that were to unfold between 15 and 19August. It consolidated the internal opposition, which was now comprised of right-wing politicians, purged military officers, and the rank-and-file of the security forces. Most significantly, it tagged along the quietist Shiite leaders who were now making common cause in an implicit clerical confederacy.

The Grand Ayatollah Boroujerdi: a retrospective sketch

In Qom, the Grand Ayatollah Mohammad-Hussein Boroujerdi – the unrivalled and revered leader of world Shiites and the main *Marja* or 'source of emulation' – was in many ways dissimilar to the lesser-ranking, but politically prominent Ayatollah Kashani. Boroujerdi (Figure 14) had inherited his mantle from the Grand Ayatollah Haj Hossein Haeri Yazdi who died in 1941. It took several years before a successor could be found. Many had their eyes on Boroujerdi who, apart from undisputed mastery of jurisprudence, was reputed for his qualities of justice and piety. He was also known to be influential among some tribes, his hometown Boroujerd being perched on the Zagros mountain range at the heartland of the Lorestān and Bakhtiāri regions. When in autumn 1944 he travelled to Tehran for prostate surgery, the Shah in person paid him a visit at the hospital,[26] a rare gesture that may have signalled a preference on the part of the monarch for his ascendancy to the supreme Shiite dignity. Boroujerdi in turn discreetly supported the Shah and at crucial moments made public gestures of sympathy. One such occasion was when the Shah survived an assassination attempt in February 1949. Boroujerdi's message of sympathy ended with a politically charged phrase: 'May God Almighty preserve your Kingdom.'[27]

Figure 14 Grand Ayatollah Seyyed Mohammad-Hussein Boroujerdi. Photo courtesy of Boroujerdi.ir.®

Under his tutelage, the Qom seminary students were enjoined to stay out of politics.²⁸ He vehemently disapproved of methods used by *Fadā'iān Islam* and had evicted from the seminary its leader, Seyyed Mojtabla Mirlohi, alias Navvab-Safavi, as well as his associate Seyyed Abdol-Hussein Vahedi, the two having formed the movement in the mid-1940s in the Qom seminary. The future leader of the Islamic Revolution, Ayatollah Rouhollah Khomeini, at that point a mid-level cleric, fell out with the Grand Ayatollah who considered Khomeini to be the *Fadā'iān*'s mentor and possible instigator of the commotions that radical seminarians were causing in the Qom *hawza* or grand centre of Shiite Islam learning.²⁹

By the same token, relations between Kashani and Boroujerdi were initially tepid. Boroujerdi was solicited and may have intervened in 1950 to obtain the lifting of Ayatollah Kashani's banishment.³⁰ Boroujerdi is authoritatively reported to have been helping Kashani financially in later years and may have bailed him out of a financial squeeze at one crucial point; furthermore, he appears to have again intervened with the Shah to obtain Kashani's release from prison in 1956 at the time when Razmara's assassination dossier was reopened.[31]

For Kashani, Mosaddeq was the enemy to beat, something that made his support for the Shah incidental. Boroujerdi on the other hand saw the monarchy as the antithesis of secular republicanism if not communist atheism. As long as Mosaddeq did not tamper with the fundamentals of the constructed state, Boroujerdi was happy to remain politically aloof. When in late February 1953 the crisis erupted, each of the two prelates saw the menace through their own prism but a common denominator had been forged. They became unchartered allies, with the difference that Kashani was vocal and dauntless while Boroujerdi was circumspect and unassuming. A political biography of Boroujerdi, published on his official website run from Qom, characterizes Boroujerdi's attitude towards Kashani as discreet support.[32] Signs of this complicity could soon be seen in *Majles* discussions and in political line ups. During the debate on the Shah's constitutional powers in early 1953 deputies who were allied with clerics who sided with opponents of Mosaddeq; a deputy reputed to be close both to Kashani and to Boroujerdi depicted the Shiite hierarchy and the Crown as the two pillars of stability along with good governance.

Yet during the early months of nationalization in 1951, Boroujerdi had been supportive of Mosaddeq and his anti imperialist struggle to safeguard the nation's rights. He had privately urged the Shah to continue his support of Mosaddeq in the face of British adversity and to keep the nation united.[33] This support, however, gradually waned. Even before the February crisis, according to Dr Mehdi Azar (a close collaborator of Mosaddeq and his minister of educational and religious endowments), the Grand Ayatollah had had a dispute with the Mosaddeq government in 1952 and served notice that he might decide to migrate, presumably to Najaf. This would have been inauspicious for Mosaddeq who immediately backed down.[34] Boroujerdi, however, was averse to public recriminations. He had discretely intervened to prevent the Shah's departure on *noh'e esfand* (the February 1953 crisis) but to maintain a façade of neutrality, he issued a declaration in which he invited Mosaddeq and the Shah to resolve their differences.[35] Mosaddeq in turn tried to placate the prelate by decreeing that insult against the Grand Ayatollah was a punishable offence.[36]

By early 1953 therefore, clerical opposition to Mosaddeq was gathering force. On *Eid Fetr* (13 June 1953) Kashani could reportedly gather a larger crowd than the pro-Mosaddeq rally a week later.[37] Closely allied with Kashani, a veteran soldier and ambitious politician, the retired

Major-General Fazlollah Zahedi had by then emerged as the front-runner opposition candidate to replace Mosaddeq if the opposition should prevail.

General Fazlollah Zahedi

A Brigadier-General at the age of 27, Zahedi was the youngest officer to ascend to that rank in Iran's modern army. A hero of several pacification campaigns under Reza Shah, Zahedi (Figure 15) had an unrivalled military track record. Zahedi's career, however, was bruised by allegations of corruption – vigorously denied by his supporters and immediate entourage – which dated back to earlier years of his military service and trailed him long after he stepped down as prime minister in 1955.[38]

His most impressive feat was to obtain the rendition of Sheikh Khaz'al of Mohammarah (later Khoramshahr) in 1924. The latter was the

Figure 15 General Fazlollah Zahedi as he emerged from his hideout on 19 August 1953. Picture from the personal collection of Ardeshir Zahedi; courtesy of IBEX publishers©

autonomous ruler of an Iranian Arab sheikhdom in the oil-rich province of Khuzestan under Britain's quasi-suzerainty. Khaz'al's allegiance to the central government in Tehran was nominal at best. The dissolution of the sheikhdom assured the central government's full authority over this oil-rich province.

As commander of Isfahan garrison in 1942, Zahedi had been abducted from his residence by a British commando detachment and whisked to Palestine. Together with some 200 other Iranian politicians, including 50 other ranking Officers, he was suspected of pro-Axis sympathies and plotting against the Allies.[39] The alleged plot, attributed to German intelligence agents, would have sabotaged the Lend-Lease supply-line to the USSR with help from *Qashqā'ei* tribesmen. This was at a time when the Wehrmacht was poised to enter Caucasia. After his release, Zahedi was reintegrated into the Army; in 1946, he commanded the expeditionary forces to the south where a revolt was afoot to obtain autonomy rights for southern provinces. We have already referred to this episode noting that British manipulation of the southern tribes was strongly suspected (see 'The Azerbaijan Crisis' in Chapter 1).

In 1949, as Chief of the National Police, Zahedi had helped prevent ballot fraud in the lower house elections in Tehran district. The National Front ticket headed by Mosaddeq swept those elections.[40] When the latter became prime minister in April 1951, Zahedi was his choice for the sensitive post of interior minister.

Shortly thereafter, he resigned over Mosaddeq's sharp criticism of the police crackdown on a *Tudeh* Party rally on the day Averell Harriman arrived in Tehran on 15 July 1951.[41] Appointed senator by the Shah – the amended constitution having empowered the monarch to fill half of the senate's seats – Zahedi joined Mosaddeq's opponents and following the *Siy'e Tyr* (21 July 1952) uprising, he progressively emerged as the chief contender for premiership.[42] In the words of the CIA internal report: 'General Zahedi stood out as the only major personality in undisguised opposition to Mossadeq [sic].'[43]

Internal conspiracies

By end March 1953 Mosaddeq had reached a point of no return. He contemplated selling oil at drastically reduced rates including to the socialist bloc, and may have obtained a promise from the Soviet government for $20 million aid.[44] As a last straw, he appealed directly to Eisenhower addressing a letter to him on 28 May.[45] He had engaged in a tug of war with the opposition over the Shah's constitutional prerogatives and

Figure 16 Court Minister Hossein Ala

moved to mobilize public opinion in order to pressure the *Majles* to ratify their curtailments. According to Court Minister Ala (Figure 16), he also attempted to drive a wedge between the Shah's supporters.[46]

The opposition was equally relentless in seeking to destabilize the government. Opposition groups had secretly contacted the court minister Ala in March. General Zahedi, for one, had met him on three occasions. Through Ala, the opposition hoped to enlist the Shah's support and trigger his intervention to dismiss Mosaddeq, but Ala was unable to convince the Shah who believed Mosaddeq's fall was a matter of time in view of his mismanagement and that he need not intervene.[47] After extensive consultations, Ala devised a plan for a smooth removal of Mosaddeq which hinged on the Shah's support. Ala's plan featured three steps:

1. Prevail upon the opposition deputies to absent themselves from the *Majles* and prevent the formation of a quorum.
2. The *Majles* Speaker Kashani would then address a letter to the Shah invoking the state of lawlessness, adding that in view of threats to their safety the deputies could not attend the *Majles* sessions rendering the parliament non-functional.
3. Invoking this letter, the Shah would then dismiss Mosaddeq and appoint a high official to ensure law and order pending the selection of a new prime minister through the usual parliamentary procedures.

The Shah, however, made it clear to all, including to Henderson, that he was unwilling to overstep the constitutional bounds. In an intuitive outburst, he remarked to Ala in mid-April that he did not wish to act as a 'cat's paw for ambitious and unscrupulous Iranian politicians on whose loyalty he could not count'. More significantly, he said he suspected the British to be responsible 'for present frictions between the Court and the Government'.[48] On his own initiative Ala personally visited the Grand Ayatollah Boroujerdi. Boroujerdi was described as sympathetic but non-committal, promising to convey his reaction at a later stage.[49] Other Iranian political figures were also looking to Boroujerdi for guidance if not intervention. Deputy Foreign Minister Meftah later recalled in his memoirs having visited the Grand Ayatollah in June, accompanied by the reputed politician, Abdollah Entezam, to warn him against the vulnerabilities of the Shah and the increasing influence of the *Tudeh* Party.[50]

The abduction of the police chief

On 20 April, Tehran woke up to the shocking disappearance of the Chief of Police, Brigadier-General Mahmoud Afshartous. Promoted by Mosaddeq, he belonged to a new breed of army officers groomed to replace the old guard. As an army major, Afshartous had served as a bailiff in the Māzandarān province under the Shah's father. Having thus been involved in an enterprise infamous for land grabbing, Afshartous had been despised in his youth and denounced as a Court henchman. Now in the sensitive post of national police chief he set out to identify mid-level pro-Mosaddeq army officers, submitting a list to Mosaddeq.[51]

Afshartous was snared in a house in mid-town Tehran, where he seemingly had a tryst with an attractive woman whose brother, Hossien Khatibi, was later said to be linked to Dr Baqa'ei. Be that as it may, the actual perpetrators – mainly retired army officers including four brigadiers – were quickly identified and arrested. At least one Iranian source has implicated the Rashidian brothers.[52] An arrest warrant was routinely issued against General Zahedi as well. The latter had to take sanctuary in the *Majles* building, helped by Speaker Ayatollah Kashani.[53] Dr Baqa'ei, also implicated, still enjoyed parliamentary immunity which Mosaddeq then sought to rescind. Baqa'ei has since vehemently denied any involvement and claims that confessions against him had been extracted under torture.[54]

The link-up: TPAJAX and the internal cabal

It will be recalled from an earlier passage ('The British Two-Prong Strategy' in Chapter 3) that the British covert track, *Operation Boot*, which had been put in abeyance while the oil negotiations were still ongoing, was reactivated by mid-March 1953.[55] On 18 March, a week after the breakdown of the oil talks, the CIA director of operations, Frank Wisner, informed MI6 that the CIA was ready to discuss details of an overthrow plan which had been raised by Woodhouse and Falle when they visited Washington a few months earlier.[56] The decision to change course had come from the State Department. General Walter Bedell Smith, Undersecretary of State, had determined that the US government could no longer approve of Mosaddeq and would prefer a successor government 'in which there would be no National Frontists.'[57]

Later in April he formally endorsed the covert approach. Clearly, it is at this crucial juncture that the internal cabal against Mosaddeq linked up with the Anglo-American overthrow plans.

It will be recalled that home-grown plots, whether pseudo-legal or seditious in character had preceded the Anglo-American scheme. Some ignition attempts by plotters in March had been cold-shouldered by Henderson. The CIA internal history, *Overthrow*, confirms that an ex-air force chief, General Guilanshah, had contacted the American Embassy with a *coup* plan which had elicited a non-committal, if mildly encouraging reaction. Similarly, Henderson was impassive when Court Minister Ala approached him on behalf of unidentified plotters in late March.[58] By mid-April, however, Henderson was all ears when Ala outlined his plan for removal of Mosaddeq.[59] The home-grown plans lacked realism, however, hinging invariably on the Shah's elusive support.

When in May 1953 MI6 and the CIA finally settled down to practical details of the planning, they were conscious of their shortcomings in terms of human assets. Those of the British consisted essentially of the Rashidian brothers and their presumed network of contacts within influential circles.[60] Nonetheless, the CIA station, which had worked with the brothers since the previous October, believed that the Rashidians 'overstated and oversold' their possibilities.[61] This was roughly the view expressed by their own treating officer, Robin Zaehner (see 'The Covert Track in Chapter 3), in a meeting with Eden in late 1952.[62] Woodhouse, who regretted Zaehner's performance in that meeting had, nevertheless, observed the involvement of the brother's in currency black-marketeering.[63] Long-tongued and corrupt as they were, the Rashidian brothers were above all political animals infatuated with Britain and, by the same token, were inveterate foes of Mosaddeq.[64] They also enjoyed a certain social standing and from that stand-point outclassed the two principal US agents who were ordinary journalists and virtually nameless. They were Farough Kayvani and Ali Jalali.[65] Through the power of the purse they must have managed the small gangs of street fighters and agitators who rammed into well-groomed *Tudeh* street formations or, alternatively, may have faked them (for evidence and details, see 'The Role of Iranian Agents' in Chapter 6). Just as the Rashidian brothers, the Kayvani-Jalali tandem must have aggrandized the extent and impact of these measures.[66] Both the CIA station and MI6 also subsidized an assortment of newspapers with virtually no readership, a topic to which we shall shortly return.[67]

Another US asset was Colonel Abbas Farzanegan, a former military attaché in Washington, who had extensive connections among the uniformed notables; these proved to be consequential. Curiously, in revealing their assets the British also named Colonel Hossien-Ali Ashrafi who, other than commanding the Third Mountain Brigade, was the martial-law administrator, thus a close military aide to Mosaddeq.[68] This turned out to be inaccurate, as we shall come to in Chapter 5, but up to early August 1953 the TPAJAX military planners had perilously relied on this bogus asset.

Details of Anglo-American planning have been chronicled and sourced in several documents and scholarly works and also revealed in the CIA's internal history, *Overthrow*.[69] The original plan drawn up in Nicosia in May 1953 underwent various changes and refinements in Beirut and London. Towards the end, a major readjustment became necessary as a result of the dissolution of the *Majles*, which was engineered by Mosaddeq through a referendum.

In its original conception, the plan was to provide a catalytic framework within which local political and social forces would be unleashed; the dynamics they generated would lead to the downfall of Mosaddeq. According to this scheme, in an inseminated crisis, the clerics were to take sanctuary (*bast*) in the *Majles* and deputies were to vote the government down following a censure motion. The military component of the plan had been conceived as a safeguard against *Tudeh* or other recalcitrant pro-Mosaddeq forces. If this pseudo-legal scenario failed, the military component would then resort to a *putsch*. As such, the plan relied on the cooperation of prominent clerics, the support of the armed forces, and that of a majority of *Majles* deputies. Further, like its home-grown homologues, the plan required the Shah's full cooperation. The budget allocated was $285,000 with the United States covering $147,000 and Britain $137,000.[70] The plan, code-named TPAJAX, was approved by Churchill and other British official on 1 July. The US hierarchy including President Eisenhower approved the plan on 11 July, the date from which it became operational.[71] To stage that scenario, the Anglo-American plan called for a campaign of destabilization, aiming to arouse angst and anger among religious leaders. They would also attempt to bribe some *Majles* deputies. These measures were to be conducted by CIA-MI6 Iranian assets whose real affiliations would remain unknown to recipients.

The military component of the plan recognized that MI6-CIA assets within the armed forces were too limited and, as such, incapable of assuring military objectives. General Zahedi, the most visible opposition figure at the time, was hence the natural choice to lead the *coup*. Another assumption made by planners was that the army would stand behind the Shah in spite of the firm control of army units by pro-Mosaddeq officers; later events vindicated this latter assumption.[72]

The summer of all dangers

As the summer set in, the war of nerves was at full swing and tension reached fever pitch. The United States was now fully in line to remove Mosaddeq through covert means. Secretary Dulles skipped Tehran during his tour of the region in the last week of May in order to play up Mosaddeq's disfavour with America. A negative response by Eisenhower to Mosaddeq's plea for aid was deliberately leaked to the press by American officials.[73] Ambassador Henderson left Tehran on an extended holiday. The Shah's loyal, if scheming, advisor Ala had to step down as Court Minister and was replaced by Abol'qassem Amini, of doubtful loyalties to the Shah.

Frequent lack of a quorum and other procedural obstructions by opposition deputies rendered the *Majles* all but non-functional. Yet, in a crucial test of strength at the end of June, Mosaddeq succeeded in stripping Ayatollah Kashani of his *Majles* speakership and replace him with Abdollah Mo'azzami, one of his own supporters. General Zahedi, who had taken sanctuary in the *Majles* compound, now went into hiding. Equally significant was the *Majles* vote to appoint the opposition heavyweight Hossein Makki as a member of the parliamentary supervisory board of the National Bank.[74] A public denunciation by Makki of illicit banknote printing was now unavoidable. Mosaddeq could ill-afford an aggravation of economic conditions that such a revelation inescapably entailed.

As mentioned earlier, the *Tudeh* rallies dwarfed those of the National Front, stirring up anxiety among conservative elements including senior clerics in Qom and Tehran. This was notably the case of the *Siy'e Tyr* uprising anniversary on 21 July.[75] More to the point, the Rashidian brothers were bribing some deputies in anticipation of a vote of no confidence that was to follow a contrived crisis as scripted in TPAJAX. One opposition deputy, Ali Zohari, had filed a censure motion, while a 'fake *Tudeh*' hate-mail campaign against clerics must have also commenced. Mosaddeq no doubt had been tipped off about the bribing efforts of British agents, a fact he brought up in his last meeting with Henderson on 18 August [76] (see also 'Ambassador Henderson's Last Meeting with Mosaddeq', in Chapter 6). Only 27 out of 79 deputies were firm Mosaddeq supporters, while roughly the same number opposed him. The loyalties of others who had voted expediently in the past were hardy incontrovertible.

To circumvent this gambit, Mosaddeq decided to close down the *Majles*. His first step was to obtain the resignation of his own supporters in mid-July. Twenty-seven deputies heeded his call and resigned; 25 others followed suit shortly thereafter. This left only 27 deputies who had opposed Mosaddeq from the outset. The much-touted bribing campaign under TPAJAX, and other covert operations before it, had yielded strictly nothing. A rule of thumb analysis in effect shows that the number of deputies voting for Mosaddeq did not really change from July 1952 to August 1953, abstraction being made of the three heavy weight National Front deputies who joined the opposition during the second half of 1952.[77] For all practical purposes the parliament was now shut down. Yet Mosaddeq decided to put the dissolution of the *Majles* to a nationwide referendum. According to the constitution, as amended in 1949, only the Shah had the authority to dissolve the parliament. Mosaddeq had never acknowledged the constitutionality of the 1949 amendments, although their validity, within the confines and shortcomings of Iran's polity, was incontrovertible. They had been enacted by an 'elected' Constituent Assembly, within the terms of the constitution itself. Later, a motion by Mosaddeq supporters in the sixteenth *Majles* to rescind the 1949 constitutional amendments was *not* carried; this was a tacit endorsement by the *Majles* of the constitutional assembly and its enactments.[78] Against such a background, Mosaddeq did not wish to resort to the monarch to obtain the dissolution of *Majles* but indicated that he would seek a royal decree for new elections once the dissolution was approved. Once more Mosaddeq was leaning on legitimacy to bypass the constitution.[79]

As August set in, Tehran was abuzz with premonition and feverish expectancy. Nocturnal anti-referendum rallies organized by Ayatollah Kashani at his residence in *Pāmenār*, a popular neighbourhood in southern Tehran and a Kashani stronghold, were punctuated with mayhem caused by presumed pro-Mosaddeq crowds. In a move seen as an act of religious encroachment in politics, Kashani issued a *fatwa* for the boycott of the plebiscite, a move that was not sanctioned either by Boroujerdi or Behbahani but, according to evidence surfaced in later years, had the blessing of the future founder of the Islamic republic, Ayatollah Rouhollah Khomeini.[80] Boroujerdi avoided any public display of partisanship. Two of Mosaddeq's close associates, Dr G. H. Sadiqi and Dr Karim Sanjabi, recall having warned Mosaddeq that the move could enable the Shah to dismiss him, given ample precedents set during the

Majles interregna earlier in the century.[81] Mosaddeq had dismissed the warnings.[82] The plebiscite was carried out in Tehran on 3 August. Separate voting booths for yes and no votes were set up, resulting in a 99.9 per cent Mosaddeq victory. In Seattle, speaking to a gathering of state governors, Eisenhower digressed to criticize Mosaddeq for closing down the parliament, an act, he specified, that had been supported by the communist party.[83] Later Woodhouse wrote that the digression had been an arranged signal to the Shah, fixed by Roosevelt, to convince the monarch of the US president's knowledge about and support of the *coup* plan.[84] A *New York Times* editorial on 4 August characterized the exercise as 'More fantastic and farcical than any ever held under Hitler or Stalin', and described it as an effort by Premier Mosaddeq 'to make himself unchallenged dictator of the country'. Likewise, Secretary Dulles said in an interview on 28 July that Mosaddeq's tolerance of *Tudeh* activities made it more difficult for the United States to give aid to his government.[85] In retrospect the referendum could be viewed as Mosaddeq's most consequential misstep in that, among other things, it propelled the Shah to join the ranks of the plotters, unleashing a chain of events that led to his downfall.

The taming of the Shah

In the midst of the turmoil described above, MI6/CIA planners had set out to convince the Shah to join their plot. This proved a frustrating undertaking. The young monarch preferred to bide his time and allow Mosaddeq to be ousted through legal means.

On 30 May, Ambassador Henderson conveyed a personal message of support from Churchill to the Shah. The British prime minister intended to dispel a deep-seated distrust the Shah was known to harbour towards Britain. This was a first move to enlist the Shah's cooperation. The Shah conveyed his gratification with a tinge of irony: the British had always advised him in the past, he remarked, 'To conduct himself as constitutional monarch in a European sense; it now seemed their policy in this regard was changing.' He went on to say that he was convinced that unless he played certain role in the political and particularly in military fields, the country would relapse into 'confusion and chaos.'[86]

When Henderson – acting under the TPAJAX scenario – sounded him on General Zahedi as a choice to replace Mosaddeq, the Shah was less than enthusiastic. He said he would agree if Zahedi could be appointed through established legal procedures and if the United States would then pledge to support the government financially so that it could function.[87]

The Shah, however, believed it was easier to achieve an oil settlement with Mosaddeq than a successor government.[88] In a display of good faith – ignored by the historians of this episode – the Shah remarked to Henderson:

> Any avenue which might lead towards settlement [of the] oil dispute with Mosadeq [sic] should not be ignored even if an attempt at settlement might result in prolongation [of the] Mosadeq [sic] government.... [The Shah] hoped in case no settlement of the oil dispute [was] possible and if Dr Mosadeg [sic] continues in power [the] US would extend sufficient financial and economic assistance [to Mosaddeq's government] to enable Iran to pass through [the] present crisis.[89]

In the ensuing weeks, TPAJAX planners showed flare and imagination in finding ways to bring pressure to bear on the Shah and co-opting him into their scheme. The first move was to get Princess Ashraf, the exiled twin-sister of the Shah, to deliver a message to her brother. The CIA agents spotted the princess in Deauville, France, and managed to convince her to fly to Tehran.[90] Her stealthy return on 25 July angered the pro-Mosaddeq press and fed speculations of a simmering conspiracy. In a public humiliation of the Shah, the new Court Minister Abol'qassem Amini issued a declaration warning the members of the royal family against breaches of protocol.[91] The Shah refused to receive his sister, but received her missive through a court official (named as a British asset in the CIA report) and may have finally deigned to grant her an audience.[92] From his sister the Shah learned that an American emissary, General Norman Schwarzkopf (Sr) was to visit him soon on behalf of the US government. Britain, for her part, began their salvos through their man in Tehran, Asadollah Rashidian. The latter visited the palace late in July with the aim of impressing upon the Shah that he was not a mere lackey, but an authentic mouthpiece for Whitehall. According to the CIA internal report, he employed signals from the BBC to establish his credentials. Eisenhower's digression in his Seattle speech on 4 August, which we referred to earlier in this chapter, is said by Woodhouse to have been another signal to reassure in the Shah.[93] The Shah must have been impressed but for now, remained unyielding.

General Schwarzkopf arrived late in July and met the Shah on 1 August. He had previously served in Iran and was credited with having organized Iran's rural police, the gendarmerie. As such, he was regarded as someone the Shah trusted.[94] The exact content of his message had

Figure 17 Princess Ashraf, the Shah's twin-sister, April 1951. Photo by Dmitri Kessel, ©Time-Life-Getty, 2009

been scripted in the plan, but was somewhat modified in view of the impending closure of the *Majles*. He wished the Shah to sign a *Farmān* (royal decree) appointing General Zahedi as the army chief of staff and another document in which the Shah would denounce Mosaddeq's decision to shut down the *Majles*. The Shah flatly refused to go along with it. On the other hand, he told Schwarzkopf that should Mosaddeq carry through his referendum (which had not yet taken place) and dissolve the parliament, he, the Shah, would be empowered under the constitution to replace him with a prime minister of his choice.[95]

This resulted in a major change in TPAJAX planning in the ensuing days. Henceforth, the plan centred on replacing Mosaddeq with General Zahedi once the dissolution of the *Majles* was accomplished. The Shah, nonetheless, remained decidedly noncommittal.

There was nothing new about the Shah's reaction. Over time, he had invoked 'legality' and parliamentary procedures with remarkable

Figure 18 Brigadier-General Norman H. Schwarzkopf Sr. Photo by AP, ©AP, 2007

consistency to shield himself against pressures to remove Mosaddeq. This was the main reason why his foreign interlocutors taxed him with being 'wavering and irresolute'. The Anglo-American planners were by then frustrated with his refusal to bend, but had yet another ace up their sleeve. Kermit (Kim) Roosevelt, the designated field commander for TPAJAX had just arrived in Tehran. He made a few secret visits to the Shah at the *Saad'ābād* Palace, the monarch's summer residence on the upper skirts of Alborz range. Faced with the Shah's continued tergiversation, Roosevelt shifted to a tough line, making the Shah an offer he could not refuse. The scene had been scripted out in the *coup* plan: in effect TPAJAX had relied on the Shah's cooperation but had foreseen the possibility that he may balk. A key passage in the plan read:

> should the Shah fail to go along with the US representative or fail to produce the [required] documents, General Zahedi would be informed that the United States would be ready to go ahead without the Shah's active cooperation...

Figure 19 Kermit (Kim) Roosevelt, as an oil executive in the 1960s. Photo by AP, ©AP, 2007

More explicitly, the plan had prescribed that the US Special Representative should, among other things, say the following to the Shah:

> If the Shah fails to go along his dynasty is bound to come to an end soon. In spite of the Shah's previous misconceptions the United States and the United Kingdom have been and continue to support him *but if the shah fails now, this support will be withdrawn* [emphasis added].[96]

On the strength of this provision, Kim Roosevelt decided to make the Shah understand that if he refused to cooperate he could ultimately be dispensed with. A plain blackmail was then performed by Roosevelt. In the CIA internal history *Overthrow* we read a passage which captures this historical moment:

> On 3 August, Roosevelt had a long and inconclusive session with the Shah. The latter stated that he was not an adventurer and, hence,

could not take the chances of one. Roosevelt pointed out that there was no other way by which the government could be changed and the test was now between Mosadeq (sic) and his force and the Shah and his army, which was still with him, but which would soon slip away. Roosevelt finally said that he would remain at hand a few days longer in expectation of an affirmative decision and then would leave the country; in the latter case the Shah should realize that failure to act could lead only to a Communist Iran or to a second Korea. *He concluded by saying that his government was not prepared to accept these possibilities and that some other plan might be carried through* (emphasis added).[97]

With the Anglo-American juggernaut now on the move, the Shah's surrender was a matter of time. Mohammad-Reza must have spent tormenting days and sleepless nights wavering. His temperament and judgement kept him from a plunge into adventurism. Yet, at that point in time, he faced two of the history's all-time colossuses – Churchill and Eisenhower – trying to lure him to their side, with an implied warning that refusal would be at his own peril.

Before the final nod, the Shah considered his options. One was to give verbal encouragement to officers involved in the plot and then leave for his Caspian resort lodge at *Kalardasht*. On 10 August, he received Colonel Hassan Akhavi, who briefed the Shah on the operation and no doubt gave him the names of key army officers involved in the plot.[98] The Shah was not reassured. Asdollah Rashidian, whose access to the palace was less complicated than that of Roosevelt, then went to see the Shah. According to the CIA's account, he told the monarch that Roosevelt would soon leave Iran *in disgust* if the Shah did not sign the two *farmāns* shortly. The Shah had already been served notice of the implications of a refusal; the blackmail was now consummated. The Shah's private secretary Rahim Hirad was given the order to prepare the texts.[99] The Shah signed them on 13 August only after he was a safe distance away from the capital in his Caspian lodge. It is likely that his wife Queen Soraya may have goaded him to overcome last minute hesitations.

The failure of the TPAJAX *coup*

Early in August Mosaddeq organized the previously heralded referendum. As mentioned earlier, he erred by having separate polling stations set up for the aye and nay voters, something that further diminished the credibility of the exercise. Only 170 voters ventured to the 'nay boots' in Tehran allowing the move to pass with 99.4 per cent overall approval. The dissolution of the *Majles* allowed the *coup* plan to be sanitized and assume an aura of legality in line with what the Shah had intimated to General Schwarzkopf a few days earlier.

The focus of the revised Anglo-American plan was thus shifted to the two royal decrees (*farmān*) dismissing Mosaddeq and replacing him with General Zahedi. Equally central to the plan was to ensure that Mosaddeq would not be in a position to counteract. Plans were made for the commander of the Imperial Guard, Colonel Nematollah Nasiri, to deliver the dismissal decree late at night, accompanied by an armoured detachment.[100] Simultaneously, the Imperial Guard units were to take over the main army command post in *Sevvom Esfand* Avenue as well as other strategic places. Chief of staff Riahi and some of Mosaddeq's left-leaning colleagues, notably Hossein Fatemi, were to be arrested.

This scenario was in effect played out in the late hours of 15 and early hours of 16 August. It failed. Colonel Nasiri was arrested in front of the prime minister's house, where he had delivered the royal fiat and obtained a handwritten receipt signed and dated by Mosaddeq.[101] General Riahi could not be arrested at his residence as planned; he had returned to his command post in downtown Tehran after Mosaddeq in person alerted him. He ordered the disarming of Imperial Guard units in their barracks in *bāq'e-shah* (literally meaning the shah's garden) and possibly the arrest of Nasiri.[102] Foreign minister Fatemi and two other Mosaddeq colleagues who had been picked up by the *putschist* units at midnight were released by daybreak and went straight to Mosaddeq's residence.

Contradictory accounts given by different participants prevent an impeachable reconstruction of what went on in the early hours of 16 August. Different actors have provided different explanations for the failure. What is certain is that the *Tudeh* secret military network, which had infiltrated key army units, including the Imperial Guard, had learned the details of the coup plot. In his memoirs, Noreddin Kianouri, at the time a key figure in the *Tudeh* leadership and its future general secretary, confirms he had personally tipped off Mosaddeq by telephone. The news of an impending *coup* had been publicly announced in *Tudeh* press on 13–14 August, but it was only late in the afternoon of Saturday 15 August that Kianouri had learned the details of the plot and could convey it to Mosaddeq. He used a back-channel to the prime minister's private quarters, given the fact that the spouses of the two men were close family relatives.[103] Mosaddeq and his army chief,

Riahi, were thus alerted enabling them to take the necessary countermeasures.[104] Other than Colonel Nasiri, a host of officers involved or implicated in the *coup* were also arrested. General Zahedi learned the news of the failure of the plan on road to the Officer's Club, which he had chosen as his temporary headquarters had the *coup* succeeded.[105] The following day, a prize was set for information leading to his arrest.

According to one account, attributed to Mosaddeq's propaganda chief Bashir Farahmand, the Prime Minister initially tilted towards compliance and even prepared a farewell address to the nation, but was dissuaded by his entourage before daybreak.[106] Whatever the truth of this account, an early-morning Tehran radio news bulletin announced that a *coup* by units of the Imperial Guard had been foiled and the plotters arrested.

In later years the issue of legality and nature of the operations has been raised and debated. Some have postulated that the Shah acted within his constitutional powers. Others deny that the Shah ever possessed such prerogatives. One thing, however, is clear. The royal decree was part of a plot hatched by two foreign powers; the head of state had been co-opted in circumstances which could be characterized as duress. These factors should divest the operation of all vestiges of legality even if, in the strictest sense, the removal procedure was in conformity with precedents established in earlier years of constitutional monarchy.[107]

Mosaddeq did not reveal the dismissal order outside a small circle of close advisors. Not even all his cabinet ministers were in the know.[108] He later explained that he had assumed the *farmān* was a forgery given the time and the manner in which it had been delivered. In his memoirs, he postulates that had the dismissal order been delivered through regular channels he would have abided by it and stepped down.[109] Mosaddeq's assertions on this subject, however, are somewhat wavering if not contradictory. In response to a query by Ambassador Henderson, whom he received on the evening of 18 August, Mosaddeq denied having received any royal decree, adding bluntly that, even if he had, '*it would have made no difference as he regarded the Shah's powers ceremonial in nature.*'[110] Still, in another passage of his memoirs, he says he would have gladly stepped down if he were not convinced that he could resolve the oil dispute in the best interest of Iran.

In reporting the failure of TPAJAX to President Eisenhower, the Under-Secretary of State (General) Walter Bedell Smith (Figure 20) attributed the failure of the plan to 'delay and vacillation by the Iranian generals concerned during which Mosadeg [sic] had found out all that was happening'. Significantly, General Smith continues: 'We now have to

Figure 20 Under-Secretary of State (General) Walter Bedell Smith. As the CIA Director under the Truman Administration and deputy to John Foster Dulles in the Eisenhower administration, he played a key role in shaping US policy towards Iran in the early 1950s. Photo by AP, ©AP 2009

take a new look at the Iranian situation and probably have to snuggle up to Mossadeg [sic] if we are going to have anything there. I dare say this means a little added difficulty with the British.'[111] General Smith's account of the failure of the *coup* had been taken from the record of the Shah's meeting with the US Ambassador in Baghdad where the monarch had given an account of the events of the previous few days and his understanding of how the *coup* had failed. We shall return to this meeting in the course of the next chapter (see the opening section 'The Gathering Storm'). It is interesting here to note that the word 'countercoup', which later became the title of Kermit Roosevelt's book, was first used in General Smith's brief note to Eisenhower.

This historical document confirms, if confirmation was needed, that the administration had no back-up plans to dislodge Mosaddeq in case the original plan failed.

5
The Downfall

This chapter is devoted to a reconstruction of events during the four critical days from the collapse of the TPAJAX *coup* in the early hours of 16 August to the actual downfall of the Mosaddeq government late in the afternoon of 19 August. The main happenings during this interval are known, but the axiom *the devil is in the detail* is eminently relevant to this brief episode. This is because, in recounting these events, some authors have assigned especial significance to certain happenings, projecting them as evidence of deliberate manipulation by the TPAJAX plotters to influence the course of events or steer them in a desired direction. Interpretative narratives reflect, at times, a view taken through an ideological prism or result from preconceived assumptions. In delving into details of this episode, therefore, we maintain a focus also on the events which have lent themselves to such interpretations and spins. A case in point is the emphasis placed on the so called *black and grey propaganda* by the TPAJAX agents or the presumed participation of some military units alleged to have been earmarked under the original *coups*. In three sub-sections, the chapter strives to shed light on all the intricate facets of responsibility versus claims of responsibility for the downfall. Combined with the ensuing Chapter 6, where additional data and analyses are provided, we strive to a present a comprehensive body of evidence on the CIA/SIS role in the actual downfall of the Mosaddeq government. Both chapters lean heavily on the declassified State Department papers as well as on the CIA's own internal history, *Overthrow*. Like other parts of this study it also benefits from the published recollections of primary actors. As in previous chapters, annotations provided in notes constitute an important source of complementary information.

The gathering storm, 16–18 August 1953

The news of the *coup* failure reached the Shah in his Caspian resort lodge, possibly by his Swiss aide Ernest Perron.[1] In panic, he flew off to Baghdad in his personal *Beechcraft*, accompanied by his wife Queen Soraya and two aides. They were received with courtesy in Baghdad and lodged in the state guest house, but their presence posed an immediate dilemma for the Iraqi government, which was served notice on 16 August by Foreign Minister Fatemi that the presence of the Shah in Iraq could adversely affect bilateral relations.[2] Both the State Department and the Foreign Office were thenceforth cautious in their attitude vis-à-vis the Shah, now a potential liability.[3] The Foreign Office vetoed a request from Darbyshire and Leavitt in Cyprus to travel to Baghdad to see the Shah. CIA headquarters informed the Station in Tehran late on 16 August that 'the State Department was firmly opposed to any American effort to contact the Shah and suggested the British do it';[4] yet at the Shah's request the US Ambassador in Baghdad, Burton Berry, met him on 16 August. After briefing the ambassador on the events of the previous few weeks the Shah said he wanted to make a public statement but before doing so, needed information and advice (presumably through American channels). His proposed statement would say in essence that he had dismissed Mosaddeq and replaced him with General Zahedi because Mosaddeq had systematically violated the constitution. He had left the country to avoid bloodshed, but had not abdicated and was ready to return when he could serve the nation.[5] Before leaving for Rome (Figure 21), he made the statement on his own initiative, adding that he was confident about the loyalty of his people.[6] In Rome, he received a message from Dulles, sent through the US Embassy there, belatedly encouraging him to make a statement. The proposed text by Dulles was, however, a rephrasing the Shah's own text; the American input may, however, have encouraged him to give interviews with an array of newsmen.[7] His departure on 16 August was the tipping point, unleashing torrents of opposing forces in the streets of Tehran; yet the Shah himself remained largely in the shadows, his contribution being confined to his press statements.

In Iran the central issue was the regime change. The *Tudeh* Party began a massive campaign to end not just the monarchy but '*all its vestiges*', which meant the feudalistic structure of power and 'bureaucratic capitalism' of which the monarchy was seen to be the symbol as well as protector. The four-point declaration issued by the executive committee of the *Tudeh* on 18 August, including advocacy for a

Figure 21 The Shah and Queen Soraya arriving in Rome, 18 August 1953. Photo by AP, ©AP 2009

'*democratic republic*', contained strong Marxist revolutionary properties.[8] It marked the ascendancy of the party's more doctrinaire leaders, notably Kianouri, who advocated a vanguard role for the party in the anti-feudal, anti-colonial phase of the struggle. The theoretical concept was termed, in their Marxist-Leninist parlance, '*proletarian hegemony*', which meant the *Tudeh* Party ascendancy at the expense of the national bourgeoisie, namely the leadership of Mosaddeq's National Front.[9] The terrain must have been judged propitious, even by the more moderate members of the *Tudeh* executive body, to henceforth pursue a power-sharing agenda in the short run that could potentially lead, as it had in many other models in Eastern Europe, to an eventual takeover of power. According to some reports on 17–18 August, the *Tudeh* leadership was in marathon contact with Mosaddeq, or his entourage, urging him to declare a republic and had requested Mosaddeq to give arms to *Tudeh* militants to counter any move by pro-Shah forces.[10] This ideological drift could be seen in other features of the *Tudeh* declaration of 18 August calling for the abolition of martial law and the legalization of the *Tudeh* Party while proposing to establish the all too familiar 'united front' with participation of all other 'anti-colonial' forces. In some provincial capitals, *Tudeh* militants occupied municipal buildings and hoisted red flags.[11] The declaration also called for the expulsion of the US military mission, Point Four, and American consulates in the provinces.[12] Some observers later pointed to eerie parallels with the episode of Edvard Beneš in 1948 when communist coalition partners ousted the bourgeois nationalist president of Czechoslovakia. The newly appointed Soviet Ambassador to Tehran, Anatoly Lavrentiev, was a specialist in Eastern European countries who had been rushed from his post as ambassador in Bucharest – where he had stayed less than a year – to Tehran. He had been deputy foreign minister in Moscow as well as an ambassador in Belgrade (during Tito's rupture with the USSR) and in Czechoslovakia (after Beneš's fall), and as such was a very senior ambassador. According to an anecdote, recounted by Abul'hossein Meftah, Deputy-Foreign Minister in Mosaddeq's government, and confirmed by *The New York Times*, Lavrentiev attempted suicide shortly after the fall of Mosaddeq and was unceremoniously withdrawn; he was said to have been blamed for the failure of the Soviet agenda in Iran. This assumption, as indeed the suicide story, is based on circumstantial evidence only. He was reinstalled and returned to his post in Tehran.[13]

The *Tudeh* campaign, which started with a march to the Reza Shah mausoleum on the morning of 17 August, culminated in the overturning of statues of the Shah and his father in the main Tehran squares (Figure 22) and continued with the removal of all other Pahlavi symbols.[14] Other pro-Mosaddeq parties also participated in this campaign and it is not excluded that TPAJAX's Iranian agents may have zealously participated as *agent provocateurs*, although it is safe to assume that these events would have occurred with or without their input. We shall return to this latter point in Chapter 6. Some of the more radical Mosaddeq advisors, notably Dr Fatemi, joined the chorus for ending the monarchy. The latter used scurrilous language in denouncing the Shah in a public rally on 16 August and in an editorial in *Bākhtar-Emrouz*, the daily he published. A climate of uncertainty reigned amidst rumours – unfounded in all likelihood – that the arrested officers involved in the plot were about to be publicly executed. Furthermore, a rumour began circulating in town that the *coup* allegation had been inspired by the government to blame the Shah and give Mosaddeq the excuse to move against him. The American Embassy reported the prevalence of this rumour to Washington.[15]

Mosaddeq was reticent at best about regime change, yet in the immediate after-shock of the *coup* had allowed things to slide. He could,

Figure 22 Crowds drag down Reza Shah's statue from Shah-Reza Square on 17 August 1953. Photo by AP, ©AP 2008

perhaps, ill-afford alienating the by then narrowed support-base of which *Tudeh* had become the most visible and vocal component. Yet he must have also dreaded a plunge into the anarchy that street scenes heralded. Several indices point to Mosaddeq's acute disquiet on this score. On his orders Fatemi, as government spokesman, formally denied the regime change even if he continued his violent anti-Shah diatribe in his paper. Mosaddeq also banned street rallies as of the *morning* of 18 August.[16] The dispersal order, as will be seen in the coming pages, was reinforced in the evening and proved consequential as events unfolded in the following 24 hours. According to the diary of one of his close associates, Mosaddeq was averse to any change that could alienate the United States and the West on whose help and support he seemed to continue to rely for solvency and the resolution of the oil dispute; Mosaddeq may also have had qualms about alienating the religious hierarchy, although nothing is documented on this point.[17] After some introspection, Mosaddeq settled for the idea of a 'Regency Council' to be endorsed by a nationwide referendum. He never got around to announcing that decision publicly, however.[18]

General Zahedi's camp, after an initial hour of dejection, decided to fight back. The CIA internal history *Overthrow* confirms that the will to fight back was expressed by General Zahedi and his son, and that Kim Roosevelt indeed *followed* that lead.[19] Details of deliberations, planning, and the immediate actions taken by Zahedi and his circle of close associates from the late hours of 15 August to the fall of Mosaddeq's government on the 19 August were chronicled and published by Ardeshir Zahdi in a 1953 article *'panj rouz'e bohrāni'* (The Five Days of Crisis) and later reproduced in his published memoirs with additional explanations and supporting material.[20] The sequence of events provided by him tally with the main thrust of the CIA internal history, but the two accounts diverge on one cardinal point as well as on a few less consequential details.[21] The major discrepancy arises from the fact that Roosevelt broadly hints that events on Wednesday 19 August were pre-planned. The Zahedi camp refers only to a *mid-term* plan for military insurgency out of Kermanshah – a city some 400 miles to the west of Tehran – and clearly denies any prior knowledge of events that occurred on 19 August. As we proceed, we shall elaborate on both points of convergence and divergence.

Both accounts confirm certain preparatory moves in the immediate aftermath of the *coup* failure. Firstly, the Zahedi camp wanted the public to learn that the Shah, in the exercise of his 'constitutional prerogative', had removed Mosaddeq and replaced him with General Zahedi.

This was accomplished by a dissemination of the photostats of the royal decree, along with a statement from General Zahedi. The accompanying statement, in a nutshell, declared that by virtue of the attached *Farmān* he, General Zahedi, was henceforth the lawful prime minister and Mosaddeq's orders were as such null and void; those carrying them out would be liable to sanctions.[22] Envelopes containing the two documents, according to the Zahedi account, were dropped off in the mailbox of as many government and press offices as feasible. The fact of the drop-offs has been independently confirmed by other sources.[23] In all likelihood, through Farzanegan, the CIA station in Tehran had also helped in a larger dissemination of Photostats. The general's son, Ardeshir Zahedi, according to both accounts, secretly met and briefed AP, UP, Reuters and *The New York Times* Tehran correspondents. Kennett Love refers to this interview in his 17 and 19 August dispatches.[24]

The CIA internal history, while acknowledging that this idea originated from the Zahedi camp, provides a somewhat different account of the way the statement was prepared. According to this version, on the afternoon of 16 August the station was working on a statement by General Zahedi *'which had been prepared on the direct advise of Ardeshir Zahedi, the Rashidian brothers and Colonel Farzanegan'*.[25] *The New York Times* correspondent Kennett Love, quoting an AP dispatch, also mentions another text in which General Zahedi would have called on Iranian military officers to be ready for ultimate sacrifice to preserve the monarchy and Islam. This language does not appear anywhere in Zahedi's own narratives – an unlikely oversight if the story was genuine. It may have been fabricated under Zahedi's name by TPAJAX agents and fed to foreign news agencies.[26] Be that as it may, *Overthrow* admits to severe limitations in their distribution possibilities, forcing them to resort to foreign outlets. The mass-circulation Tehran daily, *Kayhan*, referred to the Shah's *farmāns* in its inner pages on 16 and 17 August, citing foreign news dispatches.[27] Abdul-Rahman Farmarzi, the publisher of *Kayhan*, was a staunch Mosaddeq foe and was in direct contact with the Zahedi camp even after the *coup* failure.[28] *Shā'hed*, published by Baqa'ei, printed a photo of the Shah's *farmān* on 18 August. These two opposition heavyweights hardly needed the CIA station to prop them up. A string of low-circulation Tehran newspapers – some CIA-subsidized – followed suit on 19 August, the day of Mosaddeq's fall.[29]

The second preparatory line was to contact some provincial military commanders notably in Isfahan and Kermanshah with a view to establishing a base outside Tehran to conduct an armed insurrection. The proposal to establish a base outside Tehran had come from General

Zahedi in the course of an internal meeting with his Iranian advisors on 16 August in the general's hideout.[30] The plan was predicated on a grim assessment of human and material resources available to him in Tehran. According to a verbatim-like account of General Zahedi's words – recorded in the 1953 article published by his son – the General said that people he could count on in Tehran did not exceed 15 persons and that all military units and security forces were commanded by officers who were *a priori* loyal to Mosaddeq.[31] This was the logic of a mid-term strategy of insurrection out of a provincial capital. The insurrection plan, in substance, is confirmed in the *Overthrow* account, though the latter assigns the plan a different objective and provides a different time and setting for its adoption. According to both accounts, Ardeshir Zahedi travelled to Esfahan where he rallied the deputy-division commander, Colonel Amir-Qoli Zarghami, while Colonel Farzanegan travelled to Kermanshah where he met the brigade commander, Colonel Teymour Bakhtiar, and seemingly obtained his cooperation.[32] In all likelihood the trips received logistical support from the CIA station; false identity cards may have been issued by the station. What these secret missions reveal is that the Zahedi camp was focused on that *mid-term plan* as opposed to an immediate strike as Kim Roosevelt later claimed.[33]

In effect, in his post-facto debriefings in Washington, reflected in *Overthrow*, Kim Roosevelt referred to a different planning meeting, described as a 'council of war', held on the evening of 17 August at the US Embassy compound with the participation of General Zahedi and other key Iranian actors, as well as MI6 agents (the Rashidian brothers). According to *Overthrow*, following a four-hour deliberation, a comprehensive plan with military and political components was adopted and at the end, it was decided that *some action would be taken on Wednesday the 19th*. A detailed analysis of these assertions has been provided in Chapter 6 'Anatomy of 19 August', we will not therefore dwell on it at this point.

The backlash: events leading to the fall of Mosaddeq on 19 August

The first hint of a backlash appeared on the evening of 17 August when security elements that clashed with *Tudeh* militants reportedly manifested pro-Shah sentiments. *Overthrow* refers to this incident as the first encouraging sign. More significantly, for the first time since the departure of the Shah two days earlier, scattered pro-Shah demonstrators appeared in the streets of the capital on the evening of 18 August and clashed with the *Tudeh* militants. In his dispatch of 18 August Kennett Love also refers to a small pro-Shah demonstration in the morning. Some elements of the security forces again manifested pro-Shah sentiments and the crackdown on the *Tudeh* demonstrators was particularly severe. Curiously, the CIA narrative does not seek to link these demonstrations in any manner to the decisions adopted the previous night in Roosevelt's 'council of war.'[34] Ardeshir Zahedi for his part says, 'People poured out into the streets either on their own initiative or on instructions issued by *religious leaders*' (emphasis added).[35] Significantly, he affirms that news of that evening's happenings boosted General Zahedi's morale, who cancelled his plans to move to Kermanshah the following day (i.e., Wednesday 19 August) from where he had planned to launch his insurrection.

As of the early hours of Wednesday 19 August, initially sparse crowds gathered around the Tehran bazaar area, chanting pro-Shah slogans. Demonstrators soon grew and throngs sprouted as they moved uptown in the directions of the municipality, the Ministry of the Interior and the Post Office and later towards *Bāhārestān* Square where the *Majles* was located. A growing crowd, undeterred by the police, sacked the *Tudeh* and pro-Mosaddeq newspapers and party headquarters.[36] In his recollections, Mosaddeq's interior minister, Dr Qolam'hossein Sadiqi, notes that around 9 a.m. scant pro-Shah groups were roaming in town and some were in the vicinity of his ministry.[37] Chroniclers or eyewitnesses have described the crowds in different, at times contrasting terms. A secret British document (which is analysed in Chapter 6 of this study) maintains that the core group of demonstrators, estimated at 3000, who started the demonstration at 8 a.m. from the bazaar area, were in most part hired for this purpose, though they may have entertained genuine pro-Shah sentiments. 'Among them there were many unemployed people and many well-known hooligans... The crowd grew as time went on and a large number of well-to-do people, who resented Musaddiq's [sic] government especially his recent pro-Tudeh policy, joined the demonstrations.'[38] The American weekly *Saturday Evening Post*, in an article by Richard and Gladys Harkness, published in its issue of 6 November 1954 referred to groups of oddball athletes displaying amusing skills to attract crowds before chanting pro-Shah slogans.[39] This same impression is conveyed by Woodhouse, who later mused about a 'grotesque procession' through Teheran, 'headed by tumblers turning handsprings, weightlifters turning iron bars, and wrestlers flexing their biceps'.[40] Others, including the US Embassy in Tehran and author Richard Cottam in his early writings, conveyed the opposite impression to which we have referred under the 'US Embassy Monitoring' heading below and in other passages of this study. These contradictory observations are part of the truth of a complex event that could not be apprehended unless viewed in its full dimensions. We will try to shed light on these contrasts and provide a coherent picture as we proceed through Chapters 6 and 7. The narrative in the present chapter aims to describe the events through the lenses of several key observers including the US Embassy.

* * *

Mosaddeq had ordered a ban on all demonstrations as of the morning of the previous day, Tuesday 18 August. The police crackdown on *Tudeh* militants on Tuesday evening had been particularly severe. Mosaddeq reinforced his crackdown order possibly after the meeting with Ambassador Henderson which took place at 6 p.m on 18 August.[41] The *Tudeh* agitations, especially the call for a *'democratic republic'* (see the first section of this chapter) had no doubt troubled the quintessentially establishment politician that Mosaddeq was. He also decided on that day to shake up the top law enforcement ranks, as we shall shortly come to. On the previous evening the *Tudeh* militants had gathered in *Sepah* Square preparing to hang a gigantic placard over the municipality building calling for the end of monarchy and a democratic republic when security forces arrived. According to the top *Tudeh* official Kianouri, some 600 party cadres had been detained.[42] Now on this fateful Wednesday, *Tudeh* activists remained at home. Kianouri confirms that a meeting of the party leadership on the morning of 19 August took the decision to contact Mosaddeq and send a delegation to persuade him to call for public mobilization and the distribution of arms. Kianouri recalls having called Mosaddeq on the morning of 19 August offering to send party militants onto the streets if Mosaddeq cancelled his previous day's order. Mosaddeq, however, had told him off, citing the risks of bloodshed. He equally rejected a similar appeal by the *Tudeh* delegation which seemingly met him sometime on the morning of 19 August.[43] While the accuracy of all the above is hard to certify, it can safely be assumed that the occurrences of the morning of 19 August took the *Tudeh* leadership by surprise and that the party structure was in a state of disarray.

In those days, it was common to send truckloads of soldiers under martial-law command to the city's troubled zones; this standard practice was no doubt followed when riotous demonstrations broke out in various parts in downtown Tehran. When Mosaddeq ordered the dispersal of the crowds, it appeared that law-enforcement officials at various levels, down to policemen and soldiers deployed in the streets, disobeyed or obstructed the orders. This point is confirmed by Mosaddeq's minister of the interior, Dr Sadiqi, who in his published recollections refers to a telephone conversation (around 11 a.m.) with the outgoing martial-law administrator, Colonel Ashrafi.[44] The latter reported to the minister that units sent to disperse the crowd could not be trusted and that some had joined the demonstrators.[45] There is no doubt that within the senior police ranks there were many who deplored the turn of events following the Shah's departure and genuine pro-Shah sentiments exited among the law enforcement rank and file. Sensing foul play or incompetence, Mosaddeq had decided the previous day to replace both the police chief, General Nasrollah Modabber and the martial law administrator Colonel Ashrafi. He ended up entrusting both jobs to a family relative, General Mohammad Daftari, whose loyalties were also unclear.[46]

It is widely reported that the disarmed Imperial Guard elements requisitioned trucks and roamed the streets of the capital when the news of pro-Shah street demonstrations spread. This move might have been misconstrued by *Overthrow*, which refers to 'truckloads of pro-Shah military personnel in all main squares by 10. 15 AM'.[47] This latter assertion is not supported either by the US Embassy monitoring reports or the digest of press coverage of events published the following day in Tehran or for whatever they are worth, the recollections of the *Tudeh* official Kianouri.[48] The US Embassy in a dispatch to Washington characterized the attitude of the security forces as initially ambiguous. For his part Dr Sadiqi who drove from his ministry in a tour of the city on his way to Mosaddeq's residence in the early afternoon (Figure 23), did not come across any pro-Shah *military* units; he had, however, traversed some of the Tehran's main arteries and junctions.[49]

The CIA internal history, *Overthrow*, provides other dubious specifics about the presence on the scene of officers purportedly linked to the earlier TPAJAX *coup* attempt.[50] This subject is treated in depth under 'The Military Factor in the Fall of Mosaddeq' below. It will be seen from evidence presented there that officers earmarked for the 15 August *coup* were unknown to General Zahedi or for that matter to the CIA station. Even the most senior among active officers involved in the 15 August *coup* – Colonel Nozari, the commanding officer of the 2nd Armoured Brigade – was unknown to the CIA station judging by a key passage in *Overthrow*.[51] If anyone among the officers earmarked under TPAJAX also

Figure 23 Interior Minister Dr Golam'hossein Sadiqi arriving at Mosaddeq's house in the early afternoon of 19 August as described in his memoirs. Photo from the private collection of Ardeshir Zahedi. Courtesy of IBEX publishers®

participated in the 19 August riots it must be regarded as a feature of the haphazard pattern of events on that day. In reality military intervention in the day's events did not become visible before early afternoon, something that is uncharacteristic of planned military *coups*.

Clearly, when the news of pro-Shah demonstrations spread by word of mouth, some officers and units from garrisons in the outlying areas of Tehran, including a few armoured units, spontaneously joined the action, a point also specified in the American Embassy coverage of the day's event. In some accounts it has been mentioned that the armoured unit which decisively turned against Mosaddeq on Wednesday afternoon was originally earmarked to protect the prime minister and was sent, on Sadiqi's urging, to prevent the state radio station from falling into the hands of pro-Shah forces. Kennett Love, for his part, claimed to have tipped off the commander of the tank column which had joined the crowd around the state radio station to move to Mosaddeq's house, where pro-Shah crowds were storming the Mosaddeq residence.[52] Whatever the truth of these accounts, the entry of military units as of the early afternoon could not have been part of a pre-planned military coup. The display of élan by the military was rooted not just in the pro-Shah and anti-*Tudeh* sentiments then prevalent among officers but was also nourished by rumours that their arrested comrades-in-arms were about to be executed by the government. These rumours must have had an important psychological impact given the ethos of the Iranian officer corps, a point also made in *Overthrow*.[53] By noon on 19 August, the street movement had gathered momentum. By early afternoon, the crowd had invested the telecommunication (Telegraph and Telephone) office downtown. Its fall into the hands of the rioters must have been a factor contributing to the mobilization of pro-Shah forces in several provinces. As mentioned earlier, the American Embassy in Tehran closely monitored the situation and dispatched several cables to Washington. It is interesting to view the day's subsequent events through the embassy lens.

Monitoring by the US Embassy

The American Embassy, monitoring the situation hour by hour, described participants as *'not of hoodlum types customarily predominant in recent demonstration in Tehran. They seemed to come from all classes of people...'*[54] At about 2 p.m. the Embassy reported to Washington that a large crowd had gathered around the main radio broadcasting facility, blocking the old Shemiran Road, and intended to occupy the state radio station. Significantly, in the same report the embassy observed, *'The Embassy has not yet been able to figure out the organization and objectives of these activities.'*[55] At 4 p.m. the embassy reported that the radio station was in the hands of the pro-Shah forces and that embassy eavesdropping (presumably by the CIA) had detected that the new Chief of Police, Daftari, had been trying to draw on elements of his previous command, presumably to help Mosaddeq.[56]

The embassy confirmed that military and security forces, whose attitude was unclear at the day's onset, had now joined the crowds. The number of officers who *'individually'* were rallying to crowds was on the rise.[57] Later in the afternoon they were reinforced by armoured vehicles and a few tanks.

At around 2 p.m., according to the US Embassy, some 3000 hostile demonstrators gathered near the residence of the prime minister in *Kakh Avenue*. The military units which had joined demonstrations began an assault on Mosaddeq's residence as of 4 p.m. and were fired upon by units guarding the house. The US Embassy had sighted some six tanks displaying portraits of the Shah; they must have later taken part in the assault against the prime minister's residence.[58] In the same dispatch the embassy referred to similar incidents in front of the army's main command post in *Sevvom-Esfand Avenue* and in front of the police headquarters facing the Foreign Ministry.

The final hours

General Zahedi, who had initially planned a military revolt from Kermanshah, had seemingly modified his plans and remained in his hideout in Tehran. As mentioned earlier, the change of plan, according to his son Ardeshir, was occasioned by the news of pro-Shah street demonstrations the previous evening and the attitude of security forces, which had clearly shown pro-Shah sentiments. Now in the afternoon of the 19 August, he left his hideout to assume leadership of the street uprisings in the Capital.[59] *Overthrow* asserts that Kim Roosevelt twice visited General Zahedi during the day and urged him at the second meeting to go to Tehran radio station on board a tank that was to be obtained for that purpose. Ardeshir Zahedi vigorously contests this version of events. He insists that he personally drove his father to a rendezvous place near the Old Shemiran Road. A tank procured by Deputy Police Chief Colonel Ziauddin Khalatbari – who had rallied to the Zahedi camp – was sent there on which the general rode to the radio station to deliver his speech.[60]

Be that as it may, by 3:30 p.m. Tehran radio had fallen into the hands of the crowd. General Zahedi, riding on the tank, was able to go there and deliver a victory speech at around 5 p.m. By 4 p.m. a fierce battle was raging around Mosaddeq's residence. Casualty estimates vary but could conservatively be put at several dozen dead, all incidents included.[61] According to Kianouri, sometime after 2 p.m. he contacted Mosaddeq for the third time that day. Only a few hours earlier Mosaddeq had rejected a *Tudeh* appeal for public mobilization and distribution of arms, characterizing it as 'panic'. But the Prime Minister was now seeking help, '*Everyone has betrayed me my dear sir*', he is quoted as having complained. '*If there is anything you can do, go ahead and perform your national duty as you deem fit.*'[62] The *Tudeh* organizational structure had, however, been dealt a blow the previous night. Kianouri admits in his memoirs that at that point in time there was nothing the *Tudeh* Party could have done to save the day. Mosaddeq's eleventh-hour SOS signal to *Tudeh*, if Kianouri's testimony is accurate, remained inconsequential. The army command post appears to have fallen to pro-Shah forces by about the

Figure 24 Mosaddeq waving from his car. Photo, the US State Department ©2008, courtesy of the Truman Library®

same time. The Chief of Army Staff, General Riahi, reportedly called Mosaddeq by telephone to urge him to order a cessation of all resistance and sent an emissary to Mosaddeq's house to persuade him to follow that advice.

By 5 p.m. a dejected Mossadeq agreed to raise the white flag over the roof of the modest house he had used as both office and residence. In a brief statement he declared he was '*the lawful prime minister*', but as security forces had ceased to obey his orders, he declared his residence to be a non-combat zone, urging the assailants to desist from investing it.[63] The ceasefire request hand-carried by Riahi's emissary (Brigadier Foulanvand) did not, however, stop the assailants, who continued relentlessly to shell the house even after the white flag was raised. Accompanied by a few close associates and helped by his personal guards, Mosaddeq had to climb over the wall to the adjacent garden from where he took refuge and stayed the night in a nearby deserted house, before moving the following morning to the house of one of his ministers. His own residence at 109 Kākh Avenue was ransacked and looted by the mob before being set on fire. Mosaddeq quickly decided to present himself to the new authorities but while preparing for surrender, a police search team accidentally arrived at his hideout. The actual act of rendition took place in a dignified manner and with courtesy to a man who had left an indelible mark on the history of Iran.[64]

Figure 25 General Zahedi and close associates shortly after Mosaddeq's downfall in 1953. From left to right: Ardeshir Zahedi, Colonel Abbas Farzanegan (a CIA agent), General Fazlollah Zahedi, General Nader Batmanqelij and General H. Guilanshah. Soleiman Behboudi, a MI6 asset, is in the second row just behind Ardeshir Zahedi. Colonel Nasiri, who delivered Mosaddeq's dismissal order on 15 August, can be seen second from the left in the last row. Photo from the private collection of Ardeshir Zahedi, courtesy of IBEX publishers®

The military factor in the fall of Mosaddeq

The issue of an organic link between the TPAJAX coup of 15 August and the fall of Mosaddeq on 19 August is central to this study. To the extent that the existence of such link is at least partly predicated on the participation of officers and military units presumed to have also been earmarked in the TPAJAX operations a few days earlier, a closer look at the probability of such synchronization is called for. Appendix D of the CIA internal history on military planning (and certain passages of the main text) in effect imply that some of these officers and units may have participated in the revolt on 19 August. The proposition by itself is plausible to the extent that not all potential participants in the *coup* had been arrested following its failure. The identity of these officers, however, was unknown to foreign or Iranian plotters and equally unknown to the *Tudeh* military network which had successfully foiled the *coup* and betrayed the identities of the known *putschist* officers.[65]

Be that as it may, two observations need to be underscored. Firstly, there were no known contacts between the CIA station and these officers in the Tehran area following the TPAJAX *coup* failure on 16 August. The CIA internal history makes no claim that its main military planner Henry Carroll or General Robert McClure, heading the US military advisory group, or anyone else for that matter, had contacted anyone in the Tehran garrison after the *coup* failure. Contacts with commanders in Esfahan and Kermanshah, to which we referred in detail in the first section of the chapter, were for the purpose of setting up an insurrectional authority in a provincial capital. The fact that Kim Roosevelt in *Countercoup* and Stephen Kinzer in *All the Shah's Men* link those contacts with an alleged CIA-contrived uprising plan in Tehran on Wednesday 19 August – overlooking the logistical impossibility of such a scheme – reveals the kaleidoscopic or Pollyannaish character of their assertions.[66] If anything, Appendix D of the CIA document is specific (p. 14 of Appendix D) in saying that contacts with the line officers in the Tehran garrison was impossible following the arrest of the key liaison officer in the wake of the failed TPAJAX *coup*.[67] A copy of General Zahedi's statement of 16 August is said to have been given to 'two key army officers'[68] as well as to the friendly press. *Overthrow* does not identify the two or the manner in which this text was given to them, though it can safely be assumed that the two commanders in Kermanshah and Esfahan are meant. The declaration by General Zahedi, as it will be recalled, announced he was the rightful prime minister by virtue of the Shah's decree; his statement had no link whatsoever with plans for a new uprising. Hence, any participation by Iranian officers and units from the outlying barracks in the events of Wednesday 19 August must have been spontaneous upon spread of the news by word of mouth, as the US Embassy reports also confirm. In the next chapter we will provide evidence that no one among the plotters, whether American or Iranian, was aware of or predicted the occurrence of such turmoil.

The second point to be highlighted is that with one single notable exception, that is, Colonel Abbas Farzanegan, no Iranian officer worked for or considered himself subordinate to American or other foreign agents. Appendix E of *Overthrow* is categorical in stating that no money was spent or needed to bribe any active Iranian officers (Appendix E, p. 22, paragraph Q).[69] An in-depth examination based on *Overthrow's* own account of military planning in Appendix D and its evaluation in Appendix E in effect leads us to the conclusion that military input into the actual downfall of Mosaddeq was primarily, if not exclusively, an Iranian phenomenon, much as its political component was a product of internal dynamics. Just as the political opposition was in place and ready to act when the Anglo-American plotters sought them out, so in the military sphere the ingredients for an armed revolt among active officers existed before Carroll set out to do his military planning. This point can be demonstrated graphically through a quick review of how military planning for the TPAJAX *coup* was developed, drawing upon information mainly from the annexes of the CIA history, *Overthrow*.

TPAJAX military planning and the role of Iranian officers

A network of line officers up to regiment and deputy-brigade-commander level was already in place in the Tehran garrison – shapeless and unstructured – but looking for an outlet to act. The key figure among them was Colonel Zand-Karimi, who was in touch with every infantry battalion commander in Tehran and with most of the company commanders.[70] The outlet was found almost accidentally through a string of personal connections, at one end of which stood Colonel Farzanegan, a CIA agent. The Tehran garrison in those days was comprised of three mountain and two armoured brigades which were barracked in Tehran suburbs. Other military units included the Imperial Guard, a fairly small elite unit, as well as the army transportation branch (*Tarābary*), a cavalry squadron and also law and order organs such as the police, the gendarmerie, and squadrons attached to the martial law administration; to this cluster the militarily insignificant Custom Armed Guard could be added. The Pentagon, G2, and British army intelligence initially lacked data about this configuration and the profile of officers commanding these units, in spite of the presence of an American military advisory team headed by General McClure, a lacuna grudgingly admitted in Appendices D and E of *Overthrow*.[71]

Before coming into contact with this group, indeed up to early August 1953, the Anglo-American military planners were acting on the basis of flawed intelligence. A run of the mill *coup* plan of a Latino variety, comprising the neutralization of key strategic command and communication posts in Tehran, assorted with an arrest list had been prepared by Henry Carroll, Major Keen, and SIS military experts but the issue of military resources with which to implement the plan remained dauntingly unresolved.[72] It soon became clear to planners that General Zahedi, by then retired from the army for several years, had no significant allies, and none among the brigades. He had indicated that he could count on help from the Imperial Guard, while mentioning elements in the police and the Armed Customs Guard as well as some units from the Army Transportation branch. This was patently inadequate. The SIS in Cyprus, however, claimed *'several important friends'*, among them Colonel Hossein-Ali Ashrafi. He commanded the Third Mountain Brigade and was Mosaddeq's chief martial law administrator; as such he was the only one among presumed assets deemed to be in a position to make a difference. The initial military planning therefore relied mainly on him.[73] Carroll, however, was conscious that one out of five brigades was insufficient. He travelled to Tehran in late July hoping to build up further contacts or to snitch some assets within the brigades, helped by Colonel Farzanegan. The latter knew a lot of people in active service, among whom was Colonel Hassan Akhavi. For his part, Akhavi was closely linked with Colonel Zand-Karimi who was in contact with younger pro-Shah officers in the Tehran garrison, as we just referred to. Yet, up until early August the CIA/MI6 planners perilously pinned their hopes on Colonel Hossein-Ali Ashrafi. Zand-Karimi and Akhavi were introduced to Carroll in early August and since they knew intimately the political affiliations of their comrades, they revised Carroll's plan and the arrest list. *In extremis*, Colonel Ashrafi was dropped from the plan and added to the arrest list. The Iranian officers had just saved the TPAJAX planners from a premature fiasco.[74] That the SIS intelligence on this asset had proven to be bogus is readily admitted in Appendix D of *Overthrow*.[75]

It is worth noting that at that point this group of active officers had no link with, and did not know, General Zahedi. It is around this date, as will be recalled from 'The Taming of the Shah' in Chapter 4, that Colonel Akhavi was received in audience at Sadābād Palace to brief the Shah on the *coup* plan and the sentiments of officers in case he repudiated Mosaddeq. The latter's decision to dissolve the *Majles* afforded the Shah the legal artifice to dismiss him and the TPAJAX *coup* plan was accordingly readjusted. Colonel Akhavi himself fell seriously sick and could play no role in the TPAJAX *coup*. The brunt of the responsibility fell on the Imperial Guard, but the fact that Colonel Zand-Karimi and a few other officers from the brigades were arrested following the TPAJAX *coup* suggests that their units too had been assigned roles which had not escaped *Tudeh* vigilance. As for Ashrafi, there is indeed no evidence that on 19 August or anytime before that he played any role in helping Zahedi or the Shah. Other than the admission by *Overthrow* that the SIS claim on Ashrafi was unfounded, empirical evidence absolves him of involvement in any treacherous conduct. It must be noted that all officers who had remotely helped or were known to have been sympathetic to the Shah were later generously rewarded by promotions and assignment to sensitive posts. The annual promotion list to the rank of brigadier-general in September 1953 was unprecedentedly effusive.[76] Not only was Ashrafi not on that list but he was arrested on 20 August and was in detention till mid-November, following which he was purged from the army and faded away.[77] We do not exclude that the Rashidian brothers may have aggrandized their links with Ashrafi in their usual boastful projection of their own efficiency.[78] This is in contrast to General Daftari – a close relative of Mosaddeq – who, it will be recalled, was belatedly appointed by him as chief of the national police yet was confirmed in that same post by Zahedi and later promoted. Zahedi had already in July flagged Daftari, at that time commanding the Armed Customs Guard, as one of his allies.

From the forgoing, two conclusions are clear. Firstly, a nucleus of revolt among the line officers in the Tehran garrison already existed before CIA/SIS developed a *coup* plan. These planners did not recruit anyone from within the Iranian army; they just harvested gratuitously what was already in place and were indeed saved from premature embarrassment, thanks to the vigilance of this network. Secondly, after the *coup* failure, the plotters had no means of direct communication with those among this group who had remained at large. It is therefore unsound to presume that an organic link between the two events, that is, the TPAJAX *coup* and the fall of Mosaddeq on 19 August, had existed on account of military participation in both. In the next chapter we will probe the role claimed by foreign agents in the fall of Mosaddeq on 19 August 1953.

6
The Anatomy of 19 August

From the preceding evidence and analyses it is clear that when the crunch came on 19 August, neither TPAJAX operatives nor General Zahedi had been in a position to meaningfully harness the military resources left in the capital to launch a military *coup*. We also emphasized that General Zahedi planned to stage an armed revolt from a base in a strategic place outside Tehran. Kermanshah, a provincial capital close to Iraqi border, had been selected for this purpose.[1]

Going by the claim made in *Overthrow*, a political programme had also been envisaged by Kim Roosevelt. The relevant part of the conclusions of *'the council of war'*, as Roosevelt's Monday evening meeting on *17 August* is referred to in *Overthrow*, is quoted below in view of its central relevance to the subject matter of this study. Note that this meeting was reportedly held at the US Embassy compound without the presence or knowledge of Ambassador Henderson, who had just returned to Tehran after a long absence.[2]

> The council of war went on for about four hours, and in the end it was decided that some action would be taken on Wednesday the 19th. *As preparation for this effort*, several specific activities were to be undertaken. In the field of political action, it was planned to send the Tehran cleric [Ayatollah Behbehani] to Qum to try to persuade the supreme cleric, Ayatollah Borujerdi [*sic*], to issue a fatwa [religious decree] calling for *a holy war against Communism* and also to build up a great demonstration on Wednesday on the theme that it was time for loyal army officers and soldiers and the people to rally to the support of religion and the throne.
>
> In the field of military action, support from outside of Tehran seemed essential. Colonel Farzanegan was sent off in a car driven by a

station agent (US national Gerald Towne) to [Kermanshah, a distance of 400 miles,] to persuade Colonel Timur Bakhtiar, commanding officer of the Kermanshah garrison, to declare for the Shah. Zahedi, with Carroll, was sent to Brigadier General Zargham [sic][3] at Isfahan with a similar request. Through station facilities these messengers were provided with identification papers and travel papers which stood up under inspection. All those leaving the compound were also given station-prepared curfew passes.[4] [All emphasis added.]

The somewhat careless formulation of this passeage lends itself to different readings: According to one, all activities envisaged were *preparations* for the for the planned action on Wednesday! This is the explanation that Roosevelt himself provided in Chapter 12 of *Countercoup*. If this interpretation is accepted, then a 24-hour time allotment for preparations – which included a *fatwa* for holy war not to mention the rallying of some garrison commanders in Esfahan and Kermanshah – is bizarrely short. If, however, the alleged plan for the Wednesday was meant only as the first salvo in a process of destabilization and undermining, it is still hard to figure out why the planners accorded themselves only 24 hours to prepare such a complex plan; they could have opted more reasonably for Friday 21 August, benefiting from mosque congregations.[5] At any event, under the second hypothesis, the alleged plan for Wednesday would not amount to a deliberate and premeditated scheme to inflict a *coup de grâce* on Mosaddeq. Finally, it is not excluded that – if at all true – planning in essence may have had longer-term connotations, foreshadowing contingencies against a *Tudeh* take-over, given the wording for the requested *fatwa* and military aspects of the deliberations.

Whatever the intent of the planners, the events of Wednesday made it possible for Kim Roosevelt to link them with an alleged decision in that 'council of war', of which the Rashidian brothers were said to be among the participants. Roosevelt later wrote: 'We advised the brothers that Wednesday 19 must be the day.' *Overthrow* also confirms that on that evening the two principal agents, Keyvani and Jalali, 'were reached and given instructions'.[6] In other words, what Roosevelt claimed, in his London/Washington debriefing and later in his memoirs, was that once the target day, Wednesday 19 August, was decided on, instructions were issued to the CIA and MI6 agents and all fell into place as of then; these agents were able to deliver against all odds where TPAJAX had failed. A full subsection is devoted to these Iranian agents and their activities later in this chapter.

For reasons explained below, the claim by Roosevelt appears disingenuous and references to Wednesday a possible afterthought. Clearly no one in London or Washington tried to dig into ambiguities and inconsistencies in Roosevelt's account as success was too glowing, too precious to be spoiled. Eisenhower's sardonic remark in his diary when he finally heard Roosevelt's account first hand, implying he was a fabulist (see the reference to Roosevelt's debriefings in the Introduction of this book), is in itself telling. In London the MI6 boss, Major-General Sir Alexander Sinclair, gleefully embraced Roosevelt's debriefing, notwithstanding his grudge over Roosevelt's incommunicativeness during the interval between the two events. Was Sinclair genuinely convinced of the bona fides of Roosevelt's account or was he tight-lipped because of 'the effect this success had already and would continue to have upon SIS reputation with superiors'.[7] Tom Braden, a director in the CIA's clandestine operations, later ironized, '[That] success gave the CIA its first pair of pants.'[8]

Here are the reasons why we believe the D-Day claim by Roosevelt is questionable:

A. The claim is inconsistent with, and does not fit the pattern of a military insurrection out of a provincial capital that the Zahedi camp had planned and which by definition was a *mid-term* strategy. It would be even less credible to assume, as Roosevelt claims in *Countercoup*, that the dispatch of emissaries to Esfahan and Kermanshah following the 'council of war' was intended to persuade commanders to march their troops to Tehran on the designated D-Day, namely Wednesday 19 August, a logistical impossibility.[9]

B. Roosevelt's dispatches to Washington and Nicosia during this period were not consistent with the behaviour of an operative who seriously contemplated a strike. Just before holding the alleged 'council of war' on the evening of 17 August, Roosevelt had sent an assessment to Washington in which he opined that, 'while Mosaddegh's [sic] position will be strengthened in the coming weeks, opposition to him must continue.'[10] In another cable to Washington on the same date, Roosevelt appears to admit the impasse, at least implicitly; he requested an exfiltration plan for 15 unnamed individuals. Still in the same frame of mind, he asked CIA headquarters the following day, 'whether the station should continue with TPAJAX or withdraw'.[11]

C. Roosevelt did not ask for even a short extension of his mission to assess results of the 'planned action' for Wednesday 19 August.

He had, however, been given an express opportunity to do so. In effect, on 18 August, in a secret cable to Tehran, CIA headquarters proposed to call-off the mission 'in the absence of strong recommendation to the contrary from Roosevelt and Henderson'.[12] The fast-track *'operational immediate'* line to Washington and the time difference between the two capitals could have allowed time for Roosevelt at that moment – or before – to hint to Washington that something was in the offing requiring a short extension of his mission.

D. As will be seen in more detail in 'Surprise in Washington' and 'Ambassador Henderson's Last Meeting with Mosaddeq' below, Ambassador Henderson, who had returned to Tehran on 17 August, is categorical in denying any prior knowledge of events that were to unfold on 19 August. Henderson, however, was intimately involved in the TPAJAX scheming from the start and nothing was being done without his clearance, as Washington's cable of 18 August just referred to also illustrates. His new instructions upon his return to Tehran no doubt reflected the new thinking in Washington that Under-Secretary Bedell Smith had conveyed to Eisenhower on 16 August.

E. There are glaring inconsistencies between Roosevelt's account in his book *Countercoup* and his Washington debriefing upon return, reflected in Wilber's history, *Overthrow*. For example, there is no mention by Roosevelt of the 'council of war' that Wilber reported in detail in *Overthrow* and which was said to have taken place in the Embassy compound on the evening of Monday 17 August. In his book Roosevelt says that at that point in time, they were idle and bored with a colleague drinking vodka and irritated by the incessant chatter of Nossey and Cafron (codenames for the Rashidian brothers) who had taken refuge in the compound.[13] Farzanegan and Ardeshir Zahedi (whom Roosevelt refers to by their codenames, respectively Mohsen and Mostafa) were sent to Kermanshah and Esfahan on Sunday 16 August according to *Countercoup*; in *Overthrow* it is stated that the decision to contact local commanders in those provincial capitals was taken in the 'council of war' as part of the military plan. Roosevelt claimed he communicated with General Zahedi in broken German, a language that Zahedi did not have *at all* according to his son Ardeshir.[14] Finally, Kim Roosevelt paints a vivid description of his decisive encounter with Zahedi in his 'basement' hideout before they moved out to the street to claim victory. Zahedi is described as 'pulling on his uniform' of a general over his 'heavy woollens' and buttoning up his tunic.¹⁵ Anyone having experienced the August heat of Tehran would be stunned, especially as the existing photos of the general, the way he emerged from his hideout, show him in civilian khaki shirt and rolled up sleeves with no military insignia.

F. It is further noteworthy that in a recorded film interview with *World in Action* in 1973, in contrast to his bravado in *Countercoup* written a few years later, Roosevelt is more circumspect, almost pedestrian, in describing the CIA role in the denouement of the 19 August, although it is also fair to assume that at that juncture he had no interest in aggrandizing that role.¹⁶ There he attributes the success of the operation to a 'hardcore Iranian element which was present on the scene'. He goes on: 'all they needed was some support and professional guidance.' According to *Overthrow*, the budget allocation for the TPAJAX *coup* plan was $285,000 (US share $147,000, UK share $137,000). In the said interview, Roosevelt puts the total disbursements by the CIA station in Tehran 'during the course of operation' (i.e., 1 July to 19 August) at $10,000 only, while specifying that the number of CIA staff in Tehran was between six to eight agents.

G. Finally, unless one stretches the notion of job-related character distortions – or *déformation professionnelle* – to the extreme, it is hard to explain why Kermit Roosevelt left Iran surreptitiously – as if having himself exfiltrated – in the US naval attaché's small plane to Bahrain on 24 August, from where he was transported by Military Air Transportation Service to London. Considering his claim that he had lodged the now all-powerful prime minister of Iran, General Zahedi for three days in the basement of a CIA house, and considering his claim that he had planned and executed a *coup* that reversed the destiny of Iran and placed the now victorious Shah back on his throne, it's hard to divine why he should take such an inordinate risk of a long flight in a flimsy plane, instead of being seen off as a VIP at Mehrabad Airport on a regular flight, even if that were to be done discreetly. Yet this is the circumstance of his exit from Tehran as recorded in Chapter IX of the CIA internal history, *Overthrow*, and as also confirmed in *Countercoup*. Roosevelt had arrived in Tehran under a false identity from the Iraqi border post on 19 July under vastly different circumstances. He could now have used that false passport or any other travel document in full knowledge that the new regime was far too grateful to do any measure of hairsplitting over immigration regulations.

In contrast to Roosevelt and his cohorts, the attitude in the Zahedi camp has been far less assuming. In his 1953 article and in subsequent writings, Ardeshir Zahedi affirms that the news of pro-Shah street protests in the evening of 18 August stunned his father and made him decide instantly to change his plans. He admits, 'Things happened that none of us had predicted.'[17]

CIA station activism in Tehran, 16–19 August

If the above probe points to ambiguities and inconsistencies in the attitude and behaviour of the American master-spy, it does not follow that the CIA station under his stewardship was either inept or idle. It is conceivable that following the failure of the TPAJAX *coup* plan on 16 August, Kermit Roosevelt may have been reluctant to return to his job in Washington empty-handed. Image and career ambitions have always been important incentives, not least for those first generation 'gentlemen spies' in the CIA (Figure 26).

For this Harvard educated grandson of President Theodor Roosevelt, *amour propre* must have been a factor conditioning his behaviour in those trying days. His first instinct must have been to assess if anything could be salvaged from the TPAJAX wreckage. He must also have been genuinely concerned about the safety of the Iranians involved in the coup especially those whose identities were known to the authorities. While thus preparing to wind down and leave, Roosevelt sought to exfiltrate those whose lives may have been deemed in danger. From his contact or encounter with the Zahedis on the morning of 16 August, Roosevelt was led to conclude that, '*all was not lost*'.[18] He may have henceforth decided to give the Iranian players all the 'support, professional help and guidance' that he later spoke about in his *World in Action* interview in 1973. A flurry of activities by the CIA station in Tehran therefore followed as early as 16 August and climaxed on Wednesday 19 August. These were in essence assessment and backstopping as well as propaganda activities.[19] As will be recalled from the previous chapter, they included help in the reproduction and dissemination of the Shah's *farmān*, helping organize a hasty press conference with

Figure 26 Kim Roosevelt in his guise of the gentleman-spy in the late 1940s

foreign news agencies and providing hideouts for some *coup* figures, if the accounts given in *Overthrow* are to be taken at face value.[20] The station also advised Washington on 16 August on the press line the Shah should take while in exile, but by the time Dulles sent the Shah a message through the US Embassy in Rome the Shah had, on his own initiative, gone public.[21] These activities – plus alleged grey and black propaganda – have been widely reported and invariably credited as masterful strokes which underpinned an insidious and well-planned military *coup* against Mosaddeq. Where research and analyses conducted in subsequent years stumbles is the link between these activities and the actual happenings and their outcome. The CIA internal history *Overthrow* openly admits that, 'the extent to which the resulting activity [i.e., the fall of Mosaddeq on 19 August] stemmed from specific efforts of all our agents will never be known.'[22] Still it is worth delving into this topic in order to gauge their impact.

Among such activities figure the often-cited grey and black propaganda that supposedly outraged the clerics. This category of activities had already featured in the TP-BEDAMN programme, way before the CIA joined hands with Britain's MI6 to overthrow Mosaddeq; they were intensified under TPAJAX. If during the earlier phase the aim was to enhance the 'commie scare' among the general public through anti-Soviet propaganda, in the later phase the goal shifted to alienating clerics from Mosaddeq by projecting him as too soft on *Tudeh*. The well-known *Tudeh* animosity towards clerics was thenceforth unremittingly hammered on. Fake *Tudeh* hate-mail and telephone campaigns targeting clerics were being resorted to.[23] This may have included a mock bomb explosion near Kashani's residence in the *Pamenar* neighbourhood during the latter's campaigning against the referendum in late-July, early August and still a stink bomb in a mosque, although no mention of these incidents is made in the CIA history, *Overthrow*. The role said to have been played by Iranian agents of the CIA station in implementing such measures will be examined in the next section. Suffice it to reiterate here that the animosity between the Shiite hierarchy and the Mosaddeq government had been cemented well before the grey and black propaganda under TPAJAX was launched in July. This propaganda line imitated a reality that was already a part of the political landscape of that period as a reported pre-TPAJAX graffiti on the wall of the grand Marja Boroujerdi in Qom bears witness.[24] The TPAJAX propaganda may have enhanced visual effect and outreach, but it did not transform a mindset already permeated by fear of republicanism and its attendant drift towards atheism. The departure of the Shah on 16 August brought this angst to a paroxysm. Whether such activities continued after the Shah's flight is a legitimate subject of inquiry to which we shall shortly turn.

Another line of action by the CIA station was the dissemination of the news of Mosaddeq's dismissal and appointment of General Zahedi. This help could best be characterized as logistical in nature. *Overthrow* admits that idea came from the Zahedi camp. The latter took the initiative to prepare photostats of the Shah's *farmān* on 16 August and disseminate them.[25] The station facilities may, however, have been used for wider reproduction and dissemination among the popular press. As referred to earlier, a picture of the Shah's *farmān* initially appeared on 18 August in *Shāhed*, a daily published by Baqa'ei; it was reproduced on 19 August in a string of low-circulation, often CIA/MI6 suborned, dailies in Tehran, whose combined readership – Iranians recalling those days would confirm – hardly exceeded a thousand or two.[26] The scoop they carried could have increased their sale to a limited extent, yet insufficient for a palpable impact on public opinion. Yet a passage in *Overthrow* assigns a decisive role to this move. There we read: 'Although each of these newspapers had a normal circulation of restricted size, the news they carried was undoubtedly flashed through the city by word of mouth, for before 0900 hours pro-Shah groups were assembling in the bazaar area.'[27] To be noted that in this – or in any other passage for that matter – *Overthrow* does not attribute the gathering of pro-shah groups to crowd manipulations of the type which was later alleged by conspiracy theorists.

The role of Iranian agents

In its narrative the CIA internal history, *Overthrow*, lauds the Iranian agents working under the TPAJAX. Their efficiency and ability to act on their own, making the exact right moves are highlighted.[28] This assessment may well be true; it is not excluded that these agents may have displayed verve and creativity on Wednesday by seeking to direct street mobs or acting as *agents provocateur*. Yet like other facets of the CIA role in the actual downfall of Mosaddeq a closer scrutiny of these activities is called for.

It will be recalled from a previous chapter ('The British Two-Prong Strategy' in Chapter 3) that the British covert network was handed over to the Rashidian brothers after Mosaddeq broke off diplomatic ties with Britain in October 1952. When by May 1953 the Anglo-American *coup* plan was being elaborated, the brothers were placed under the supervision of the CIA station in Tehran. They were known by both the American and British services for unethical business practices. The levelheaded CIA station chief in Tehran, Roger Goiran, and his successor

Figure 27 Asadolloh Rashidian, successful businessman, in the early 1960s

Josef Goodwin both believed their potentials had been exaggerated by their British handlers; a point seemingly conceded by [their handler] Robin Zaehener himself in his meeting with Eden to which we referred in an earlier chapter ('The Link-Up' in Chapter 5). They were, however, well-connected in Tehran's society and as such deemed useful assets. The brothers were also inveterate anti-Mosaddeq activists in their own right.

The two principal CIA agents recruited in Tehran, on the other hand, were ordinary journalists with no particular social standing. Farouq Kayvani and Ali Jalali were staunch anti-communist activists who had, a couple of years earlier, volunteered their services to Goiran. At the time, the CIA station chief had noted that the two had a knack for covert tradecraft and ran some network of their own. This may have come from a background either in the British or Nazi intelligence.[29] They were sent to Washington for evaluation and training by the CIA. Wilber himself reportedly came to Tehran on a six-month assignment in January 1952 to work with Jalali and Kayvani and learn more about their network.[30] When their anti-communist credentials were fully established, they were assigned to the TP-BEDAMN project for which the station had an allotment of half a million dollars a year. In April 1953 when the anti-Mosaddeq campaign was added to the CIA station responsibilities, this budget was raised to one million, a disproportionately high chunk from the then CIA's 82 million dollar budget.[31]

Kayvani and Jalali were by all accounts smart operatives who had impressed their superiors, both in Tehran and Washington. An angle barely explored is what their touted network consisted of. Their *modus operandi* had little in common with that of the Rashidian brothers, who had entrée in Tehran's influential milieus and were capable of sleek political manipulations. Kayvani and Jalali, while journalists by profession, were operating from a front commercial firm they had created in downtown Tehran.[32] From descriptions given of their activities, it could be concluded that the two had links within *Sumkā* – a Fascist pack of fanatical anti-*Tudeh* activists wearing black shirts and Nazi-like insignia – as well as with a quaint bunch of ultra-nationalists known as Pan-Iranists. This group, also with a strong anti-communist bent, fantasized about the return to Iran of the 17 Caucasian cities that the country had lost to Russia in the early nineteenth century; they also campaigned for the restoration of Bahrain to the Iranian sovereignty, which had not been exercised since the late eighteenth century. Membership in either group was scant, making it hard to cover their operational expenses through cardholder subscriptions. In his memoirs the *Tudeh* leader Kianouri has rounded the size of the *Sumkā* membership at about one hundred, a reasonable guestimate.[33] Membership in the *Pan-Iranist* Party was only a trifle higher, especially after the pro-Mosaddeq elements in their midst formed a splinter group under Daryoush Forouhar.[34] All indications suggest that the two main CIA agents paid stipends from the TP-BEDAMN funds to the *Sumkā* boss Davoud Monshi'zadeh and in all likelihood to the *Pan-Iranist* leader Mohsen Pezeshkpour.[35] The Jalali-Kayvani tandem may have also had contacts with the Baqa'ei thugs or the likes of Shaban Jafari (alias *bimokh* or brainless) who, incidentally, was serving a prison term when Mosaddeq was overthrown on 19 August and could not have played a role in that day's events as the current literature has broadly assumed.[36] These groups armed by clubs, knifes, and even machetes rammed into well-groomed *Tudeh* formations at every turn when the latter organized a public demonstration.

Figure 28 A scene from a well-groomed *Tudeh* Party procession in Tehran, c. 1951. Photo *Life* magazine. ©Time-Life-Getty, 2009

The faces of these thugs were familiar to the authorities as well as to *Tudeh* itself, something that must have rendered the faking of the *Tudeh* crowds all the more complicated. Another facet of the Jalali-Kayvani work consisted of liaison with suborned the anti-*Tude*, later anti-Mosaddeq press, implanting propaganda material and cartoons, some of which was reportedly produced in Washington. Hate mail and a telephone campaign against clerics must have been carried out by these two, helped by a coterie of sub-agents to smear *Tudeh*. The reality of the hate-mail campaign against clerics in this period has been confirmed independently by eye-witness Iranian sources.[37] In short, as an important feature of the original *coup* plan, psychological warfare was carried out with limited effectiveness till mid-August.

What happened next after the TPAJAX *coup* failed should be treated with greater circumspection. In the maze of expedient claims, denials, enflamed egos and tarnished memories it is hard to tell facts from factoids, some of which have unfortunately crept into serious scholarly works in the United States. Both the veracity and the impact of these activities on the final outcome must therefore be probed. In the CIA internal history Wilber wrote: '*The extent to which the resulting activity* [i.e. fall of Mosaddeq on 19 August] *stemmed from specific efforts of all our agents will never be known.*'[38]

What did those specific efforts consist of? Were they part of a structured plan with a defined goal or haphazard moves and improvisations? For starters, Roosevelt was later reported to have threatened Nerren and Cilley – pseudonyms for Kivani and Jalali – at gun-point when on 16 August they wanted to quit the operations following the failure of the TPAJAX *coup*.[39] *Overthrow* obliquely refers to the incident (p. 51), but elsewhere it makes the point that the station had no contact with the two agents in the first two days following the failed *coup*. This contact would be re-established only on *Monday* evening (17August). According to another claim – not corroborated by Wilber's internal CIA history *Overthrow* – these same agents on *Sunday* 16 August received a sum of $50,000 from a CIA officer to mobilize fake *Tudeh* crowds to create negative sentiments towards Mosaddeq and precipitate an uprising. The fake crowd, according to this narrative, joined by unsuspecting real *Tudeh* and nationalist militants attacked the Reza Shah mausoleum and tore down statues of the Shah and his father.[40] Later Kayvani and Jalali are thought to have led gangs of fake *Tudeh* to ransack some shops in Lāleh'zār Avenue, faked threats by telephone to some clerics in the name of *Tudeh*, and incited the crowds to ransack or set fire to the *Tudeh* newspaper offices on 19 August.[41]

Figure 29 *Tudeh* boss Noreddin Kianouri in a pose in the early 1980s

A cross-check of these assertions with a statement by the *Tudeh* leader, Noreddin Kianouri, is edifying.[42] For whatever it is worth, Kianouri flatly denies the existence of fake *Tudeh* crowds or infiltration by foreign agents in their midst. Reacting to an article by Professor Mark Gasiorowski in the *International Journal of the Middle East Studies* in 1987, Kianouri addressed the key questions relating to grey and black propaganda and the role the CIA agents would have played during the crucial days from 16 to 19 August 1953. To the question whether the *Tudeh* executive committee had ordered the deployment of *Tudeh* cadres into streets during these days, Kianouri responded: 'After the failure of the 25 August [TPAJAX] *coup* and the Shah's flight the party leadership adopted the slogan of *"Democratic Republic"* and instructed the party members to celebrate this victory [the Shah's departure] *in a militant fashion* through widespread street demonstrations' [emphasis added].

Kianouri then turns to the issue of 'fake *Tudeh*' saying: 'Not only did we not sense the slightest trace of fake Tudeh in our demonstrations or have any report to that effect but, on the contrary, we learned of the presence of anti-Tudeh groups like Zahmatkeshān [the Baqa'ei Party], the Pan-Iranists and Sumkā which under the protection and with the help of the security forces physically assaulted the Tudeh cadres as reported by Kayhan.'[43] Clearly, if the dismantling of the Pahlavi statues in the main squares of Tehran and in the provinces, the desecration of the Reza Shah mausoleum (see Chapter 5 under 'The Backlash') or the destruction of the Pan-Iranist main office and other acts of vandalism attributed to the CIA Iranian agents had not been sanctioned by the leadership, a modicum of suspicion would have been aroused, given the iron-clad discipline for which the *Tudeh* cadres and its leadership were known.[44] What transpires from the Kianouri statement is that the CIA-subsidized groups did not fake the *Tudeh* crowds; they assaulted them as they had done on so many other occasions in previous several years. Note that at the time he made this statement in the early 1990s, Kianouri had every reason to try to deflate guilt for the party's failures, by playing up the presumed CIA manipulations, thus shielding himself against criticism by the more moderate faction of the party leadershipin later years.[45]

Another unsubstantiated claim, which has crept into an otherwise well-respected scholarly work, concerns the bribing of clerics by the Rashidian brothers. Based on interviews with former TPAJAX agents, Professor Gasiorowski chronicles the following from the 19 August morning activities of the CIA station:

> The Rashidians suggested that they seek help from Ayatollah Kashani and said he could be contacted through their ally Ahmad Aramesh. In the early morning of August 19, two CIA officers therefore went to Aramesh's home and gave him $10,000 to give to Kashani to organize demonstrations. It is not clear whether Kashani received this money and, if so, whether he used it for this purpose.[46]

Apart from the fact that the alleged occurrence is *not* recorded in the CIA internal history and is questionable on that ground alone, a critical fallacy in its main thrust is evident: It is easy to note that by the time these alleged activities were being contemplated, the fate of the Mosaddeq government was all but sealed. The train had left the station. To try to reach Ayatollah Kashani on the morning of 19 August through an intermediary and bribe him to amass crowds is above all an indication – assuming that the anecdote could have had any basis – that the CIA station was running behind the events, not creating them. The payment of $10,000 to Kashani is, furthermore, incompatible with Roosevelt's recoded interview in *World in Action*, where, for whatever it is worth, he estimates the cost of the entire TPAJAX (mid-July to 19 August) to be $10,000 (see also 'The CIA Money' below).

A careful examination of the CIA's own narrative reveals that the purported activities of the Iranian agents were not part of a structured and coherent plan foreseen in advance and could at best be characterized as improvisations. From *Overthrow* (p. 66) we learn that the CIA Iranian agents had *not* expected the pro-Shah crowds in the streets of Tehran on Wednesday 19 August; the agents had planned a trip outside Tehran only to change this plan '*as soon as they noticed that the pro-Shah groups were gathering.*'[47] The planned trip to Qazvin was in connection with rumours of an upcoming *fatwa* from the grand Shiite magnate, Boroujerdi, about which the agents allegedly intended to print broadsheets. Equally elucidating is the passage on page 63 of the same CIA narrative. Describing the CIA's reaction to the initial pro-Shah demonstration on the evening of 18 August, we read: 'Just what was the major motivating force [behind these demonstrations] is impossible to say, but it is possible to isolate the factors behind the disturbances.' Curiously, Wilber's ensuing analysis of the crowd's motivation *does not in any* way link these demonstrations to CIA manipulations or other subterfuges. Clearly, the CIA station appeared puzzled by occurrences which were not of its making.

Surprise in Washington

The foregoing must logically lead to the conclusion that American officialdom in Washington at all levels was equally surprised by the end-result. Sceptics may, however, benefit from some irrefutable evidence that proves this point. Here are the main points to retain:

The first to point to highlight is that following the failure of TPAJAX on 16 August, CIA headquarters in Washington called off the mission. In a telling message on 18 August copied to some other CIA stations, the CIA acknowledged that, 'the operation has been tried and failed'.[48] This was in line with positions adopted by the State Department as well as the Foreign Office. It will be recalled that Under-Secretary Bedell Smith recommended to President Eisenhower on the 16 August to 'snuggle up' to Mosaddeq even at the risk of annoying Britain. Ambassador Henderson hurriedly returned to Tehran on 17 August, possibly with new instructions.[49]

The CIA headquarters, according to Wilber's narrative in *Overview*, had its first word of what that day (19 August) was to bring just before 9 a.m. 'when someone burst in from the hall pouring out what at first seemed to be a bad joke in view of the depression that still hung on from the day'.[50]

Other US archive documents confirm that neither CIA headquarters, nor the State Department or the White House, not even the American Ambassador in Tehran were aware of events that were to unfold on 19 August or had knowledge of any prior planning to foment trouble on that day. As will be seen below, the downfall of Mosaddeq came as a complete surprise to them all.

Confidential reporting by the US Embassy to the State Department suggests that the US Ambassador and embassy officials in Tehran while monitoring events of 19 August were at a loss to apprehend '*the cause and motives*' of pro-Shah demonstrations.[51] In a post-facto confidential round-up cabled to the State Department on 20 August, for example, Ambassador Henderson admits *among other things* that the (19 August) uprising succeeded *'with high degree of spontaneity'*. Significantly, among the five factors that the embassy moots as motives for the uprising, none is related to foreign manipulation.[52]

Equally revealing is Henderson's affirmations in an Oral History interview conducted by the Truman Library in 1972. He says:

> When I returned to Tehran [17 August 1953], I was under the impression that Mossadegh [sic], at least for a time, had won his long conflict with the Shah. I was surprised by the events that took place the next day, and I think that if they are ever published, my telegrams to the Department will support what I am saying.[53]

The telegrams to which Henderson refers here were later declassified and some are quoted in this study; they indeed vindicate what Henderson said in the above interview.

The most revealing document on this score, however, is a brief 'secret' memorandum addressed by the Acting Director of the CIA, General Charles Cabell to President Eisenhower, clearly filed late on 19 August (although the document is undated). There we read: 'An unexpectedly strong upsurge of popular and military reaction to Prime Minister Mossadeq's [sic] Government has resulted, according to late dispatches from Tehran, in the virtual occupation of that city by forces proclaiming their loyalty to the Shah and his appointed prime-minister Zahedi.'[54] He goes on, *'our sources'* have confirmed press and radio reports that *'pro-royalist forces* [are] *in control of city of Teheran...'*. General Cabell's memorandum to Eisenhower, which is based on press dispatches as well as the CIA's own 'sources' is remarkable for what it does *not* say. It should be recalled that since at least April 1953, the US government had been engaged in delicate covert operations designed to oust prime minister Mosaddeq. Now on the day of victory, the acting director of the agency in charge of this operation reports the event to the president of the United States, but is silent about the role his agents would have played in that outcome. It would not have been inappropriate for Roosevelt, who later wrote *Countercoup*, and by extension, for the CIA acting director Cabell, to claim at least some credit for this victory. There is no hint of such a claim in General Cabell's memo to Eisenhower.[55]

In later debriefings in London and Washington, Kim Roosevelt claimed that he deliberately withheld his plans and activities from them because, he said, 'had he told everyone what they were up to he would have been called crazy and asked to stop and return'.[56] It is true that following the failure of TPAJAX on 16 August the mood among the higher officials in both London and Washington was such that they may not have brooked further tergiversation on the part of Roosevelt. What Roosevelt has overlooked, however, is the fact that not only had he made no serious attempt to persuade the two capitals to extend his mission but, as was shown earlier in this chapter, he himself enquired whether the *'the station should continue with TPAJAX or withdraw.'* He also requested exfiltration plans for up to 15 individuals.[57]

Many years later Richard Helms, who directed the CIA during the Johnson and Nixon administrations, reportedly recalled in an interview that the CIA decided in the early1960s not to deny having played a major role in Mosaddeq's downfall because after the Bay of Pigs, the CIA needed to show victories to justify its soaring budget.[58]

Ambassador Henderson's last meeting with Mosaddeq

In most accounts of the collapse of Mosaddeq's government, a meeting that Henderson held with the prime minister late on 18 August is cited as CIA scheming designed to intimidate Mosaddeq and force him to keep the *Tudeh* Party off the streets in preparation for the presumed CIA plan for the following day. Kim Roosevelt in *Countercoup* does not go as far as saying that the meeting was a part of the *coup* plan, but claims that he had astutely coached and steered the ambassador in a direction that would serve that purpose. This was to be achieved by strongly warning Mosaddeq about the US reaction to *Tudeh* harassment of American citizens. Further, Henderson was to tell Mosaddeq point-blank that the United States supported the Shah and his departure was a tactical move in the Moslem tradition of *hejrah* akin to prophet-Mohammad's retreat to Medina.[59] This claim – which has largely been echoed in the literature – is not backed by the State Department's record of the meeting and Henderson's own recollections.[60] Nor is there *any* reference in the CIA's own internal report *Overthrow* to this meeting, much less to the alleged coaching by Roosevelt. It would have been appropriate for the CIA internal history to make a mention of Henderson's visit to Mosaddeq had the visit been ingeniously used by Roosevelt to further the objectives of the plan.[61]

Reminiscing some 20 years later for the historical records of the Truman Library, Henderson (Figure 30) says, 'When I talked with Mosaddeq on the evening of August 18, I had no idea that an attempt would be made to overthrow him by force.'[62]

Figure 30 Loy Henderson US Ambassador in Tehran 1951–55. Photo, US State Department, courtesy of the Truman Library®

To elucidate the point it is important to reiterate that Henderson had deliberately absented himself from his post in Tehran since early June as part of the TPAJAX war of nerves. Just before the *coup* attempt on 15 August, he left the Austrian Alps where he was vacationing, to move to Beirut in order to remain in contact with events. When the news of the failure of the *coup* arrived, Henderson was urged by the US Chargé in Tehran, Matisson – and no doubt by Washington – to return to Tehran immediately. Regular flights to Tehran being scarce in those days, Henderson used a US military plane to return, something that gives a measure of the urgency which the Department accorded to his return. It should also be recalled that the failure of the *coup* brought an about-turn in Washington, reflected in Undersecretary Bedell Smith's prop to '*snuggle up*' to Mosaddeq '*if we are going to save anything there*'. The Department's attitude was made known in the field by the end of the working day on 16 August as *Overthrow* cheerlessly confirms.[63] The United States no doubt continued to be alarmed by a creeping Soviet intrusion in Iran through its proxy, the *Tudeh* Party. To forestall it, they now had to work through Mosaddeq, at least in the immediate future. This must have been the brief Henderson was given when he was rushed back to Tehran on 17 August.

It will also be recalled from an earlier chapter that Mosaddeq, while suspecting American complicity in the plot, was still anxious to keep in their good graces. Henderson was met at the airport by Mosaddeq's son as well as by a cabinet minister, a treatment way above normal diplomatic practice. In the meantime, *Tudeh* had stepped up the harassment of American personnel in Tehran and provinces. This was being done by threatening phone calls, vandalizing of property as well as physical assaults on individuals. On 16 August, prior to Henderson's return to Tehran, Mosaddeq's office advised the embassy to close down all its offices, keen as the government was to avoid untoward incidents.[64] Just before Henderson's arrival the embassy had urged all Americans in Iran to remain in their residences.[65]

It was against such a backdrop that Henderson met Mosaddeq on 18 August. The first point to underline is that this meeting started at

6 p.m. and lasted an hour and a half. By 10 p.m., Henderson had transmitted his report to the State Department.⁶⁶ In his report there is no modicum of a hint that the meeting was a scripted step in preparations for the following day's uprising. While in *Countercoup*, Kim Roosevelt speaks about *'the quasi-apologetic tone of a frightened Mosaddeq'*.⁶⁷ This is contradicted by Henderson's report to Washington, which depicts the prime minister as defiant and sardonic. Henderson in effect complained to Mosaddeq about the widespread insecurity felt by American personnel and citizens given the background just referred to. Mosaddeq had retorted that such violent behaviour was inevitable as the Iranian people had observed that the US government acted against them. Mosaddeq clearly wished to seize the occasion to vent a pent-up resentment over the US attitude over the previous several months and their suspected involvement in the *coup*.⁶⁸ For his part Henderson used the issue of insecurity and harassment, in order to gauge Mosaddeq's attitude on the continued functioning of American missions in Iran, and hinted at the possibility that the United States might withdraw Americans *'en masse'* if they were not wanted. It will be recalled from 'The Gathering Storm'in Chapter 5 that the *Tudeh* organ *Shojā'at* had among other things called, on that very day, for the expulsion of the US military as well as the Point Four missions from Iran. After some jibes and sarcasm, Mosaddeq had finally said he did not want the American missions in Iran to leave *and promised to look further into the subject of a better protection*. There is no reference in the report of the meeting to a telephone call by Mosaddeq to the police chief ordering the dispersal of the *Tudeh* demonstrators as was later claimed. It is fair to assume that Henderson would have flaunted such a clear gain, had a call gone out in his presence.⁶⁹

It could be safely assumed that some time that evening – in great likelihood as a result of the Henderson demarche – Mosaddeq reinforced his earlier orders for a crack-down on all demonstrations. Independent of Henderson's demarche, the prime minister was, by all accounts, alarmed by the extent of agitations and had already decreed a ban on all street rallies as of the morning of 18 August 18.⁷⁰ The *Tudeh* party secretary, Kianouri, confirms that martial law agents dispersed *Tudeh* gatherings *'as of the morning of 18 August'*. The police clampdown, he goes on, peaked late in the afternoon when some 600 party cadres were detained.⁷¹ The CIA internal account, *Overthrow*, also records a government bulletin broadcast in the *morning* of 18 August banning all street demonstrations.⁷² The relevant point here, therefore, is not whether such orders were issued or reinforced during or subsequent to Henderson's visit, but whether that demarche was part of a prepared plan to clear the streets of Tehran in anticipation of a pro-Shah uprising the following day. Our study does not subscribe to that latter hypothesis; yet it is also fair to observe that the crack-down order by Mosaddeq that night, which may have been influenced by Henderson demarche, allowed the security forces to vent their anger against *Tudeh* while making a clear show of support for the Shah; the ripple effects were non-negligible and no doubt encouraged pro-Shah forces at various levels. From this angle, the meeting may have had an unintended impact on the events of the following day, all the more so as the *Tudeh* activists stayed home on orders issued by their leadership.

Other than the issue of the security of US citizens, Henderson was keen to gauge Mosaddeq's attitude towards recent events, notably the Shah's dismissal decree and appointment of Zahedi. Mosaddeq was evasive in his response, denying he had received a dismissal order. He went on to say that even if he had received such an order, it would not have made a difference as the Shah's powers were ceremonial in nature. Mosaddeq was keen to air his complaints about the deliberate leak of Eisenhower's letter to him (see under 'The Summer of All Dangers' in Chapter 4) and the British bribing of the deputies that had prompted him to close down the *Majles*. When he asked Henderson's opinion about this decision, the ambassador cautiously responded that it would be best for Iran if state organs *foreseen in the constitution* could work with a minimum of harmony. Here was a hint of preference for preservation of the monarchy, the abolition of which was the hottest topic of the day, given the *Tudeh* campaign and Mosaddeq's own deliberations on the fate of the Shah on that very day, as we reported under 'The Gathering Storm' in Chapter 5.

Finally, Henderson tried to placate Mosaddeq by boasting that he had set rules to discourage potential political refugees seeking sanctuary in the US Embassy compound. To this Mosaddeq reacted caustically, saying he did not mind; in fact he urged the ambassador to allow political refugees to stay at the embassy compound and went as far as saying that he would be willing, despite his government's penury, to pick up the tab![73] This was a rejoinder to a niggardly remark by Henderson who raised the issue of the expense of keeping the refugees at the compound. Henderson clearly had not expected such spontaneity on Mosaddeq's part.

The CIA money

Some commentators have pointed out that CIA money was spent to recruit crowds, characterizing them as ruffian mercenaries. The CIA crowd-manipulation claim partly emanates from scattered remarks by some former covert agents interviewed by historians which we analysed earlier in this chapter. The claim was no doubt implied and may also be rooted in Richard and Gladys Harkness's article in the *Saturday Evening Post* of November 1954 entitled *'Mysterious Doings of the CIA'*, to which we also referred in the Introduction.

The most robust evidence refuting this claim emanates from the CIA's own internal history, which makes no such claim. This has not prevented two subsequent publications in the United States covering the CIA role in the overthrow of Mosaddeq from repeating the old claims. In a similar vein, some Iranian authors have maintained that clerics, notably Behbahani and Kashani, used CIA money to mobilize thugs in popular neighbourhoods on the day of Mosaddeq's fall. There is little doubt that some manipulation took place along familiar crowd-mobilization methods by clerics, a point that we shall take up next in Chapter 7 under the rubric: 'Where did the spark come from?' It may not be totally excluded – although there is strictly no evidence to support the contention – that prior to the TPAJAX *coup* and as part of its preparations, some CIA or MI6 money may have reached Kashani or Behbahani through channels created by the Rashidian brothers, who would not disclose the source to the recipients. Needless to say, anyone could make a payment to a top cleric in the Shiite system of religious taxes or alms for the poor (*Khoms, Zakāt, kheyrāt and Nazr*).[74] This study contests the prevailing assumption that CIA money could have been disbursed to recruit crowds after the failed 15 August *coup*. Here are the reasons why such an assumption is deemed farfetched:

- As just noted Wilber, who detailed all CIA station activities in Tehran before and after TPAJAX *coup*, makes *no* reference to any payment made by the CIA for crowd mobilization. This same source, however, makes mention of bribery attempts to win over the *Majles* deputies and efforts by the CIA to plant propaganda material and cartoons in the popular and subsidized press in Tehran *prior* to the failed *coup*.
- The same CIA account specifically mentions that attempts under TPAJAX to get the religious leaders to play a specific role, notably staging *bast* (taking sanctuary) in the *Majles*, were inconclusive. These activities had been envisaged to create a favourable climate for the *putsch*. Had Behbahani or Kashani been bribed for that purpose it would have been recorded in that secret internal document like other similar activities.

- Appendix E of *Overthrow* (dealing with the evaluation of military aspects of the plan) categorically states that no money for bribery was needed or used to recruit Iranian army officers.[75]
- For whatever it is worth, Kim Roosevelt has put the total CIA disbursement for the entire TPAJAX operations at about $10,000.[76] Though Roosevelt's pronouncement ought to be taken with caution, even a multiplication of this estimate hardly leaves room for financing a contrived uprising and other 'master strokes' that brought the government down.
- Strictly from an accounting point of view, it is questionable whether Roosevelt could have disbursed additional funds for undeclared, hence unauthorized, activities of which the outcome was far from certain. As noted earlier in this chapter, Kim Roosevelt later claimed that he had deliberately withheld from the CIA and SIS/MI6 headquarters all information regarding activities he initiated following the *coup* failure on 16 August for fear of being disavowed or reprimanded.
- It must be noted that ruffian types and mercenaries recruited by the likes of the Rashidian brothers rarely put their lives on the line. As stated before, the clashes around the Mosaddeq residence and elsewhere resulted in several dozens of dead and many more wounded among civilians.[77] Kennett Love of *The New York Times* put this figure at 300 dead in his dispatch of 19 August, which made a banner headline. Most casualties occurred in front of Mosaddeq's residence. While the assailants must have mostly originated from the urban underclass in southern neighbourhoods – given the fact that they proceeded to a strip-to-the-wire pillage of Mosaddeq's house – it is inconceivable that they risked their lives for the few bucks that conspiracy theorists claim was their prime motive. Mosque-driven crowds, on the other hand, have a different behavioural pattern. At its roots, back in the seventh century, war booty was the flipside of martyrdom.
- A final point merits reiteration. In their respective reporting, both Henderson and Wilber – as indeed Richard Cottam in his 1964 book[78] – described the crowd in positive terms, differentiating them from the '*hoodlum types*' presumably seen in previous day rallies. While the opposite view has gained currency, a careful examination of evidence reveals a motley crowd from different walks of life. Among them notorious underworld figures were later identified and named, but it is incorrect to dismiss the crowds as a whole as ruffian mercenaries.[79]

Figure 31 A scene from the 19 August pro-Shah demonstrations in Tehran. Photo from the personal collection of Ardeshir Zahedi; courtesy of IBEX publishers©

An orphan British secret document

Our analyses of foreign input in the fall of Doctor Mosaddeq would not be complete without a close scrutiny of a succinct report from an unknown British government entity to which we alluded in the preface of this book. Given its purview and content, the document could be regarded a microcosm, if not the precursor, of the CIA's *Overthrow* by Donald Wilber. Dated 2 September 1953, only two weeks after the fall of Mosaddeq, the eight-page, top-secret document must be regarded as the earliest assessment from an official source, though its exact origin and authoritativeness could not be certified by the State Department which later declassified it. The FRUS editors are unable to determine by whom, or through what channel, it had been transmitted to the State Department and profess to be equally in the dark about the source of the information it contains.[80] To our knowledge, this document has not been noted or referenced in any published study made on Mosaddeq's downfall. As the document does not seem to exist in Britain's Public Record Office, it could cautiously be assumed that it may not have originated with the Foreign Office whose files, unlike those of MI6, are declassified. According to the FRUS editors, however, the document resembles in format those emanating from the Foreign Office or the British Embassy in Washington. As the document refrains from directly implicating the British government and makes only oblique references to an American role, it may have been a chapter from a broader country-by-country review, possibly intended for high government officials and key embassies abroad. But these are all conjectures and somewhat secondary in importance. Before probing its substance, we highlight its salient points described in two phases.

The narrative of 'Phase 1', comprising 16 paragraphs, is mainly background information about the events leading up to the TPAJAX *coup* and its immediate aftermath. Two elements in this section of the document contain intelligence then unavailable to the general public. Paragraphs 6 and 8 stated that the trip by Princess Ashraf to Tehran on 27 July and General Schwartzkopf's visit and audience with the Shah shortly thereafter were both linked to a *coup* plan. Rumours to this effect were in fact circulating in Tehran at the time, but the British note also contains a piece of intelligence to which only insiders were privy. '*Certain personalities who are in very close contact with the Shah*', states paragraph 8, '*were reported to have stated on 3rd August that the Shah had declared that great changes would take place shortly.*' The date mentioned corresponded to the time when, following tense discussions with Roosevelt and Assadollah Rashidian, the Shah finally decided to issue the two royal decrees dismissing Mosaddeq and appointing Zahedi in his place.

The Phase 2 narrative, comprising an additional 16 paragraphs, covers the period from 17 August to Iran's post-Mosaddeq relations with the United States and the United Kingdom. Apart from a description of known events, the document makes the following key points:

- On 17 August General Zahedi had succeeded in winning over the commander of the motorized regiment as well as the chief of police. 'It was also established that a second attempt would shortly be made to overthrow Musaddiq's [sic] government.'
- The *Tudeh* leaders warned Mosaddeq that a second military *coup* against him was in preparations. They asked for 10,000 rifles and small arms, which Mosaddeq refused.
- The meeting between Henderson and Mosaddeq on 17 August ended abruptly. (No explanation is given and a few dots in the released document suggest that words from the text at this point may have been omitted as is usually the case in FRUS when an explicit reference to the TPAJAX *coup* is made.)
- Quoting 'well-placed sources', the secret document observes that it was soon after Henderson's meeting with Mosaddeq that the plans for the events of 19 August were put into operation. This is clearly a reference to the events on Tuesday evening, 18 August, when security forces clashed with *Tudeh* militants and pro-Shah demonstrations were reported.
- On this occasion only the chief of the police, commanders of regiments, and Ayatollah Behbahani, who was responsible for organizing demonstrations, knew of the plan and *Tudeh* had no chance of discovering the plot beforehand.
- Most of the crowd of 3000 armed with clubs and sticks, although possibly inspired by royalist sentiments, had obviously been hired for the purpose, among them well-known hooligans.

Analysis of the British secret document

A careful examination of this document reveals a mix of some good intelligence on peripheral issues, but errors and misinformation on crucial points. It will be recalled that following the rupture of diplomatic relations in October 1952, Britain had no diplomatic representation in Iran and when, after a short lull, planning for TPAJAX got underway the Rashidian brothers were placed under the authority of the CIA station in Tehran. Britain, however, had other sources of intelligence, including in high places. In addition to a number of influential Anglophile politicians and notables who volunteered their views and information to British officials, there were those who could be described as formal agents and/or informers. The two most prominent in the latter category were Soleiman Behboudi, the head of the Shah's household, as well as another individual seemingly in semi-ministerial position in the Mosaddeq cabinet, whom the MI6 station chief in Tehran, Christopher Woodhouse, referred to in his autobiography as 'Omar', and who seemingly reported some of the inner circle discussions in the cabinet or elsewhere to MI6.[81]

In retrospect, one may venture an educated guess about the sources of this document, hazardous as such guesswork is. The intelligence about Princess Ashraf and General Schwarzkopf as well as the Shah's indiscretion on August 3 are likely to have been reported by Soleiman Behboudi, the Rashidian brothers not fitting the description given of the source, namely personalities in very close contact with the Shah. In her memoirs, *Faces in a Mirror* (referred to in 'The taming of the Shah' in Chapter 4), Princess Ashraf identifies the intermediary for her first contact with the TPAJAX agents in Europe as 'my friend Mr B'; and although this also must remain a matter of conjecture, it is likely that Behboudi is the person she refers to, something that justifies the affirmative language in document about the link between Ashraf's trip to Tehran and *coup* plans.

As for the intelligence on events subsequent to the TPAJAX *coup* of 15 August, the subject requires more careful examination. The part in the document on intensive *Tudeh* lobbying with Mosaddeq and his entourage about the abolition of the monarchy on the days prior to Mosaddeq's fall – a reality little known at the time – is likely to have come from sources close to the cabinet. 'Omar' – if he is not a figment of Woodhouse's imagination – may be designated as a likely source. For the rest, information in the British secret document is either flatly wrong or distorted. To start with, the claim to the effect that on Monday 17 August General Zahedi won over the police chief and the commander of a motorized regiment seems apocryphal. Apart from the inordinate risk that contacting the police chief entailed for a political fugitive like Zahedi or his entourage, factual evidence refutes this claim. Mosaddeq's chief of police at that point was Brigadier Nasrollah Modabber. Though Mosaddeq did not fully trust the latter and ended up replacing him on 19 August, there is no doubt that on 17 August he was still in his job. This is known because in his memoirs Mosaddeq's interior minister, Sadiqi, mentions him by name as the outgoing police chief with whom he had a telephone conversation on the morning of Wednesday 19 August. Had Zahedi managed to win Modabber over, the latter would have received commendation and promotion after the fall of Mosaddeq, the way other participants and sympathizer's did. Instead, when he became prime minister Zahedi had him arrested together with other pro-Mosaddeq officers.[82] As for winning over the commander of a motorized regiment, there is no reference to any such officer either in *Overthrow* and its annexes or in the Ardeshir Zahedi memoirs, the latter flatly denying this information as well as any material possibility for his father being able to make recruitment efforts from his hideout.[83]

The secret document also claims that *Tudeh* leaders warned Mosaddeq that a second military *coup* was in preparation and asked for '10,000 rifles and small arms which Mosaddeq refused'. According to the *Tudeh* leader Kianouri, the party *had not* predicated a second *coup* in Tehran not at least in the immediate future. A passage from his memoirs is informative in this respect:

> We learned about the commencement of the *coup d'état* only in the morning of 19 August.... Moreover, our previous information was that the *putschist* forces planned to establish Zahedi's government in Esfahan; this assured us that at least for the days to come nothing would happen [in Tehran] but all of sudden we learned that the *coup* had been started by hooligans from downtown.[84]

The above passage refutes the claim made in the secret document that *Tudeh* warned Mosaddeq about the second *coup*; but the untruths do not stop there. The secret document claims that the meeting between Henderson and Mosaddeq on 17 August ended abruptly. We have already devoted a substantial part of this chapter to this meeting, laying out in minute detail its content and possible impact on the events of the following day. Suffice it to mention here that not only did the meeting not end abruptly, but Henderson in his report to Washington observed that 'Mosadeq [sic] seemed to be in a much better frame of mind when I left him.'[85] Finally, the observation about the role played by Ayatollah Behbahani in crowd mobilization – and the presence among the core group of demonstrators of gangs of traditional athletes and/or some hooligans – tallies with the findings of this study. We, nevertheless, view this rabble-rousing as a separate act of clerical defiance aimed at arresting the momentum then afoot towards an unwanted regime change, rather than a move scripted in a foreign plot. We have devoted the next chapter to describing the crucial role played by the clerical leadership in sparking the events of 19 August.

It is inconceivable that the authors of the secret report would have knowingly diffused inaccurate, indeed false information in a document seemingly intended for the consumption of British officials. It is noteworthy that the preparation of the secret document did indeed coincide with the arrival of Kermit Roosevelt in London on 25 August. The secret document is dated 2 September. It will be recalled that Roosevelt was warmly received by the head of MI6 and an array of top officials in the Foreign Office, including acting Foreign Secretary Lord Salisbury, before briefing the ailing Churchill. As noted earlier, any attribution of source in this context is a hazardous act of guesswork. While the presence of Roosevelt in London is an important indicator, it cannot be excluded that one of the Rashidian brothers may have been the source of some misinformation. It will be recalled that the London draft operational plan for the TPAJAX *coup*, prepared in early June, stated that SIS agents could amass a crowd of 3000 for the first phase of the destabilization campaign, termed 'religious refuge' or *Bast* in the *Majles* building.[86] That claim had emanated from one of the Rashidian brothers who, in spite of travel restrictions, managed to go to Geneva and meet with Darbyshire, a TPAJAX planner, about the time the Nicosia draft was being prepared.[87] The same figure of 3000 was now put in the British secret document as the estimated number of the club wielding *hired* crowd that roamed the bazaar area in the morning of Wednesday 19 August, a curious coincidence that may provide another clue about the source of this information. What is certain is that the line adopted in this secret report – including the assertion that the *coup* had been decided on Monday 17 August – resembles in its main thrust what later emerged from Roosevelt's debriefings as reflected in *Overthrow*, creating an enduring myth about the CIA role in the actual fall of Mosaddeq on 19 August.

A *coup d'état*, a popular uprising or something else?

The main point that emerges from the foregoing chapters is that unlike a military *coup* where objective and specific moves are meticulously designed in advance, the fall of Mosaddeq was unplanned. The day's events took turns that no one had predicted. It was the product of a haphazard combination of circumstances and deliberate strokes that achieved the ultimate aim of the TPAJAX *coup*. When this happened, the scenario for the assumption of power by General Zahedi, foreseen under the original *coup* plan, was put into effect. The latter emerged from his hideout and drove on board a tank to the Tehran radio station to deliver a victory speech. General Batmanqelij, released from detention by the crowds, occupied his post as the army chief of staff and proceeded to appoint *putschist* officers to key command posts.

Much, but not all of what happened was spontaneous. The indigenous character of the event was acknowledged not just by Henderson in his evaluation report to Washington on 20 August but, a week later, also by Secretary Dulles. He commented on 27 August, in a meeting of the National Security Council chaired by Vice-President Nixon, that while what happened in Iran 'was spontaneous, a number of people in Iran had kept their heads and maintained their courage when the situation looked very tough.'[88] At the time of this meeting, Kermit Roosevelt was still in London debriefing the British officials. Having remained proactive during the four crucial days, however, Roosevelt was able to claim credit.

The second main point in the body of evidence presented in this chapter is that while the political climate following the Shah's flight was propitious for manipulation by plotters, neither the TPAJAX machinery nor the Zahedi camp had such a crowd-rousing capability or the military means to produce a major power permutation in so brief a period of time. When the objective set for TPAJAX were attained by other means, intelligence organs in London and Washington took things at face value. They were too eager to score points. Iranians of all persuasions took the bait: according to a deep-seated societal credo, the traces of which have not fully disappeared even to this day, nothing of significance could ever possibly happen in Iran without a foreign hand. A parallax formed from an optical illusion came into the vision and anchored in the collective consciousness of Iranians. It also became a fixture in Western literature on US-Iranian relations.

Reading between the lines, American protagonists recognize this fact. The CIA account, *Overthrow*, tacitly admits – as does Roosevelt himself in the *World in Action* interview in 1973 – that the backlash was the result of specific internal events. On page 48 of *Overthrow* we read:

> It was this statement [Mosaddeq's announcement of the official dissolution of the Majles], together with the following day's violently anti-Shah remarks by Fatemi [16 August rally] and the undisguised and freely-preached republican propaganda of the Tudeh Party, that

was instrumental in persuading the general public that Mosaddeq was on the verge of eliminating the monarchy.

In a telling retrospective reflection years later, Christopher Woodhouse (one of the architects of TPAJAX) mused:

> There may be reason for not being dogmatic in claiming that the revolution of August 1953 in Tehran was planned and executed by the one Anglo-American team. We may have done no more than mobilizing forces which were already there, but that was precisely what needed to be done.[89]

Yet assuming a pure coincidental gathering of all adverse forces on Wednesday 19 August is equally naïve. In the next chapter we will dwell on forces which *sparked* the event. We will examine the body of evidence, according to which the amassing of crowds was an intuitive reaction by the Shiite clerical establishment as a gesture of disapproval of the course Mosaddeq had embarked on.

7
Where Did the Spark Come From?

The issue of spontaneity – or lack thereof – in the events of 19 August is one of the main topics of our enquiry. There is no doubt that at that point in history the Shah enjoyed a residual support among ordinary Iranians. Random, but incontestable evidence, worth glancing at, is the attitude of people on the balconies (Figure 32) of their houses in the following snapshot taken on 19 August.

Many Iranians hoped the Shah and the Prime Minister could work together, and their rift was greeted with desolation. Many tribes, notably the Afshāris, the Bakhtiāris, the Zolfaqāris and the Shahsavans, as well as ethnic groups such as Turkmans and Baluchis, were reputed to be pro-monarchy, while some others such as Qash'qāis and Sanjābis were Mosaddeq supporters.

The Shiite religious establishment had its own reasons for supporting the monarchy. The demise of the Ottoman Empire some three decades earlier had begotten a resolutely secular regime in Turkey, and Egypt was gravitating towards a similar course following the Free Officers *coup* in 1952. This left the staunchly anti-Shiite Wahhabi kingdom in the Arabian Peninsula as the only traditional pole of Moslem power in the region outside Iran. The fledging kingdoms in Iraq and Jordan were still being seen as subservient to Britain.

The Iranian monarchy had been closely associated with Shiism since the onset of the sixteenth century, leaving aside the brief reign by Nader Shah in the eighteenth century and Reza Shah's undisguised hankering for secularism. Among many titles that the Iranian monarchs tagged along with them was *'pādeshāh'e shi'eh-panāh'* or 'the Sovereign protector of Shiites.'

The all-pervasive fear of a communist takeover was another factor. *Tudeh* was being seen by the clerical establishment as the long arm of

Figure 32 A sparse group of pro-Shah demonstrators fraternizing with the military on 19 August while ordinary people applaud from the balconies of their houses. Photo from the Steven Langlie Collection, courtesy of Steven Langlie and the Middle-East Centre Archive, St. Anthony's College, Oxford University. ©Middle-East Centre Archive, 2007

the Comintern and the party's support for the irredentist campaign in Azerbaijan had not been reassuring. Added to the mix was the fact that *Tudeh* appealed to the downtrodden masses, a social stratum which had its traditional allegiance to clerics.

For the Shiite hierarchy therefore, monarchy spelled continuity and traditionalism. The Shah was seen as antipodal to republican secularism of the Turkish variety, and atheism was associated with *Tudeh* and its insidious penetration into the hearts and minds of the oppressed masses. By mid-1953, with minor exceptions, the rank and file Shiite clerics resented Mosaddeq; by the same token, most ranking ayatollahs supported the Shah. Other than the supreme leader Boroujerdi and the maverick activist Kashani, the most prominent among the Shah's supporters were Ayatollahs Mohsen Hakim Tabatabaei, Mohammad Behbahani and Kazem Shahrestani.[1]

For his part, Mosaddeq remained popular among segments of the middle class and the bazaar, the politicized youth and the intelligentsia. A few lesser clerics also supported him, of whom the most prominent was Haj Agha Reza (later Ayatollah) Zanjani and Seyyed Mahmoud (later Ayatollah) Taleqani.[2] The *Tudeh* Party had also shifted its support to Mosaddeq. To firm his grip on power Mosaddeq had, furthermore, placed his supporters in key command posts in the army, police and national gendarmerie.

It was against the backdrop of such polarization and social rifts that events in August 1953 took shape. The news of the unexpected departure of the Shah on 16 August brought the simmering tensions to a boiling point. According to a rumour making the rounds in Tehran and Qom, the news of the military *coup* had been trumped up by the government in order to rid itself of the Shah and the monarchy.[3] The hate-mail campaign against clerics conducted under TPAJAX had climaxed and was an added factor of irritation. Another rumour, unfounded in all likelihood, suggested that the arrested officers were to be executed shortly. These factors awakened the worst fears among Mosaddeq opponents, notably the clerics and the younger military officers.

It must also be stressed, as it has been also observed in *Overthrow* and US Embassy dispatches to Washington, that both the *Tudeh* Party and the more radical Mosaddeq supporters overplayed their hands, stoking up a furnace which was ready to explode. The sight of the toppled statue of a mounted Reza Shah, a man many Iranians remembered with a mix of admiration and awe, and that of the fouled-up Sepah square – which in those days still kept its original splendour – must have incensed many Iranian urbanites. The injurious remarks by

Foreign Minister Fatemi at the 16 August rally, and the proclamation by the *Tudeh* central committee, calling for a 'democratic republic',[4] were all building blocks for a backlash.

However, those ordinary citizens resentful of these excesses were not the types who would impulsively rise up and put themselves in harm's way. The embryo of the pro-Shah crowds which gathered on the evening of 18 August and early morning of 19 August was made up of frenzied, vindictive, often club-wielding groups from the urban underclass in the southern neighbourhoods. That bore the trademark of the clerics. Others from different walks of life, described in the US Embassy round-up cable of 20 August no doubt joined in and swelled the street throngs as the morning wore on.[5] Yet again the nucleus *sparking* the event were bands of dauntless daredevils originating from popular neighbourhoods. Ayatollah Kashani, the unrelenting political foe of Mosaddeq, and his peer, the top ranking Tehran ayatollah, Seyyed Mohammad Behbahani, had between them a formidable crowd mobilization capability, and they used it. There are no gainsayers among historians of the period on the role the two played in bringing about the downfall. Traditional scholarship has, however, presumed that the two acted as instruments of TPAJAX, or were bribed. No evidence either in the CIA's own history or other reliable documents allow us to support that claim.

Esoteric inner councils of the Shiite clerical hierarchy, on the other hand, could create dynamics of frightening potency through mosque networks, independent of the will and actions of foreign powers. The rabble-rousing ability of *ulama* had nothing new to it. It was the same phenomenon that so many times in the previous 50 years had been brought into play at crucial cross-roads when the interests of Islam had been seen to be in peril.[6] It was the same clout which a quarter of a century later ignited *the Islamic revolution* against the very man *'their crowds'* proclaimed on that fateful day in August 1953.[7]

The missing link: the Boroujerdi factor

As we saw in the two opening sections of Chapter 4, since the previous February, Shiite clerics had closed ranks. The quietist strain led by the Grand Ayatollah Seyyed Mohammad-Hossein Boroujerdi had tacitly sided with Kashani and other anti-Mosaddeq activists. We noted that Boroujerdi's rift with Mosaddeq had indeed predated the February 1953 crisis.[8] If the tiff in late 1952 was over trivialities, it must nevertheless be viewed as symptomatic of an underlying resentment felt by the grand Shiite magnate. Boroujerdi had perceived Mosaddeq as being too apathetic in matters related to the faith. He used an archaic clerical jargon, *'lā'beshart'* (indifferent) to describe the prime minister's attitude towards religion.[9] Government in a Shiite state, he believed, should not be *'lā'beshart'*, towards Islam, it should promote it. Mosaddeq's secular liberalism was an irritant to clerics of all strains. If for *Fadā'iān* that spelled rupture and enmity, it inspired mere alienation in most other clerics. Woodhouse synopsized the phenomenon in his narrative of the Mosaddeq episode, 'Since the Tudeh party, still nominally outlawed, was openly supporting Mosaddeq, the religious leaders turned away from him to form an alliance with the Shah.'[10] What vexed the mild-mannered apolitical Boroujerdi was the free sway Mosaddeq had allowed the *Tudeh* Party to enjoy. Ayatollah Hossein-Ali Montazeri (heir apparent to Khomeini during the 1980s) describes Boroujerdi as having been *overly sensitive* to communism although to shield Boroujerdi from a pro-monarchy smear in the early days of the Islamic revolution, Montazeri blamed foreigners and Court intrigues for that sentiment.[11] As a younger cleric in the late 1940s and early 1950s, Montazeri had been a student as well as a scribe in Boroujerdi seminars, and relatively close to him. He recalls that just before Mosaddeq's downfall, presumed *Tudeh* militants had gone as far as demonstrating in front of Boroujerdi's summer residence (in an adjacent village to Qom, called *Voshnouh*).[12] We earlier referred to a passage from Meftah's memoirs, which referred to Tudeh graffiti already on Boroujerdi's wall in June.

Mosaddeq was alive to the potential risk of alienating Qom, and as early as March 1953 – well before the TPAJAX black and grey propaganda campaigns – had passed legislation declaring affronts to Boroujerdi a felony.[13] Clearly such measures could not have been envisaged in a void and incidents of insult to the top prelate must have been occurring.[14] The incident in *Voshnouh* village has *not* been disclaimed by Kianouri, who makes a reference to it in a footnote in his memoirs.[15] Nor has the incident been claimed by Roosevelt in *Countercoup*, or by Wilber in *Overthrow*, in spite of its potential significance; the actual truth is unlikely to ever be known. Regardless of who was responsible for outrages of this sort, it is wrong to assume that these or similar acts were anything more than irritants that stirred a more profound malaise in Boroujerdi. Not even the secularism displayed by Mosaddeq could by itself make the Grand Ayatollah come out of his quietist reserve.

Since the saga of the Shah's abortive trip abroad in February 1953, Qom was watching the developments in Tehran with a mix of anguish and frustration. The spectre of a fundamental change and a drift towards republicanism and beyond had suddenly appeared in Iran's political horizon. The historical context within which such an eventuality was being viewed has already been explained. It will also be recalled that Behbahani and other dignitaries such as Ala had been in contact with the Grand Ayatollah during and in the aftermath of the February crisis (*noh'e esfand*).[16] In that crisis, the same phenomenon, namely the departure of the Shah, had sparked off a reaction from Qom. At that juncture the TPAJAX had not yet come into existence to deploy its panoply of dirty tricks.

The Shah's precipitous departure on the morning of 16 August brought things to a head. It must have awakened in the grand Shiite magnate the same fears that the spectre of a secular republic had set off among the Shiite *ulama* a generation earlier in 1924. Reza Khan, then prime minister, was forced to retract his project for the creation of an Ataturk-style republic; the clerics had organized massive protest rallies and managed to tip the balance in their favour.[17] The CIA/MI6 planners of TPAJAX had measured well the potency of faith as an instrument of political manipulation, and correctly concluded that nearly all religious leaders with a significant following were opposed to Mosaddeq.[18] The TPAJAX plan drawn up in London had envisaged contact with Ayatollahs Boroujerdi through Ayatollah Behbahani, and no doubt hoped to work indirectly with Ayatollah Kashani. They had further assumed that through *Fadā'iān Islam,* the terrorist group led by Navvab-Safavi, they could intimidate pro-Mosaddeq deputies and politicians.[19]

The TPAJAX experiment with clerics proved inconclusive to the extent that its outcome could not be demonstrated in a tangible way. This is at least how the CIA post-mortem in Chapter X of *Overthrow* has recorded the matter. Under the original plan drawn up in London, Behbahani was expected to persuade Boroujerdi to issue a religious decree (*fatwa*) of some kind against Mosaddeq. The TPAJAX plan subsequently changed. The core element became an outright Mosaddeq dismissal by the Shah; a shift resulting from the dissolution of the *Majles* by Mosaddeq through the referendum. The royal *farmāns* were to be backed by enforcement measures to ensure Mosaddeq's compliance. After the *coup* attempt failed, Roosevelt and the others had seemingly hoped – if affirmations in *Overthrow* can be taken at face value – to obtain a *Fatwa* for a *holy war,* this time against the communists.[20] In a broad sense, the failure of plotters to interact with Boroujerdi one way or the other was taken as a failure by the Grand Ayatollah to act.

Clearly, the TPAJAX planners lacked familiarity with the idiosyncrasies and *modus operandi* of high Shiite prelates. For years Ayatollah Boroujerdi had kept a tap on the vast network of clerics with diverse or contrasting outlooks through an apolitical minimalist approach marked by restraint and reticence. He would not let himself be used as a pawn in foreign intrigues. In his own subtle way, however, Boroujerdi used to act when action was called for.[21]

Although the evidence is circumstantial, it appears that in the immediate aftermath of the Shah's flight to Baghdad on 16 August, religious leaders swiftly moved to forestall a drift towards republicanism. In response to a query, presumably from Behbahani – and possibly from some Bazaar dignitaries[22] – the Grand Ayatollah had emitted a succinct opinion, which may not amount to a binding *fatwa* but was enough to set the redoubtable clerical apparatus in motion. Mosaddeq or his immediate entourage, it was presumed, had engineered the *coup* plot to abolish the monarchy. In a three-word statement therefore, Boroujerdi opined, '*mamlekat Shah mikhahad*' or 'the country needs a king.[23] This was not a call for *holy war* and may just have been intended as a preliminary warning to Mosaddeq that a change of regime would not be brooked. Aware of Boroujerdi's strong position – and possibly reassured by this injunction – Ayatollah Behbahani, in tandem with Kashani, must have signalled the '*usual crowds*' to move into the streets *as of the evening of 18 August*, and followed up on the ensuing day. While close to the Shah's Court, Behbahani was quintessentially linked to Qom, much in the same way as a cardinal is linked to the Vatican. He would not have taken risky initiatives on his own, especially after the Shah left the country and the outcome of the political gambit launched against Mosaddeq was far from certain, just as the monarch's return was universally deemed improbable.[24] It bears a mention in passing that the Qom hierarchy was not bereft of financial resources that may have been used on this occasion.

This little-known facet of the drama is, however, a clue to the 19 August jigsaw. The CIA internal report confirms that the agency's local contacts had heard about '*a pro-Shah statement from the ranking Shiite cleric Boroujerdi*[25] *in the morning of 19 August and had planned to travel to Qazvin, some 80 miles away, to prepare broadsheets.*'

In his memoirs, Ayatollah Montazeri recounts an historical anecdote of relevance to this chapter. On 19 August, he writes, 'we were about 30 or 40 (clerics) in *Voshnouh* [Boroujerdi's summer residence] debating *Jāmee' ul ahādīs*,[26] when news came that Mosaddeq's government had been overthrown.' Montazeri does not mention the reaction of Boroujerdi *per se*, but writes, '*One of the acolytes suddenly fell on the ground prostrating in a gesture of pleasure and good-riddance, thanking the almighty.*'[27] Clearly the acolyte must have been aware of the position of the grand ayatollah to venture an ordinarily banned display of political zeal.

Of relevance also are occurrences in the provinces. On Wednesday afternoon, even before the outcome of the showdown in Tehran was sealed, protests broke out in major Iranian cities like Tabriz, Esfahan and Shiraz. In a pattern similar to Tehran, mixed crowds of military and civilians poured out into the streets, occupied government offices and declared allegiance to the Shah through the local radio. The occupation of the telecommunication building by the crowd in the early afternoon in Tehran had no doubt facilitated contacts with the provinces, but telegrams by the populous on occasions of this sort were traditionally addressed to community leaders, that is, senior clerics. Needless to say, such a coordinated onslaught was beyond the means – even wildest hopes – of the TPAJAX planners. *Overthrow* refers to these developments without claiming credit.[28] The clerical network led from Qom was, however, in a position to produce such an orchestration. In a less structured way, the network of pro-Shah officers may also have intervened, although a resort to military communication channels would have been risky to say the least.

In his memoirs, Ardeshir Zahedi refers, albeit in passing, to the role played by the religious leaders in rallying the pro-Shah crowds, 'People poured out either on their own or following instructions from religious leaders.'[29] In an interview with the author, Zahedi stressed the importance of the role played by these leaders, and *emphatically confirmed* the role played by the Grand Ayatollah Boroujerdi in person.[30] Americans knowledgeable about the event have also stressed the point. In his seminal work, *Nationalism in Iran*, Richard Cottam – then an insider – emphasizes the role of the clerics, refuting in the same breath, CIA involvement in the events of that particular day.[31]

Shortly after the news of the Mosaddeq downfall reached the Shah in Rome he wired two messages, one was to Grand Ayatollah Boroujerdi and the other one to Ayatollah Behbahani. In these messages, the Shah thanked the nation for the support given him and requested all concerned to support the new prime minister, General Zahedi. The response by Boroujerdi (the Persian wording of which is reproduced in the note flagged here) reads: '*I hope the well-augured return of your majesty to Iran will put an end to [temporal] ills therein and will bring glory to Islam and welfare to Moslems.*' The telegram then ends with a more familiar tone in a phrase that more than anything said before reveals his inner thoughts: '*Do return, as the Shiism and Islam need you. You are the Shiite sovereign.*'[32]

8
Summary and Conclusions

The main premise of this study is that internal political dynamics more than foreign intrigues were responsible for the ultimate blow to Mosaddeq and his national movement. No significant organic link could be established between the failed CIA-MI6 plot to oust Mosaddeq in mid-August and his actual downfall on Wednesday 19 August 1953. The first part of the book was devoted to understanding the background and nature of internal forces, namely the power structure and polity in Iran at the time of Mosaddeq's rise to power. The study then followed developments in the oil dispute and reviewed reasons for the Eisenhower administration's decision to join with Britain to remove Mosaddeq through covert means. The last part of the study focused on operation TPAJAX and the ensuing events that brought about Mosaddeq's downfall on 19 August 1953. Having carefully examined documents and other relevant sources we have come to conclude that claims by Kermit Roosevelt and others to have pre-planned and played a decisive role in the downfall of Mosaddeq borders on prevarication.

In this final chapter we will try to sum up our findings in relation to each of the above three facets. In so doing we need to underscore the fact that the world's political climate and the internal situation in Iran were vastly different then, making it inconceivable to judge Mosaddeq's conduct both on the oil issue and internal reforms, by to-day's standards and values.

Power structure and internal dynamics in the early 1950s

The key question to address here is whether Dr Mosaddeq misunderstood or underestimated the complexities of the internal political environment in which he had to wage a campaign against the superpower that Britain still was in those days. The study concludes that while Mosaddeq was a product of the system and familiar with its characteristics, he did not assess obstacles realistically. In retrospect, his parallel struggles on several fronts appear quixotic, and instrumental in causing his downfall. Let us first recapitulate the broad characteristics of the system:

1. By the time Mosaddeq became prime minister in the spring of 1951, the socio-political structure in Iran still retained much of its oligarchic properties. Tribal chieftains, major landlords, and influential families – sometimes referred to as *Hezār fāmīl* – coalesced to form the ruling elite. Some rudiments of democracy existed. Behind the benign façade of a constitutional monarchy the parliament (*Majles*) played a pivotal role. The landed provincial notables or their surrogates got elected by herding peasants to the polling stations or through other devices.

2. Monarchy as the kingpin of the system was the guarantor of the privileges of that elite, but this reality did not translate into unswerving loyalty from its various components towards the Crown. Plots, insurgencies, and assassinations were rife. The Shah, in his early thirties at the time, was the product of tumults that had placed him on the throne in September 1941, at the age of 21. Still in those days keen to remain a constitutional monarch, the Shah nevertheless was apprehensive about the vulnerabilities that beset the country and the Crown. He felt uneasy about strong prime ministers who he felt could squeeze him out of all vestiges of power, worse, dethrone him. Yet there is no denial of his patriotism and pragmatic lucidity in confronting adversities. He tried to contain the British influence without stepping over the tripwire that could provoke severe British retributions. These factors shaped his attitude towards Mosaddeq and the oil nationalization drive; they explain his ambivalence, and his at times unsteady behaviour towards the prime minister.

3. The military, while below par as a fighting force, was strong enough to maintain a semblance of law and order. Having been created by the Shah's father, its loyalty was by and large to the monarch. Its officer corps was drawn from middle-class families, though scions of *hezār fāmīl* were also visible among the top brass.

4. The Shiite clerical hierarchy directed from Qom remained highly influential. It wielded power through a vast network of mosques, informal neighbourhood associations and alliance with well-to-do bazaar

merchants. *Ulama* hence had immense crowd-manipulation ability. At the helm of the hierarchy, the Grand Ayatollah Boroujerdi discouraged the involvement of clerics in politics. He nevertheless supported, albeit discreetly, the institution of monarchy as the embodiment of tradition as well as the antipode of a secular republicanism of the Turkish variety. By the mid-twentieth century, however, a strain of politicized clerics had emerged. Although not homogenous – some practising terror – a certain complicity bound them together. Ayatollah Kashani was their symbol and the lightning rod. He sided with Mosaddeq's *National Front* initially, but like most right-wingers in this loose alliance, later turned around to become a venomous foe and an instrument of Mosaddeq's undoing.

5. A high-voltage British neo-colonial influence ran through and contaminated the system. This influence drew its potency from several factors. Through the nineteenth and early twentieth century, a debilitated Iran under the *Qājār* dynasty had had its own brushes with the British Empire but mostly felt her crushing weight due to geography and the empire's enduring presence in the region. Iran was flanked on three sides by a power which had emerged victorious from all the adversities of the Napoleonic wars in the early nineteenth century to the two world wars in the first half of the twentieth. Britain, for all practical purposes, owned Iran's oil resources and industry, giving Iran a paltry share. Reza Shah, the first Pahlavi monarch, was humiliated and cowed when in the early 1930s he gambled to snatch back control of the oil industry. British officials viewed Britain as a virtuous power with a civilizing mission and regretted that Iran had escaped the rigour of a British colonial rule that would have straightened its many flaws and blemishes. Some Iranians agreed and without lacking in patriotism believed that Iran should throw in its lot with Britain. The perceived ubiquitous presence and overarching influence of Britain overwhelmed Iran's body politic. In many ways it was a psychosomatic affliction, exquisitely satirized in later years by an Iranian novelist Iraj Pezeshzad.[1] Mosaddeq's attempt to stamp out that influence was all the more daring in view of the prevalence of this psyche.

6. The emerging middle class and intelligentsia drifted either to the pro-Soviet communist movement, embodied in the *Tudeh* Party, or to the centrist National Front. Created in 1941, *Tudeh* had grown to become a formidable political force by the time of Mosaddeq's rise to power in 1951, having weathered serious adversities and reverses during the previous decade. The most damning of these reverses came when, during the Azerbaijan crisis, the *Tudeh* Party sided with the USSR (see 'The

Azeraijan crisis', in Chapter 1). The party was also implicated by the government in an assassination attempt against the Shah and was outlawed only to return in force through a slew of front organizations and newspapers.

7. For its part, the National Front, comprising secular democrats with strong anti-imperialistic leanings, formed a loose coalition of parties and personalities in 1949 around Doctor Mosaddeq, with large mass appeal but poor political structures (see 'The Rise of the National Front' in Chapter 2).

Mosaddeq's rule

1. A septuagenarian of noble stock, trained in Switzerland, Mosaddeq was in his element as a parliamentarian, though he had held ministerial and gubernatorial posts during the 1920s. Mosaddeq as such was first and foremost a product of the system described above, and his rise to power in April 1951 had been filtered through this same semi-oligarchic structure. The *Majles* that voted Mosaddeq into office was not itself a democratically elected body in the Western understanding of the term. Once in power Mosaddeq pursued two objectives: The acquisition of Iran's rights over its natural resources through the Nationalization of the British owned Anglo-Iranian Oil Company, and reforming the state apparatus.

2. Britain's knee-jerk reaction to Mosaddeq's nationalization and seizure of the company's assets was to resort to force. In the British Labour Cabinet two key ministers, Foreign Secretary Morrison and Defence Secretary Shinwell, advocated military means while Prime Minister Attlee was more circumspect. A plan for the seizure of Abadan, code-named *Operation Buccaneer*, was prepared and initial preparatory steps were taken. The Truman administration firmly opposed the use of force and succeeded in dissuading Britain. This reality is little noticed in history books and almost absent in the collective memory of Iranians. Parallel with military planning, Britain seized the International Court of Justice and imposed a naval embargo to prevent the sale of Iranian oil. But the Labour government ended up recognizing, shortly thereafter, 'the principle of nationalization of the oil industries' and engaged in dialogue. These intermittent negotiations spanned a period of 15 months from June 1951 to March 1953. The conclusions drawn from different phases of oil talks are discussed under a separate heading below.

3. Riding on the crest of his immense popularity and impressive successes at the UN Security Council and the International Court of Justice – where he successfully defended the rightfulness of Iran's cause and her grievances against Britain – Mosaddeq set out also to reform the system and its institutions. In so doing, he stepped over the interests of virtually all elements in the power structure described earlier. His model was a secular Western-style democracy in which the monarch plays a ceremonial role and the will of the people, embodied in the parliament, should rule supreme. This noble, if idealistic, goal was hardly adaptable to the political system and power structure of the time.

4. Out of power in earlier years, Mosaddeq had always blamed the central government for rigging the *Majles* elections. Now, as the all-powerful prime minister, he tried but failed to pull off clean, nation-wide elections for the seventeenth *Majles*. He suspended the polls after only 79 out of 136 seats had been decided on. The system just did not lend itself to an unblemished electoral process.

5. Mosaddeq's first year in office brought the nation much pride but few concrete results. With oil talks gridlocked and the economy stagnating, jittery signs of discontent in higher state echelons and among interest groups began to emerge. Already by spring of 1952 the US Ambassador, Loy Henderson, had joined the British chargé in lobbying the Shah to replace Mosaddeq. The Shah did not cave in, but soon got embroiled in a dispute with Mosaddeq over the control of the armed forces triggering the latter's resignation in July 1952. He was replaced by Ahmad Qavam. This led to a crisis which culminated in the *Sey'e Tyr* (21 July 1952) popular uprising (see 'The Qavam Hiatus and the *Si'ye Tyr* Popular Uprising' in Chapter 3).

6. Ahmad Qavam could be regarded a Machiavellian figure in Iran's contemporary history. He had already managed the Azerbaijan crisis in 1946 when he tried to obtain results by appeasing Stalin. But in so doing Qavam brought the country to the verge of chaos and disintegration. Possibly encouraged by Britain, southern tribal regions demanded the same autonomy rights that Qavam had accorded to the Soviet proxies in the north. The country seemed to relapse into the wobbling pre-constitution state where de facto zones of influence had been created by Britain and Russia. Qavam reversed course only after a dramatic face off with the young Shah who, with the possible encouragement of the American Ambassador in Tehran, brandished the army to force the hand of his prime minister. Now in early 1952, at the high point

of Mosaddeq's successes, Qavam lobbied with Britain to replace him. He had promised British officials that as prime minister he would establish a dictatorship in Iran and settle the oil dispute in a manner compatible with British and Iranian interests. Once appointed prime minister he proceeded along that line, only to be thwarted by a national uprising that forced his resignation.

7. Back in power, Mosaddeq defiantly pursued his domestic agenda and oil talks. He rightly saw the *Siy'e Tyr* as a plebiscite that had returned him to power. He was further vindicated by a landmark International Court of Justice decision in Iran's favour. From this unparalleled position of legitimacy and strength Mosaddeq embarked on a daring programme of reform. He deemed it fit to circumvent the seventeenth *Majles* in which he nevertheless retained an adequate majority. He sought and obtained emergency powers which allowed him to rule by decree. This alienated the conservative wing in his National Front coalition and narrowed his support base. Unperturbed, Mosaddeq went on to curb the Shah's prerogatives as commander-in-chief, purge the army, close the Senate, and shake up the judiciary. State institutions were thus tampered with and interest groups disenfranchised. The stakeholders saw Mosaddeq reforms as a budding threat to their political survival. Compounding this alienation, Mosaddeq also allowed the communist party, *Tudeh*, not just to resume its activities and growth, but to become a formidable political force.

8. Allowing the *Tudeh* party a free sway was in part a scarecrow tactic *vis-à-vis* the United States. Mosaddeq counted on American support and sought to convince the United States that his nationalist enterprise was the only alternative to communism. This tactic eventually backfired. *Tudeh* showed no restraint in exhibiting its prowess in Tehran's streets. The fiercely anti-communist minuscule parties, some possibly subsidized by the CIA under the TP-BEDAMN secret project, clashed with *Tudeh* cadres in the streets of the capital. Tehran became the scene of daily unrest, rallies and strikes. People who went about their daily lives were not amused. Mosaddeq's efforts to sell the nationalized oil in the international market had all but failed. The oil-less economy did not bode well for the country in spite of the valiant strides made by his government to readjust the economy through austerity measures and a boost in domestic products.

9. Interest groups bristled; resentments gradually fermented into conspiracies. An unchartered alliance among Mosaddeq opponents

gradually took shape, comprising his erstwhile National Front allies, right-wing or anglophile deputies, politicized clerics, and purged army generals as well as the Shah's own entourage, including notably the court minister Hossein Ala. Princess Ashraf, the Shah's plucky twin sister, his brother Ali-Reza, and the Queen mother were all among Mosaddeq's ferocious foes.

The handling of the oil crisis and stalemate

1. By the time Mosaddeq took office in the spring of 1951, the Supplemental Oil Agreement negotiated by his predecessors was off the table. Britain had discreetly made an offer of a fifty-fifty deal to Prime Minister Razmara and, following his assassination in February 1951, to his immediate successor Prime Minister Ala. Mosaddeq's nationalization of Iran's oil industries was intended not just to redeem the legitimate rights of Iran but also to put an end to the British neo-colonial influence. The oil nationalization created unanimity among Iranians – taking no account of initial negative *Tudeh* Party reaction. The move was also supported, ostensibly at least, by the quasi-totality of Iran's body politic.

2. Initially, Mosaddeq and his advisors did not have an adequate understanding of the intricacies of the oil market including the nexus and interaction among the Oil Majors. He wrongly assumed that once the flow of Iranian oil was suspended, the market would face a shortfall and customers would attempt to circumvent the British naval blockade to procure it. In actual fact, the Oil Majors quickly increased production elsewhere. Helped by an existing market glut, the hoped-for supply deficit was quickly offset. Mosaddeq also misjudged the politics of the Cold War and the nature of the alliance between the United States and Britain.

3. Over time, several compromise proposals for the resolution of the oil dispute were presented to Mosaddeq by Britain, by the International Bank for Reconstruction and Development (IBRD), and jointly by Truman and Churchill. One final proposal, worked out between the newly installed Eisenhower administration and the Foreign Office, was presented to Mosaddeq in February 1953. Merits and demerits of these proposals are examined in the main body of this volume.

The proposal by the IBRD had the advantage of being an interim arrangement *without prejudice to the position of either party*. It would have given Mosaddeq a badly needed breathing space and financial relief. The subsequent Churchill-Truman offer had gone a long way to meet Mosaddeq's concerns, but it fell short of Iran's requirements. By then the key stumbling block was the issue of compensation to AIOC resulting from the Nationalization Act. Mosaddeq had agreed to submit the determination of the amount of compensation to arbitration by the International Court of Justice in The Hague, but had wrongly assumed that the proposed '*terms of reference*' for the arbitration would enable Britain to reopen the issue of validity of the Nationalization Act. Based on this assumption, he rejected the Truman-Churchill proposal. Mosaddeq was also concerned – and here he judged correctly – that Britain sought compensation for '*future losses*' resulting from the Nationalization Act. He feared that Iran might be saddled with an onerous long-term debt that would keep the nation under foreign yoke.

4. In reality, Mosaddeq judged oil proposals by two yardsticks. One was whether they were consistent with the Nationalization Act and satisfied Iran's legitimate interests. The second criterion was more complex. It had to do with the political, even emotional, side of things. Would the end of the oil dispute with Britain also eradicate its influence in Iran? Would the terms of settlement measure up to Mosaddeq's exalted image and the nationalistic expectations he had aroused? Would he be able to stand up to abusive tirades of his erstwhile allies or the 'sell-out' outcry by *Tudeh* if American conglomerates were allowed in as the proposed packages foresaw? These concerns prevented Mosaddeq from analysing the situation with the needed serenity.

5. When in March 1953 Mosaddeq rejected the final oil proposal and put a unilateral end to the oil negotiations, the Eisenhower administration despaired. That, in fact, proved to be the last straw. The US government shifted to a different line of action; that of joining hands with Britain to remove Mosaddeq through underhand means.

External and internal conspiracies

1. Britain had followed a two-pronged strategy towards Mosaddeq and the oil crisis, comprising negotiations and subversion. Sapping the government started when Labour was still in power. Foreign-Secretary Morrison in particular was keen to confront Mosaddeq by brute force and, short of that, to undermine him through covert means. The Foreign Office under Eden had privileged diplomacy, but efforts to sap the Mosaddeq government hardly ever stopped. By March 1953 the new American administration was ready to cross the line from diplomatic engagement to subversion. Diplomacy lost all its allure when the Dulles brothers reached the conclusion that the rise of communism in Iran was inescapable while Mosaddeq remained in power. Iran's rejection of the American-backed Churchill oil proposal and its withdrawal from negotiations in March 1953 created a watershed. The British needed little convincing to revert to a one-stroke approach to deal with the 'nationalist nuisance' in Iran. The *coup* plan codenamed TPAJAX thenceforth became the Anglo-American agenda in Iran.

2. In late February squabbles and tension between the Shah and his prime minister came to a head. Mosaddeq saw the imperial Court as a hub of conspiracy and wrongly attributed an insurgency by a *Bakhtiāry* tribal chief to court intrigues. He threatened to resign and publicly blame the Shah for his decision. To what extent this was a genuine concern or an alibi to further curtail the Shah's powers it is hard to gauge. On his part, a forlorn Shah had his heart set on a break from what must have been felt as a climate of tension and humiliation. His natural tendency was to escape problems rather than confronting them. He volunteered to go on extended travel to Europe. Mosaddeq initially objected or feigned reluctance; he ended up supporting the idea. The decision to travel abroad was, however, the Shah's. This was not the way matters were perceived at the time by Mosaddeq opponents or by top clerics in Qom and elsewhere. For them the move was a gambit by Mosaddeq, possibly intended to bring about a regime change. Among clerics concerned with such a prospect was the Shiite world's highest religious authority, the Grand Ayatollah Boroujerdi.

3. Matters were different for Ayatollah Kashani. He saw in the crisis an opportunity to enfeeble the government or bring about its collapse. For Boroujerdi, the aim was just to prevent the Shah from leaving. They both intervened. So did a cohort of right-wing politicians, retired army officers and a coterie of courtiers and pedigreed elders including Mosaddeq's own half-brother, Heshmattol'doleh Valatabar and Ahmad Qavam. Foreshadowing what was to come in August, a crowd of pro-Shah demonstrators was rushed to the front entrance of the palace. The Shah finally caved in but Mosaddeq was convinced that the incident had been orchestrated with a view to assassinating him. He had not ruled out US connivance in such a plot.

4. The *noh'e esfand* crisis, as it is known to Iranians, became yet another watershed. Above all it alerted the quietist Shiite hierarchy in Qom to a scenario they dreaded: A drift towards secular republicanism, if

not communist atheism, inherent in forcing the Shah out. As of that date faint signs of a rapprochement between Qom and the activist cleric Kashani could be detected (see 'The Grand Ayatollah Boroujerdi' in Chapter 4). The unchartered alliance between different stripes of right-wing opposition to Mosaddeq was also consolidated.

5. Documents at hand reveal that by then some in the right-wing politico-military milieus already entertained the idea of a *putsch* against Mosaddeq. Even before the United States had come fully on board, a former Iranian air force chief, General Hedayatollah Guilanshah, had approached the American Embassy in Tehran with that idea. After the *noh'e esfand* crisis, the court minister Ala had his own schemes to bring about a collapse of the government through an inseminated parliamentary crisis. He had discussed his plan with the American Ambassador, but had been unable to convince the Shah whose role would have been pivotal in any such scheme. At some point in the late spring of 1953 internal and external conspiracies merged.

6. A retired general turned politician, Fazlollah Zahedi was known to harbour political ambitions. He had an unrivalled track record in the Iranian army. Moreover, as the national police chief he had helped in the rise of the National Front, something that earned him the Interior portfolio in Mosaddeq's first cabinet. He subsequently turned against Mosaddeq and became one of his daring critics. As such, he was an obvious choice to lead the *coup* plan.

7. The Shah had originally hesitated to name Zahedi. The monarch's attitude was that of wait-and-see and constitutional expediency. He had repeatedly voiced his aversion to cabalistic games. Already in June 1952 the Shah had resisted Anglo-American pressures to oust Mosaddeq. As late as May 1953 the Shah continued to back Mosaddeq in a discussion he held with Henderson. There was surely no love lost between the Shah and his prime minister, but the Shah hoped that Mosaddeq would step down once the oil dispute was successfully resolved; conversely, if the dispute dragged on, Mosaddeq could be voted down, having eroded his capital of popularity.

8. The TPAJAX plan for the unseating of Mosaddeq, drawn up in Nicosia and London in late spring, had a political as well as a military component. The political part foresaw a campaign of destabilization to be culminated in a sanctuary (or *bast*) by clergy-led crowds inside the *Majles enceinte* where a censor motion and bribing of deputies would have brought about the fall of Mosaddeq through parliamentary procedures.

The military component was a contingency to protect the outcome against resistance by *Tudeh* or Mosaddeq supporters. This plan hinged on the Shah's support and active involvement but Mohammad Reza refused his blessing when solicited by an array of emissaries. The CIA field manager, Kermit Roosevelt, and the MI6 Iranian agent Assadollah Rashidian then resorted to blackmailing the Shah according to a line scripted in the TPAJAX plan. The exact circumstances are detailed in 'The Taming of the Shah' in Chapter 4. The Shah finally succumbed. Once on board, he proposed a different course of action. He postulated that the *Majles* dissolution, envisaged by Mosaddeq, empowered him to dismiss the prime minister in line with established precedents during parliamentary interregna. The London draft *coup* plan was readjusted in its political component accordingly.

9. In effect, Mosaddeq, fearing a manoeuvre designed to unseat him, had decided to dissolve the parliament through a referendum. He was aware that the deputies were being bribed to vote him down. Some of his close advisors warned him against this move and the latitude it accorded the Shah to dismiss him. Mosaddeq had rebuffed that advice.

10. The *Majles* disposition towards the prime minister, in spite of the bribing campaign, showed virtually no change, not on the surface at least. In late June 1953 deputies voted to oust Ayatollah Kashani as the Speaker and to replace him with a Mosaddeq loyalist. When in July Mosaddeq asked the deputies to voluntarily resign, 52 deputies, or a two-thirds majority, meekly obliged. A year earlier some 40 deputies had voted in favour of Qavam when Mosaddeq resigned. If these voting patterns could be taken as a yardstick, it should be concluded that TPAJAX bribing was patently ineffectual, producing no change in the voting pattern. This notwithstanding, Mosaddeq resorted to a highly controversial referendum to formally close down the seventeenth *Majles*. By then Kermit Roosevelt had arrived in Tehran and preparations for the TPAJAX *coup* were in full swing.

The TPAJAX *coup* and its aftermath

1. In the main body of this essay, we examined details of the revised TPAJAX plan and its execution on the night of 15 to 16 August. The Shah had signed two royal decrees, one dismissing Mosaddeq and the other appointing General Zahedi in his place. The military component of the plan had been modified to assume a peremptory character, designed to forestall any attempt at resistance by Mosaddeq supporters or *Tudeh*

cadres. It had all the trappings of a *putsch*. In retrospect it is fair to conclude that even if the Shah's dismissal order was not *stricto sensu* unconstitutional, the fact that it was a feature of a foreign scheme to bring about a change of government, divested the operation of any vestige of legitimacy. The *coup* plan unravelled when the commander of the Imperial Guard who had gone to Mosaddeq's residence to deliver the Shah's dismissal order was arrested and his detachment disarmed.

2. Why the plan failed is clear in hindsight: The *Tudeh* secret military network had penetrated most military units, including the Imperial Guard which had been slated under the plan to carry the brunt of the operation. *Tudeh* had published the news of an impending *putsch* in its official organ and no doubt tipped off Mosaddeq and his army chief of staff, General Riahi, in a timely fashion. The Shah, who had been following the event from his hunting lodge in the Caspian, flew to Baghdad in panic.

3. Mosaddeq may have initially hesitated to reject the dismissal order; he did not publicly announce it. Later, he explained his rejection in different, even contrasting, terms. To Ambassador Henderson he said on 18 August that the Shah was not entitled to dismiss him; he did not acknowledge having received such an order. In his trial months later, Mosaddeq said he had presumed the *farmān* was a forgery, given the manner in which it had been delivered to him. Elsewhere in his memoirs, Mosaddeq intimated that he would have accepted the royal fiat had it been delivered through regular channels. Finally, Mosaddeq has also said he would have accepted it were it not for the fact that he was confident he could pull off the oil dispute in the best interests of the nation.

4. Upon the Shah's flight on 16 August a new political climate set into the country. Manifestations of unbridled radicalism alarmed the conservative segments of society, including, notably, the clerical establishment. On the opposite end of the spectrum, the *Tudeh* leadership appeared to be veering further to the left. Up to that point they seemed to be conceding to bourgeois nationalists, led by Mosaddeq and the leadership of the anti-colonial and anti-feudal mass movement. In an ideological drift reflected in the *Tudeh* executive committee's four-point declaration on 18 August, the party appeared to be moving to what in their jargon was later described as the '*proletariat hegemony*' in the first phase of the revolution, assorted with a power-sharing agenda in the short-run. The newly appointed Soviet Ambassador, Anatoly Lavrentiev, a Balkan and East-European specialist, had been rushed to Tehran a few month earlier from his post to Bucharest; an indication – surely no proof – that a scenario similar to Czechoslovakia 1948 was not to be excluded. Only days after the fall of Mosaddeq in August, Lavrentiev was mysteriously withdrawn from his post in Tehran amidst strong indications that he had attempted suicide (see 'The Gathering Storm' in Chapter 5).

5. Mosaddeq was not keen on a regime change. He rejected the idea of a republic partly because he was keen to retain the good will of the US government. He may also have had the sensitivities of high clerics in mind, although no evidence to this effect has surfaced. He appears not to have given up hope until the very end to enlist American financial aid and its help to resolve the oil dispute. Paradoxically, he also suspected American involvement in the *coup*. He finally opted for a Regency Council to be endorsed by a referendum, but did not get around to publicly announcing this decision. However, he had to explain and convince his more radical collaborators who were urging the abolition of the monarchy in concert with the *Tudeh* Party. Later, Mosaddeq wrote that he had intended to invite the Shah to return. The rupture with the monarch, however, had been consummated, and such a retraction appears in retrospect to have been an afterthought.

6. Mosaddeq banned all rallies as of the *morning* of 18 August. The fierce crackdown and the roundup of *Tudeh* activists, however, peaked during the later hours of the evening, after Henderson's call on Mosaddeq. Some authors – Kim Roosevelt notably – later postulated that Henderson's meeting with Mosaddeq in the late afternoon of 18 August was used to lay the ground for the overthrow of Mosaddeq, foreseen for the following day. According to this claim, the meeting became an instrument to scare Mosaddeq into ordering *Tudeh* crowds off the streets, thus paving the way for an unhindered execution of the second phase of TPAJAX. Our evidence, presented in Chapter 5, does not support this presumption. Undoubtedly when Henderson returned to Tehran on 17 August from his prolonged absence he must have met and exchanged views with Roosevelt prior to meeting Mosaddeq. Nothing in his report to Washington or in subsequent communications with the State Department could remotely be construed as an indication of prior knowledge by Henderson of the events that were to unfold the following day. Henderson himself flatly denied any knowledge of a second *coup* plan when he sat to testify for history, some 20 years later, in an interview with the Truman Library Oral History Project. There he

confidently predicted that if one day his dispatches to Washington were declassified, the truth of his statement could be seen by all.

7. TPAJAX had no back-up plan. Solid documentary evidence to this effect exists and was presented in the relevant chapter of this study. In Washington neither CIA headquarters nor the State Department nor the White House was aware of any plans for Wednesday 19 August. The news of Mosaddeq's fall on Wednesday took everyone in Washington by surprise. Ample evidence was presented to support our central contention that the *fall* of Mosaddeq on August 19 had not been scripted by the CIA or its duty station in Tehran as was later claimed and broadly accepted. It follows that Kim Roosevelt's claims in later years were disingenuous. Embassy dispatches to Washington on the day Mosaddeq fell and subsequently – now declassified – clearly demonstrate not just a lack of prior knowledge, but an avowal of puzzlement about what was happening in the streets of Tehran on that day. Henderson's prediction in the Truman Library interview was fully vindicated.

8. When the TPAJAX *coup* on 15–16 August failed, the State Department recommended a rapprochement with Mosaddeq. Later in the week, in an internal cable, CIA headquarters acknowledged that the subversion plan had been tried and failed and a new policy course was to be adopted.

9. In the camp of the opposition, General Zahedi was equally in the dark. His strategy was twofold: to widely disseminate the news of Mosaddeq's dismissal and of his own appointment, thus denouncing Mosaddeq as a usurper. The second part of his plan was to set up a military base in a remote province – Kermanshah was finally selected over Esfahan – from where he intended to launch an insurrection. This inherently *mid-term* plan must have been discussed and coordinated with the CIA station. Colonel Farzanegan, a CIA agent, acted as a military aide to Zahedi. The former travelled to Kermanshah and obtained the agreement of the garrison commander, Colonel Teymour Bakhtiar. General Zahedi had reportedly set out to leave for Kermanshah in the early hours of Wednesday 19 August but the news of pro-Shah street demonstrations on the evening of 18 August made him change his plans. Roosevelt, however, claimed that the purpose of contacting the military commanders in Esfahan and Kermanshah was to get these garrisons to move to Tehran on 19 August, a logistical impossibility.

10. The CIA internal history *Overthrow* claims that in a '*council of war*' on 17 August, Kermit Roosevelt planned the Wednesday event.[2] The latter

Summary and Conclusions   169

admits that he had kept Washington and London in the dark because he feared a negative reaction on their part. Since the subject of the credibility of Kim Roosevelt is a central theme of this essay, detailed evidence and analyses have been provided in Chapter 6. The main conclusions are recapitulated below:

- If Kim Roosevelt was intent on dealing a fatal blow to Mosaddeq on Wednesday, 19 August, it is reasonable to expect that he would have given his team more than *24 hours* to prepare such a feat. As noted, his *'council of war'* was convened in the evening of Monday, 17 August.
- The dispatch of emissaries, discussed in the 'council of war', to Esfahan and Kermanshah, at prohibitive distances from the Capital, could only have been aimed to establish anti-Mosaddeq-*Tudeh* insurrectional bases. Further, the purported *fatwa* to be solicited from the grand Shiite magnate in Qom, would have called, according to *Overthrow*'s own wording, for a *'holy war against communism'*, again an indication of mid- to long-term planning.
- Some of the activities later claimed to have been performed by the MI6-CIA Iranian agents to *prepare* the blow were bizarrely tardy. They are said to have been performed on *Wednesday 19 August*. If true, they should have been undertaken at an earlier date if Wednesday had indeed been set as the target day.
- There is no evidence – certainly *no* claim in the CIA's internal history – that any CIA money was disbursed for crowd manipulation *or any other purpose* after the failure of TPAJAX. The claim in existing literature that the two principal Iranian CIA agents were given $50,000 on 16 August or any date after that for crowd mobilization, for grey or black propaganda, or a *Tudeh* smearing campaign is not supported by evidence at hand and must be deemed bogus.
- The contents of Roosevelt's communications with Washington are inconsistent with the attitude of someone who had planned a second strike. He did not request *any* extension of his mission – something that would have been natural if he had had plans for Wednesday. Instead, he opined that Mosaddeq's position had been fortified for the time being and inquired from Washington if the operations should be called off. In a separate cable, he asked for exfiltration of 15 unnamed individuals.
- This study independently confirms the existence of a hate-mail campaign to scare and alienate clerics in the period prior to the TPAJAX *coup* on 15 August. The study is more circumspect about claims by the

Iranian agents of the CIA to have faked the *Tudeh* crowds – notably in the days following the *coup* failure – in an attempt to smear the *Tudeh* Party. The study maintains that the two principal CIA agents, Kayvani and Jalali, were manipulating a network comprising small fascist and ultra-nationalist gangs and possibly a few mobsters, who systematically harassed the *Tudeh* crowds rather than faking them. The full size of the network did not exceed a few hundred individuals whose faces were known to security authorities as well as to *Tudeh* cadres. The *Tudeh* leader Kianouri has flatly denied the existence of fake *Tudeh* in their ranks during that episode. His denial came some forty years later, in reaction to specific claims in existing American literature about fake *Tudeh* moves in the days prior to the fall of the Mosaddeq government. We noted in this connection that Kianouri had strong personal reasons to confirm, even aggrandize, the *fake Tudeh* phenomenon to shield himself from criticism levelled against him by his *Tudeh* peers for his role within the party leadership during that episode.

- A careful examination of *Overthrow* shows a high degree of reticence in crediting the activities of the CIA field station in Tehran for the final outcome, in preference to internal dynamics. Specific citations from *Overthrow* to this effect, has been provided in relevant passages of this volume. The way they are detailed in the CIA narrative, these activities could essentially be characterized as support and backstopping in nature. Some may have produced an enhanced visual effect of an existing condition such as the *Tudeh* animosity for clerics.

- In his secret evaluation of the event submitted to Washington on 20 August 1953, Ambassador Henderson goes to great length to elucidate the causes of Mosaddeq's downfall; yet there is no modicum of a hint that the event may have been linked to or in any way the result of foreign meddling. Likewise, in his succinct report of the event to Eisenhower, the Acting CIA director *claims no credit* whatsoever, even if the downfall of Mosaddeq was what the administration had meticulously planned for.

- Finally, it bears repetition here that according to his biographer, President Eisenhower judged Roosevelt a fabulist when he finally heard his debriefing. Furthermore, in his earlier pronouncements – that is to say prior to the publication of his book *Countercoup* in 1979 – Kim Roosevelt had appeared less assuming, attributing, as it were, the lion's share of credit to internal factors, while citing the incredibly modest sum of $10,000 for expenses of the entire TPAJAX operation.

11. Limited in scope and impact as the CIA activities in the crucial four days were, the fact that they existed caused an optical illusion; they helped create an impression that the CIA had concocted the overthrow on 19 August as a follow-up to its earlier *coup*. Such claims were hard to contradict even by American field staff, as the nexus between those activities and the outcome could never be established or denied. Washington and London took things at face value. Their intelligence organs were too eager to score points; no one was willing to pick on success. Iranians of all persuasions took the bait: According to a deep-seated societal credo, nothing of significance could ever happen in Iran without a foreign hand – as was noted earlier.

12. The issue of an organic link between the TPAJAX *coup* of 15 August and the fall of Mosaddeq on 19 August was carefully examined *from a military angle*. Some passages from *Overthrow* imply that officers originally earmarked for the 15 August *coup* – and still at large – might have participated in the revolt against Mosaddeq on Wednesday 19 August. While deemed plausible, our study did not find any evidence of an organic link between the TPAJAX *coup* and the participation of some officers and military units in the events that led to the downfall of Mosaddeq on 19 August; the study, accordingly, does not sanction such a hypothesis. The *Overthrow* narrative in this connection was scrutinized and its fallacies discussed under 'The Backlash' in Chapter 5.

13. This study found that a nucleus of revolt among the line officers in the Tehran garrison already existed before CIA/SIS developed their plan for the *coup* of 15 August. The TPAJAX planners did not bribe or recruit anyone from within the Iranian army; they harvested gratuitously what already was in place and managed to establish loose links with this group of officers through a liaison mechanism. This mechanism was dismantled when the TPAJAX *coup* failed on the night of 15 to 16 August. By its own admission, neither the CIA station in Tehran nor the Zahedi camp knew the identities of, and had no means of communication with, those among this group of officers who had remained at large. Any participation by such officers/units in the riotous events that resulted in the downfall on 19 August should therefore be considered unpremeditated.

14. Prior to establishing contact with the leaders of these officers in early August, the TPAJAX planners had planned their *coup* on the basis of flawed intelligence. It was the Iranian network that saved them from a premature fiasco (see under 'The Military Factor in the Fall of Mosaddeq' in Chapter 5). This is not to say that the officers who participated in the

revolt had not been influenced by the general climate that reigned following the departure of the Shah and the ensuing chaos, including the psychological warfare waged against Mosaddeq. In this latter category of activities the CIA station in Tehran had played a role.

15. To complete the survey of all evidence related to foreign plots and manipulation in relation to the fall of Mosaddeq, the study has delved into a top secret document of British origin drafted only two weeks after the fall of Mosaddeq. While this document contained good intelligence on peripheral issues occurring prior to the TPAJAX *coup*, it is seriously flawed on the main lines related to the subject matter of this study. In all likelihood, the secret document reflected in part a debriefing by Roosevelt, who was in London about the time the document was prepared. This appears, notably, to be the case in respect of occurrences following the failure of the TPAJAX *coup* on 16 August. A detailed analysis of its content can be found under 'An Orphan British Secret Document' in Chapter 6.

The involvement of *ulama*

1. If the street commotions on Wednesday 19 August were *not* choreographed by the CIA, does it follow that they were spontaneous manifestations of revolt by a segment of opinion in Iran? The study does not subscribe to this hypothesis either. To be sure, a segment of opinion was disillusioned, some were dismayed by the turn of events; among them the Shah had genuine support. Yet the study maintains that the uprising was *sparked* by religious leaders, probably as a first warning shot in an upcoming confrontation with Mosaddeq. This does not suggest that the clerics had planned a fatal stroke on that day or the crowds they amassed were tasked to overthrow the government. The evidence regarding the precise role played by top clerics remains circumstantial; it may, as such, be seen as interpretative or deductive. But the *analytical* assumptions made rely on a body of hard facts; the cumulative evidence is compelling. The gist could be summarized as follows:

- The study retraced landmarks in Iran's recent past where the clerics changed the course of history ('The Ulama as a Socio-Political Force' in Chapter 1). Their influence on the masses and their rabble-rousing capacity cannot be overstated.
- In Chapter 4, 'The Clash at the Helm' and 'The Grand Ayatollah Boroujerdi' together with 'The Missing Link' in Chapter 7 underscore the perennial link between the Shiite establishment and the Iranian

monarchy. There we dwelled on reasons why the Shiite hierarchy in Qom and some of the top clerics in the provinces had became alarmed by the course of events of February 1953. To them the removal of the Shah spelled secularism of the Turkish variety, not to say outright atheism if at the end of the road the communist *Tudeh* gained the upper hand. The evidence provided suggests that as of that date the two main tendencies within the clerical establishment in Iran, namely the activist faction headed by Kashani and the more influential quietist strain led by Grand Ayatollah Boroujerdi, tacitly coalesced, even if their style and public posturing radically diverged. For different reasons, they had concluded that the course Mosaddeq had embarked on portended a threat to Islam and/or to their own socio-political standing.

- The study concludes that the top Shiite leader Boroujerdi, who, already in the previous February (*noh'e esfand*) had acted to prevent the Shah's trip abroad, again intervened when the Shah left Iran on 16 August. The cacophony about a republic that followed the Shah's flight was indeed the clincher; it unleashed forces which only the clerics were capable of delivering. Ayatollah Behbehani, a clerical figure widely recognized as having played a pivotal role in mobilizing crowds, was quintessentially linked to Qom and would not have taken initiatives of his own without the full consent of Boroujerdi at a time when the return of the Shah was generally deemed improbable. The study reveals the terms of a succinct pro-Shah opinion issued by the Grand Ayatollah Boroujerdi following the departure of the Shah on 16 August. The CIA account also refers, albeit in oblique terms, to rumours of Boroujerdi's intervention and *fatwa*. For his part, Ardeshir Zahedi, a key player in that episode, emphatically confirmed the role played by Boroujerdi (discussed under 'The Missing Link' in Chapter 7). In the same vein, the victory of pro-monarchy forces was heartily hailed by Boroujerdi and the clerical establishment.

The causes of Mosaddeq's defeat

1. Ignited by religious leaders, the event on 19 August succeeded through a confluence of disgruntled military and civilian crowds of diverse profiles and motivations; present among them were some notorious underworld figures but also many ordinary citizens. The blend was toxic and dealt the final blow. The most important factor in the government's defeat was the fact that the security forces dispatched to quell the riots and disperse the crowds refused to do so; some even joined them.

From early afternoon, some armoured units from the outlying military barracks joined the crowed, making the trend irreversible. Unlike the usual pattern observed in military *coups d'état* elsewhere, in which military units intervene at dawn to secure strategic localities and pre-empt resistance, armed units on that day did not come onto the scene before early afternoon, by which time crowds had already paved the ground for a final blow. Later the *Tudeh* leader Kianouri referred to this reality in order to explain why his party was caught off guard in spite of its vast military network.

2. In retrospect, strategic misjudgements by Mosaddeq led him astray and brought upon him a defeat he had not deserved. A dearth of realism, laxity about power structure in Iran, insufficient understanding of Cold War politics and oil market forces, coupled with a perfectionist attitude towards the resolution of the oil crisis, aligned internal and external forces and made his downfall a matter of time. His quest to reform institutions along unadaptable Western lines against the backdrop of an oil-less economy, and confrontation with the superpower that Britain still was in those times, was quixotic. His moves to divest the Shah of all vestiges of power and prestige were short-sighted and could only have fostered instability in the longer run, independent of events of August 1953. A monarchy reduced to ceremonial functions is no doubt a hallmark of a people's sovereignty in advanced democracies, but for the Iran of the 1950s it was a recipe for chaos and instability. Between 1951 and 1970, close to 40 military *coups d'état* took place in all continents across the globe. None of Iran's immediate neighbours (including eventually the USSR) was spared. While the Shah's presence and his role as commander-in-chief of the armed forces was no safeguard *per se* against militarist or communist *coup* attempts, his drastically reduced prestige or total absence of power fostered such eventualities. It is not excessive to postulate that the humiliation that the Shah suffered during Mosaddeq's tenure prodded him to opt for an authoritarian rule following Mosaddeq's overthrow.

3. Characteristically, American officials viewed Mosaddeq and his nationalistic enterprise through the prism of the cold war. The Eisenhower administration had a poor understanding of Iran and its body politic. Anxieties about communism and an inevitable or impending takeover by *Tudeh* bordered paranoia even if it was not totally unfounded. While the post-Stalin leadership in Moscow was certainly disinclined to engage in an existential face-off with America over Iran, opportunistic and low-risk adventurism or mere miscalculations by the

Kremlin could not be excluded. The study concluded that after the flight of the Shah on 16 August, the *Tudeh* Party moved into a higher gear for power sharing. The scenario which unfolded some 20 years later in Afghanistan inevitably flashes though the mind, although drawing such parallels remains speculative and conjectural.

4. The overthrow on 19 August had essentially an indigenous character and resulted from Iran's internal dynamics although, viewed from a different angle, the chain of events emanating from the Shah's flight a few days earlier links the downfall inexorably to the TPAJAX plot. To the extent that the failure of the TPAJAX *coup* in the early hours of 16 August triggered the Shah's flight, one could indeed establish a direct *lineage* between the Anglo-American plan and the downfall of Mosaddeq on 19 August. The TPAJAX failure set off a chain of events which led to the downfall. In other words, the CIA indeed had a role in the Mosaddeq overthrow, but mainly by default.

5. The TPAJAX plot was an inappropriate intrusion into Iran's politics that marred America's image, especially among informed opinion in Iran. Yet that meddling was never the cause or in any way related to the hostility that the Islamic Republic of Iran harbours against the United States, and has displayed since its inception in 1979. It is possible to trace an ideological lineage, linking the post-war clerical militancy to the Islamic revolution (1978–79). Activist clerics of the period, including the future leader of the Islamic Revolution, Ayatollah Khomeini, invariably opposed Mosaddeq. If anything, in that chapter of Iran's history the clerical establishment was complicit. After the success of the Islamic Revolution the by-then-defunct Ayatollah Kashani became an iconic and venerated figure among the revolutionaries. So were the *Fadā'iān* who were sanctified as martyrs. These actors had played a crucial role in Mosaddeq's defeat.

6. Mosaddeq was not humiliated by that defeat; he became a legend. To this day – perhaps more in future – Iranians of all generations proudly cherish his memory and laud his accomplishments. He certainly deserves great praise, unvarnished by the hero worshipping and adulations characteristic of his unconditional supporters that at times, alas, touches on apotheosis.

Notes

Preface

1. William Roger Louis, 'Britain and the Overthrow of the Mosaddeq Government', in Mark Gasiorowski and Malcolm Byrne (eds), *Mohammad Mosaddeq and the 1953 Coup in Iran* (New York: Syracuse University Press, 2004), p. 126.
2. Kermit was the grandson of President Theodor Roosevelt; his account of the events was narrated in his book, *Countercoup: The Struggle for the Control of Iran* (New York: McGraw-Hill, 1979).
3. This CIA internal report, entitled *'Clandestine Service History; Overthrow of Premier Mossadeq [sic] of Iran, November 1952–August 1953'* (hereinafter referred to as *Overthrow*). The author is Donald Wilber who, as Iran point-man at CIA headquarters in Washington, had a hand in the drafting of the *coup* plot against Mosaddeq codenamed TPAJAX. He was not, however, in Iran at the time of the events in August 1953.

Introduction

1. On 13 March 1983, commemorating the twenty-first anniversary of the death of Ayatollah Kashani, Iran's parliamentary Speaker, later President, Ali-Akbar Hashemi-Rafsanjani made the following statement: 'We honour the memory of the exalted Ayatollah Kashani and request the Iranian nation to participate in the commemoration ceremonies that will be held tomorrow and in the following days; on the same occasion we should express indignation over the injustice done to him and to the Islamic movement by the nationalists [i.e., the Mosaddeq supporters] and the blow inflicted by them on the Islamic movement in one episode in Iran's history. On this historical day, we express our sorrow to his honourable family and to the Iranian nation and celebrate the life of this great man.' See, Hashemi-Rafsanjani and Sara Lahooti, *Omid va Delvāpasi, kārnameh va khāterāt'e Hashemi Rafsanjani, sāl'e 1364* (*Hope and Preoccupation, the Balance-Sheet and Memoirs of Hashemi-Rafsanjani, year 1364/1985*), (Tehran: Daftar'e Nashr'e Ma'āref'e Eslami publishers, 2008), p. 446 fn.
2. The Doctrine enunciated in Guam on 25 July 1969 by Richard Nixon stated that the United States, while respecting its security commitments would henceforth expect its allies to take care of their own military defence. The Doctrine argued for pursuit of peace through a partnership with American allies. The doctrine permitted the Shah to pursue a highly ambitious armament procurement programme and to expand his power and influence, notably in the Persian Gulf region.
3. In James Bill's *The Eagle and the Lion: The Tragedy of American-Iranian Relations* (New Haven, CT: Yale University Press, 1988), we read: 'This direct

covert operation left a running wound that bled for twenty-five years and contaminated America's relations with the Islamic Republic of Iran following the revolution of 1978–79', p. 86.
4. A case in point is Stephen Kinzer's *All the Shah's Men* (Hoboken, NJ, John Wiley & Son, 2003).
5. A Tom Seligson and Susan Werbe CBS News production for History Channel cable TV, 2000, hosted by Arthur Kent.
6. For the full text, see <http://www.fas.org/news/iran/2000/000317.htm>, retrieved in May 2007.
7. Kermit Roosevelt, *Countercoup: The Struggle for the Control of Iran* (New York: McGraw-Hill, 1979), ch. 12.
8. 'Moscow Says U. S. Aided Shah's Coup', *The New York Times*, 20 August 1953.
9. Foreign Relations of the United States, [FRUS] 1952–54, vol. X, Iran, document 351, p. 759.
10. Woodhouse wrote in his autobiography (*Something Ventured*, p. 122) that in 1954 the CIA took active steps publicizing its role in the August 1953 events in Iran.
11. Richard Cottam, *Nationalism in Iran* (Pittsburgh: Pittsburgh University Press, 1964), ch. XIII. Richard Cottam (1925–1997) had studied in Tehran as a Fulbright scholar before a stint at the American Embassy in Tehran (probably with the CIA station) in the mid-1950s. He subsequently joined the faculty of Pittsburgh University and in 1964 published his magnum opus *'Nationalism in Iran'*. Thenceforth he was recognized not just as an Iran expert, but as a beacon in American academia speaking on behalf of the pro-Mosaddeq opposition. He became a vocal critic of the American foreign policy that had cast its lot with the Shah. He befriended some of the exiled activists including two of the icons of the Islamic Revolution, Sadeq Qotb'zadeh and Ibrahim Yazdi; see his obituaries in <http://www.pitt.edu/utimes/issues/30/091197/04.html>.
12. Reference to this article, entitled 'Imperial Regime in Iran: Why it Collapsed' in *l'Iran d'Hier et Demain*, is taken from a citation by Nikkie Keddie in *Roots of Revolution* (Yale University press, New Haven, 1981), p. 289. In the article referred to by Keddie (as in his subsequent works, *Khomeini: The Future and U.S. Options* in 1987 and *Iran and the United States: A Cold War Case Study* in 1988), Cottam reversed his earlier assessment of the events in August 1953. The extent to which he might have been influenced by Roosevelt's *Countercoup* published in 1979 and/or by his own image as a leading advocate in American academia of Iran's nationalist aspirations is hard to assess.
13. *The Invisible Government* (New York: Random House, 1964).
14. Roosevelt first hinted at his project in a handwritten letter to the Shah when he was in Tehran in February 1976 in connection with his business lobbying for Northrop. He had not obtained an audience from the Shah, but was received by Court-Minister Alam through whom he submitted a letter to the Shah. Characteristically, he was less than candid when he casually raised the subject of his memoirs. He linked it to his wartime experiences with the Office of Strategic Services (CIA's precursor), adding, that he had been asked by 'several publishers' to write about his *'various post-war activities in related fields'*. Roosevelt added he did not want to make any decision before *'discussing it with, and receiving guidance from, Your Majesty'*. In August,

Alam reported to the Shah that Roosevelt was trying to get his memoirs, which he characterized as a 'complete load of nonsense', published. Alam entered the following words in his 18 August log, *'HIM was amused, instructing me to do as I see fit'*. It was only when Alam read the manuscript in May 1977 and reported that Roosevelt was portraying the Shah as a *'waverer forced into various crucial decisions'* that the Shah agreed with his minister that they should try to prevent its publication. See, Alinaghi Alikhani, (ed.) *The Shah and I: The Confidential Diary of Iran's Royal Court, 1969–97 Asadollah Alam* (London: I. B. Tauris, 1991), pp. 502 and 540. For a reproduction of Roosevelt's handwritten letter of 11 February 1976 to the Shah, see Volume 5 of Alam's diaries in the Persian language, edited by Alikhani, published by IBEX in the US and Ketabsara in Tehran; pp. 496–97 in the latter edition.
15. Roosevelt, *Countercoup*, see the (unnumbered) Foreword.
16. Ibid., 207; Wilber, *Overthrow*, ch. IX, p. 81.
17. Stephen Ambrose, *Eisenhower*, vol. II, *The President* (New York: Simon & Schuster, 1984), p. 129 n. 73, p. 685. The Eisenhower biographer says that the president was reluctant about seeing Roosevelt publicly. Roosevelt puts the date of his White House debriefing as 4 September, contradicted by Ambrose. What's more to the point is that Eisenhower appears to have assessed Roosevelt as a fabulist.
18. For the way Major-General Sir Alexander Sinclair greeted Roosevelt's debriefing, see the CIA internal history in Wilber, *Overthrow*, ch. IX 'Report to London', pp. 78–85. For the Foreign Office attitude towards MI6, see several references in Woodhouse's autobiography, *Something Ventured* (pp. 106–23) and Chapter 4, section 'The link-up: TPAJAX and the internal cabal' as well as Chapter 6 in this volume.
19. The four broad tasks assigned to the Agency under its 1947 statute were: To advise the NSC on matters related to national security; to make recommendations to the NSC regarding the coordination of intelligence activities of the Departments of State and Defense; to correlate and evaluate intelligence; and provide for its appropriate dissemination. Finally, the agency was to perform such other functions as the NSC will from time to time direct it to undertake. In spite of some improvement in 1952, inter-departmental rivalries continued to impede the CIA from playing a direct role in intelligence gathering and clandestine operations. This was the main reason why the CIA needed to show gains to boost its clandestine action potential. It is not farfetched to assume that material in articles and books published on the CIA in the USA was being deliberately leaked by Agency officials for this purpose. See also note 23 below.
20. Woodhouse, 1982: 122. For his part, Richard Helms reportedly admitted in an interview with the BBC that in the immediate aftermath of the Bay of Pigs disaster in 1961, the CIA exaggerated its role in the overthrow of Mosaddeq because it needed feathers in its cap. Quoted by Ardeshir Zahedi, *Khāterāt'e Ardeshir Zahedi (Ardeshir Zahedi's Memoirs)*, Vol. I (Maryland: IBEX, 2006), p. 269.
21. The National Security Archive filed a lawsuit in 1999.
22. See the National Archive Electronic Briefing Book no. 28 at the following link: <http://www.gwu.edu/~nsarchiv/NSAEBB/NSAEBB28/>.

23. According to an account given to this author by a credible source, the report may have been found among personal belongings of its author Donald Wilber who died in 1997. This version does not explain why the document was given away three years after Wilber's death, presumably by relatives.
24. The declassified CIA records are hosted on the *CIA Records Search Tool* (CREST), which is an electronic search and retrieval system. CREST now includes more than 10 million pages of records declassified under Executive Order 12958.

1 The Context

1. The term was familiar in pre-Revolution Iran political vocabulary. It referred to the ruling class, reputed to be interlinked through marriage and/or blood kinships. It was comprised of old *Qājār* aristocracy and officialdom as well as landed bourgeois families. Almost all known political figures and persons in the top echelon of government bureaucracy belonged to this group. Under Reza Shah, the group had lost part of its prominence without being totally sidelined.
2. For an excellent study of this period, see Ervand Abrahamian, *Iran between Two Revolutions* ((New Jersey: Princeton, 1983), pp.169–267.
3. Seventy per cent of the population lived in rural areas; 0.2 per cent of the population possessed 33 per cent of cultivable land., see Mohammad G. Majd, 'Reform Policies in Iran', *American Journal of Agricultural Economics*, Vol. 69, No. 4 (Nov., 1987), pp. 843–8; Mohammad Reza Pahlavi, *Pāsokh be Tārīkh* (*Answer to History*), (privately published in 'Imprimerie Aubin', France, 1980), p. 1
4. They were: Mohammad-Ali Forouqi (27 Aug. 1941–9 March 1942); Ali Sohayli (9 Mar.–9 August 1942); Ahmad Qavam (9 Aug. 1942–15 Feb. 1943); Ali Sohayli (2nd mandate, Feb. 1943–6 Apr. 1944); Mohammad Sa'ed-Maraqe'i (6 Apr.–25 Nov. 1944); Mortezaqoli Bayat (Dec. 1944–May 1945); Ebrahim Hakimi (May 1945–June 1945); Mohsen Sadr (July–Oct. 1945); Ebrahim Hakimi (2nd mandate Oct. 1945–Jan. 1946); Ahmad Qavam (2nd mandate, 27 Jan. 1946–Oct. 1947); Ebrahim Hakimi (3nd mandate, Oct. 1947–June 1948); Abdol'hossein Hazhir (17 June 1948–1 Nov. 1949); Mohammad Sa'ed (2nd mandate, Nov. 1949–Apr. 1950); Ali Mansour (Apr. 1950–25 June 1950); Ali Razmara (June 1950–7 Mar. 7 1951); Hossein Ala (Mar. 1951–26 Apr. 1951).
5. For the text, see Sir Percy Sykes, *A History of Persia*, Vol. II (Basingstoke: Macmillan, 1963), pp. 410–12.
6. This party was created by a cleric named Sheikh Mohammad Khiabani, who established an autonomous government in Azerbaijan during the First World War. For a detailed history of the *Tudeh* party and its growth, see: Abrahamian, 1983: 281–325. See also Sepehr Zabih, *Communist Movement in Iran*, (Berkeley: University of California Press, 1966). For a useful account in Persian of the *Tudeh* Party's roots, evolution and activities, see Fuad Rouhani, *Zendegui'e Siāsi Mosaddeq dar Matn'e Nehzat'e melli'e Iran* (*The

Political Biography of Mosaddeq in the Context of the Iranian National Movement), (Paris: 'Nehzat'e Moqāvemat'e Melli, 1366/1987), pp. 5–122. For a well-researched account and review of the background and activities of the *Tudeh* in the French language, see Houshang Nahavandi, *Iran, le Choc des Ambitions* (London: Aquilion, 2006), pp. 125–52.

7. The main figure in the group, Dr Taqi Arani, died in hospital in 1939 under suspicious circumstances. Others were released upon the Allied occupation of Iran in 1941. Among them, 18 withdrew from political life while the rest joined the *Tudeh* Party (Abrahamian, 1983: 158–61).

8. Since the second Comintern in 1920, the dominant trend in both the USSR and Iran was that non-industrialized Moslem societies should take account of the local conditions and privilege pragmatism over ideological purity. The *Tudeh* founders also believed the communist label would reduce the party's appeal among social-democrats, the less indoctrinated members of the intelligentsia, and Moslem masses. Finally, they were mindful of the still unrescinded legislation promulgated by Reza Shah that banned communist ideology.

9. The *Tudeh* Military wing was discovered in 1954. It comprised some 500 officers, of whom 466 were arrested and prosecuted. In all, 27 *Tudeh* officers were executed. This included Khosro Rouzbeh who – seemingly unbeknown to the *Tudeh* leadership – had committed several politically motivated acts of murder during the 1940s). The rest received prison terms. All were released within a few years and helped to reintegrate. While in prison, their salaries were paid to their families; for this latter point, see Morteza Zarbakhat and Hamid Ahmadi, *Khāterāti az Sāzemān'e Afsarān'e Hezb'e Tudeh Iran* (*Recollections from the Military Organization of the Tudeh Party of Iran*), (Tehran: Qoqnous Publishers, 2004), p. 241.

10. The Trilateral Accord was signed by the USSR, UK and Iran on 29 January 1942.

11. Assertion by some American scholars (among several others, Keddie, 2003: 112) to the effect that the referral of the matter to the UN was with American encouragement is not supported by archive documents. The initial American attitude was to resolve the problem through the tripartite arrangement proposed by Bevin, see the record of the Iranian Ambassador's talk with Henderson (at the time director of NEA at the State Department), *Foreign Relations of the United States* (FRUS), *Near-East and North Africa*, 1946, Vol. VII, *Iran* (Washington: United States Printing Office, 1970), pp. 295–8. At the Moscow Conference late in 1945, Bevin proposed a tripartite UK, USSR, USA commission, rather than the UN to tackle the Azerbaijan Crisis. The Russians eventually rejected this idea.] Once the US realized that Qavam was tempted to cede to Soviet pressure to withdraw Iran's complaint in February/March 1946, the US played a more proactive and supportive role. For the British attitude related to tripartite commission (see FRUS 1946, Vol. VII, pp. 299–301).

12. Byrnes's speech at the Overseas Press Club, New York, *The New York Times*, 9 March, 1946. Note that in his memoirs President Truman claimed he issued an ultimatum to Stalin to withdraw, of which no trace could later be found in the State or Defense Department files. (This point was underscored by the author in a study of the Azerbaijan Crisis in 1971 for Columbia

University/SIA, to which he no longer has access, but the point about the Truman memoirs was highlighted in the printed edition of FRUS 1946, vol. VII).
13. Soviet troops evacuated Iran under pressure from the US and the Security Council but also because Qavam's oil concession was an attractive spin-off to Stalin. Unlike the zealous Soviet Azerbaijan boss, Mir-Jaafar Baqerov, who dreamed of annexing the Iranian Azerbaijan, Stalin was not keen to risk confrontations with the West. For some insights on the role of Baqerov, see Kianouri, *Khāterāt'e Noureddin Kianouri (Kianouri Memoirs)*, (Tehran: Moasseseh'e tahqiqāti va entesharāti 'e Didgah, 1371/1992), pp. 121–5. The oil concession by Qavam fell through, however, when it was presented to the *Majles* (fifteenth session) for ratification. On Mossadeq's initiative, an earlier session of the Parliament (the fourteenth session) had passed legislation forbidding governments to grant oil concessions to foreigners without the express approval of *Majles*. Deputies used this legislation to vote down Qavam's concession to Stalin.
14. The Iranian government went as far as declaring the British Consul-General in Ahvaz, A. C. Trott, *persona non grata*. The British vehemently denied their involvement and evidence remains circumstantial. See also note 19 below.
15. See, FRUS 1946, Vol. VII, pp. 517–18.
16. See, Fuad Rouhani, citing memoirs of Anvar Khameh'ei (a leftist intellectual and prominent member of *Tudeh* who later joined the splinter group led by Khalil Malaki), 1987: 113.
17. Keddie, 2003:.113; according to Abrahamian, 1983: 174, Sheikh Jasseb the elder son of Khaz'al had returned to Iran in 1942 and convened a meeting of (Iranian) Arab Sheikhs making noises about independence of the 'Emirate of Arabestan'; see also Nahavandi, 2006: 162.
18. The cable traffic between the US Embassy in Tehran and the State Department in September–October 1946 (FRUS 1946, Vol. VII) reveals the serious nature of the risk of dismemberment of the north and south. According to a policy paper prepared by a senior Foreign Office official, Robert Howe, given the events in Azerbaijan and the Russian posture, the disintegration of Iran was inevitable. Howe had recommended a series of measures that would be tantamount to the creation of a breakaway authority in the south with the help of southern tribes. For all practical purposes this scenario was the concretization of the model conceived in the Anglo-Russian division of Iran into two zones of influence in 1907, see William Roger Louis, 1984: 61. While, according to Louis, Foreign Secretary Bevin did not approve the plan, events that took place in the south, known as *fetneh'e jonoub* (or the southern cabal) corresponded closely to the scenario drawn up by Howe. It is conceivable that after the *Tudeh* show of strength in Abadan and Aqājāri in May and June 1946, Bevin's initial reservations were overridden or that local British officials may have acted on their own.
19. The Soviet haste for elections was to get the oil concession ratified by the new *Majles*. Qavam's nod may have been partly for selfish political reasons. By then he had formed a political party and may have reckoned that his supporters would sweep seats in Tehran and most provinces under his complaisant watch.

20. Director of Near-East and Africa Office (Henderson) to Acting Secretary of State Acheson, 15 October 1946, FRUS, Vol. VII, p..534. The passage in Henderson's memo reads: 'It has become clear to our Ambassador and to us that Qavam is virtually a prisoner of his own policies of retreating before Soviet pressure and that Iran is daily losing what remains of its independence.'
21. Qavam had estimated Iranian needs in military and developmental aid at $250 million. The US was prepared to consider a loan by EXPORT/IMPORT bank for $10 million, FRUS 1946, Vol. VII, Ambassador Allen to Secretary of State, 30 September 1946, pp. 518–19.
22. Although no trace of Allen having goaded the Shah could be found in declassified State Department documents, some authors (possibly based on an unpublished manuscript by Allen deposited in the Truman Library) have postulated that Allen in effect encouraged the Shah to confront Qavam and force his hand. See Bruce R. Kuniholm, *The Origins of the Cold War in the Near East*, pp. 324–35, cited in Mostafa Dabiri, *Bohrān'e Azerbaijan* (*The Azerbaijan Crisis*), (Tehran: Parvin Publishers, 1386/2007).
23. Rumours of an impending clash at the top, even a palace *coup*, spread around the town. Qavam, who by then had realized his errors and was discontent with the *Tudeh* ministers' *'truculent'* attitude, did not put up any resistance, especially as the War Minister Amir-Ahmadi warned him that the army would back the Shah in any face-off. See US Ambassador Allen's report to the State Deptartment dated 20 October 1946, FRUS 1946, Vol. VII, pp. 537–8. For army support of the Shah in confronting Qavam, see Amir-Ahmadi, *Khāterāt Nakhostin Sepahpod'e Iran Amir-Ahmad Amir-Ahmadi* (*Memoirs of Iran's First Lieutenant-General Amir-Ahmad Amir-Ahmadi*), (Tehran: Centre for Research and Cultural Studies, 1378/1999), p. 513.
24. Firouz belonged to a top patrician *Qājār* family. His father, Nosrat'dolleh Firouz, was arrested and killed in prison on orders from Reza Shah. His paternal aunt, Mariam Firouz, known as the 'Red Princess', married the future Secretary-General of the *Tudeh* Party, Noureddin Kianouri. In June 1946, Firouz had signed (on Qavam's behalf) an agreement with Pishevari, the leader of the Azerbaijan insurrection, meeting the bulk of their demands. The outstanding issue was the reintegration of rebel officers – many of whom had fled army ranks to join the insurrection – into the Iranian army to which the Shah violently objected. According to a US embassy report of 20 October cited earlier, Qavam pleaded and the Shah agreed that Mozafar Firouz be appointed Ambassador to Moscow.
25. George Allen was instrumental in sensitizing Washington. The US attitude towards the second phase of the Azerbaijan Crisis could be described as initially laid-back. Material support to Iran (financial or military hardware) was next to nil but as a result of vigorous lobbying by Allen, *moral support and encouragement* was finally given in abundance by Washington around late-November; see the cable traffic between mid-October to mid-December 1946 in FRUS 1946, Vol. VII, pp. 520–65. Secretary of State Byrnes recognized Allen's contribution and sent him a citation (ibid., p. 563.
26. Qavam's War Minister, General Amir-Ahmadi recalled in his published memoirs that Qavam was lukewarm and ambiguous about the dispatch of the

army to Azerbaijan and 'when on his majesty's orders the army moved to Zanjan, Qavam went to Lāhijān [a town in the Caspian region where Qavam had a state] pretending he was sick', 1999: 518. (This statement could not be cross-checked for accuracy.) The Shah's preference for military intervention is widely reflected in Allen's reporting to Washington, FRUS, 1946, Vol. VII, May–November.

27. For a vivid account of the liberation of Tabriz and the climate that reigned in the city just before the arrival of government troops, see the report of the US Consul General in Tabriz (Sutten) dated 12 December 1946 (21 Āzar 1325), FRUS 1946, Vol. VII, p. 561.
28. According to some authors, the Azari senior cleric Seyyed Kazem Shariat'madari – who three decades later as a Grand Ayatollah was instrumental in the Islamic revolution – played a part in the Tabriz uprising (see, Nahavandi, 2006: 176). The Shah, on the other hand, was later categorical in denying that religious leaders played any role in the public mobilization, adding that even (the top-ranking Shiite prelate) Boroujerdi, whom he had personally solicited, refused to take a stand. See, Alam diaries, in Alinaqi Alikhani (ed.), *Yāddāsht'hāy'e Alam, sale 1354 (Diaries of Alam 1975–76)*, Vol. 5 (Tehran: Ketabsara Publishers, 1382/2003), p. 477.
29. Qavam's defeat was in part the result of his own manipulative moves to form a political party from heterogeneous political figures often with no genuine loyalty to him. Elections of the fifteenth *Majles* had been held under Qavam's watch and allegedly rigged by him. Some 60 deputies from Qavam's Democratic Party of Iran were elected, while doctor Mosaddeq, the most popular politician in Tehran, was excluded. This did not prevent the *Majles* from voting down his oil deal with Russia in October 1947 and voting him out of office shortly thereafter.
30. The circumstances surrounding this assassination attempt were never fully clarified. The would-be assassin, Nasser Fakhrara'ei, appears to have been a freakish character who had decided on his own to kill the Shah. He had, however, revealed his intention to a *Tudeh* party cadre and the party leadership was accordingly informed. The party secretary Kianouri insists in his memoirs that *Tudeh* had not goaded or in any way helped Fakhrara'ei, 1992: 183–5.
31. A cable from Anthony Eden to the British Minister in Tehran, Sir Reader Bullard, dated 19 September 1941, reflects the British unwillingness to accept the ascension of Mohammad Reza to the throne. In this message Eden clearly states that due to his known pro-German sympathies, the Crown Prince should be prevented from succeeding his father, something that according to Eden would result in continuation of anti-Allied policies by Persia. Eden proposes two alternatives: either one of the younger Pahlavi's (e.g., one of the half-brothers from a Qājār mother] or a restoration of the Qājār dynasty. See Sir Reader Bullard, *Letters From Tehran: A British Ambassador in World War II Persia* (I. B. Tauris, 1991), cited from the book's Persian translation by Mahmoud Toloui: *Pedar va Pesar* (Tehran: Elmi publishers, 1372/1992), p. 521. The British plan to block Mohammad-Reza did not work, due to the political savvy and agility of Iran's then prime minister, Mohammad-Ali Forouqi, (Zoka'olmolk), who speedily arranged the swearing-in ceremony for the Crown Prince on 17 September 1941, thus presenting the Anglo-Russians

with a *fait accompli*. Their envoys refused to attend the parliamentary swearing-in ceremony, prompting the government to retract invitations already sent to the diplomatic corps. The aim was to avoid a public show of displeasure by the occupying powers over Mohammad-Reza's accession to the throne, something that would have compromised the succession. See also the memoirs of General Hussein Fardoust (the childhood friend of the Shah), *Zohour va Soqout'e Saltanat'e Pahlavi; Khāterāt'e Arteshbod'e sābeq Hossein Fardoust*. (The Rise and Fall of the Pahlavi Dynasty; Memoirs of ex-General Hossein Fardoust), (Tehran: Tehran Political Research Institute, 1369/1990), Vol. 1, pp. 100–1. Fardoust claims that he acted as intermediary with the British Embassy on behalf of Mohammad Reza, but the Embassy had the details of the Shah's daily routine, including the fact that he listened to foreign broadcasts in three languages and had a war map on his wall, carefully tracing *Wehrmacht's* advances in the war front. Note that the Fardoust memoirs were published in Tehran after the Revolution under censorship and duress, and its contents must be viewed with caution. Part of the British hesitation about Mohammad-Reza may be related to a genuine British preference, at that point in time, for restoration of the Qājār dynasty. British exploratory contacts with the Qājār Prince Hamid Mirza had revealed little enthusiasm on the latter's part, compounded by his inability to speak the Persian language (Nahavandi, 2006: 115); Farmanfarmaian suggests that Bullard had offered the crown to another Qājār prince, Sarem'odolleh; see Manucher and Roxane Farmanfarmaian, *Blood & Oil: Memoirs of a Persian Prince* (New York: Random House, 1997), ch. VIII, in the Persian translation by Mehdi Haqiqat-Khah (Tehran, 1377/1999), p. 170.
32. Abrahamian, 2003: 176; Toloui, 1992: 516–20.
33. Asadollah Rashidian, a British agent who played a significant role in Britain's sapping efforts against Mosaddeq and was involved in the TPAJAX *coup*, had entrée to the Shah's Court in spite of the fact that he formally presented himself to the Shah as the agent and mouthpiece of the British government in early August 1953 (see Chapter 4 under the title 'infra'). There is little doubt that the Shah knew about the affiliation of this family with the British Embassy even before that date. Asadollah's father, Qodratollah, had spent many years in prison during the reign of the Shah's father who, unlike his son, had no tolerance for foreign agents. Another case is Soleiman Behboudi, head of the Shah's household and a veteran courtier, who is identified as a British agent in the CIA internal report; see the CIA internal report by Wilber, '*Overthrow*', 2000: 23. There are grounds to believe that the Shah must have known at least of Behboud's close – if not organic – links with British officials. Further, reminiscing for the *Harvard Oral History Project*, Dr Mozafar Baqa'ei recalled that at one point the Shah had told him that Qaem-maqam Rafiee, at the time a *Majles* deputy, was indeed a British agent (no independent verification could be made). Baqa'ei was surprised to see that the deputy was later appointed senator by the Shah after Mosaddeq's fall, recollections recorded by Habib Ladjvardi: <http://www.fas.harvard.edu/~iohp/middleton2.html> tape 17.

34. The Shah had made two known attempts to make Mosaddeq accept premiership. The first was in early 1945. In his published memoirs Mosaddeq acknowledges this offer and explains why he brought up excuses to decline it. See Iraj Afshar (ed.), *Khāterāt'e va Ta'alomāt* (*Recollections and Sorrows*), (Tehran: Elmi Publisher, 1365/1986), pp.133–8). The second attempt – also confirmed by Mosaddeq – was in early 1951, ibid.: 176–8; see also Toloui, 1992: 633–5. Jalal Matini, *negāhi be kārnāmeh'e sīasi doctor mohammad mosaddeq* (A Glance at the Political Balance-Sheet of Dr. Mohammad Mosaddeq), (*Negāhi be Kār'nāmeh'e Sīsasi doctor Mohammad Mosaddeq* (*A Review of Dr Mohammad Mosaddeq's Political Balance-Sheet*), (Los Angeles: Sherkat Ketāb Publishers, 2005).
35. These emissaries included but were not limited to his Swiss confidant Ernest Perron, his childhood friend Hossein Fardoust, Court Minister Hossein Ala, Deputy Court Minister Ahmad Houman, and Bahram Shahrokh (a shadowy figure who during the Second World War had run the Persian Language broadcasts from Berlin).
36. For the nexus between Sunnite-Shiite rivalry and the Afghan revolt, see Sir Percy Sykes, 1963: 219.
37. Ahmad Ashraf, *Mavāne'e Tārīkhi'e Roshd'e Sarmāyeh-gozāri dar Iran dar doreh'e Qājārieyeh* (*Historical Barriers for Growth of Capital Investment in Iran during the Qājār Period*), (Tehran: Peyyam Publishers, 1359/1980), p. 112; Keddie and Richard, 1981: 21.
38. Accounts of the tobacco boycott are largely chronicled in numerous published studies. For samples, see Ashraf, 1980: 110–12; Keddie-Richard, 1981: 66–7. For a more thorough account in English of bazaar discontent and reaction to the Qajār Shah's economic policies, see Abrahamian, 1983: 58–9.
39. The victorious constitutionalists executed Sheikh Fazlullah Nouri, the leader of the anti-constitutionalist clerical movement. Following the 1979 Islamic Revolution, some 70 years later, he was rehabilitated and glorified.
40. Abrahamian, 1983: 134.
41. Kashani's father was a senior cleric by the name of Seyyed Mostafa who had migrated to Najaf just before the turn of the century. His death, possibly in 1919, took place in circumstances which have not been clarified with precision, but it is presumed he was killed in Shiite protests against the British Mandate over Mesopotamia. Yann Richard, 'Ayatollah Kashani: Precursor of the Islamic Republic?' in Keddie, 1983: 106. For a succinct sketch of Kashani, see Fakhroddin Azimi, 'Unseating Mosaddeq', in Mark Gasiorowski and Malcolm Byrne (eds): *Mohammed Mosaddeq and the 1953 Coup in Iran* (New York: Syracuse University Press, 2004), pp. 56–7.
42. For a folksy account of such interaction, narrated by the notorious mob honcho *Shaban bimokh* (Shaban the brainless), see Homa Sarshar, *Khāterāt'e Shabān Jafary* (Memoirs of Shaban Jafary), (Tehran: Sāles Publishers, 1381/2002), pp. 77–89. Homa Sarshar's laid-back account of Shaban's recollections, supported by an album of photos, provide some interesting insights into activities carried out on the political fringes, apart from enriching Persian-language folk literature.

43. In 1946 *Fadā'iān Islam* assassinated Ahmad Kasravi, a secular intellectual and iconoclast historian (epithet used appropriately by Abrahamian, 1983: 258). Kasravi had been publicly denounced as an apostate and *mahdoum-ul-dam* (liable to be lynched under *Sharia*), notably by the future founder of the Islamic Republic, Rouhullah Khomeini, then a mid-ranking cleric. This happened shortly after the publication in 1945 of Kasravi's essay on *Shiism*. [See Khomeini's statement declaring Kasravi as 'corruptor on earth', cited from Khomeini's book *kashf'al' asrar* by Hamid Ahmadi, in *Tahqiqi darbāreh'e tārikh'e enqelāb'e Iran*, (A Study on the History of Iran's Revolution), (Frankfurt: Enghelāb'e Islami Zeitung, 1380/2001), Vol. II, pp. 658–9. and 653. The charge carries the death penalty in Shiite Islam. *Parcham'e Islam* (*The Banner of Islam*) a daily newspaper, associated with Kashani, became the instrument of Islamist agitations in the immediate aftermath of the assassination. Kashani and Khomeini links are said to go back to the 1930s when Kashani would have arranged the marriage of Khomeini with the daughter of a prominent Shiite scholar (Yann Richard, in Keddie and Richard, 1981: 123). Paradoxically, while Kashani was banished for fomenting religious agitation, the government succumbed to pressure by clerics and freed Kasravi's assassin.
44. See the first two sections of Chapter 4 and the first section of Chapter 6. It bears mentioning here that the Grand Ayatollah strongly disapproved of this radical group and their terrorist methods. Ayatollah Khomeini and one of his closest disciples, Morteza Motahhari (also prominent in the Islamic revolution), fell out with the top Shiite leader because Boroujerdi viewed them as instigators of *Fadā'iān Islam*. See the Montazeri memoirs, pp. 139–44.
45. At the time of the attempt against the Shah's life and in subsequent years conspiracy theories abounded. The British Ambassador in Tehran, Le Rougetel, blamed the *Tudeh* (Louis, 1984: 640). The Shah blamed the British (on flimsy evidence that the would-be-assassin's girlfriend was the daughter of a British Embassy employee). Many, including the Shah himself, suspected the army chief, General Ali Razmara, who became prime minister in 1950 under possible British lobbying. Those who implicate him claim Britain wanted to create a dictatorship through Razmara to resolve the oil issue in a convenient manner. Mohammad Sa'ed, the incumbent prime minister at the time of the assassination attempt against the Shah, later disclaimed responsibility for the arrest of Kashani and a few other personalities which, according to him, had been ordered by Razmara, possibly as a diversion to conceal his own involvement (Tolou'ei, 1992: 605–6). This hypothesis is not backed by any reliable evidence. Like all conspiracy theories, all blame attributions referred to above should be taken with outmost caution.
46. In Qom, the seminary students set up a registry for recruiting volunteers to be sent to the war-fronts in Palestine. See Ayatollah Hossein-Ali Montazeri's memoirs in *Majmoueh'e kāmel'e khāterāt'e Ayatollah Montazeri* (Full Compilation of the Memoirs of Ayatollah Montazeri) at: <http://www.montazeri.com/>, pp. 146–7.
47. For an account of Prime Mister Sa'ed's efforts in relation to Israel and and allegations of bribery, see William Shawcross, *The Shah's Last Ride*

(New York: Simon & Schuster, 1988), pp. 81–2 in the French translation by Françoise Adelstain (édition Stock 1989) In his memoirs, the *Tudeh* Party secretary-general, Kianouri, plausibly argues that the banning of the party in 1949 had more to do with the oil negotiations with Britain (over the Supplemental Oil Agreement) than the failed assassination attempt, which served as an alibi to rid the government of *Tudeh* agitations among oil-workers in the South (Kianouri, 1992: 179). In the same breath, Kianouri opines that Kashani's arrest and banishment was related to Israel and the bribery scheme later alleged by Shawcross.

48. In his autobiography published in his official website in English, the current Supreme Leader of the Islamic Republic of Iran, Ayatollah Ali Khamenei, reveals that he was propelled into activism and militancy inspired by Navvab Sadavi (see <http://www.leader.ir/langs/EN/index.php?p=bio>).

49. Between 1951 and the better part of 1952, *Fadā'iān* turned against Kashani. Khomeini also became critical of Kashani and wrote him a letter expressing disapproval of Kashani's involvement in temporal affairs at the expense of militancy for the rule of Islam (direct quote from Ayatollah Khomeini, cited in Kianouri memoirs, 1992: 254-5; Ahmadi, 2001: 603-4. This changed, however, when Kashani turned against Mosaddeq by year-end. For confirmation of special relations between Khomeini and Kashani, see the memoirs of Montazeri, <http://www.montazeri.com/>, pp. 152–3; see also Yann Richard (Keddie and Richard, 1981: 123) who cites eyewitnesses saying that Khomeini was a frequent visitor to Kashani's house and was there on 31 July, 1953 (1 August) when 'Mosaddeq supporters' attacked Kashani's house. For details of this latter incident, see Kennett Love's piece in *The New York Times* 2 August 1953. For background on Khomeini's early support of *Fadā'iān Islam*, see Hamid Ahmadi, 2001: 653–65. After the Islamic revolution in 1979, *Fadā'iān* leaders – who were executed in 1955 – were sanctified as martyrs of Islam; some of the group's surviving members – including the would-be-assassin of Mosaddeq's closest ally and foreign minister Hossein Fatemi – reached high state positions. The by-then-defunct Ayatollah Kashani became an iconic and venerated figure among the revolutionaries.

50. Yann Richard, in Keddie and Richard, 1981: p.123.

51. One such letter pretends that Kashani, on the eve of Mosaddeq's fall, had warned him of the plots lamenting that the prime minister had not heeded his numerous warnings. For explanations about this forgery, see Ali Qarib, '*Kashani, Mosaddeq, Tafāhomāt va Taqābolāt* (*Kashani and Mosaddeq; Understandings and Confrontations*), available on the web: <http://asre-nou.net:80/1386/mordad/27/m-kashani-mossadegh.html>. Kashani is on record as having called for the death penalty for Mosaddeq following the latter's detention in August 1953. On this latter point, see Yann Richard, in Keddie, 1983: 121.

52. For a spirited eyewitness account of this delirious welcome, see Sarshar, 2002: 80; see also Yann Richard, in Keddie, 1983: 109–10.

53. Mosaddeq read out a message from the Ayatollah in the *Majles* a week after his return, proclaiming that Iranian oil belongs to Iran; cited in Matini, 2005: 211.

54. In a binding resolution dated 21 October, 1947 the fifteenth *Majles* mandated the government, then headed by Qavam, to take appropriate action or enter into negotiations 'to restore Iran's national rights in all cases where the rights of the nation in respect of its national wealth, notably the southern oil resources, have been infringed on'. Qavam's successors (see p. 179n.4), notably Prime Minister Sa'ed, pursued the negotiations with the AIOC. Faustian and myopic, the latter refused meaningful concessions. The country was in dire economic straits as a result of two successive bad harvests. The cabinet gave the treasury minister Abas-Ali Golshayegan full powers to obtain the best terms he could. The latter concluded an agreement on 17 July 1949 which was submitted for ratification to the *Majles*.
55. Iran's Seven-Year Development programme had been budgeted at $650 million. Government had reckoned to obtain some $250 million through loans. Two consecutive bad harvests added to a myriad of difficulties. The main item in the US package of aid was a $10 million loan from EXIMBANK, which was later raised to $25 million with a 3.2 interest rate and foresaw a supervisory role for the US.
56. For the British position on a package of reforms proposed to the Shah and the importance attached to the SOA ratification, see the records of bilateral Anglo-British discussions in London in May 1950, FRUS, Vol.III, p. 988 (working level) and p. 1030 (ministerial).
57. See memorandum of conversation between Iran's Ambassador Ala in Washington and Undersecretary McGhee, 1 May, 1950, FRUS, Vol. V, *Near East*, pp. 536–8.
58. For a vivid account of internal British debate involving, notably, deputy-assistant-secretary of the Foreign Office for the Near-East Michael Wright and Britain's Tehran ambassador, Le Rougetel, on the need for pushing the Shah to appoint a strong prime minister, see Louis, 1984: 632–5.
59. There is no reference in the records of the Acheson-Bevin meeting in London about need for nomination of a *strong prime minister* but, apart from some nuances, the two had identical analyses of the situation in Iran. The American side could not persuade the British negotiators at different levels to be more forthcoming on oil negotiations with Iran and ended up agreeing that the ratification of the SOA was an essential step in the immediate term. For the summery record of the discussion in London on Iran, see FRUS 1950, Vol. III, p. 1030. For reservations of McGhee on SOA, expressed to UK officials, see the record of the 21 September 1950 discussion between Michael Wright and Undersecretary McGhee in the Foreign Office, London, FRUS 1950, Vol. V. pp. 593–5.
60. See the Washington cable to the embassy in Tehran, 22 May 1950, FRUS, Vol. V. 1950, p. 549. For a reference to Dooher's interventions, see Bill, 1988: 52–3.
61. Ambassador Wiley reported on 26 May that the Shah intended to appoint Razmara unless Britain objected! Razamar himself confirmed the Shah's decision and the concern over the British attitude to Dooher (FRUS 1950, Vol. V, p. 558). In an earlier conversation with Wiley, the Shah had referred to the candidacy of Seyyed Zia, rejecting him off-hand as ineffectual (ibid.:

p. 557). From this evidence it could be construed, albeit with due caution, that the UK officials in Tehran may have been lobbying for their favorite Iranian politician, Seyyed Zia, something that was intensified after Razmara's assassination.
62. For the attitude of the British Embassy and Razmara's lobbying, see the British Embassy minutes to the Foreign Office, cited by Abbas Milani, *Eminent Persians: The Men and the Women Who Made Modern Iran, 1941–1979* (Syracuse, NY: Persian World Press, 2008),Vol. I., p. 486.
63. The Shah's criticism angered Washington: it was voiced in an interview with *Reuter* on 27 November 1950, timed to coincide with the departure of Ambassador Grady to Washington for consultations where the latter was expected to take up the US aid package to Iran (FRUS, Vol. V, pp. 618–20). It is not inconceivable, although this is a mere conjecture, that the Shah may have timed his interview to give Grady a boost in his difficult task of persuading Washington to put Iran on the same aid scale as Greece and Turkey. In his memoirs Dean Acheson confirms that Grady was unhappy about the volume of aid the US was willing to dispense (see *Present at the Creation: My Years in the State Department* (New York: W. W. Norton, 1969), p. 502).
64. FRUS, Vol. V, 1950, p. 615 fn. 2. In his book on the Pahlavi dynasty, the Iranian author/translator Mahmoud Tolou'ei cited a relevant passage of Rubin's *Paved with Good Intentions* (of which, incidentally, he is the Persian translator), where Rubin refers to Razmara's disappointment over the EXIM-BANK loan and highlights the government decision to restrict travel freedom for American diplomats (Tolou'ei, 1992: 621–2).
65. Acheson to Grady, 20 November 1950, FRUS 1950, Vol. V, p. 615.
66. Acheson to Grady, November 18, 1950, ibid., pp. 613–15.
67. Razmara may have known some *Tudeh* leaders through his brother-in-law Sadeq Hedayat, a renowned Iranian writer who was a *Tudeh* sympathizer. Razmara was also reputed to have been close to Khosrow Roozbeh, a radical *Tudeh* military officer among the escapees, from his days as a cadet in the Tehran military academy. These were factors that fed rumour-mongering in Tehran's political circles, then, and induced some authors in later years to implicate him in the failed attempt against the Shah's life (e.g., Tolou'ei, 1992: 609–10). There is no evidence or reasonable grounds to lend credence to either accusation.
68. For samples of such public reactions, see Matini, 2005: 222–4. In 1955 Kashani openly admitted that he had issued the *Fatwa* authorizing Razmara's assassination, cited by Matini from *Rouzshomari* (i.e., *The Countdown*), authored by Baqer Aqeli (ibid.: 382).
69. Acting-Secretary James Webb to the embassy in Tehran, doc. 4, 7 March 1951, FRUS, Vol. 10, *Iran*, p. 8.

2 The Advent of Mosaddeq and the Oil Crisis

1. Most authors have projected this move as essentially anti-Shah, implying that the court had rigged the elections. See Abrahamian, 1983: 251; Kinzer, 2003: 69–70; Kenneth M. Pollack, *The Persian Puzzle: The Conflict Between*

Iran and America (New York: Random House, 2005), p. 52. A letter dated 14 October addressed to the Shah by Mosaddeq contradicts this assumption. He wrote, 'For people whose rights are violated and infringed on there is no other recourse but to seek refuge to and beg help from your imperial majesty' (full text cited by Matini, 2005: 205). Recollections by some sit-in participants, such as Makki, Zirakzadeh, Sanjabi and Ahmad Malaki, make it clear that the protesters wished to publicize their cause and had hoped to enlist the Shah's support against the perceived government interference. Zirakzadeh, in making this point, adds: 'The court was neither able nor willing to ensure free elections.' A similar point is made by another participant in the sit-in (and future leader of the National Front), Dr Sanjabi. He writes in his memoirs that the reception at the Court was pretty good and the Shah received and parleyed with Mosaddeq. Then he goes on to say that the real decision-maker then was not the Shah not even the government but the court minister Hazhir who, Sanjabi claims, was connected with foreign interests. See, Karim Sanjabi, *Khāterāt'e doctor Karim Sanjabi* (Memoirs of Dr. Karim Sanjabi); (Seday'e Mo'āser publisher, 1381–2002, Tehran), p.107. According to Makki, for the first two nights of the sit-in the group was treated to sumptuous dinners hosted by the court minister Hazhir. Then the group decided to go on a hunger strike to press for a response to their petition. The official declaration of the group at the end of the inconclusive four-day sit-in, dated 18 October 1949, speaks of a complaint launched *to the Shah* (emphasis added) against government interferences. See, Ahmad Malaki, *Tārīkhcheh'e Jebhe'e Melli* (The History of the National Front); (Stockholm 2005), pp. 4–8.

2. Here again a point of clarification is called for. By law, Prime Minister Sa'ed was unable to cancel polling results and acted through the Supervision Commission which alone was able to do so on the grounds of irregularities. Some authors have wrongly attributed this decision to the Shah.

3. Foreign Secretary Morrison, in the course of a speech before the House of Commons in July 1951, confirmed that the UK had proposed such a deal to Prime Minister Razmara on 10 February 1951 (cited by Mostafa Fateh, *Panjah Sāl Naft (Fifty Years of Oil)*, (Tehran: Kavosh Publishers, 1358/1980), p. 584. Another authoritative source is Fuad Rouhani, 1987: 182–7. For another insider's detailed account of that episode – and confirmation of the 50-50 deal – see Farmanfarmaian, Manucher and Roxane, 1997), Persian translation, pp. 305–6. To be noted that already in 1946 foreign secretary Bevin had toyed with the idea of 50-50 profit sharing when Qavam signed an oil agreement with the USSR, based on that principle (Louis, 1984: 69).

4. Britain quietly agreed to a 50-50 deal for two reasons mainly: firstly, the Truman administration, concerned that political agitation in Iran may benefit the *Tudeh* and by extension the USSR, was pressing Britain for more concessions; officials like McGhee openly supported the equal split of revenue in line with the ARAMCO arrangement concluded with Saudi Arabia on 30 December 1950. The second motive had to do with internal Iranian politics reflected in the *Majles* proceedings. Mosaddeq and other nationalist deputies demanded full and unhindered control of Iran over its oil industries through nationalization or alternatively the cancellation of the 1933 oil agreement, which Mosaddeq argued had been obtained under duress and

hence legally invalid. This agreement would expire in 1993, whereas if cancelled and returned to its predecessor D'Arcy Concession, it would last only to 1963. Legal niceties apart, from a strictly political angle these growing tendencies were galling for Britain and induced it to take a more flexible line. Prime-minister Razmara skilfully played up these leverages. He did not, however, reveal the deal in *Majles* for reasons that remain unclear. Fateh, a well-respected oil expert and historian, attributes this delay to Razmara's desire to find an appropriate opportunity to present this proposal as a triumph to *Majles* thus consolidating his own position (1980: 407).

5. Twelve signatures were necessary for a bill to be receivable and placed on the *Majles* agenda. When Mosaddeq first attempted to place the oil nationalization bill on the *Majles* agenda on 29 November of the previous year, he could not obtain the requisite 12 signatures.
6. The deputy in question was Jamal Emami who later became a cantankerous opposition figure to Mosaddeq. The common assumption is that Emami challenged Mosaddeq to accept the premiership, hoping he would decline. This reasoning is plausible and based on Mosaddeq's own writing; it overlooks, however, a key factual point which has prompted some Iranian biographers and historians to postulate that the Shah actually engineered Mosaddeq's rise to power. In his memoirs, *Khāterāt va Ta'alomāt* (1986: 176–8 and succinctly on p. 362), Mosaddeq recalls that a few days before the assassination of Razmara, the Shah offered him, *through the same deputy*, the position of prime minister, which he declined. Mosaddeq's son, Dr Gholam-Hossein Mosaddeq, in his memoirs, *Dar kenār'e pedaram* (*By the Side of My Father*) confirms the identity of the intermediary as being Jamal Emami (cited by Matini, 2005: 222; Toloui, 1992: 632–3). According to this hypothesis, the Shah's support for Mosaddeq's premiership was in part designed to thwart British pressures for the appointment of the anglophile politician Seyyed Zia'uddin Tabataba'ei as prime minister (see the passage on 'Anglophiles' in Chapter 1 in the present volume, and 'The British two-pronged strategy' in Chapter 3).
7. FRUS 1952–54, Vol, X, *Iran*, doc. 18, p. 46.
8. Acheson to McGhee (then on a visit to Cairo), 28 March 1951, ibid.: 26–7.
9. Zia had led a *coup d'état* in 1921 with the indispensable help of the Shah's father, Colonel Reza Khan, then commander of the Kazak brigade. Shortly thereafter Reza rid himself of Zia and became Iran's strongman leading to the creation of the Pahlavi dynasty in 1925.
10. Many Western observers at the time confused his anti-British campaign, which was central to his nationalist struggle, with xenophobia and hatred. Woodhouse called him a xenophobe, first against the Soviets (in 1944) and then Britain. This accusation is unfounded. As an indication, when Mosaddeq broke off diplomatic relations with Britain he treated the British Chargé George Middleton with outmost civility, to which Middleton himself later testified in his Harvard Oral History Iran project: <http://www.fas.harvard.edu/~iohp/middleton2.html> (interview with Lajvardi, tapes 1 and 2). Abdolhosein Meftah, Mosaddeq's deputy foreign minister, later complained in his memoirs that Mosaddeq, against all norms of diplomatic protocol, ordered him to go to Karaj, then a small town some 50 km outside Tehran, to see Middleton's convoy off, the latter

leaving Iran by road: Meftah's memoirs, *Haqiqat Bi'rangue Ast* (*Truth Has No Colour*) was written in Persian and published in London. A rough mimeographed English translation of these memoirs was examined by this author (pp. 25-6). Mosaddeq had also expressed willingness to keep the AIOC British staff (if they agreed to work under the new Iranian management) and later accepted maintaining the AIOC as bulk purchaser of Iranian oil in an eventual oil settlement. For another such indication, see the report of Henderson's conversation with Mosaddeq, 20 May 1953, FRUS, Vol. X, p. 726. Mosaddeq confirms Iran would welcome friendly relations with UK if the latter abandoned its ambition to dominate Iran.

11. Shepherd to Furlonge, 6 May 1951, cited by Louis, 1984: 652; Woodhouse called him a 'wily, theatrical tragic comic figure', 1982: 106.
12. In his memoirs Dean Acheson observed: 'Another of Mosadeq's [sic] characteristics was his distrust of his own countrymen.' Acheson goes to some length, quoting Harriman and McGhee as well, to explain how Mosaddeq excluded Iranians from his talks with foreigners (Acheson, 1969: 504).
13. In his book Nour-Mohamad Asgari (not a Mosaddeq sympathizer) cites statements made *on record* by two of Mosaddeq's ministers, namely Abdol'ali Lotfi, Minister of Justice, and Dr Ebrahim Alemi, Minister of Labour; they criticized Mosaddeq after his fall for his hot and fluctuating temper (Lotfi) and for dissimulating facts from his cabinet ministers (Alemi). Asgari, *Shah, Mosaddeq, Sepahbod Zahedi* (Stockholm, 2000), pp. 146-50. Other evidence of Mosaddeq having been temperamental is reflected among others in the sixteenth *Majles* proceedings (27 and 29 June 1950) and US archive documents.
14. Since his student days in Paris, Mosaddeq had developed a not well-diagnosed health problem that in his later years effected his sensory organs and produced occasional fainting spells.
15. For a summary of abusive reporting by British diplomats and epithets used to describe Mosaddeq, see Louis, 1984: 135-6.
16. For a thorough intra-cabinet discussion of these issues, see Louis, 1984: 670-90.
17. The arbitration proposal was contained in a note dated 2 May; Mosaddeq rejected this in his response dated 8 May. The 19 May note contained a proposal for direct talks, failing which serious consequences may arise. See Clifton Daniel, *The New York Times*, 20 May 1951; FRUS, Vol. X, doc. 21, pp. 51-2, including the fn. on p. 52.
18. For a detailed account of British war preparations and internal British debate, see Louis, 1984: 672-3.
19. See the summary of the British cabinet decisions shared with the State Department on 21 June 1951, which included the 'use of force if necessary' (FRUS, Vol. X, p. 67 fn.). A year later, Churchill, by then prime minister, looking back at that episode lamented, '*if only a few salvos had been fired, the cabal would have ended there*' (paraphrased from the citation in Persian by Rouhani, 1987: 236).
20. FRUS, Vol. X, p. 56 fn., and pp. 59-61; Rouhani, 1987: 236; Barry Rubin, *Paved with Good Intentions* (Oxford: Oxford University Press, 1980), p. 65; Louis, 1984: 672-3. According to the latter source, the Atlee government

decided to desist from an all-out attack in a cabinet meeting in late July, but kept open the option of occupying and keeping Abadan.
21. Acheson memoirs, 1969: 506.
22. Acheson asked Harriman to arrange a meeting on his hilltop veranda looking down over Potomac with Sir Olivier on 4 July to discuss Iran (ibid.: 507).
23. Louis, in Gasiorowski and Byrne, 2004: 133.
24. For a full and excellent account of the British boycott of Iran's oil, see Mary Ann Heiss, 'International Boycott of Iranian Oil', in Gasiorowski and Byrne, ibid.: 178–200.
25. See, document 32, dated 27 June 1951, entitled: 'Statement of Policy Proposed by The National Security Council', FRUS, Vol X, pp. 71–6.
26. Acheson, 1969: 507.
27. Mosaddeq characterized this as interference by the US in Iran's internal affairs. See FRUS, Vol X, pp. 56–7.
28. As an example among several others, see Memorandum of Secretary's [Acheson] Conversation with the President dated 10 October 1951, doc. 112, ibid., p. 223; and US comments on the World Bank proposal, doc. 134, ibid.,p. 288; see also Heiss, in Gasiorowski and Byrne, 2004: 186.
29. While in New York, Mosaddeq, referring to this constraint, remarked to McGhee that he believed the US government would not ultimately support a settlement that could jeopardize the interests of American oil firms in Venezuela and Saudi Arabia. Mosaddeq had assumed that, as was the case with the British Government, the US had a direct interest in American oil firms. McGhee did not deny the constraint but pointed out that all American firms were strictly private. FRUS, Vol. X, doc. 113, p. 229.
30. Heiss, in Gasiorowski and Byrne, 2004: 187.
31. Acting Secretary Webb to Acheson, November 6, 1951, FRUS, Vol. X, doc.121, p. 260.
32. The Farsi-speaking Dooher, married to an Iranian woman (Zahedi, 2006: 68), was the deputy chief of mission under Ambassadors Allen and Wiley. For his anti-British outbursts, see Farmanfarmaian and Farmanfarmaian, 1997: 287; for the way he arranged regular contacts between embassy staff and National Front politicians, see Kianouri, 1992: 328–9. Dooher was something of an unguided missile, having enjoyed wide latitude when Wiley was ambassador (Bill, 1988: 52–3). He left when Henry Grady arrived in Tehran to become head of the Middle-East division of the Voice of America.
33. Among many sources that have referred to this sympathetic envoy, see Rouhani, 1987: 240–3. Woodhouse (1982: 106) speaks of Grady in a contemptuous tone. For negative British attitude towards him in general, see Louis, 1984: 654. Mostafa Fateh (1980) adds to the list of sympathetic Americans the name of Max Thornburg, a rich oilman who was recruited by Iran and played a key part in developing Iran's first Seven-Year Development Programmme in the late 1940s; he was removed under British pressure.
34. Mc Ghee, other than having married the daughter of Everett De Golyer, a well-known Texas oil baron, was an oil magnet on his own right before he made a highly successful career in foreign affairs.
35. Summary record of McGhee's talks with the UK ambassador in Washington, Olivier Franks, 17 April 1951, FRUS, Vol. X, doc. 12, pp. 30–7; see, in particular, the attachment to this document, pp. 35–6.

36. Louis, citing a British memorandum from Foreign Office records, 1984: 655.
37. For the attitude of the Foreign Office towards McGhee, see *ibid.*: 655–6 and 664.
38. For an example, see the memoirs of the National Front leader Karim Sanjabi, *Khāterāt'e Doctor Karim Sanjabi* (*Memoirs of Dr Karim Sanjabi*) (Tehran: Seday'e Mo'āser Publisher, 1381/2002), p. 113.
39. The first clear signal of this strategy appeared in a background paper that Iran submitted to Averell Harriman in Tehran in July 1951. The report contains a passage which reads, 'Should, as a result of disagreement over the full implementation of the nationalization of the oil industry, the western powers withhold technical assistance to Iran, which would bring oil production to a halt and cause large-scale unemployment among oil workers... the poor, who constitute over 95 per cent of the population would ineluctably gravitate towards communism in spite of their patriotism and religious bonds' (cited by Fuad Rouhani, 1987: 291). For another explicit use of this tactic, see (among many other examples) FRUS, Vol. X, p. 323 f.n. 2. Kim Roosevelt has also attributed this line to Mosaddeq (1979: 151). The emphasis on this point is important since some commentators (e.g., *End of Empire*, BBC film version) have suggested that Britain inculcated this idea in US policy-makers to lure them in the *coup* plot.
40. The pro-Mosaddeq press in Iran constantly highlighted a presumed conflict of interest between the US and the UK, and expressed the opinion that Iran should take full advantage of it for her own ends. Fateh, 1980: 507
41. Mosaddeq's speech in the *Majles*, 11 December 1951. For an audio record of this speech, see the National Front website at link: <http://www.jebhemelli.net/mossadegh/index.html>. Note that Mosaddeq's intuitive remark about the departure of Henry Grady from Tehran was inaccurate, although the British dislike for him was real (Louis, 1984: 654). According to an administrative note printed in FRUS, Vol. X, p. 162, Grady had accepted the assignment to Tehran for one year only. At the end of May 1951, he signalled to Washington that he would want to be relieved by 15 July. He left Tehran on 19 September, coinciding with the failed Stokes mission (see 'Early Conduct of the Oil Dispute' in Chapter 3); he was replaced three days later by Loy Henderson, transferred from his post as ambassador in India. Grady later became a vocal critic of America's siding with Britain in the oil dispute.
42. Years later, the *Tudeh* leadership, which finally abandoned its hostility during the latter part of Mosaddeq's tenure, conceded that the party's earlier analysis of Mosaddeq's nationalist campaign and their own attitude towards his government had been an error. In his memoirs, the party Secretary-General, Kianouri, insists – citing certain evidence – that the Soviet authorities, as opposed to a few Soviet CPSU apparatchiks and Comintern bureaucrats, did not share *Tudeh*'s negative analysis of the Mosaddeq government (1992: 224).
43. Mosaddeq, fearing an attempt against his life, took sanctuary in the *Majles* for two weeks at the outset of his government. For a reference to this threat in British archive documents, see FO371 EP 91460, dated 13 June 1951, cited by two Iranian authors from the original research conducted by Fakhreddin Azimi.

44. Minute by R. C. Zaehner, FO 248 1548, dated 1 March 1952, cited by Ahmadi, 2001: 611–13.
45. For more information on the latter two, see Chapter 3 on the, 'Rift Among Mosaddeq Supporters'.
46. FRUS, Vol. X, p. 46. As stated in a previous passage, the Shah's misgivings were related to potential upheavals, including possible military reaction by Britain. It was equally due to Mosaddeq's desire to curtail the Shah's control over the army and reduce its budget. For confirmation of this latter point, see ibid., p. 50 fn. 2.
47. Barring a hiatus in July 1952, he maintained this position up until late July 1953. When considering a replacement, the Shah favoured someone from Mosaddeq's own circle, notably Allah'yar Saleh. For further details, see Chapter 3 and Chapter 4 on 'The Taming of the Shah'.
48. See Atlee's letter of 25 September to Truman, FRUS, Vol. X, doc. 89, pp. 167–9.
49. For the text of Foreign Office instructions to Ambassador Shepherd, see ibid., doc. 92, dated 27 September 1951, pp. 173–4. For the Shah's reaction, see Henderson to Acheson, 30 September, ibid., doc. 98, pp. 185–6.
50. Jackson proposed to transfer AIOC assets to the Iranian National Oil Company (NIOC); in return the latter would delegate operational responsibilities to a new London-based company which would produce and sell the Iranian oil and share profits on a 50-50 basis (Rouhani, 1987: 277–8; Louis, 1984: 676).
51. For a more thorough explanation of the legal position of the two sides (in the Persian language), see Rouhani, 1987: 331–4.
52. Mosaddeq's summary rejection of the Truman proposal on the ICJ injunction was not without the zest of bitterness on Mosaddeq's part, accusing the US of 'always taking the British side and giving Iran no aid'; minutes of Grady's meeting with Mosaddeq on 11 July 1951 (FRUS, Vol. X, doc. 38, pp. 86–7). On 11 July, Mosaddeq responded to Truman's letter welcoming the mediation proposal.
53. See the text of Morrison's letter of 7 July 1951, ibid., pp. 82–3.
54. For Attlee's arguments and debate in the Labour cabinet, see Louis, 1984: 662–3.
55. Ibid.: 680–2.
56. FRUS, Vol. X, doc. 90, pp. 169–70.
57. Acheson, 1969: 510.
58. Mosaddeq presented some documents to the Security Council pointing to the contrived character of the ninth *Majles* which had ratified the 1933 accord. See Mosaddeq's report in the *Majles* proceedings of 11 December 1951. (The audiotape of this speech can be accessed through The National Front USA website: <http://www.jebhemelli.net/mossadegh/index.html>, retrieved in March 2008).
59. Details of the American oil proposal could be found in FRUS, Vol. X, doc.119, pp. 249–55. In view of its immediate rejection by Eden, we have not attempted to summarize its substance here. Suffice it say that it covered the full range of issues, i.e., management, marketing, price structure, etc. The proposal excluded AIOC from any role in management. For Eden's reaction, see ibid., doc. 120, pp. 256–8.

60. Ibid., doc. 132. p. 284 fn. 2.
61. Telegram 2432, dated November 20, from Clifford is referred to in fn. 2 of doc. 133, ibid., p. 285. Washington responded that, 'Definitive reply to Mosadeq's [sic] recent request for direct financial assistance will not be made for some time, if at all' (ibid.).
62. Ibid., doc. 132, p. 284.
63. See Acheson's record of talks with Eden on 4 November in Paris (ibid., doc. 120, pp. 256–8); and Acheson's complaint to Eden about 'British inaction' on the American oil proposal and its consequences, described by the State Department as having been expressed in 'very strong' terms (ibid., p. 260 fn. 4).
64. Acheson 1969: 511.
65. For Mosaddeq's remarks about US policies, see the record of his talks with McGhee on 9 November (ibid., doc. 126, pp. 269–72). The profuse praise of the US is on page 272.
66. Ibid., doc. 134, pp. 287–8.
67. For an excellent and expert analysis (in Persian) of the IBRD package, see Rouhani, 1987: 319–22. Dr Rouhani (who was the first secretary-general of OPEC) arrives at the conclusion that the IBRD proposal was lopsided in favour of Britain and its rejection justifiable.
68. For indication of Mosaddeq's favourable disposition towards the IBRD approach, see his remarks to Henderson on 28 November (FRUS, Vol. X, doc.135, pp. 288–90). See also the minutes of internal discussions in Mosaddeq residence on 9 March 1952 (cited by Rouhani, 1987: 318).
69. The language used in Persian was 'na'khāstam lakkeh'e nangu'i bedāman'e khod va shoma begozāram' (cited in ibid., p. 323).
70. Fateh, 1980: 522 fn.1; Rouhani, 1987: 256–61.
71. It is difficult to pinpoint the moment when Mosaddeq became convinced that Iranian oil had lost its markets. The American interlocutors had pounded him with this reality during different phases of talks. In his report to Washington dated 17 July 1951 (FRUS, Vol. X, doc. 42, p. 93), Harriman reported that his oil expert Walter Levy gave the two Mosaddeq oil advisors, Hasibi and Saleh, 'probably their first frank detailed education on the technical aspects of how the worldwide oil business was conducted'. A second lecture on the same topic came from Mostafa Fateh, an Iranian director of AIOC, who in a meeting with the prime minister on 16 August 1951 briefed him on the realities of the oil market and the intricate relationship among major oil companies. See Fateh, 1980: 529–30; cited also by Matini, 2005: 254.
72. For a sample of haughty Tory attitude, see FRUS, Vol. X, doc. 197, pp. 434–5.
73. Abrahamian, 1983: 189.
74. See, FRUS, Vol. X, pp. 336–7. In spite of the country's dire needs, the total volume of aid, including amounts under Point Four, did not exceed $50 million in two years. For a summary of US aid during this period, see Rouhani, 1987: 484–7. It is noteworthy that in June 1952, in response to the Shah's query about US willingness to support a successor government to Mosaddeq,

the State Department estimated that the US might be able to come up with a total of $110 million, encompassing military ($30–35 million), Point Four ($25 million) and another $60 million against emergency needs (FRUS, Vol. X, doc. 177, p. 387).
75. Mosaddeq memoirs, 1986: 182.

3 Mosaddeq's Second Government, July 1952 to August 1953

1. Note that by this time, Under-Secretary McGhee had been reassigned as ambassador to Turkey and could no longer exert a moderating influence.
2. FRUS, Vol. X, doc. 181, pp. 396–99.
3. Conversation with Henderson, ibid.: 397.
4. The volume of printing of banknotes during Mosaddeq's tenure was later varyingly put between 300 to 400 million *Tumāns* or about $33 million (at, by then, increased exchange rates); Rouhani puts this volume at 350 million *Tumāns* (1987: 476). Dr Karim Sanjabi, a close associate of Mosaddeq, has mentioned 300 million, 2002: 218.
5. FRUS, Vol. X, doc. 178, pp. 389–92.
6. See report of the Shah's conversation with Henderson on 12 June (FRUS, Vol. X, doc. 181, pp. 396–400). Pressed by Henderson, the Shah mooted three hypothetical scenarios but ended up opting for none: (A) Appoint someone from Mosaddeq's own circle (Allahyar Saleh) to resolve the oil problem honourably. (B) Appoint someone who would be able to understand and work with Mosaddeq's National Front. For that, he mentioned the former prime minister Ali Mansour. (C) Short of the above, a strong figure like Qavam could take the helm and confront the situation head-on.
7. It will be recalled that Sir Francis Shepherd had unsuccessfully lobbied the Shah for the appointment of Seyyed Zia, a notoriously pro-British politician. See the Foreign Office document FO371/91472/73486, cited by Rouhani, 1987: 301; Louis, in Gasiorowski and Byrne, 2004: 139.
8. For details, see in this chapter the section titled 'The British Two-Prong Strategy'.
9. Telegram 4812 from Henderson, dated 12 June 1952, cited in FRUS, Vol. X, p. 392 fn. 3.
10. Ibid.: 404.
11. For a lively post-mortem, see Henderson's report to Washington, ibid., document 185, pp. 409–12.
12. Ibid., doc. 185; and Gifford's (the US ambassador to the UK) report, ibid., doc. 186, pp. 409–12, and 413–14 respectively. For the substance of the US response on aid to a potential successor to Mosaddeq, see ibid., p. 387.
13. The Persian term used in the constitution in referring to the Shah's status is '*maqām'e qeyr'e mas'oul*' (or 'the unaccountable authority'). The word '*mas'oul*', of Arabic derivation, has a double-sense: responsible or accountable. Clearly, the first sense would divest the Shah of all state responsibilities except rubber-stamping and ceremonial functions. The second sense of 'non-accountability' could be interpreted as empowering the Shah to

exercise certain substantive functions within constitutional bounds in as much as he could maintain harmony with government and *Majles*.

14. For the names of prime ministers appointed during this interval, see Matini, 2005: 363.
15. The Shah's dislike of Qavam was known. In his book *Mission for My Country* (New York: McGraw-Hill, 1961), the Shah effectively confirms his reluctance and misgivings about naming Qavam. The latter had, however, obtained 40 out of the 42 ballots cast in the *Majles* inclination vote. Some 30 pro-Mosaddeq deputies had stayed away. In his diaries Kazem Hasibi, the National Front *Majles* deputy and Mosaddeq's oil advisor, recorded that when on 19 July a team of deputies pleaded with the Shah to restore Mosaddeq, the monarch replied, 'look for legal means to unseat Qavam' (see Mohammad-Ali Movahed, *Khāb'e Âshofteh'e Naft: Doctor Mosaddeq va Nehzat'e Melli Iran* (*The Oil Nightmare: Dr Mosaddeq and Iran's National Movement*), (Tehran: Nashr'e Kar'namah, 1378/2000), Vol. I., p. 474. After the revolution in 1979, Dr Movahed obtained from Hasibi the notes the latter had intermittently logged on his journal; Movahed has used these notes in his well-documented two volume work cited above.)
16. Meaning: 'Most Exulted Excellency' or a rough Spanish equivalent of 'Excelentésimo'.
17. Diary of Hassan Arsanjani, a close associate of Qavam, quoted by Tolou'ei, 1992: 642. For more details about Qavam's lobbying and the pledges he had made to British officials, see 'The covert track' later in this chapter.
18. Nahavandi, 2006: 207. According to another account, the Shah had dispatched his brother prince Ali-Reza to monitor the situation in the streets and give him a firsthand account. The latter would have been recognized by the rioting crowds and his car attacked. He would tell the Shah the country was at the verge of revolution (Tolou'ei, 1992: 642).
19. As referred to above the Shah had predicted massive popular support for Mosaddeq and postulated that his replacement would not be tenable in case of his victory in The Hague (FRUS, Vol. X, doc. 181, pp. 396–400).
20. For the attitude of the two embassies, see FRUS, vol. X, p. 415. For the Foreign Office reaction, see Azimi, in Gasiorowski and Byrne, 2004: 54 and p. 292 fn.103.
21. *The New York Times*, 23 July 1952.
22. FRUS, doc. 189, pp. 416–21.
23. The point had strongly been made by the British Chargé Middleton in the course of several meetings which he held with Mosaddeq as of 25 July (see ibid., doc. 190, pp. 423–4).
24. Ibid., conversation with Henderson, 30 July.
25. A UN advisory mission headed by Camille Gutt visited Iran during November and December 1952 to make recommendations on requisite measures to handle the oil-less economy (FRUS, Vol. X, p. 494 fn. 3).
26. Mosaddeq supporters in the *Majles* tried to dissuade Kashani from running for speakership, inflating his ego by flattering remarks (see Movahed, citing Hasibi's unpublished diary, 2000: vol. II. p. 566; Matini, 2005: 302).
27. FRUS, Vol. X, doc. 198, p. 438. Bushehri had played a prominent role during Harriman's mission in the previous summer. Some observers did not exclude Kashani's own personal ambitions for the job (ibid., doc. 183, pp. 404–6).

28. Kashani was against three of the Mosaddeq appointees: Foreign Minister Navvab, Agriculture Minister Akhavi and the deputy-defence minister, General Vosouq (Mosaddeq himself carrying the defence portfolio). Vosouq was a nephew of Qavam and as such also a relative of Mosaddeq. The general was accused by his detractors of a harsh crackdown on crowds during the *Siy'e Tyr* (21 July) uprising against Qavam.
29. According to a Mosaddeq minister (Amir'ala'ei) about 1500 letters of recommendation in favour of individuals had been written by Kashani and his sons to various government ministries and structures during the period from July to December 1952 (see Ali Gharib's article on the web: <http://asrenou.net:80/1386/mordad/27/m-kashani-mossadegh.html>).
30. In his memoirs, Ayatollah Montazeri confirms Kashani's meddling in the *Majles* elections and relates some anecdotes in connection with the candidacy of one of his sons (<http://www.montazeri.com/>, pp. 153–4). See also Ahmad Maleki's history of the National Front, *Tārīkhcheh'e Jebhey'e Mellī* (*A History of the National Front*), (Stockholm: 2005); Maleki confirms that Mostafa Kashani (the older son of the Ayatollah) was a candidate from Abadan, whereas another of his sons was running from Sāveh (ibid.: 46).
31. For an example of such an exchange, see Movahed, 2000: 559.
32. The list of prominent deserters would not be complete without a mention of Ha'eri-zadeh, Zohari, Qanatabadi, all associated with the right wing of the National Front.
33. He obtained a record number of popular votes in Tehran's electoral circuit in the seventeenth *Majles* elections, exceeding that of Ayatollah Kashani; this performance itself was a cause for certain irritations and jealousies within the Mosaddeq camp.
34. This is the opinion given by Karim Sanjabi, a cabinet minister and close advisor of Mosaddeq who, as the leader of the National Front in 1978, played a key role by throwing the Front's weight behind Ayatollah Khomeini (see, Sanjabi, 2002: 205).
35. Matini, 2005: 185–7, citing from Hussein Makki's memoirs, Azimi in Gasiorowski and Byrne, 2004: 60.
36. See Chapter 1 note 52.
37. In an interview published in Iran in 1997, Makki describes his mediation efforts (Asgari, 2000: 70–5).
38. See Azimi, in Gasiorowski and Byrne, 2004: 60–2, citing from the Mehdi Bazargan recollections.
39. In a speech on 28 October, Dr Baqa'ei lambasted the government for laxity towards the *Tudeh* Party, leaving it a free hand to conduct propaganda and allowing its militants to occupy sensitive posts (cited by Rouhani, 1987: 363).
40. In November 1953, when Mosaddeq was being prosecuted by a military court, Baqa'ei protested a breach of the constitutional provision according to which crimes attributed to a defendant in the exercise of ministerial functions could only be prosecuted by the Supreme Court, and hence supported Mosaddeq's own line of defence which argued that the military court lacked competence to deal with his case. This is in contrast to the attitude of Ayatollah Kashani who called for the death penalty for Mosaddeq. In April 1975, at the height of the Shah's power, Baqa'ei was the first Iranian politician to protest at the creation of a unique party

system, *Nehzat'e Rastakhiz*, in a telegram to the Shah (Alinaqi Alikhani (ed.), *Yāddāsht'hāy'e Alam, sale 1354 (Diaries of Alam 1975–76)*, Vol. 5 (Tehran: Ketabsara Publishers, 1382/2003), p. 52 fn. 20.
41. FRUS, Vol. X, Eden to Acheson 9 August, doc. 197, p. 435.
42. Ibid., doc. 190 through 197, pp. 421–37.
43. Ibid., Eden to Acheson, doc. 197, pp. 434–5.
44. For Acheson's reaction to Eden, see, ibid., doc. 199, pp. 439–43.
45. The tonnage was not mentioned in the text but, according to Rouhani, the volume of oil products stored and ready for market just before the oil dispute was two million tons.
46. FRUS, Vol. X, doc. 211, pp. 464–9.
47. It is not totally excluded that Eden may still at that stage have entertained the hope of revisiting the validity of the Nationalization Act based on a provision in the 1933 accord. If such hope was pinned on the language in the terms of reference, it only reveals undue optimism on the part of British lawyers. It is true that, according to the 1933 agreement, Iran forfeited the right to *cancel* the agreement unilaterally and disputes had to be referred to arbitration. On the strength of this forfeiture, Mosaddeq (or his advisors) may have reckoned that 'having regard to the juridical position prior to 1951', stated in the terms of reference, could enable Britain to challenge the validity of the Nationalization Act. The language of the terms of reference, however, did not take the parties *back* to the juridical situation prior to the nationalization. If Britain argued otherwise, she could have been refuted on three grounds. Firstly, the object of arbitration was determination of the compensation which arose from the act of nationalization; so the exercise of arbitration by ICJ could not deny its *raison d'être*. Secondly, Iran had not cancelled the 1933 agreement, it had nationalized the AIOC. The ICJ award of 22 July 1952 had already recognized that the 1933 agreement was nothing more than a 'concessionary contract' between Iran and a company and not an international agreement. Companies could legitimately be nationalized, a measure Britain herself had amply resorted to. Finally, the Labour government itself had already solemnly recognized the principle of nationalization and hence the ICJ could not entertain any retraction.
48. In his analysis, Faud Rouhani – having not had access to Henderson's confidential report of the 27 August meeting with Mosaddeq – attributes the rejection of the Truman-Churchill proposal by Iran to *inclusion* in the said proposal of a provision for compensation of *future losses*. No such provision, in explicit terms, was included in the terms of reference, though future developments made it clear that such intention was indeed implicit in the Truman-Churchill proposal. See Rouhani, 1987: 379.
49. For Iran's counter-proposal, see FRUS, Vol. X, doc. 216, p. 476–9. For the US and British separate responses and the follow-up correspondence, see ibid., pp. 486–98.
50. Mosaddeq later estimated that from August 1952 to August 1953 his government decreed some 200 bills under emergency powers (see Mosaddeq memoirs, 1986: 238). After Mosaddeq's downfall the *Majles* rescinded all his bills on the ground that they were illegally legislated.

51. By the end of 1952, the government had succeeded in reversing the negative non-oil balance of trade, posting a 626 million rials surplus. For details, see Heiss, in Gasiorowski and Byrne, 2004: 126–7.
52. The Mosaddeq associates in the *Majles* proposed a bill to enfranchise women. This provoked vociferous opposition by clerics inside and outside the *Majles* (Abrahamian, 1983: p. 276).
53. Under his emergency powers Mosaddeq un-benched some 200 judges. The commission, set up to implement judicial reforms, however, refused to act in respect of the seating judges of the Supreme Court (*divān'e āli'e keshvar*). A decree under the emergency powers was then issued to dissolve the Supreme Court and replace it with a new composition (see Matini citing Dr Mohammad-Hussein Moussavi, a judge involved in Mosaddeq's judicial reforms. 2005: 321–3).
54. Senators, according to a law promulgated in 1949, were elected for a six-year term. The constitution, on the other hand, had anticipated that the periods of legislation in the *Majles* and the Senate should be made harmonious. Mosaddeq took advantage of this ambiguous provision to allow the *Majles*, which by law had the prerogative of interpreting the constitution, to pass a law reducing the Senate's term to two years *applied retroactively*. The Shah signed the bill and the senate was dissolved, having already served out its term.
55. The seventeenth *Majles* was functioning with only 79 deputies. If applied retroactively, the provision could prevent the formation of a quorum. Mosaddeq vigorously denied any intention of foul play. Yet some deputies, notably Makki and Baqa'ei, introduced a resolution to block the bill. Their action was polemical in nature, but served as a reminder that non-retroactivity could not be taken for granted given the Senate's fate (see the preceding note). Rouhani, 1987: 364; Movahed, 2000: Vol. II, p. 674.
56. Makki, Baqa'ei and Ha'eri'zadeh were formally excluded from the National Front and formed a rival caucus named 'The Freedom Front'. Shams Qanatabadi, a cleric-cum-deputy close to Kashani, formed the '*Fraktion Islami*'.
57. See Wilber, *Overthrow*, 2000: appendix E, p. 9. Note that Mosaddeq's first choice for that job, Brigadier-General Mahmud Amini, was universally respected but opted out due to the guarded attitude of the Shah. He was made head of the National Gendarmerie and later became Mosaddeq's deputy in the defence ministry.
58. According to *Overthrow* (ibid., appendix D. p. 3): 'Colonel Ashrafi, military governor of Tehran and commanding officer of the Third Mountain Brigade, could be relied upon; this later turned out to be incorrect but for staff planning purposes in June it had to be assumed correct.' In his memoirs, Ardeshir Zahedi (2006: 146–7) confirms that during the summer of 1953 both Colonel Ashrafi and Colonel Naderi, the chief of the police intelligence branch, had been in secret contact with him. He could not however vouch for their loyalty to the Shah or to his father. Further elaboration on this point has been provided in Chapter 5 (see 'The Backlash'), note 18.
59. The designated man was Abol'qassem Amini from a patrician Qājār family and a relative of Mosaddeq. He was the brother of General Amini, referred to in note 57 above. Another brother, Dr Ali Amini, had served in a streak of post-war governments, including that of Qavam and Mosaddeq before

becoming minister of finance in the Zahedi government, whence he negotiated the Oil Consortium agreement which replaced the AIOC. In spite of a deep distrust by the Shah towards the family, Ali Amini became prime minister in the early 1960s and initiated certain reforms, including land reforms, which were reputedly inspired by the Kennedy administration; these reforms included a mild relaxation of the political climate.

60. The text (cited by Tolou'ei, 1992: 643) reads: 'I would be the enemy of the Koran if I were to act in contravention of the Constitution or accept becoming president of the republic if [others] violated the Constitution by a regime change.'
61. Louis, 1984.
62. Woodhouse (1982); and Sam Falle, *My Lucky Life in War, Revolution, Peace and Diplomacy* (Sussex: Book Guild, 1996); Brian Lapping, *End of Empire* (London: Granada, 1985) and the BBC series: <http://ftvdb.bfi.org.uk/sift/title/436592>; Donald Wilber, *Adventures in the Middle East: Excursions and Incursions*. (Darwin Press, Princeton, 1986).
63. HIOHP, tapes one and two: <http://www.fas.harvard.edu/~iohp/>.
64. Dr Lambton was the author of an authoritative book entitled, *Landlord and Peasant in Persia: A Study of Land Tenure and Land Revenue Administration* (Oxford: Oxford University Press 1953; London: I. B. Tauris, 1991). She died at the age of 96 in July 2008. In a commentary on her death, published in *Middle East Strategy at Harvard (MESH)*, Martin Kramer laments that her obituaries in the British press failed to mention her role in the Mosaddeq episode. See the link: <http://209.85.135.104/search?q=cache:Q98lynqZAawJ:blogs.law.harvard.edu/mesh/2008/08/miss_ann_lambton_advice/+Dr.+Ann+K.S.+Lambton+%2B+wm+Roger+louis&hl=fr&ct=clnk&cd=1&gl=ch>.
65. Acheson, 1969: 509. Woodhouse also expresses a low opinion of his ambassador (1982: 109).
66. Cited by Louis, in Gasiorowski and Byrne, 2004: 136. For a sample of opinion from Shepherd, see his report to the Foreign Office: 'A Comparison between Persian and Asian Nationalism in General', 2 October, 1951, FO, 371/91464/EP1015/361, cited by Louis, 1984: 639–40.
67. Louis, in Gasiorowski and Byrne, 2004: 130–5.
68. Ambassador Shepherd's cable in this regard is cited by Louis, ibid.: 140. Shepherd's predecessor Sir John le Rougetel back in 1949 had described Seyyed Zia as 'one of the few, in fact the only, outstanding personality in public life who is both competent, honest and sincere' (ibid.: 139).
69. Ibid.: 141.
70. 'Intervention of Mr Julian Amery', 7 February 1952, FO/371/98683, cited in Mark Gasiorowski, 'The 1953 Coup d'état in Iran', *International Journal of Middle East Study*, No. 19 (1987); Amery, the son-in-law of Harold Macmillan and an MP was influential in the Tory government. He later confirmed contacts with Qavam, saying the latter visited him in his London apartment in Eaton Square (cited by Lapping, 1985: 214).
71. Louis, in Gasiorowski and Byrne, 1984: 142; Gasiorowski, 1987: fn. 21.
72. Richard, in Keddie and Richard, 1981: citing Kashani's son, ibid.: 111.
73. For the background of the Rashidian brothers, see p. 184n. 33; see also 'The Link-Up' in Chapter 4.

74. During talks that led to the joint Truman-Churchill proposal, some blunt words were exchanged between the two (see FRUS, Vol. X, doc. 202, pp. 445–7). Tension between the two allies was also palpable in the November–December 1952 bilateral consultations, during which Eden vehemently objected to an American proposal for the settlement of the compensation through an agreed lump sum. On other related topics, however, Eden was conciliatory (ibid., p. 556 fn. 2).
75. Eden personally intervened to dump the US efforts to revive a $25 million loan from IMEXBANK (ibid., doc. 254, p. 556).
76. Gasiorowski and Byrne, 2004: 158 and 227.
77. Wilber, *Overthrow*, 2000: 1; Woodhouse, 1982: 117.
78. Britain had just submitted its American-backed oil proposal, the final offer to Mosaddeq as will be seen shortly in this chapter. Woodhouse attributes the suspension of Operation Boot, of which he was the main architect, to Eden. Louise (in Gasiorowski and Byrne, 2004: 162ff.) believes the decision came from Dixon. The two versions are not contradictory. One way or another the suspension decision was linked to the oil proposal submitted to Mosaddeq in February 1953.
79. Britain argued that the AIOC had entered this amount in her ledgers in relation to payments which would have been due under the Supplemental Oil Agreement which was never ratified by the *Majles*. Iran disputed this reasoning.
80. The alleged plot, in the light of later evidence, appears to have been exaggerated by the government in order to cow the opposition and *potential* conspirators, based on *prima facie* presumption of plots. Rumours were then circulating in Tehran, which although imprecise were not totally unfounded. The Rashidian brothers and General Abdol'hossein Hejazi were arrested, while an array of civilian personalities from the opposition, including Senator Fazlollah Zahedi, were implicated. The fact that the detainees were released shortly thereafter suggests that nothing concrete had taken place. This point was later confirmed by the then Chief of Police, Brigadier General Kamal (cited in the Zahedi memoirs, 2006: 162–3). According to General Kamal when he enquired from Dr Fatemi (who as the government spokesman had announced the discovery of a plot) about the evidence, the latter responded, *'it's all hot air, there is no need for material evidence'*.
81. FRUS, Vol. X, doc. 208, pp. 458–9. Mosaddeq referred to this possibility in a public broadcast (see Rouhani, 1987: 351).
82. While the Mosaddeq government does not seem to have had precise information, plots and subversion at low level continued. Woodhouse recalls that in July 1952 he flew from Habbanieh base in Iraq with a RAF plane and brought back a pack of small arms for eventual use by northern tribes (1982: 116). The anecdote by Woodhouse seems strange, as he claims the consignment was destined to northern tribes as a contingency against a USSR intervention in Iran. He says, however, that the plane got lost in the Zagros mountain range, which is located in central Iran where some pro-British tribes were located. It is particularly surprising that Britain, which hardly believed in the possibility of a direct Soviet intervention in Iran, would take such an inordinate risk for so little impact on such an improbable contingency. Note that not long thereafter, elements in the Bakhtiāri tribe in South

Esfahan started a short-lived insurgency against the Mosaddeq government. We have no way of judging whether the Woodhouse account is accurate or altered due to memory failures of other motives.
83. FRUS, Vol. X, doc. 231, pp. 503–4.
84. As an example of this attitude by Britain, see the report of the meeting of 16 December 1952 between Eden and Acheson, in which the former agreed with the bulk of American oil proposals submitted earlier by Paul Nitze, director of policy planning staff at the State Department (ibid:, doc. 250, pp. 550–1).
85. When the US proposed a participation in the purchase of Iranian oil to American firms, they thought Shell and the French oil concerns should also be invited and that Kuwait should take the brunt of production cutbacks to reduce the glut (ibid., doc. 249, p. 548).
86. An incredulous Mosaddeq responded if that was indeed so and the ICJ used it as a criterion for the settlement of the AIOC compensation, 'he would not object' (ibid., doc. 256, p. 560).
87. When this opinion was shared with Eden on 6 March, Henderson took exception and remarked that the Shah 'might emerge from this crisis with a certain vestige of influence' (ibid., doc. 314, pp. 703–4 fn. 4).
88. In a meeting on 6–7 March in Washington, Secretary Dulles informed an appalled Eden that if Mosaddeq rejected the current oil proposal, the US would have to go his own separate way – meaning accommodation. Eden pleaded that if the US wished to keep Mosaddeq afloat, it was best doing it in ways 'not directly related to the oil'(ibid., doc 314, p. 702).
89. Ibid., p. 704 fn 4.
90. Ibid., p. 705.
91. Rouhani, 1987: 375.
92. Ibid.; while Rouhani has chosen not to disclose the names of the two advisors, circumstantial evidence points to Karim Sanjabi and Kazem Hassibi. In a dispatch to Washington the same day, Henderson quotes his well-connected Iranian advisor and interpreter, Ali-Pasha Saleh, naming Sanjabi as one of Mosaddeq's oil advisors 'believed to be against any kind of settlement which could possibly be accepted by [the] British' (see FRUS, Vol. X, doc. 317, 11 March 1953, p. 709). Ali-Pasha Saleh was the brother of Allahyar Salleh, a close ally of Mosaddeq and his Ambassador to Washington. Kazem Hassibi was also known as a hard-line oil advisor to Mosaddeq.
93. Ibid., doc. 318, pp. 711–13.

4 The Downslide

1. General Azizollah Kamal, who was Mosaddeq's Chief of National Police in1952, designates Fatemi as the person in Mosaddeq's kitchen cabinet who advised him on repressive measures. See Kamal's article in *Khāndanīhā* magazine, cited by Asgari, 2000: 148–9. Kamal is also cited in Ardeshir Zahedi's memoirs in connection with arrests made in October 1952, in which Fatemi's role is highlighted (ibid.: 149–50). Moharam-Ali Khan, head of the police censorship unit, is quoted by Matini to the effect that he received orders for closure of a number of newspapers from Fatemi (ibid.: 318). See

also, Homa Sarshar, the compiler-editor of Shaban Jafari's recollections citing the latter to the effect that Dr Fatemi was reputed to be the man behind the court decisions when Jafari and a group of co-agitators were being prosecuted after the *'noh'e esfand'* crisis (Sarshar, 2002: 150–1). Note that some of the comments above may have been politically motivated.
2. Haeri'zadeh, Qanat'abadi, Baqa'ei, Makki, Kashani.
3. *The New York Times*, 17 August 1953; the passage in Kennett Love's article reads: 'According to a completely reliable source, the Shah first became seriously worried about the conduct of the Mossadegh [sic] Government after the gigantic *Tudeh* (Communist) demonstration, held with Government approval in Parliament Square July 21.'
4. Several sources have recorded Maleki's position. In the minutes of his interrogations by SAVAK in August 1965, Maleki, while proudly recalling his long association with Mosaddeq and while lauding the latter's contribution and place in history, says he had two differences with him: one was over his tolerance of, and relations with, *Tudeh*, and the other over Mosaddeq's perfectionist approach to the resolution of the oil dispute. See *Khalil Maleki Be'ravāyat'e Asnād'e SAVAK* (*Khalil Maleki as Depicted by SAVAK Archives*) (Tehran: Markaz'e Baresy'e Asnād'e Tarikhi, 1379/2000), p. 388.
5. Mohammad-Reza Pahlavi, *Mission for My Country* (New York: McGraw-Hill, 1961), p. 123; Mosaddeq, 1986: 211–13.
6. The tribal chief in question was Abol-Qassem Bakhtiari, from the same tribe as Queen Soraya. The Bakhtiari tribes had sustained relations with the British. It will be recalled from the Woodhouse memoirs, cited earlier, that he had shipped some small arms for the tribes in a small plane from a base in Iraq, though Woodhouse is vague about the recipients.
7. Zahedi, 2006: 121
8. The Crown lands were mainly properties arbitrarily confiscated by the first Pahlavi monarch, Reza Shah, from landlords. It is not quite clear why Mosaddeq objected to their distribution among peasants, but it could have had something to do with his vision of the Shah's constitutional functions or alternatively with the legitimacy of their acquisition, or both.
9. Ala reminded Mosaddeq in connection with the Bakhtiāri insurgency that some time back, the pro-Shah Bakhtiāri leaders had urged the government to prevent Abol-Qassem (the leader of the insurgency then afoot) to return to the region but the government had not paid attention (FRUS, Vol. X, doc. 301, pp. 674–7).
10. Ibid., doc. 305, pp. 681–2.
11. Movahed, 2000: vol. II, pp. 675–6; Matini, 2005: 331.
12. Mosaddeq told the Shah on 24 February that it was a good idea for him to leave after all and to stay away until the situation became calm (FRUS, Vol. X pp. 681–2). It is not excluded that his initial objection may have been insincere in the spirit of *'ta'āroff'*, an Iranian cultural habit that allows courtesy to take the better of candidness.
13. Ibid.
14. At that time the scheming by Prime Minister Reza Khan (the Shah's father), which led to Ahmad-shah's definitive departure from Iran and the change of dynasty, was still fresh in memories.

15. Zahedi, 2006: 121; Matini, quoting Behbahani's son, 2005: 333–4. Ernest Perron may have tipped-off the American Embassy (FRUS, Vol. X, doc. 306, p. 683).
16. Cited by Yann Richard (Keddie and Richards, 1981: 113) from the ex-queen's memoirs, '*Ma Vie*'.
17. The relevant passage from the Ardeshir Zahedi memoirs (in Persian) is translated in view of its relevance to the main theme of this study: 'at first I had been assigned to travel overnight to Qom and inform Ayatollah Boroujerdi. A letter had also been prepared which I was supposed to deliver. Later there was a change of plan and they talked to Boroujerdi by telephone. The latter was of the opinion that action must be taken to prevent the Shah from leaving.... He instructed Behbahani to pass on his message to His Majesty' (Zahedi, 2006: 121–2).
18. Mosaddeq, 1986: 264–5.
19. Reported by Behbahani's son, Seyyed Jafar, cited by Matini, 2005: 334.
20. In his published memoirs, the mob leader Shaaban Jafari confirms that he received his marching orders on the morning of 28 February directly from Kashani; Jafari quotes Kashani as having said that, 'if the Shah goes so goes our turbans' (see Homa Sarshar, 2002: 123–4).
21. Mosaddeq memoirs, 1986: 265.
22. FRUS, Vol. X. doc.308, pp.685–8.
23. Mosaddeq emphatically refers to this matter in two different sections of his memoirs (1986: 211–13). Judging by his writings, Mosaddeq was convinced that the 28 February incident was an assassination plot and hints that the Shah and/or his entourage might also have been involved.
24. For whatever it is worth, the mob-leader Shaban Jafari, who, together with a quirky army colonel, Aziz Rahimi, rammed his jeep into the gate of the prime minister's residence, insists (in his recollections collated by Homa Sarshar, 2002: 126) that he had no intention whatsoever of harming Mosaddeq and only wished to plead with him to prevent the Shah's departure. Mosaddeq's guards, he goes on, would not let them in so they tried to force the entrance!
25. An eight-member parliamentary committee subsequently held several meetings with the Shah and Mosaddeq and made recommendations for stripping the Shah of the Crown lands, the Mashad-Shrine revenues, and of his role as army commander-in-chief, save during time of war. In his memoirs Baqa'ei recalls that Mosaddeq had in return agreed to give up part of the emergency powers he had obtained from the *Majles*, but later reneged. Richard Cottam, quoting the *New York Times* of 17 March 1953, confirms Baqa'ei's claim (1964: 281). The commission's recommendations were never ratified by the *Majles* because of obstruction tactics used by Baqa'ei himself prior to the full suspension of the *Majles* (see Baqa'ei's oral memoirs, Harvard Oral History Project, tape 17, pp. 9–13).
26. Ayatollah Montazeri's memoirs: <http://www.montazeri.com/>, p. 110; Ahmadi, 2001: 669; A historical picture of the Shah's 1944 hospital visit is on display on the Grand Ayatollah's official website: <WWW. Broujerdi.ir> (retrieved in December 2008).
27. Cited by Shahrough Akhavi, 'The Role of the Clergy in Iranian Politics,1949–54' in James Bill and William Roger Louis (eds), *Musaddiq, Iranian Nationalism and Oil* (London: I. B. Tauris, 1988), p. 93.

28. Ibid., Akhavi states that shortly after the assassination attempt against the Shah, Boroujerdi convened a major conference in Qom in which he enjoined clerics to stay out of politics. In his memoirs, Ayatollah Montazeri does not refer to this conference, but recalls that in 1948–49 when rumours circulated in Qom that Iran was about to recognize Israel, there were commotions among seminarians and a registry was established for volunteers to fight on the side of Arab legions. When a government emissary assured Boroujerdi that no (*de jure*) recognition was contemplated, the latter moved to dampen the enthusiasm of the seminarians and discouraged all political agitations (see Montazeri's memoirs, <http://www.montazeri.com/>, pp. 146–7).
29. In his memoirs Montazeri stresses that both Khomeini and his acolyte Morteza Motahari were maliciously denounced to Boroujerdi as supporting the *Fadā'iān*; he himself narrowly escaped denunciation because he worked as a scribe for Boroujerdi and hence was considered close to him. Montazeri does not, however, conceal his admiration at that time (and thenceforth) for the *Fadā'iān* leaders and their cause, nor does he criticize their terror; he only refers, disapprovingly, to their insolence and non-reverential attitude towards Boroujerdi and other high clerics in Qom (see ibid.: 142–4). Later, in 1979, Morteza Motahari, as a jurisprudent close to Khomeini, occupied a highly revered place within the ranks of revolutionaries; he was assassinated by an esoteric Islamist group called *Forqān* in May 1979. *Fadā'iān* leaders were sanctified as heroes and martyrs. For background on Khomeini's early support of *Fadā'iān Islam*, see Ahmadi, 2001: 653–65.
30. Akhavi, in Bill and Louis, 1988: 93.
31. Ayatollah Montazeri speaks of a possible financial stipend that Boroujerdi may have allocated to Kashani in 'later years', by which he probably means after the fall of Mosaddeq. In a more precise and affirmative language, Montazeri recounts (quoting a fellow cleric) a concrete case where Boroujerdi could have accorded Kashani a gratuity of 12,500 *Tumāns*, a considerable sum in those days, in order to bail him out of a mortgage debt. According to this account, Kashani had mortgaged his house to take out a loan from some Mosaddeq supporters who later turned against him and began to make noises to seize the house (Montazeri, <http://www.montazeri.com/>: 149–50. Though no precise date for these episodes is given by Montazeri, it's likely that they correspond to the period after the fall of Mosaddeq, possibly in late 1956 or 1957 when Kashani was arrested in connection with the prosecution of *Fedāiān Islam* and the reopening of the Razmara's assassination file in which Kashani was implicated. See Yann Richard, 'Ayatollah Kashani', in Keddie, 1983: 119 n. 46, where Boroujerdi is quoted as confirming that he had done the necessary for Kashani (see also Matini, 2005: 381). While support of Boroujerdi could be explained by sheer clerical solidarity, it is more likely that it was based on convergence of interests at a crucial political juncture.
32. Mohammad Quchani, *Zendegui'nāmeh'e Sīāsi Ayatollah Al-ozma Boroujerdi; Shah va Faqih*, (*Political Biography of Grand Ayatollah Boroujerdi: The Shah and the Shiite leader*): <www.broujerdi.ir>, Part II (retrieved 14 December 2008).
33. Boroujerdi made his position known to the Shah through an unnamed emissary on 29 September 1951 when Mosaddeq was about to expel British employees of the AIOC and was embroiled in a dangerous stand-off

with Britain. The Shah intimated this to Henderson in a meeting on 30 September 1951 (FRUS, Vol. X, doc. 98, p. 186).
34. See Dr Mehdi Azar's recollections in the *Harvard Oral History Project*, tape 3. pp. 16–17. According to Dr Azar, the Grand Ayatollah requested a passport to leave the country (presumably to Najaf in Iraq) in protest. Mosaddeq averted the crisis by instructing his minister to ensure the Grand Ayatollah's satisfaction on the subject in dispute (explained at length in Dr Azar recollections): <http://www.fas.harvard.edu/~iohp/AZAR08.PDF4->.
35. Akhavi, in Bill and Louis, 1988: 106–7.
36. Quoted from *Etelā'āt* daily, 3 March 1953 by Ali Gharib: <http://asrenou.net:80/1386/mordad/27/m-kashani-mossadegh.html>. The daily that cited him was the semi-official gazette.
37. Woodhouse, 1982: 125.
38. See Nour-Mohammad Asgari, 2000: 201 and 214. See also Ahmad Kasravi, *Afsarān'e Mā* (*Our Military Officers*), quoted in Tehran Political Research Institute,*Zohour va Soqout'e Saltanat'e Pahlavi* vol. II Tehran 1369/1990, p. 255, accusing Zahedi of corrupt practices. William Louis wrote in 2005 that Zahedi received one million dollars from the CIA in 1953 but does not provide a source (Louis, in Gasiorowski-Byrne, 2004: 169). General Zahedi and his son Ardeshir have vehemently denied any financial wrongdoing (see Zahedi, 2006: 423–8).
39. For the list of names of all detainees, see Hossein Makki, *Tārīkh'e Bīst-sāl'eh Iran*, Vol. VIII (Tehran: Elmi Publishers, 1987), pp. 400–2.
40. General Zahedi's help to the National Front by ensuring free elections in Tehran is confirmed by several sources (see Makki's article dated 26 February 1952 in *Khāndanīhā* (a weekly digest magazine), issue no. 42, xiii year, February 1952, cited by Zahedi, 2006: 104–7. The fact that he was named interior minister in Mosaddeq's first cabinet, confirms the point.
41. It will be recalled that Harriman came to Tehran as Truman's personal representative for oil mediation. By coincidence, on the day of his arrival the *Tudeh* Party had organized a rally marking the anniversary of a strike by oil-workers in Abadan back in 1946 in which several *Tudeh* militants had been killed. The fact that it coincided with Harriman's arrival provided the *Tudeh* Party an occasion for anti-American demonstrations (Kianouri memoirs, 1992: 219). Miniscule anti-*Tudeh* political formations, including the Baqa'ei's Toilers Party, the *Pan-Iranist* Party, the Fascist *Sumkā* group, some of them presumably in the CIA payroll under the TPBEDAMN operation (see 'The Role of Iranian Agents' in Chapter 6) were out to agitate and provoke confrontations. Demonstrations degenerated into violent clashes and security forces fired into the crowd mainly to protect the *Majles* premises. Mosaddeq was unhappy. He vented his wrath on the Chief of Police, but Zahedi as the responsible minister saw himself targeted.
42. For an account of Zahedi's emergence as the opposition leader in1952, see Nahavandi, 2006: 221–3. Some authors have plausibly postulated that Zahedi was the key figure in a secret society formed by the retired officers, called *Komite'e Nejat'e Vatan* (Committee for Salvation of the Fatherland) (see Abrahamian, 1983: 278).

43. Wilber, *Overthrow* (CIA internal report), 2000: 6.
44. Dwight D. Eisenhower, *Mes Années à la Maison Blanche* (My Years at the White House), Vol. I, *1953–56* (Paris: Robert Laffon, 1963), p. 197
45. Ibid. Mosaddeq first raised the possibility of writing to Eisenhower at the 4 April meeting with Henderson when he could not extract a pledge for a loan from the US. He sent Eisenhower a letter on 28 May. As part of a war of nerves, Washington decided to delay the response by Eisenhower and when by the end of June a negative response arrived, its content was allowed to leak to the press in order to embarrass Mosaddeq.
46. FRUS, Vol. X, doc. 322, p. 719.
47. The Shah's recorded words were: 'Mosaddeq has led the country to bankruptcy and will be losing his political capital without his [the Shah's] intervention' (ibid.: 716).
48. Reported to Henderson by Ala on 15 April (FRUS, Vol. X, doc. 324, p. 723).
49. Ibid.: 720
50. Meftah wrote in his memoirs: 'Boroujerdi thought the National Front would not repeat the same mistake [trying to force the Shah out as on 28 February]. After listening carefully to strong warnings by the visitors about the dangers of Iran going behind the 'iron curtain,' a dejected Boroujerdi said he would see what he could do' (n.d.: 46–7).
51. This information is based on the author's personal information obtained directly from the sources involved. The list was found in Mosaddeq's safe-cabinet after the ransack of his residence on 19 August. It is not clear whether the abduction and subsequent murder of the police chief was linked to his involvement in cherry picking for Mosaddeq or was an act designed to destabilize the government. The latter hypothesis is more plausible. Later there were claims, including from Baqa'ei as well as an anecdote attributed to Afshartous's son, alleging that Mosaddeq's relations with his police chief had soured towards the end. This point must be taken with utmost caution.
52. Matini, 2005: 347, quoting from the recollections of Parviz Etesami, a presumed confidant of the Rashidian brothers. Woodhouse (1982: 124) attributes the murder to private motives, something that reveals either his ignorance or cynicism.
53. No evidence then and nothing since have linked General Zahedi to the Afshartous killing. The fact that Dr Mo'azami (a close associate of Mosaddeq who replaced Kashani as the Speaker of the *Majles*) personally escorted Zahedi from his sanctuary in *Majles* building to his residence in a Tehran suburb could be taken as a tacit acknowledgement by the Mosaddeq government of Zahedi's non-involvement.
54. Baqa'ei's memoirs, Harvard Oral History Project, tape 17, p. 13. As the prosecution of the case was suspended after the overthrow of Mosaddeq, the secrets of this abduction and murder were never brought to full light.
55. Woodhouse attributes the lifting of the suspension to Eden's ailment (which had taken him to Boston for a gall bladder operation and then to a Mediterranean resort for convalescence), adding that Churchill, who replaced him in the Foreign Office, had a feel for covert action (see Woodhouse, 1982: 125). Earlier in his narrative Woodhouse acknowledges that

Operation Boot came back to life when Mosaddeq rejected the final oil proposal (ibid.: 124). There is no reason to doubt that the resumption of covert action resulted from the collapse of oil talks and that Eden would have opted for the same course. See also Louis, in Gasiorowski and Byrnes, 2004: 168.
56. Ibid.; Woodhouse, 1982: 123; Wilber, *Overthrow*, 2000: 2.
57. Wilber, *Overthrow*, ibid.
58. Ibid.: 3. Equally on 31 March, when Ala sounded Henderson on behalf of unidentified conspirators, the ambassador sat on the fence: 'He [Ala] should understand [that] United States government could not be associated with a coup d'état.' He went on to say that Iranians planning a coup 'should act on their own responsibility and not expect any foreign power to become involved in such a venture' (FRUS, Vol. X, doc. 322, p. 719).
59. For details, see the earlier section 'Internal Conspiracies' in this chapter.
60. In *Countercoup* (1979) Kermit Roosevelt referred to the brothers as Nossey and Cafron.
61. Wilber, *Overthrow*, 2000: 7.
62. Louis, in Gasiorowski and Byrne, 2004: 162; Woodhouse, 1982: 117.
63. Ibid.: 112.
64. Darbyshire confirmed the Brother's devotion to the anti-Mosaddeq cause to Wilber during TPAJAX planning. His praise of the brothers was in contrast to the negative view of Woodhouse (Wilber, *Overthrow*, 2000: 7).
65. They were referred to in Roosevelt's *Countercoup* as Boscoes brothers. For more details on the two principal CIA Iranian agents, see 'The Role of Iranian Agents' in Chapter 6.
66. This will be shown at a later stage of this study in connection with the result of the bribing campaign under TPAJAX targeting the *Majles* deputies among others (see the first two sections of Chapter 5). Both the CIA and MI6/the FO may have been taken for a ride by their Iranian agents. As in all bureaucracies, achievement was partly measured by disbursement of funds which is often confused with results.
67. These papers, listed in Wilber, *Overthrow*, 2000: 65, survived by obtaining paid government advertisement or subscription quotas through favour-trading and other illicit means. Payola from foreign sources was no doubt an added income which they embraced with no scruples.
68. See ibid.: Appendix D, p. 3; Ardeshir Zahedi also confirms that Col. Ashrafi had been in contact with their camp prior to the coup. He also names Colonel Naderi, head of the police intelligence bureau, although he doubts his *bona fides* (Zahedi, 2006: 146–7).
69. The CIA internal report, *Overthrow*, is the main source. A scholarly work '*Mohammad Mosaddeq and the 1953 Coup in Iran*, ed. Mark Gasiorowski and Malcolm Byrne (2004) was published subsequent to the leak and publication by *The New York Times* of the CIA internal report in 2000. It combines elements of this document with an impressive volume of earlier research and publications by various contributing scholars. Numerous other works and memoirs – some by direct participants (e.g., Kim Roosevelt, Woodhouse) refer to preparations for the *coup d'état* with varying degrees of detail and credibility.

70. The Nicosia plan, May 1953, codenamed TPAJAX comprised of six points:

   1. Destabilization campaign against Mosaddeq.
   2. Creation of a military network under General Zahedi,
   3. Obtaining the Shah's cooperation,
   4. Shiite *ulama* taking sanctuary (*Bast*) in *Majles* provoking a censure vote.
   5. A military network to prevent *Tudeh* and *Qashqais* from intervening.
   6. If the above scheme failed, the military wing would take over through a *putsch*.

71. Wilber, *Overthrow*, 2000: 18.
72. Ibid.: Appendix D: 'Report on Military Planning Aspect of TPAJAX', p. 1.
73. Eisenhower's response took a full month to finally arrive on 29 June. In it Eisenhower explained why the United States was unable to provide financial aid to Iran or purchase its oil. Later Mosaddeq bitterly complained about the leak to Henderson, who tried to turn the blame on Iranian officials (FRUS, Vol. X, doc. 347, 18 August, p. 750).
74. No central bank existed yet and the issue of banknotes as well as foreign currency management and control were functions performed by the National Bank. Through a watchdog committee, the parliament monitored both the monetary reserves and issue of banknotes.
75. *The New York Times*, 22 July and 17 August 1953, article by Kennet Love.
76. FRUS, Vol. X, doc. 347, pp. 748–52. Mosaddeq cites this corrupting of the deputies as the reason for dissolving the *Majles*. The CIA internal history confirms the bribing of many deputies by US agents and the Rashidian brothers.
77. For the purposes of this study it is interesting to analyse the voting pattern in the *Majles* as a means of gauging the effectiveness of the Anglo-American bribing campaign. Without attempting to engage in a detailed analysis – lacking sufficient data – one can note that in early July 1952, when Mosaddeq routinely resigned (see the section on the Qavam hiatus in Chapter 3), 53 *Majles* deputies cast an 'inclination vote' for his reappointment. Two weeks later, 40 deputies cast an inclination vote for his political foe, Qavam. Some 30 pro-Mosaddeq deputies boycotted that vote (three of them from Mosaddeq's camp, namely Makki, Baqa'ei and Kashani, subsequently joined the opposition). In July 1953, a month before his overthrow, when Mosaddeq requested deputies to resign, 52 deputies complied. This very superficial analysis indicates that the number of deputies voting for Mosaddeq did not really change between July1952 and August 1953. It also confirms the existence of a large floating block of votes which could easily be swayed in one direction or the other. Although details on bribery under TPAJAX are not revealed, it is hard to see any major impact from the bribing campaign in the *Majles* voting pattern. All this is not to state that Mosaddeq's fears of a censure vote by opposition deputies were unfounded.
78. The constitutional amendments were designed to increase the Shah's prerogatives. The Shah had adroitly moved to bolster his authority in 1949 in the aftermath of an assassination attempt in February of that year when he was at the apex of his popularity.

79. In his memoirs, Mosaddeq writes how he was confronted with two options: one was to accept the verdict of a vote of no-confidence in the *Majles* which the opposition had prepared. This was against Iran's interests and spelled the doom of national aspirations. The second option was to let the people, namely the real owners of the country, decide whether he should stay or go. This was the option he retained (see Mosaddeq, 1986: 269–70).
80. Kenneth Love, *The New York Times*, 2 August 1953. For the involvement of Khomeini in Kashani's campaign, see Richard, in Keddie and Richards, 1981: 123, who cites eyewitnesses saying that Khomeini was in Kashani's house on 31 July 1953 (1 August) when 'Mosaddeq supporters' attacked Kashani's house.
81. Between the third and the fourth legislatives, a prolonged interregnum had occurred during which Ahmad-Shah, the last of the *Qajār* kings (or the regent on his behalf) had appointed and dismissed governments at will on several occasions.
82. Mosaddeq had retorted that the Shah 'would not dare' or was not empowered due to a virtual plebiscite given him during the popular uprising of the previous July (*Siy'e Tyr*); cited from the original sources by Matini, 2005: 351–5.
83. *The New York Times*, 5 August 1953.
84. Woodhouse, 1982: 127.
85. FRUS, Vol. X, doc. 339, p. 740; Wilber, *Overthrow:*, 2000: 29.
86. FRUS, Vol. X, doc. 329, p. 730.
87. Ibid: 730–1.
88. Ibid.
89. Ibid.
90. Wilber, *Overthrow*, 2000: 23. Several versions of this historical anecdote have appeared in various narratives including in her own memoirs, *Faces in a Mirror, Memoirs from the Exile* (Englewood Cliffs, NJ: Prentice Hall, 1980). While some details do not tally with the version cited here, the thrust of the story is confirmed by all sources.
91. Gerard de Villiers, citing Tehran's French language daily, *Journal de Téhéran* of 27 July, in *L'Irresistible Ascenssion de Mohammad Reza, Shah d'Iran* (Paris: Plon, 1975), p. 225.
92. The Court official named is Soleiman Behboudi. Behboudi, who is referred to in Ashraf's memoirs as my friend 'Mr B', may have originally set the rendezvous between TPAJAX agents and the princess (see Princess Pahlavi, 1980: 135).
93. Wilber, *Overthrow*, 2000: 24. Woodhouse and his replacement as MI6 Iran point-man, Norman Darbyshire, arranged the BBC signal; Woodhouse also claims the Eisenhower digression in Seattle was a prearranged signal to the Shah (1982: 127); see also Louis, in Gasiorowski and Byrne, 2004: 174.
94. A West Point graduate, General Schwarzkopf had gained fame in the US as a key figure in the Lindbergh kidnapping case when he was the New Jersey police chief in 1930's. His stint in Iran from 1942 to 1946 drew him close to the Shah, but the claim by Stephan Kinzer in *All the Shah's Men* (2003: 66) to the effect that Stalin 'withdrew his soldiers [from Azerbaijan] as General Schwarzkopf's gendarmes marched to Tabriz' is utterly baseless. Soviet troops had long before withdrawn from Azerbaijan and the Iranian

Gendarmerie played only a minor, if any, role in the Azerbaijan expedition of December 1946.
95. Wilber, *Overthrow*, 2000: 30. See also the report of the US Ambassador in Baghdad dispatched to Washington following his meeting with the Shah on the evening of 16 August (FRUS, Vol. X, doc. 345, pp. 746–7).
96. Wilber, *Overthrow*, 2000: Appendix B, pp. 6–7 and 10.
97. Ibid., the main text, pp. 33–4.
98. See ibid.: Annex D, pp. 14–15. Colonel Akhavi, a key figure in the TPAJAX *coup* plot could not play a direct role in actual events having fallen sick during the crucial days. This did not prevent him from becoming an influential cabinet minister in the Zahedi government.
99. The assertion in the CIA history *Overthrow* (p. 36) that Rashidian in conjunction with Behboudi, (a UK asset and head of the Shah's household) prepared the *farmāns* is unfounded. These *farmāns*, like all other royal fiats, were handwritten in Persian calligraphy by the Shah's personal secretary Hirad. Existing photostats of Zahedi's appointment *farmān* confirm this point; for its reprint, see Asgari, 2000: 137. For the manner in which the Shah instructed Hirad to write the two *farmāns*, see Zahedi, 2006: 152. The error in the CIA account (*Overthrow*) has prompted some authors to suggest that the two *farmāns* were actually prepared by the CIA-linked agents. See Gasiorowski and Byrnes, 2004: 248. The point has some historical relevance as Mosaddeq later, during his trial, raised the issue of authenticity of his dismissal *farmān* (see the explanations given by Mosaddeq in his memoirs referred to in subsequent passages of this study). Note that the photostat of a *farmān* printed in Stephen Kinzer's *All the Shah's Men* and described as the Zahedi's appointment *farmān* (2003: 114–15) is also an error.
100. Ardeshir Zahedi has provided certain details in his memoirs (2006: 154, 156) about deliberations in their camp on15 August which, according to him, led to determination of modalities for the delivery of the Shah's dismissal *farmān* to Mosaddeq. According to this narrative, early in the morning that day General Zahedi convened a meeting in his hideout in Mostapha Moqdam's property in Tehran suburbs, where in addition to his civilian and military aides, some *Majles* deputies had been invited; they included opposition deputies Abol'hassan Haeri-Zadeh and Aabdol'rahman Faramarzi (the publisher of the mass-circulation daily *Keyhan*). General Zahedi informed the meeting of his appointment as prime minister and consulted the group on how best the dismissal order could be delivered to Mosaddeq, taking into account the possibility that the latter might disobey, leading to serious public disorder. The meeting lasted several hours and certain decisions were taken. According to this narrative, the timing for delivery by Colonel Nasiri of the dismissal *farmān* was fixed at 23: 30 on Saturday 25 August, shortly after the council of ministers in Mosaddeq's residence would have ended. From this account, it is not clear whether or to what extend the CIA team in Tehran had been involved in the determination of actual operational details. It is reasonable to assume that coordination with Carol and Roosevelt was being assured by Colonel Abbas Farzanegan (a CIA asset) who was present at the Zahedi meeting.
101. A photostat of Mosaddeq's handwritten receipt was later published in Iranian press articles and books.

102. The circumstances of the arrest of Nasiri remain murky. It is not certain that the arrest was ordered by Mosaddeq, who had no reason to issue a receipt if he wanted to disobey the Shah's *farmān* and arrest the messenger. *Tudeh* sources have claimed that a *Tudeh* officer by the name of Lt. Shoja'eian took the initiative to arrest him helped by the military unit that was guarding Mosaddeq's residence/office. Kianouri of the *Tudeh* Party affirms that Lt. Shoja'eian changed sides and joined Mosaddeq's guards (1992: 264–6). Nasiri attributes the failure to a delay in the arrival of a reinforcement detachment from the Third Mountain Brigade. The CIA internal report *Overthrow* provides accounts by various sources, but admits that contradictions are too flagrant to allow a clear picture (see Wilber, *Overthrow*, 2000: ch. VI, pp. 39–43); this is a view that we share.
103. Mosaddeq memoirs, 1986: 379; Kianouri memoirs, 1992: 264–5. In tipping off Mosaddeq, Kianouri had apparently told him that the imperial guard detachment was tasked to arrest him; this is confirmed in the memoirs of both men (Mosaddeq, 1986: 379–80; Kianouri, 1992: 265–6).
104. The *Tudeh* Party secretary, Kianouri, later recalled that he personally telephoned Mosaddeq to inform him of the *coup* plan. Kianouri, who had close family links to Mosaddeq from his wife's side, had established a discrete back-channel which Mosaddeq never acknowledged (ibid.).
105. Again, certain details are provided by Ardeshir Zahedi (2006: 156–7). General Zahedi, who had meanwhile changed his hideout (to Hassan Kashanian's property near Shemiran), started a meeting at 7: 30 p.m. which lasted until 11 p.m.. He was informed at this point, by an Imperial Guard officer by telephone, that Colonel Nasiri was on his way to Mosaddeq's residence. General Batmanqelij, the chief of staff-designate, Colonel Farzanegan (named minister of post and telegram), and the brigade commander-designate were at hand. Batmanqelij in his military uniform (he had been retired as major-general in Mosaddeq's purges) then headed to Army Headquarters to take up his post, presuming that the designated units had by then sanitized the place. When he reached there, he saw the premises surrounded by forces loyal to Mosaddeq and learned Mosaddeq's army chief of staff, General Riahi, was present at his command post. He therefore returned to report to Zahedi. Meanwhile General Zahedi, assuming that all had gone according to the plan, headed to his own designated headquarters at Tehran's main Officer's Club. They accidentally crossed one another in the after-hours deserted Pahlavi Road, where Batmanqelij informed Zahedi of the failure of the plan.
106. Bashir Farahmand recalls that he was called into the prime minister's house in the middle of the night when Mosaddeq made him record a valedictory statement for early morning broadcast. According to this account, Mosaddeq changed his mind when Fatemi (and two other close associates) arrived in pyjamas, having just been released from detention by pro-government security forces. Fatemi would have convinced Mosaddeq that he should ignore the *farmān* and consider himself the rightful head of government. Bashir Farahmand was reportedly interviewed by an Iranian journalist, Ahmad Anvari. The anecdote is quoted in Asgari, 2000: 107. In Mosaddeq's own memoirs there is no reference to this account. Mosaddeq

in effect says that he would have seized the opportunity of this dismissal order to step down had it not been for the fact that he was sure to be able to resolve the oil issue at a 100 per cent gain for Iran.
107. As discussed earlier in this volume, ambiguities in the language in which the Constitution of 1906 was redacted allowed for contrasting interpretations of the Shah's prerogatives in appointing governments. Since his ascension to the throne, Mohammad-Reza Shah recognized that he could not appoint and dismiss governments at will and that the prior concurrence of the *Majles* was required for a nomination. On the other hand, ample precedents, dating back to the last Qajār king, clearly allowed the Shah to dismiss the government during parliamentary interregna. This had its own logic, as a prime minister with a dictatorial bent could procrastinate in holding new elections or rig them to his own advantage. In respect of Mosaddeq's dismissal, one legal *technicality* could, however, be invoked to dispute the validity of the Shah's *farmān*. In fact, since the Shah had not signed into law the dissolution of the *Majles*, voted for in the referendum of 4 August, it could be argued that technically the seventeenth *Majles* still existed. Mosaddeq formally announced the dissolution of the *Majles* only on 16 August, namely after the Shah's flight to Baghdad. This argument hardly holds water given, among other things, the fact that 52 out of 79 deputies had resigned even before the referendum. For a different view on juridical niceties related to this issue, see Rouhani, 1987: 522–9.
108. Dr Alemi, the labour minister in Mosaddeq's cabinet, later denounced Mosaddeq's non-disclosure of the Shah's *farmān*. The text of Dr Alemi's letter is published in Asgari, 2000: 146–7. Dr Mehdi Azar, minister of education and endowments, also confirmed that he was unaware of the dismissal order, although in his case he did not criticize Mosaddeq for dissimulation (see Dr Mehdi Azar, Harvard Oral History Project interviews, 1983).
109. Mosaddeq, 1986: 294.
110. FRUS, Vol. X, doc. 347, p. 751.
111. Ibid., doc. 346, dated 18 August, p. 748. According to a footnote on the same page, General Smith had attached the report of the Baghdad meeting to his report to the president.

5 The Downfall

1. For details of the flight of the royal couple and their arrival in Baghdad around 10:30 a.m. on16 August, see Gérard de Villiers, *L'Irresistible Ascension de Mohammad Reza, Shah d'Iran* (Paris: Plon, 1975), pp. 231–2; Shawcross, 1988: 68–70.
2. Other than a circular sent to Iranian embassies abroad, specifying that the Shah had no longer any status, the Iranian Ambassador in Baghdad, Mozafar Aalam, received direct instructions from Fatemi. The ambassador had called Deputy-Foreign Minister Meftah to seek instructions about the Shah's presence; the call was redirected to Foreign Minister Fatemi, who seemingly told him to warn the Iraqi government (Meftah, n.d.: 65). The cases of Mozafar Aalam and Iran's ambassador in Rome, Nezamul'molk Khajeh'nouri, who equally ignored the Shah when he arrived in Rome from Baghdad

on 18 August, became a *cause célèbre* in the annals of Iran's pre-revolution foreign service.
3. Wilber, *Overthrow*, 2000: 51.
4. Ibid.: 51–2.
5. Ambassador in Iraq, Berry, to the Department of State, FRUS, vol. X, doc. 345, pp. 746–8. On a personal note, the Shah confined to Berry that he wished eventually to settle down in America and, 'will have to look for work shortly as he has a large family and very small means outside Iran'. Note that contents of Berry's cable to Washington appears to have been truncated in the FRUS probably to delete explicit references by the Shah to the TPAJAX plot.
6. Wilber, *Overthrow*, 2000: 53.
7. For the contents of Dulles message, see Zahedi, 2006: 236, reproducing cable 1790, 18 August, from Dulles to the US Embassy in Rome. For the Shah's interview spree in Rome, see Shawcross, 1988: 69.
8. For a post-facto *Tudeh* ideological analysis of the role of monarchy and Iran's body politic at that juncture, see Kianouri, 1992: 261.
9. A few months after the fall of Mosaddeq (April 1954), Kianouri wrote an article entitled, 'The Main Lines of the Cooperation of our Party with Bourgeois Organizations', in which he expounded his views about the 'proletarian hegemony'. This article was later discussed in the Fourth Plenum of the party held in Moscow in June–July 1957 and while some aspects of the paper were criticized, the central concept of 'proletarian hegemony' during the anti-colonial anti-feudalistic phase of the revolution (i.e., the phase of Iran under Mosaddeq) was endorsed. Another party paper, analysing the 19 August 1953 events, in which such leadership was deemed to be the legitimate prerogative of bourgeois leadership was now deemed theoretically incorrect (see ibid.: 372–3).
10. In his memoirs Kianouri confirms the Tudeh request for arms (ibid.: 277). A top secret British report, while referring to these contacts, claims the *Tudeh* requested 10,000 rifles from Mosaddeq who refused (printed in FRUS 1952–54, Vol. X, doc. 362, p. 784).
11. Abrahamian, 1983: 324.
12. For the full translation in English of the *Tudeh* declaration, see Kennett Love in *The New York Times*, 19 August 1953.
13. See Robert Doty, 'Suicide Attempt by Russian Envoy Reported After Red Defeat', *The New York Times*, 31 August 1953; Meftah (n.d.) written in Persian and published in London. A rough mimeographed English translation of these memoirs was examined by this author. The detailed account of the Soviet envoy's apparent suicide attempt – the news first came in a telephone call from the Soviet Embassy, but was subsequently denied – is given on p. 68, although Meftah may have confused the actual date of the incident that he records as on the night of 19 August; see also Nahavandi, who other than recounting the anecdote (2006: 257–8) observes that Lavrentiev was presumed to be from the Soviet secret service and known as a specialist in abrupt and brutal changes of government (p. 214).
14. Robert Doty, 'Statues of the Shah Overturned', *The New York Times*, 18 August 1953; Kianouri, 1992: 267.
15. The US Chargé Gordon Matisson cable to the department on 16 August (see FRUS, Vol. X, doc. 343, p. 745); *Overthrow* confirms the rumour, using identical wording as in the embassy cable (Wilber, 2000: 46).

16. Ibid.: 61; Kianouri, 1992: 268.
17. A tip about the inner councils of Mosaddeq's advisors and the latter's own thinking at that juncture is given in the diary of Dr Kazem Hasibi, Mosaddeq's ally and oil advisor. He says Mosaddeq refused to declare a republic in order not to give the impression that Iran was gravitating towards the left as well as to keep the flow of American aid. Other items considered in the inner council were the dismissal of the Shah, the ending of the Pahlavi dynasty and the formation of a regency council through referendum. Mosaddeq finally settled for a regency council. This passage from Hasibi's diaries is reproduced in Zahedi, 2006: 227, from Movahed, 2000.
18. In his memoirs Mosaddeq states that he intended to request the Shah to return to Iran and if he refused then set up a referendum for deciding on the composition of a Regency Council as foreseen in the constitution (1986: 272). Interior Minister Dr Sadiqi has on the other hand asserted that early on 19 August, Mosaddeq issued tentative orders for a nationwide referendum related to the formation of a 'Regency Council'. The Sadiqi recollections (published in *Ayandeh*, in 1367/1988) are fully reproduced in Matini, 2005: 469–88. This particular point is separately mentioned on p. 368. See also the reference to Hasibi's diary in note 17 above.
19. In *Overthrow* we read: 'Roosevelt drove up to Shimran – the summer resort section north of Tehran – to hear that Areshir [sic] and his father felt that there was still hope in the situation. It was immediately decided that a strong effort must be made to convince the Iranian public that Zahedi was the legal head of the government and that Mossadeq [sic] was the usurper who had staged a coup' (Wilber, 2000: 46). In his memoirs, A. Zahedi describes in minute detail all action that was being taken, as of the early hours of that same morning (16 August), to produce photostats of the appointment *Farmān* for distribution among the press (2006: 175). *Overthrow* (p. 48 decrypted version) confirms this action but states that the CIA station later reproduced additional copies, kept the original in its safe, and ensured wider circulation. In a different passage *Overthrow* states, 'The station continued to feel that the "project was not quite dead" since General Zahedi, General Guilanshah, the Rashidian brothers, and Colonel Farzanegan were still determined to press action' (Wilber, *Overthrow*, 2000: 52).
20. Zahedi's article *'panj rouz'e bohrāni'* first appeared in *Etela'āt Māhīāneh* in 1953 and was later reproduced in his memoirs (2006: 169–295). It was written when the author's memories were fresh and the protagonists named were all alive and active in public life.
21. On certain details, the CIA account and that of Ardeshir Zahedi diverge: Where his father and he himself were hiding. Where and at what date the strategy of resistance was decided on and who the participants were. How General Zahedi's statement to the press was drafted and how foreign correspondents were assembled. However, both accounts confirm that these events actually took place. This point is the subject of thorough investigation in the main body of this study. Furthermore, Zahedi does not acknowledge any knowledge of, or contact with, foreign agents even before the failed TPAJAX coup.
22. In his 17 August article in *The New York Times*, correspondent Kennett Love quotes the ending phrase of the message as: 'Anyway, at the present time

I am the legal Prime Minister and any action Dr Mossadegh [sic] takes in the name of the Government is against the law.'
23. In his memoirs the *Tudeh* boss, Kianouri, quotes the publisher of *DĀD*, Amidi Nouri, who, on 18 August, had received one of those envelopes containing the photostat of the *farmān*, which he decided to publish the following day, Kianouri, quoting Amidi Nouri (an erstwhile Mosaddeq ally, turned foe), 1992: 274.
24. In his 1953 article, later in his memoirs, Ardeshir Zahedi states that the interview was arranged through the Iranian correspondent of Associated Press, a former classmate of his, Parviz Ra'in, who he located in their hangout at the Park Hotel. The secret rendezvous place was at Velenjack Heights in the northern outskirts of Teheran. Youssef Mazandi, the Iranian correspondent of United Press and an unnamed Reuters correspondent are mentioned, but Zahedi omits the names of Kennet Love of *The New York Times* and Donald Schwind of AP who must have been on the briefing.
25. Wilber, *Overthrow*, 2000: 49.
26. In several of his dispatches on 17, 18 and 19 August, Kennett Love and AP have referred to another Zahedi statement, this time addressed to officers of the armed forces, saying the time was approaching for them to make the ultimate sacrifice, 'even of your lives, to maintain the independence and the monarchy of Iran and preserve the principles of the holy religion of Islam.' *Overthrow* confirms AP had wired this message on 18 August (ibid.: 60). Note that, were it true, the statement would have been played up by the Zahedi camp in various postmortems; it is mentioned in none of such narratives. The CIA account separately refers to a bogus Zahedi interview forged by its two main Iranian agents, Keyvani and Jalali (ibid.: 50).
27. See ibid.: 47 and 52.
28. Zahedi, 2006: 154.
29. Further details including the list of these newspapers are provided under the title 'CIA Station Activities in Tehran, 16–19 August'in Chapter 6. Note that an arrest warrant against Baqa'ei had been issued. While it cannot totally be excluded that he may have benefited from CIA money during the previous 12 months, he was more than capable of taking initiatives of his own (such as publishing the *farmān*) independent of the CIA or anyone else for that matter.
30. Described in the 1953 article as the 'Residence of a relative, named Seif'ul-Saltaneh Afshar' (Zahedi, 2006).
31. Ibid.: 208–9.
32. See Wilber, *Overthrow*, 2000: 56–7; Zahedi, 2006: 213–14. Colonel Farzanegan was a military aide to Zahedi appointed under TPAJAX. He was a CIA agent who later became a cabinet minister in Zahedi's government. There is no certainty, however, that at that time either Zahedi or the Shah knew of Farzanegan's organic link to the CIA.
33. Note that if Wednesday 19 August really was designated as the D-Day in Kim Roosevelt's 'council of war' held on the evening of 17 August, Farzanegan and Ardeshir Zahedi could not, in the space of one day only, have gone to the places in their mission and returned in time to report on the military component of Roosevelt's plan. Short of having used a plane – something

that is not claimed in *Overthrow* or by Zahedi – the distances were prohibitive for such a time span.
34. Wilber, *Overthrow*, 2000: 62.
35. Zahedi, 2006: 188.
36. Party headquarters looted and destroyed by the crowd included *Hezb'e Iran* (Iran Party), and the Pan-Iranist Party (the pro-Mosaddeq branch). Newspapers ransacked were *Besouy'e Āyandeh* (the main *Tudeh* mouthpiece), *Bākhtar Emrouze* (published by Dr Fatemi), *Neyrouy'e Sevvom* (the official organ of the socialist party of the same name led by Khalil Maleki) *Shouresh* (a violently anti-Shah paper published by Karim Pour Shirazi), and *Haji-Bābā* (a satirical pro-Mosaddeq daily).
37. Sadiqi's recollections are cited in full in several published works in Iran, see Aqeli, 1997: Annex to vol. II. pp. 419–24; Matini, 2005: Annex 4, pp. 469–88.
38. FRUS, Vol. X, p. 784. For an analysis of the British Secret document, see 'An Orphan British Secret Document' in Chapter 6.
39. Reference to this article is already made in the Introduction of this book.
40. Woodhouse was at the time in post in the Far-East and followed the events from there. The above description, which resembles that of the Harkness couple in the *Saturday Evening Post* is quoted by the *Telegraph* on Woodhouse's obituary, who died the 5th Lord of Terrington on 22 November 2001.
41. For the details and relevance of this meeting to the events of 19 August, see 'Ambassador Henderson's Last Meeting with Mosaddeq' in Chapter 6.
42. The claim by Kim Roosevelt, echoed by several authors, to the effect that Mosaddeq acted unwittingly on Ambassador Henderson's behest is treated separately in Chapter 6, under the heading, 'Ambassador Henderson's Last Meeting with Mosaddeq'.
43. The delegation was headed by Mohammad-Reza Qodveh, chairman of the 'National Committee to Struggle Against Colonialism' (one of several *Tudeh* front organizations), Kianouri, 1992: 276–77.
44. Mosaddeq had replaced Colonel Ashrafi the previous day, 18 August, with a family relative General Daftary, but the handover had not fully taken effect. As mentioned under 'The Link-Up: TPAJAX and the Internal Cabal' in Chapter 4, Colonel Ashrafi had been named in Appendix D, p. 3 of *Overthrow* as someone the British planners of TPAJAX considered an ally. This assumption did not prove accurate as Appendix D has noted. For elaboration, see Chapter 6.
45. Dr Sadiqi's recollections are integrally reproduced as Annex IV in Matini, 2005. Reference to this call is on p. 472. While Colonel Ashrafi's name was mentioned in *Overthrow* as an MI6 asset (and later retracted in the same document (see under 'The Military Factor in the Fall of Mosaddeq' below), nowhere in the CIA account is there the slightest hint that he may have played a role in the events of 19 August. More to the point Ashrafi was purged from the army following Mosaddeq's fall, unlike scores of other officers who were promoted on the remotest evidence of pro-Shah sentiments.
46. According to *Overthrow*, General Zahedi had included Brigadier-General Daftari among his assets when Carol was drafting the military plan. Daftari is not mentioned by name in *Overthrow* but the command he held, i.e., 'The Custom's Guards', is mentioned in Appendix D. Ardeshir Zahedi implicitly confirms that Daftari was linked with his father (2006: 154). Dr Sanjabi

recalls that the army chief, General Riahi, had warned Mosaddeq about Daftari's doubtful loyalties but Mosaddeq had been dismissive (cited from Dr Sanjabi, Harvard Oral History, by Matini, 2005: 370).
47. The passage from p. 67 (decrypted) reads as follows; 'By 1015 hours there were pro-Shah truckloads of military personnel at all the main squares.' Clearly the CIA account conveys the impression that a military *coup* was afoot at that moment. But in its internal history there *no hint* of any preparations or contacts with the *active* army rank and file for such a military *coup* in the period from 16 to 19 August. In all likelihood, the truckloads observed were those of the security forces that Ashrafi had been reporting to the interior minister.
48. For a digest of Tehran press coverage of the day's events, see *Khāndanī'hā*, 20 August 1953. Kianouri asserts that it was at 2 p.m. that they received news of intervention by some military units from the outlying barracks (1992: 277).
49. The following passage from Sadiqi's recollections (Annex IV, in Matini, 2005: 473–5) contradicts the observation in *Overthrow* that by 10:15 a.m. there were truckloads of pro-Shah units at all the main squares. It also suggests that by the time he reached Mosaddeq's house at Kakh Street around 3:30 p.m. the major fighting, including the tank duel, had not yet started:

'At 14.45 hours I left the Interior Ministry compound in an unmarked car.... We took the road from Sepah Avenue passing though Shapour, then Shahreza Avenue till we reached the Pahlavi Avenue junction. [Note: All these streets are among Tehran's main arteries. The trajectory included two of the Tehran's principal squares] My intention in making this detour was to assess conditions in the streets and [to size up] crowds but on this trajectory we did not come across any group. We were stopped by a police officer at that [Shahreza-Pahlavi] junction... He allowed us to continue when he recognized me. Then at the junction of Pasteur Avenue and Kakh Street [where both the Shah's Winter Palace and Mosaddeq's residence were located] tanks and soldiers were stationed. A young lieutenant stopped us and when the driver introduced me, he politely enjoined that no car could be allowed from this point on. I then decided to walk to Mosaddeq's house.'
50. *Overthrow* asserts, 'Fairly early in the morning [Colonel Demavand?], one of those involved in staff planning, appeared in the square before the Majlis [sic], with a tank which he had secured from the Second Battalion of the Second Armoured Brigade, a battalion originally committed to the operation. Lt. Colonel Khosro-Panah and Captain Ali Zand were on hand and were joined by two trucks from the same battalion, while members of the disbanded Imperial Guard seized trucks and drove through the streets.' While it is plausible that some among those named above may have been proactive on that day, the CIA internal account is utterly silent about prior contacts, if any, between the plotters and Iranian officers in Tehran during the three-day interval. Colonel Demavand is not named anywhere in the text or the Annexes of *Overthrow*; nor does his name appear anywhere subsequent to the overthrow of Mosaddeq government; we do not exclude a name confusion by *Overthrow*'s authors or those who decrypted the leaked CIA internal history.

51. From p. 54 of *Overthrow* it is clear that few among the arrested officers involved in the 15 August *coup* where known to the CIA station in Tehran. The list of officers and civilians arrested in connection with the TPAJAX *coup*, including Colonel Nozari, is printed there and those previously known to the station are marked by an asterisk. During the planning phase of TPAJAX, the name of Colonel Nozari had been mentioned in a cursory way as *neutral*. On p. 55 of *Overthrow* his name is flagged as one of those unknown to the station (see also Annex D, p. 16 of Wilber, *Overthrow*, 2000. Nor is there any mention in *Overthrow* of Colonels Khajeh'nouri and Navvabi who had been appointed by Zahedi for specific tasks in connection to the 15 August *coup*, as confirmed in Zahedi, 2006: 156, 157.
52. In a 1960 unpublished paper Kennett Love, the *NYT* correspondent in Tehran in 1953, wrote that he was responsible, 'in an impromptu sort of way', for speeding the final victory of the royalists. 'Seeing a half-dozen tanks parked in front of Tehran's radio station', he said, "I told the tank commanders that a lot of people were getting killed trying to storm Dr Mossadegh's house and that they would be of some use instead of sitting idle at the radio station.' He added, 'They took their machines in a body to Kokh [*sic*] Avenue and put the three tanks at Dr Mossadegh's house out of action' (quoted in James Risen: 'C.I.A. Tried, With Little Success, to Use US Press in Coup', *The New York Times*, 16 April 2000).
53. Overthrow has also picked up this point and states on p. 54: 'Rumors circulated to the effect that the arrested officers were to be hanged on 20 August, and throughout the unit commands of the Tehran garrison, the police, and the gendarmerie, officers met to discuss the situation. Several of them resolved to risk all to attempt to rescue their friends.'
54. The roundup telegram sent by Henderson on 20 August (FRUS, Vol. X, doc. 348, pp. 752–5).
55. A Persian translation of this confidential report, signed by Henderson and dispatched at 2 p.m. on 19 August and numbered 398, is produced in Zahedi, 2006: 243–4. For unknown reasons this document and a few others produced by the same source were not included in FRUS, Vol. X, Iran, 1952–1954; they must have been obtained through other channels; their authenticity is not to be doubted.
56. Ibid. Upon learning that General Daftari had been confirmed as Chief of Police in the Zahedi government, the embassy was confounded. It had earlier reported that Daftari was a Mosaddeq appointee as Chief of Police and martial law administrator and that he was trying to draw on elements of his previous command to help Mosaddeq. When Zahedi confirmed him, the embassy sent a correction to Washington saying, '*either our earlier message was an error or else Daftari had changed loyalty in the last minute*'. As mentioned earlier, the unit under Daftari's earlier command (the Custom Guard) had been flagged during TPAJAX planning exercise as a Zahedi asset. Clearly this point was unknown to the embassy.
57. Report filed at 2 p.m., ibid.: 243–4.
58. This account is fairly consistent with the narrative given in *Overthrow*. On p. 68 we read, 'About noon, five tanks and 20 truckloads of soldiers joined it, the movement took on a somewhat different aspect. As usual, word spread like lightning and in other parts of the city pictures of the Shah were

eagerly displayed. Cars went by with headlights burning as a tangible indication of loyalty to the ruler.' *The New York Times* correspondent in Tehran, Kennett Love, later confided that he personally, but unwittingly tipped off the tank units around the radio station to move to Mosaddeq's residence where people, according to Love, were being fired on by the unit guarding the residence.

59. According to Ardeshir Zahedi, at the time of these events his father was hiding in a relative's house, Saiful–Saltaneh Afshar. He would have changed places several times during the time he was a fugitive. Henderson contradicts the affirmation by Kim Roosevelt according to which Zahedi was harboured in the house of a CIA agent. See his report to the State Department (FRUS, Vol. X, doc. 351, p. 759). Roosevelt, on the other hand, claims that he had withheld from Henderson the fact that he harboured Iranian fugitives.
60. Zahedi, 2006: pp. 188–9.
61. *The New York Times* correspondent, Kennett Love, put the number of dead at 300, which appears to this author to be an exaggeration. See his article published on 20 August 1953.
62. Kianouri, 1992: 277
63. Dr Sadiqi's recollections, reprinted in Matini, 2005: 477.
64. Kennett Love, 'Mossadegh Quits Teheran Hideout; Is Held for Trial', *The New York Times*, 21 August 1953; Dr Sadiqi, who was by Mosaddeq's side during the siege of his residence and the ensuing 24 hours, has provided minute details from the time Mosaddeq left his residence to the moment he confronted General Zahedi in the latter's headquarters in the main Officer's Club in Sevvom Esfand Avenue. Mosaddeq had spent the night in an empty house belonging to an Azari merchant in the vicinity of his residence. From there he moved to the house of his Minister of Post and Telegram Seyf'ollah Mo'azzami and made arrangements for surrendering to the new authorities. Sadiqi confirms that the arrival of the search team in the afternoon of 20 August was accidental. He also mentions the courtesies proffered by the new authorities to Mosaddeq when he was brought to the main police headquarters and the civil exchange of pleasantries between Mosaddeq and Zahedi when the two came face to face.
65. Officers arrested included General Batmanqelij, the Zahedi chief-designate of army staff Colonel Nasiri (commander of the Imperial Guard), Colonel Zand-Karimi deputy commander of the Second Mountain Brigade, and Colonel Nozari commander of the Second Armoured Brigade. It's significant that of some 20 military officers arrested, only six were known to the CIA station as participants in the *coup* plot (see Wilber, *Overthrow*, 2000: 54).
66. *Overthrow* states that Carroll accompanied Ardeshir Zahedi to Esfahan (some 400 km south of Tehran) to enlist 'Brigadier General Zarghami'[sic]. In his memoirs Zahedi confirms the trip and the fact that he met and enlisted the support of Colonel (Amir-Qoli) Zarqami, deputy division commander, but denies having been accompanied. In his book *All the Shah's Men*, Kinzer claims, without mentioning his source, that on Sunday 16 August, Roosevelt sent General McClure with a plane to Esfahan 'with instruction to try to enlist the garrison commander there' (2003: 171). This anecdote appears to be apocryphal. Such reckless conduct on the part of an accredited head of military mission in Tehran at the time when the US administration was

making an about-turn to mend relations with Mosaddeq (see Undersecretary Smith's note to Eisenhower earlier under 'The Gathering Storm') is unlikely to say the least. There is at any event no reason why such a mission would have been omitted from the secret CIA report *Overthrow* or in Appendix D, just as McClure's official visit to the Chief of Army Staff General Riahi on Roosevelt's behest on that same date has been noted in that document. There we read that Roosevelt sent McClure to see Riahi to gauge his attitude and understood that Riahi was fully loyal to Mosaddeq: 'It was not until a number of hours later that McClure reported to Roosevelt on this meeting, and from the time of the meeting on, McClure seemed disposed to go along with Riahi in the hope that Riahi himself might *eventually* try to overthrow Mossadeq' (emphasis added). It will be seen from this passage that after meeting Riahi on 16 August, McClure's attitude was no longer aligned with that of Roosevelt.

67. On p. 14 of Appendix D, we read: 'The weakness in our plan lay in the fact that the station would not be in a position to contact battalion and company commanders but would have to depend upon Colonel Zand-Karimi to do the job.' Zand Karimi's role was thus pivotal in the operation of TPAJAX but when he was arrested on 16 August, the possibility of communication between the CIA station and Iranian officers at regiment and battalion level vanished. Note that in the General Zahedi camp, neither Colonel Farzanegan nor Akhavi were privy to the identity of lower echelon officers with whom Zand-Karimi alone – among the inner circle of *putschist* officers – was in contact.
68. It is also possible, though unlikely, that these two officers may have been Colonels Khajeh'nouri and Navabi, who Zahedi had designated as brigade commanders should he have succeeded in the 15 August venture; these two, however, did not have any command posts in the Tehran garrisons and had no role in that event.
69. In Appendix E, p. 22, paragraph Q, we read: 'In Iran we did not spent one cent in the purchase of officers.'
70. Setting aside four fairly senior officers associated with the TPAJAX-Zahedi *coup* of 15 August (Colonel Nozari, the commanding officer of the Second Armoured Brigade; Colonel Hamidi of the Tehran police; Colonel Ordubadi of the Tehran Gendarmerie district; and Colonel Mansurpur, commanding officer of the cavalry squadron), Zand Karimi's friends were regimental and battalion commanders: Colonel Rohani, deputy commander of the Third Mountain Brigade; Lt. Colonel Khosro-Panah, commanding officer of the Second Mountain Brigade Infantry Regiment; Lt. Colonel Yusefi, who was soon to be named commanding officer of the Third Mountain Brigade's Infantry Regiment. Through these officers Colonel Zand-Karimi was in touch with every infantry battalion commander in Tehran and with most of the company commanders (see Wilber, *Overthrow*, 2000: Appendix D, p. 12).
71. Ibid.: 2; and Appendix E, p. 8.
72. Ibid.: 6.
73. Ibid.: 4.
74. According to Carroll, it was Colonel Akhavi who said he did not trust Colonel Ashrafi (ibid.: 11).
75. Ibid.: Appendix D, Military Planning, p. 3

76. *Etelā'āt* and *Keyhan* mass-circulation dailies in Tehran published these lists on their front page. See issues corresponding to 1 Mehr 1332 in the Iranian calendar, (23 September 1953).
77. Asharafi was arrested with a number of Mosaddeq military aids including General Riahi and Colonel Momtaz (see Aqeli, 1997: Vol. II, p. 9).
78. Colonel Ashrafi could have been one of those opportunistic individuals who would flirt with opposition figures hoping to outplay everyone. Ambiguities in his conduct and discourse may have been the reason why Ardeshir Zahedi in his memoir also mentions him, without elaboration, as someone who was in contact with their camp during the summer of 1953 (Zahedi, 2006: 146).

6 The Anatomy of 19 August

1. Wilber, *Overthrow*, 2000: 54–6. In his memoirs, Ardeshir Zahedi (2006: 187) provides details of how this decision was reached: on his return in the early hours of 18 August from Kermanshah where he had obtained the cooperation of the brigade commander, Bakhtiar, Colonel Farzanegan strongly argued in favour of selecting that province as the locus for establishing an insurrectional authority. General Zahedi went along and overruled his son, who had gone to Isfahan and was arguing in favour of that location. The selection of Kermanshah was based on its contiguity with Iraq, the existence of an oil refinery, and the fact that Zahedi's own Hamedan birthplace was in the vicinity.
2. *Overthrow* confirms the point that Roosevelt sought to mislead Henderson at this point (ibid.: 56–7).
3. Note that the commander of the Esfahan garrison then was Brigadier-General Davalu and 'Zargham', a colonel, was his deputy.
4. Ibid.: 56–7.
5. In his article 'The 1953 Coup d'État in Iran', in the *International Journal of Middle East Studies* (Number 19, 1987), Mark Gasiorowski attributes this precipitation to a fear by Kim Roosevelt that 'Mosaddeq's net would soon close in around them'. He explains that the Mosaddeq security forces were close to discovering General Zahedi's hideout. This does not tally with the claim by Roosevelt that the general was lodged in Fred Zimmerman's basement. General Zahedi had decided to launch an insurrection from Kermanshah and was about to leave Tehran for that destination that same week.
6. Wilber, *Overthrow*, 2000: 56.
7. Ibid., ch. IX, Report to London.
8. For Sinclair's reaction, see ibid.: 78–85. Tom Braden's remark was made in an interview with *World in Action* in 1973: <http://www.youtube.com/watch?v=_y_TjO44Rx0&NR=1>.
9. It will be recalled that the distances between these provincial capitals (Esfahan and Kermanshah) and Tehran are roughly 400 and 600 km respectively. Given the state of preparedness of the Iranian army and road conditions in those days, it would have taken weeks to prepare such a feat, assuming that other prerequisites were met. Roosevelt's own account in *Countercoup* is explicit in describing the move as intended to have these

garrisons storm Tehran on his designated D-Day. 'The best thing we could hope for' [for the success of the 19 August plan], he wrote, was to have the troops move 'from offstage either from Isfahan or Kermanshah, if possible both'; when Frazanegan returned from his mission, Roosevelt wrote, he reported that [Brigade Commander Teymour] Bakhtiar will move his troops with tanks and armored vehicles at dawn tomorrow 19 August (1979: 181). Even in the CIA internal history, *Overthrow*, we read a totally fanciful account to the effect that the Kermanshah brigade commander, Bakhtiar, upon receipt of a coded message from Farzanegan, started to move his troops to Tehran on Wednesday 19 August and reached Hamadan in time to interrupt a *Tudeh* rally before learning about the fall of Mosaddeq (Wilber, *Overthrow*, 2000: 73).

10. Cable sent by Roosevelt at 1630 hours, 17 August (Wilber, *Overthrow*, 2000: 56).
11. Ibid.: 61
12. Ibid.: 61and 64.
13. Roosevelt,1979: 180
14. In his memoirs Ardeshir Zahedi recalls his father had some Turkish and Russian but no German at all (2006: 267).
15. Ibid.: 193.
16. This recorded interview done by *World in Action* in 1973 is available on the Internet web in two videos under the title 'US Overthrows Iranian Government 1953': <http://www.youtube.com/watch?v=_y_TjO44Rx0&NR=1>. *World in Action* was one of Britain's most prestigious and long-running (1963–1998) current affairs programmes and a pioneer in investigative TV journalism. It was produced by Granada TV. The interview referred to here contains misleading information from both the narrator and some of the other guests. Kim Roosevelt's statement in this interview is nevertheless revelatory, though the contents of this interview should be viewed with caution given the fact that in 1973, the Shah was at the zenith of his power and Roosevelt may have deliberately understated the impact of the CIA.
17. The full passage in Zahedi's memoirs (2006: 188) translates as follows: 'It had been convened that we set out to Kermanshah at dawn on Wednesday 19 August, in order to begin the operations; yet while we were discussing the details, things took an unexpected and unbelievable turn. *Things happened that none of us had predicted.* On Tuesday evening groups of people, shaken by the events of the previous three days and no doubt worrying about the nation's destiny, *either on their own or following instructions from the religious leaders* poured out into the streets and clashed with the Tudeh militants'(emphases added).
18. Wilber, *Overthrow*, 2000: 46; Ardeshir Zahedi denies this encounter and in fact asserts that his father had never seen Kim Roosevelt till after Mosaddeq's fall (Zahedi, 2006: 180).
19. *Overthrow*, (p. 46, decrypted version) asserts that as a first step General McClure, head of the US military advisory mission in Tehran, was sent to see the Iranian army chief of staff, General Riahi. The purpose was to *assess* General Riahi's attitude in the light of rumours about the Shah's dismissal order. This errand was not helpful as Riahi broadly hinted that he and the army would support Mosaddeq.

20. In his 1953 article Ardeshir Zahedi provides a more plausible account of how the interview with foreign news outlets was arranged on 16 August. See page 218n. 24.
21. Wilber, *Overthrow*, 2000: 53. In cable 1790, 18 August, Secretary Dulles sent word to the Shah through the embassy in Rome to issue a public statement clarifying that he had acted to dismiss Mosaddeq within his constitutional prerogatives, that he had staged no *coup d'état* but had been the victim of one. Washington believed such a statement would strengthen the Shah's position '*if one day he were to return to Iran*'. In the meanwhile, the line taken by Walter Bedell Smith to give concessions to Mosaddeq was re-endorsed (translated in Persian and cited by Zahedi, 2006: 236). Note that Dulles's message is more likely to have been prompted by Ambassador Berry's cable of 17 August reporting his conversation with the Shah than by Roosevelt's advice (see 'The Gathering Storm' in Chapter 5; FRUS, Vol. X, doc. 345). There the Shah had intimated his intention to make a statement along the lines that Dulles later adopted.
22. Wilber, *Overthrow*, 2000: 67.
23. For a thorough description of the CIA/MI6 propaganda campaigns during this period, see Gasiorowski and Byrnes, 2004: 242–6; Professor Gasiorowski concludes that the campaign probably played some role in turning the clergy and others against Mosaddeq, although Kashani, most other leading clergymen and most Iranians in general had already chosen sides by this time (ibid.: 246).
24. The then Deputy foreign minister Meftah recalled in his memoirs (n.d.: 48) that coming out of Boroujerdi's residence in Qom where he had visited the prelate in early June (i.e., before the TPAJAX launch), he saw a Tudeh slogan written on the wall in front of the gate of Boroujerdi's house, which read '*Tudeh* Republic is victorious'; Ayatollah Montazeri has made similar observations to which we shall refer in Chapter 7.
25. Zahedi, 2006: 175; Wilber, *Overthrow*, 2000: 46 (decrypted version); see also page 210n. 67.
26. The Shah's fiat was published on Wednesday 19 August by *Āsīā'ye-Javān*, *Ārām*, *Mard'e Āsīā*, *Melat'e Mā*, *Dād* and *Setāreh'e Islam* and the French language daily, *Journal de Téhéran*. *Setareh Islam* was the mouthpiece of Fadāiān Islam. *Journal de Téhéran* belonged to a large chain of which the publisher may have been bribed. See *Overthrow* p. 65 (decrypted version). Some of the above press was linked through subsidies with CIA/MI6. *Dād* was being published by Abol-Hassan Amidi-Nouri, an ex-National Front deputy turned bitter foe of Mosaddeq. Later he claimed that he had found a copy of the *farmān* in the newspaper's mailbox with a note from Ardeshir Zahedi, a credible claim since we know a mailbox drop-off effort had taken place.
27. Wilber, *Overthrow*, 2000: 65.
28. On p. 50 of *Overthrow* we read: 'In this instance, as in a number of others, the high-level [Iranian] agents of the station demonstrated a most satisfying ability to go ahead on their own and do just the right thing.'
29. Gasiorowski, in Gasiorowski and Byrne, 1987: 236.
30. Ibid.
31. Ibid.: 236; Wilber, *Overthrow*, 2000: 2; Byrne, in Gasiorowski-Byrne, 2004: 217.

32. The two were known as syndicated journalists and translators during the late 1940s and early 1950s. They operated out of a fictitious commercial firm in Lalezar Avenue where *Tehran-Mossavar* magazine (a fiercely anti-communist weekly) was also located (see Asgari, 2000: 333). It's likely that they wrote some of the anti-USSR propaganda of that weekly. Ali Jalali was also on the editorial staff of *Etelā'āt Māhīāneh* (a monthly journal published by the *Etelā'āt* chain whose publisher Abbas Masoudi is named in *Overthrow*, p. 26, as having received a $45,000 loan from the CIA). The two agents faded away after the fall of Mosaddeq and according to Asgari established a business in Europe.
33. Kianouri, 1992: 94.
34. The Pan-Iranist party had been split into two segments, a pro-Shah and a pro-Mosaddeq faction. The pro-Shah faction led by Mohsen Pezeshkpour obtained a seat in the *Majles* in the 1970s – while the other faction *Hezb'e Melat'e Iran bar Bonyād'e Pan-Iranism*, under Daryoush Forouhar, joined the revolution with Forouhar becoming minister of labour in the first transitional government formed by Mehdi Bazargan. Forouhar was assassinated in the late 1990s in the notorious serial murders of intellectuals and dissidents in Tehran.
35. For certain insights in this respect, see the recollections of Darioush Homayoon, a prominent journalist and politician in the Shah's regime, titled '*Man va Rouze'gāram*' (*Me and My Life*), a compilation of interviews conducted by Bahman Amir-Hosseini (Hamburg: Talāsh publishers, 2008). As a young man in his early twenties Homayoon was a senior member of *Sumkā*. He confirms that Monshizadeh had been receiving money from Nerren and Cilley (Ibid.: 45–6), codenames for the Jalali-Kevani tandem.
36. Gasiorowski, 1987: 236; based on interviews with former CIA operatives, the author confirms TPBEDAMN payments to *Sumkā* and Pan-Iranist and Baqa'ei groups and a string of popular news papers. For the situation of Shaban Jafary during the August 1953 events, see Homa Sarshar, 2002: 160.
37. Montazeri,: <http://www.montazeri.com/>, p. 160; Kianouri, 1992: 252 fn. 45.
38. Wilber, *Overthrow*, 2000: 63.
39. See ibid.: 49 and 56; Gasiorowski and Byrne, 2004: 250.
40. Gasiorowski, 1987.
41. Wilber, *Overthrow*, 2000: 63.
42. Kianouri was the general secretary of the *Tudeh* Party in the late 1970s. He is the man who maintained a backchannel to Mosaddeq in 1952–53 due to family ties.
43. Kianouri, 1992: 270–1. He refers to the coverage of events from *Keyhan*, 20 August 1953.
44. *Tudeh* was widely known in Iran for order and discipline. For a confirmation by foreign observers, see Kennett Love's piece in *The New York Times*, 22 July 1953; US chargé Mattison's telegram 142, same date, observed the 'Tudeh demonstrations the previous day [21 July] were large and well organized and that Tudeh masses displayed a high degree of discipline' (FRUS, Vol. X, p. 838 fn.2).
45. Other historical leaders of *Tudeh*, like Ehsan Tabari in 'Kaj'rāheh' ('Deviation'), and Fereydoun Keshavarz's 'Man Mottaham Mīkonam' ('I Accuse') as

well as Iraj Eskandari and Anvar Khamenei in their respective memoirs, have severely criticized Kianouri in relation to the *Tudeh* Party's line notably during Mosaddeq. The party's Fourth Plenum in 1957 in Leipzig (East Germany) criticized the party leadership's conduct during the critical days from 16 to 19 August; Kianouri personally came under fire for errors during those days, notably the inaction during 19 August (Kianouri, 1992: 373).'

46. See Gasiorowski, 1987; Gasiorowski and Byrnes, 2004: 254.
47. The passage on p. 66 reads: 'Their plan was to print broadsheets at this town [Qazvin], some 85 miles west of Tehran, should it appear that the Mossadeq [sic] government had increased its attempted stranglehold on the urban press. As soon as they noticed that the pro-Shah groups were gathering [Djalali, Majidi, and Rezali, another sub-agent] rushed to supply the needed leadership.'
48. Wilber, *Overthrow*, 2000: 64.
49. Both Wilber in *Overthrow* (pp. 51 and 64) and Roosevelt in *Countercoup* confirm that the State Department had taken the position that the game was over and all covert operations against Mosaddeq must stop. From his resort vacation place in the Austrian Alps, Henderson had gone to Beirut in mid-August to follow events and must therefore have been in contact with the Department after the failure of the TPAJAX *coup*.
50. Ibid.: 77.
51. See cable 398, cited under heading 'US Embassy Monitoring' above.
52. FRUS, Vol. X, doc. 348, pp. 752–5.
53. See the Truman Library Oral History project, the 1974 interview with Henderson: <http://www.trumanlibrary.org/oralhist/hendrson.htm>. The full paragraph by Henderson is quoted here for the record: 'It has been charged that the CIA inspired the uprising that started with the march of the members of the athletic club in Tehran. Whether it did or did not, I honestly don't know. When I returned to Tehran, I was under the impression that Mossadegh [sic], at least for a time, had won his long conflict with the Shah. I was surprised by the events that took place the next day, and I think that if they are ever published, my telegrams to the Department will support what I am saying. I am sure of one thing, however. No matter how skilled the CIA might be, it could not have engineered the overthrow of Mossadegh [sic] if the people of Iran had not overwhelmingly been in favour of the return of the Shah.'
54. FRUS, Vol. X, doc. 349, pp. 755–6.
55. In his memoirs Eisenhower (1963: 199) later wrote that during those days the Americans officials in Tehran had done all they could to help. Eisenhower's remark here, though tacitly disclaiming responsibility for the outcome, appears to result from subsequent Roosevelt debriefings which were personally given to Eisenhower on the latter's request. It should be read against the backdrop of the comment the president made when he was actually briefed by Roosevelt, analogizing his account to a dime novel. See the Introduction and p. 177n. 17.
56. See Roosevelt, 1979: ch. IX, pp. 78–85.
57. Ibid.: 61.
58. Cited in Zahedi, 2006: 269.
59. Roosevelt, 1979: 183–5.

60. Many authors have echoed Roosevelt's claim to the effect that he coached Henderson before the latter saw Mosaddeq on the evening of 18 August. In their writings they have underscored the impact of this meeting on the events of the following day to the extent that, as the result of Henderson's demarche, Mosaddeq ordered the police to crack-down on *Tudeh* demonstrators; this purportedly facilitated the pro-Shah uprising the following day. (Although not everyone explicitly claims that it was a deliberate move. See Gasiorowski and Byrne, 2004: 253.) In some narratives this factoid has taken on melodramatic proportions (e.g., Kinzer, 2003: 174; Villiers, 1975: 241).
61. The passage in *Overthrow* about the events of Tuesday evening 18 August – corresponding to the time of Henderson's visit to Mosaddeq – reads as follows: 'Security forces were given orders to clear the streets and serious fighting resulted. Friends of Colonel [Hamidi] in the Police Department exceeded instructions in preventing Tudeh vandalism by beating up Tudehites and shouting for the Shah.' Clearly, if this event was the outcome of Henderson's demarche and Roosevelt's coaching, a mention in the CIA internal report would have been in order.
62. Henderson's 1972 Oral History interview with the Truman Library in 1972: <http://www.trumanlibrary.org/oralhist/hendrson.htm>.
63. Wilber, *Overthrow*, 2000: 51.
64. Mattison's cable to the State Department, 16 August, FRUS, Vol. X, doc. 343, p. 745.
65. Reuters dispatch dated 16 August, carried in *The New York Times*, 17 August 1953.
66. See FRUS, Vol. X, doc. 347. pp. 748–52.
67. Roosevelt, 1979: 183.
68. In his report to Washington, Henderson had detected in Mosaddeq's attitude a certain amount of '*smouldering resentment*', suspecting Anglo-American complicity to change the government (FRUS, Vol. X, doc. 347, pp. 747–52).
69. In his oral history interview 20 years later, Henderson affirmed that Mosaddeq had called the police chief in his presence. Why didn't he mention it in his report to Washington? Could that be an oversight or a deliberate omission then or a mix up 20 years later? This is hard to judge. What is known is that, in the same breath, he disclaims any prior knowledge of plans for the following day, Wednesday 19 August.
70. Mosaddeq later recalled having ordered the dispersal in the afternoon of 18 August (1986: 273–4).
71. Kianouri, 1992: 268.
72. Wilber, *Overthrow*, 2000: 61.
73. Ibid.
74. Further, a reasonable presumption could be made that these religious leaders may have indeed spent money in their crowd-mobilization efforts on 18–19 August, as has always been the case for organizational expenses and incentives. Such traditional methods should not be confused with bribing and a CIA-funded crowd-mobilization effort.
75. Wilber, *Overthrow*, 2000: Appendix E, p. 22, paragraph Q. This source was also citedearlier in the chapter under 'The Role of Iranian Agents'.

76. We have already referred to Kim Roosevelt's World in Action interview, retrievable from: <http://www.youtube.com/watch?v=QBs8WFNdSdQ&aNR=1>, video 2.
77. Other death figures cited are: (a) Tehran coroner's office (*pezeshk'e qā'nouni*) which put the death 'in front of the Mosaddeq house' at 75 (cited by Matini, 2005: 375). A *provisional* figure of 35 dead was given by a digest of Tehran press published on 20 August in *Khāndanī'hā* (reproduced in Zahedi, 2006: 252–60).
78. Cottam, 1964: 228–9; Cottam rejected the characterization of the crowd by a *Saturday Evening Post* article in 1954. For his position in later years, see the explanations given in the Introduction chapter (pp. 6 and 177n. 12).
79. As noted earlier, contrary to a widely held assumption, the notorious mob leader Shaban Jafari was serving a prison term at that time and could have played no role in crowd mobilization.
80. A footnote by the FRUS editor while making the above caveats states that Under-Secretary Henry Byroade had seen and personally inscribed his initials on the document (see Vol. X, doc. 362, pp. 780–8).
81. Suspicion has long been focused on Abdol'hossein Meftah, the Mosaddeq-appointed deputy foreign minister. Mosaddeq's son and personal physician, who had known and may have recommended Meftah to his father, later lamented in family circles that Meftah had betrayed his father and was a British informer (information obtained in private discussion with a close family member of Dr Mosaddeq). Author Fakhreddin Azimi also believes that Meftah's profile fits the description given by Woodhouse of his high-level contact 'Omar' and regards Meftah as the most likely candidate (Gasiorowski and Byrne, 2004: 290). As deputy, and frequently acting, foreign minister, Meftah was a frequent participant in cabinet meetings especially as his minister Fatemi, having escaped an assassination attempt by *Fadā'iān Islam* in February 1952 with serious injuries, was occasionally on sick leave and more interested in internal politics than his role as foreign minister. What makes the conjecture about Meftah rather lame, however, is the fact that he took up his post as deputy foreign minister in mid-October 1952, coinciding with the rupture of diplomatic relations and the departure of British diplomats including the MI6 chief Woodhouse. Woodhouse claims that 'Omar' spontaneously presented himself to him and for several months directly reported to him (1982: 111–12). Meftah's memoirs, written in Persian, described the date and circumstances of his appointment (assigned from his post in Hamburg as of October 1952; a rough mimeographed English translation of these memoirs was examined by this author), n.d.: 18–21. As memoirs in general are liable to memory lapses and/or deliberate spin, we refrain from making a definitive judgement on this issue.
82. The news of Modabber's arrest is recorded in Aqeli's chronology (1997: Vol. 2, p. 17).
83. Interview with Ardeshir Zahedi, Montreux, 31 March 2008; a list of pro-Shah officers who were known to TPAJAX planners is given in note 51 in Chapter 5. Figuring among them is a Colonel Mansurpour, commander of a cavalry regiment (which is not the same thing as motorized), yet this officer's allegiance was not newly acquired as his name appears in the list prepared between Carroll, Farzanegan and Zand-Karimi in the TPAJAX context.

84. Kianouri, 1992: 276.
85. Telegram 788.00/8 by Henderson to the Department of State (FRUS, Vol. X, doc. 347, p. 752).
86. Wilber, *Overthrow*, 2000: Appendix B, London draft plan of operations, p. 20.
87. Ibid.: ch. II, p. 10.
88. FRUS, vol. X, doc. 358, pp. 772–3.
89. Woodhouse, 1982: 130. This summing up by Woodhouse is in fact in line with Kim Roosevelt's own assessment made in the afore-cited interview with *World in Action*: <http://www.youtube.com/watch?v=_y_TjO44Rx0& NR=1>.

7 Where Did the Spark Come From?

1. Zahedi: 2006: 265 and 273.
2. For a list of clerics who supported Mosaddeq – of whom none then carried the title of Ayatollah – see Katuzian, in Gasiorowski and Byrne, 2004: 14.
3. Wilber, *Overthrow*, 2000: 46; the US chargé Mattison to Department of State, FRUS, Vol. X, doc. 343, p. 745.
4. The proclamation by the Central Committee was published in the 18 August issue of *'shojā'at'*, which had replaced *'Besouy'é Āyandeh'* as the party mouthpiece. Kianouri in his memoirs laments this proclamation as an error by the party leadership (1992: 267).
5. The embassy cable reads, 'Participants not of hoodlum type customarily predominant in recent demonstrations in Tehran. They seemed to come from all classes of people including workers, clerks, shopkeepers, students, etcetera' (FRUS, Vol. X, doc. 348, p. 758).
6. See *'Ulama* as a Socio-Political Force', in Chapter 1.
7. Some of the more notorious mob leaders such as Tayyeb Haj-Rezaie, known to have played a role in the 19 August anti-Mosaddeq riots, reappeared in a pro-Khomeini uprising ten years later on 5 June, 1963 (15 Khordad 1342).
8. See the reference to Dr Mehdi Azar (Chapter 4, section 2)
9. Montazeri memoirs: <http://www.montazeri.com/>, p. 161
10. Woodhouse, 1982: 122.
11. Montazeri: <http://www.montazeri.com/>, p. 160.
12. In the immediate aftermath of the Islamic Revolution, assessments in Iran tended to shield Boroujerdi from pro-monarchic or anti-Mosaddeq sentiments, shifting the blame to foreign efforts to aggrandize the communist menace. Ayatollah Montazeri attributes such moves, including a hate-mail campaign against clerics in the summer of 1953, to complicity between the Shah's Court and *Tudeh'e Nafti*, a term predating TP-BEDAMN in Iran's political lexicon that referred to disingenuous pro-British parallel *Tudeh* or other fake *Tudeh* groups. In the course of a speech in December 1979, Montazeri blamed the Shah's Court for unleashing the fake *Tudeh* against the clerical establishment to drive a wedge between Mosaddeq and Boroujerdi (cited from *Keyhan*, 10 Deymah 1358 (31 December 1979), in Kianouri's memoirs, ibid.: 252 fn. 45). Note that at that point in time the revived *Tudeh*, under the leadership of Kianouri, had allied itself to Khomeini and the Islamic revolution.

13. *Etelā'at* daily, 3 March 1953; the full citation is given on page 208n. 36.
14. It is far fetched, though not excludable, to assume that TP-BEDAMN, or its British *Operation Boot*, may have instigated such insults to smear *Tudeh*.
15. In footnote 45, p. 252 of his memoir, Kianouri cites Montazeri's remarks referred to in note 12 above, but does not confirm or deny the allegation of fake *Tudeh* having been launched by the CIA. Elsewhere in his memoirs, he has flatly denied infiltration of fake *Tudeh* groups in their ranks at that epoch (Kianouri, 1992: 270–1).
16. The Ala conversation with Henderson, 30 March 1953, FRUS, Vol. X, doc. 322, pp. 719–20; Zahedi, 2006: 120–1.
17. See 'The *Ulama* as a Socio-Political Force', in Chapter 1.
18. Wilber, *Overthrow*, 2000: Annex B, pp. 20–1.
19. Ibid.: Annex B, the London Plan.
20. For details, see Chapter 6, 'Anatomy of 19 August'.
21. See Chapter 4, the section on Boroujerdi.
22. In his account of the events of 19 August, Professor Housahang Nahavandi, a top official under the Shah writes, '*Les chefs du Bazar avaient appelé le grand ayatollah de Qom, Boroujerdi, pour lui demander ce qu'ils devaient faire*' ('The Bazaar dignitaries had called upon the grand ayatollah of Qom, Boroujerdi, in order to ask him what they should do') (2006: 245).
23. The exact wording was related to this author by a key government official in post in Qom shortly after the events of 19 August, who had frequent contacts with the Grand Ayatollah (whose identity I am not at liberty to disclose). See also Wilber, *Overthrow*, 2000: 65–6.
24. Behbahani's support for the Shah and his role in the February and August 1953 events is acknowledged across the board. Professor Mark Gasiorowski observes: 'Ayatollah Behbahani apparently played a key role in organizing the demonstrations of August 19' (in Gasiorowski and Byrnes, 2004: 254). *See also* Azimi, ibid.: p. 67, Bill, 1988: 101; Wilber, *Overthrow*, 2000: 57; Homa Katuzian, *Musaddiq and the Struggle for Power in Iran* (London and New York: I. B. Tauris 1999), 178–9. Woodhouse, Kianouri, Zahedi and a host of other authors also refer to the supportive role played by Behbahani, notably during the 28 February 1953 crisis.
25. Wilber, *Overthrow*, 2000: 66.
26. A compilation of *hadīs*, or accounts of the sayings and conduct of the prophet and the 12 Shiite *imāms*, handed down by word of mouth. *Hadīs* ranks second only after the Koran and are used as jurisprudence by *Marja* (or source of emulation).
27. Montazeri: <http://www.montazeri.com/>, p. 160.
28. The passage on p. 74 of *Overthrow* reads,' Reactions were also being reported from the provinces. At 14.50 hours the regional station at Sanandaj in Kurdestan suddenly went off the air. At 15.55 hours Radio Tabriz reported the capture of the station itself by forces loyal to the Shah, and stated that all of Azerbaijan was in the hands of the army.... By 1800 hours the station at Isfahan was on the air with strong statements in favour of the Shah and Zahedi by such elements as local editors, a member of Baghai's [*sic*] Toilers Party, religious leaders, and staff officers – all groups which we had hoped would react in this fashion. Not until 2000 hours did the radio station at Kerman proclaim loyalty to the new government. Meshed Radio was

not heard from at all, but the religious-minded town turned royalist almost immediately after the news of the change had been sent out over Radio Tehran. Known Tudehites were pursued and shops of Tudeh sympathizers looted'. As a personal observation, this author was eyewitness to commotion in Shiraz by around 1500 on 19 August.
29. Zahedi, 2006: 188
30. Interview, Montreux 31 March 2009. Zahedhi's words in Persian were 'Sherāfatan agar dekhālat'e rohaniyon naboud in etefāq nemī'oftād' ('In all honesty, had it not been for the intervention of religious leaders this occurrence [19 August, 1953] would not have happened'). When asked whether Ayatollah Boroujerdi had personally played a role the answer was 'Albateh! Behbahani bedoun'e ejāzeh'e eīshan hich karī nemīkard' ('Of course! Behbahani would do nothing without his permission').
31. Richard Cottam had been a Fulbright scholar in Iran just before the rise of the National Front to power. He served at the American Embassy (probably as part of the CIA station) 1956–57. For reference to Cottam's modified stance in later years, see the relevant passage in the Introduction.
32. Due to its historical relevance, the original wording of the Boroujerdi response to the Shah is cited here from *Etelā'āt* (the authoritative Tehran daily which could be regarded as an official gazette), 25 August, 1953 (cited in Ali Gharib article, see note 29 in Chapter 3):

' پیشگاه اعلیحضرت همایونی شاهنشاهی خلد الله ملکه، امید است ورود مسعود
اعلیحضرت به ایران مبارک و موجب اصلاح مفاسد ما فیه و عظمت اسلام و آسایش مسلمین باشد.
بیایید که تشیع و اسلام به شما احتیاج دارد . شما پادشاه شیعه هستید.

Seyyed Mahmoud Kashani (the late Ayatollah Kashani's son) has made a reference to this message in an article in *Sharq* reproduced in *Nimrouz* (London, no. 827, 18 March 2005/28 Esfand 1383) but does not provide the full text.

8 Summary and Conclusions

1. Iraj Pezeshkzad has lampooned this character trait in his exquisite novel *Dā'i Jān Napoleon* (Uncle Napoleon) written in 1970s and available online.
2. Or 'an event on Wednesday was planned', depending on how one reads the passage in the CIA's account (Wilber, *Overthrow*, 2000).

Direct Sources of the Study

(Includes material reviewed for data cross-checking.)

Abrahamian, Ervand (1968), 'The Crowd in Iranian Politics', *Past and Present*, No. 41 (December).
Abrahamian, Ervand (1983), *Iran Between Two Revolutions* (New Jersey: Princeton University Press).
Acheson, Dean (1969), *Present at the Creation: My Years in the State Department* (New York: W. W. Norton).
Alikhani, Alinaghi, ed. (1991), *The Shah and I: The Confidential Diary of Iran's Royal Court, 1969–1997 Asadollah Alam* (London: I. B.Tauris).
Ambrose, Stephen (1984), *Eisenhower*, vol. II, *The President* (New York: Simon & Schuster).
Ansari, Ali M. (2003), *Modern Iran since 1921* (London: Pearson Educational).
Bakhtiar, Shahpour (1982), *Ma Fidélité*, (Paris: Albin Michel).
Bill, James (1988), *The Eagle and the Lion: The Tragedy of American-Iranian Relations* (New Haven, CT: Yale University Press).
Bill, James and Louis, William Roger, eds (1988), *Musaddiq, Iranian Nationalism and Oil* (London: I. B. Tauris).
Cottam, Richard (1964), *Nationalism in Iran* (Pittsburgh: Pittsburgh University Press).
Eisenhower, Dwight (1963), *Mes Années à la Maison Blanche* (*My Years at the White House*), Vol. I, 1953–56 (Paris: Robert Laffon).
Falle, Sam (1996), *My Lucky Life in War, Revolution, Peace and Diplomacy* (Sussex: Book Guild).
Farmanfarmaian, Manucher and Roxane (1997), *Blood & Oil: Memoirs of a Persian Prince* (New York: Random House).
Gasiorowski, Mark (1987), 'The 1953 Coup d'État in Iran', *International Journal of Middle East Study*, No. 19 (August).
Gasiorowski, Mark and Malcolm Byrne, eds (2004), *Mohammmad Mosaddeq and the 1953 Coup in Iran* (New York: Syracuse University Press).
Griffiths, Sir Eldon (2006), *Recollections, Revelations and a Plan for Peace* (California: SLP).
Katuzian, Homa (1999), *Musaddig and the Struggle for Power in Iran* (London and New York: I. B. Tauris).
Keddie, Nikki, ed. (1983), *Religion and Politics in Iran: Shi'ism from Quietism to Revolution* (London and New Haven, CT: Yale University Press).
Keddie, Nikki (2003), *Modern Iran: Roots and Results of the Revolution* (London and New Haven, CT: Yale University Press).
Keddie, Nikki and Yann Richard (1981), *Roots of Revolution: An Interpretive History of Modern Iran* (New Haven, CT: Yale University Press).
Kinzer, Stephen (2003), *All the Shah's Men: An American Coup and the Roots of Middle East Terror* (New York: John Wily).

Lapping, Brian (1985), *The End of Empire* (London: Granada).
Louis, William Roger (1984), *British Empire in the Middle-East1941–1951: Arab Nationalism: The United States and Post-War Imperialism* (Oxford: Oxford University Press).
McGhee, George (1984), *Envoy to the Middle World; Adventures in Diplomacy* (New York: Harper & Row).
Milani, Abbas (2008), *Eminent Persians: The Men and the Women Who Made Modern Iran, 1941–1979* (Syracuse, NY: Persian World Press).
Nahavandi, Dr Houshang (2006), *Iran, Le Choc des Ambitions* (London: Aquilion).
Pahlavi, Mohammad-Reza (1961), *Mission for my Country* (New York: McGraw-Hill).
Pahlavi, Princess Ashraf (1980), *Faces in a Mirror, Memoirs from the Exile* (Englewood Cliffs, NJ: Prentice Hall).
Pollack, Kenneth M. (2005), *The Persian Puzzle: The Conflict Between Iran and America* (New York: Random House).
Roosevelt, Kermit (1979), *Countercoup: The Struggle for the Control of Iran* (New York: McGraw-Hill).
Rubin, Barry (1980), *Paved with Good Intentions* (Oxford: Oxford University Press).
Shawcross, William (1988), *The Shah's Last Ride* (New York: Simon & Schuster).
Sykes, Sir Percy (1963), *A History of Persia*, Vol. II (Basingstoke: Macmillan).
Villiers, Gérard de (1975), *L'Irresistible Ascenssion de Mohammad Reza, Shah d'Iran* (Paris: Plon).
Wilber, Donald (1986), *Adventures in the Middle East: Excursions and Incursions* (Princeton, NJ: Darwin Press).
Woodhouse, Christopher Montague (1982), *Something Ventured* (London: Granada).
Zabih, Sepehr (1982), *The Mossadegh Era: Roots of the Iranian Revolution* (Chicago, IL: Lake View Press).

Books and publications in Persian language

Ahmadi, Hamid (1380/2001), *Tahqīqi darbāreh'e tārikh'e enqelāb'e iran* (*A Study on the History of Iran's Revolution*), Vol. II (Frankfurt: Enghelāb'e Islami Zeitung).
Alikhani, Alinaqi, ed. (1382/2003), *Yāddāsht'hāy'e Alam, sale 1354* (*Diaries of Alam 1975–76*), Vol. 5 (Tehran: Ketabsara Publishers).
Amir-Ahmadi, General Amir-Ahmad (1378/1999), *Khāterāt Nakhostin Sepahpod'e Iran Amir-Ahmad Amir-Ahmadi (Memoirs of Iran's First Lieutenant General)*, ed. Gholam-Hossein Zargari-Nejad. Published by 'Markaz Motāle'āt va Pazhohesh'hay'e Farhangui' (Tehran: Centre for Research and Cultural Studies).
Aqeli, Baqer (1376/1997), *Rouzshomari'ye Tārīkh'e Iran Az Mashroutieh tā Engelab'e Eslāmī* (*Chronology of Iranian History from Constitution to the Islamic Revolution*), (Tehran: Nashr'e Goftār).
Asgari, Nour-Mohammad (2000), *Shah, Mosaddegh, Sepahbod Zahedi* (Stockholm).
Ashraf, Ahmad (1359/1980), *Mavāne'e Tārīkhi'e Roshd'e Sarmāyeh-gozāri dar Iran dar doreh'e Qājārieyeh* (*Historical Barriers for Growth of Capital Investment in Iran during the Qājār Period*), (Tehran: Peyyam Publishers).
Dabiri, Mostafa (1386/2007), *Bohrān'e Azerbaijan* (*The Azerbaijan Crisis*), (Tehran: Parvin Publishers).

Fardoust, General Hossein (1369/1990), *Zohour va Soqout'e Saltanet'e Pahlavi; Khâterât'e Arteshbod'e Sabegh Hossein Fardoust* (*Memoirs of Ex-General Hossein Fardoust*), (Tehran: Tehran Political Research Institute).
Fateh, Motafah (1358/1980), *Panjah Sāl Naft (Fifty Years of Oil)*, (Tehran: Kavosh Publishers).
Hashemi-Rafsanjani, Sara Lahooti (2008), *Omid va Delvāpasi, kārnameh va khāterāt'e Hashemi Rafsanjani, sāl'e 1364* (*Hope and Preoccupation: The Balance-Sheet and Memoirs of [Ali-Akbar] Hashemi – Rafsanjani,1364/1985*), (Tehran: Daftar'e Nashr'e Ma'āref 'e Eslami Publishers).
Homayoon, Daryoush (2008), *Man va Rouze'gāram* (*Me and My Life*), a compilation of interviews with Homayoon conducted by Bahman Amir-Hosseini (Talāsh Publishers, Hamburg).
Kianouri, Noureddin (1371/1992), *Khāterāt'e Noureddin Kianouri* (*Kianouri Memoirs*), (Tehran: Moasseseh'e tahqiqāti va enteshārāti 'e Didgah).
Makki, Hossien (1366/1987), *Tārīkh'e Bīst-sāl'eh Iran*, Vol. VIII (Tehran: Elmī Publishers).
Malaki, Ahmad (2005), *Tārīkhcheh'e Jebhey'e Mellī* (*A History of the National Front*), (Stockholm).
Matini, Jalal (2005), *Negāhi be Kār'nāmeh'e Sīsasi doctor Mohammad Mosaddeq* (*A Review of Dr Mohammad Mosaddeq's Political Balance-Sheet*), (Los Angeles: Sherkat Ketāb Publishers).
Meftah, Abul'hossein (n.d.), *Haqiqat Bi'rangue Ast* (*Truth Has No Colour*), (London, 1983). (An unpublished mimeographed English translation of this book was available to this author for this volume).
Montazeri Ayatollah Seyyed Hassan-Ali, *Majmou'eh kāmel'e khāterāt'e Ayatollah Montazeri* (*Full Compilation of the Memoirs of Ayatollah Montazeri*), online: <http://www.montazeri.com/>.
Mosaddeq, Doctor Mohammad (1365/1986), *Khāterāt'e va Ta'alomāt* (*Recollections and Chagrins*), ed. Iraj Afshar (Tehran: Elmi Publishers).
Movahed, Mohammad-Ali (1378/2000), *Khāb'e Āshofteh'e Naft: Doctor Mosaddeq va Nehzat'e Melli Iran* (*The Oil Nightmare: Dr Mosaddeq and Iran's National Movement*), (Tehran: Nashr'e Karnamah).
Pahlavi, Mohammad-Reza (1980), *Pāsokh be Tārīkh* (*Answer to History*), (Ligugé, France: Aubin).
Qarib, Ali, *Kashani, Mosaddeq, Tafāhomāt va Taqābolāt* (*Kashani and Mosaddeq; Undestandings and Confrontations*). Web article: <http://asre-nou.net:80/1386/mordad/27/m-kashani-mossadegh.html>.
Rouhani, Fuad (1366/1987), *Zendegui Siāsi Mosaddegh dar Matn'e Nehzat'e melli Iran* (*The Political Biography of Mosaddeq in the Context of the Iranian National Movement*), (Paris: Nehzat'e Moqāvemat'e Melli).
Sanjabi, Karim (1381/2002), *Khāterāt'e Doctor Karim Sanjabi* (*Memoirs of Dr Karim Sanjabi*), (Tehran: Seday'e Mo'āser Publisher).
Sarshar, Homa, ed. (1381/2002), *Khāterāt'e Shabān Jafary* (*Memoirs of Shaban Jafary*), (Tehran: Sāles Publishers).
Toloui, Mahmoud (1372/1992), *Pedar va Pesar; Nā'goftehā az Zendegui va Rouzegār'e Pahlavi'ha* (*The Father and the Son; Untold Accounts of the Life and the Epoch of the Pahlavis*), (Tehran: Elmi Publishers).
Zahedi, Ardeshir (2006), *Khāterāt'e Ardeshir Zahedi* (*Ardeshir Zahedi's Memoirs*), Vol. I (Maryland: IBEX).

Zarbakhat, Morteza and Hamid Ahmadi (2004), *Khāterāti az Sāzemān'e Afsarān'e Hezb'e Tudeh Iran (Recollections from the Military Organisation of the Tudeh Party of Iran)*, (Tehran: Qoqnous Publishers), p. 241.

From Iranian archives

Khalil Maleki Be'ravāyat'e Asnād'e SAVAK (Khalil Maleki as Depicted by SAVAK Archives), (Tehran: Markaz'e Baresy'e Asnād'e Tarikhi, 1379/2000).
Tehran Political Research Institute, *Zohour va Soghout'e Saltanat'e Pahlavi (The Rise and Fall of the Pahlavi Dynasty)*, Vol. II (Tehran, 1369/1990).

Archive documents, press and periodicals

Foreign Relations of the United States (FRUS, 1970), *Near-East and North Africa*, 1946, Vol. VII, *Iran* (Washington: United States Printing Office).
Foreign Relations of the United States (FRUS); *Near-East and North Africa*, 1950, Vol. V (Washington: United States Printing Office).
Foreign Relations of the United States (FRUS), *Europe, 1950*), Vol. III (Washington: United States Printing Office).
Foreign Relations of the United States (FRUS, 1989), *Iran*, 1952–54, Vol. X (Washington: United States Printing Office).
Harvard Oral History Project: Interview with Dr Mehdi Azar, 1983: <http://www.fas.harvard.edu/~iohp/AZAR08.PDF4->.
Harvard Oral History Project: Interview with Doctor Mozaffar Baqai'ei Kermani, 1983: <http://www.fas.harvard.edu/~iohp/baghaie.html>.
Iran files: Public Record Office, London.
National Front website: <http://www.jebhemelli.net/mossadegh/index.html>.
Truman Library Oral History Project: Interview with Loy Henderson (American Ambassador in Tehran 1951–54): <http://www.trumanlibrary.org/oralhist/hendrson.htm>.
Wilber, Donald (2000), *Clandestine Service History: Overthrow of Premier Mossadeq [sic] of Iran, November 1952–August 1953*. This internal CIA document written in 1954 was published by *The New York Times* in 2000. <http://cryptome.org/cia-iran-all.htm#VIII>.
World In Action, Granada TV channel; 'US Overthrows Iranian Government 1953', Interview with Kim Roosevelt, 1973. Available on web in two video tubes: <http://www.youtube.com/watch?v_y_TjO44Rx0&NR1>.
The New York Times, May 1951–August 1953.

Index

Aalam, Mozafar, 215n.2
Acheson, Dean, 23, 34, 36, 45–6, 48, 60, 66, 182n.20, 188n.59, 189 nn.63–5, 66, 191n.8, 192n.12, 193nn.21, 22, 26, 28, 31, 195n.49, 57, 196nn.63–4, 200n.41, 43, 44, 202n.65, 204n.84, 234
Afshar, Seiful-Saltaneh, 218n.30, 222n.59
Afshāri tribe, 147
Afshartous, Brigadier-General Mahmoud, 63, 84, 209n.51, 53
Akhavi, Colonel Hassan, 94, 213n.98
Akhbārīs (religious sect), 18
Ala, Hossein, x, 25–6, 29–30, 40, 42 (fig. 8), 52–4, 57, 64, 75–6, 83 (fig. 16), 85, 87, 152, 161, 164, 179n.4, 185n.35, 188n.57, 205n.9, 209n.48, 210n.58, 232n.16
Alam, Asadollah, 7, 177n.14, 178n.14, 183n.28, 200n.40, 215n.2, 234n.35
Albright, Secretary Madeleine, 3
Alemi, Doctor Ebrahim, 192n.13, 215n.108
Allen, Ambassador George, 15, 182nn.21, 22, 23, 25, 193n.32
Amery, Julian, 202n.70
Amidi-Nouri, Abol'hassan, 226n.26
Amini, Abol'qassem, 87, 90, 201n.59
Amini, Ali, 201–2n.59
Amini, General Mahmoud, 201nn.57, 59
Amir-Ahmadi, General Ahmad, 182n.23, 235
Anglo-Iranian oil company (AIOC), 12, 13, 20, 23, 25–30, 33–7, 40–6, 48–9, 58, 60–1, 68–71, 162, 183n.54, 192n.10, 195n.50, 196n.71, 200n.47, 202n59, 203n.79, 204n.86, 207n.33

Anglophile, 13, 33, 37, 66, 142, 191n.6
Ārām, newspaper, 226n.26
ARAMCO, 25, 28, 37, 190n.4
Aramesh, Ahmad, 130
Arani, Taqi, 180n.7
Arbenz Guazman, President Jacobo, 7, 9
Arsanjani, Hassan, 198n.17
Ashrafi, Colonel Hossein-Ali, 63, 86, 108, 116–17, 201n.58, 210n.68, 219n.44, 220n.47, 223n.34, 224n.78
Āsiā'ye-Javān, newpaper, 226n.26
Attlee, Clement, 34, 41, 43, 158, 195n.54
Austin Warren, 43
Azar, Doctor Mehdi, 80, 208n.34, 215n.108, 231n.8
Azerbaijan Crisis, vii, 14, 16, 21, 136 and Qavam 55, 82, 157, 158, 159, 180n.11, 180n.12, 182n.22, 182n.25, 235

Baharmast, General Mahmoud, 63
Bakhtiar, Colonel Teymour, 105, 119, 168, 224n.1, 225n.9
Bākhtar Emrouz, newspaper, 101
Bakhtiari Aboul'qassem, 147, 205n.6, 205n.9
Bakhtiāri tribe, 14, 75, 147, 205n.6, 205n.9
Baluchi, ethnic group, 147
Baqa'ei, Dr Mozaffar, xvi, xvii, 40, 58–9, 76, 84, 104, 125, 127, 129, 184n.33, 199nn.39–40, 201nn.55–6, 205n.2, 206n.25, 208n.41, 209n.51, 209n.54, 218n.29, 227n.36
Baqerov, Mir-Jaafar, 181n.13
Batmanqelij, General Nader, 113 (fig. 25), 145, 214n.105, 222n.65

Bayat Mortezaqoli (Saham-Sultan), 72–3, 179n.4
Behbahani, Ayatollah Seyyed Mohammad, 76–8, 137, 141, 143, 149, 150, 152–4, 206n.15, 206n.17, 206n.19, 232n.24, 233n.30
Behboudi, Soleiman, 113 (fig. 25), 142, 184n.33, 212n.92, 213n.99
Berry, Ambassador Burton, 99, 216n.5
Besouy'e-āyandeh, Tudeh newspaper, 219n.36, 231n.4
Bevin, Ernest, 14, 23, 180n.11, 181n.18, 188n.59, 190n.3
Boīr'ahmadi tribe, 14, 147
Bolshevik Revolution, 12
Boot, UK covert operation, 35, 69, 84, 203n.78, 210n.55, 232n.14
Boroujerdi, Grand Ayatollah Mohammad-Hossein, viii, ix, x, 4, 21, 76, 78–80, 124, 130, 149, 150–4, 157, 163–4, 172–3, 183n.26, 186n.44, 206n.17, 207nn.28, 29, 31, 32, 39, 209n.50, 226n.24, 231n.12, 232nn.21–2, 233nn.30–3
  and Kashani, 79–80, 150
  and Khomeini, 79
  and Mosaddeq, 80, 124, 150–1
  and *noh'e esfand* crisis (28 Feb. 1953), 76
  as Grand Shiite *marja'* , 78
  attitude towards communism, 151
  attitude towards *Fada'ian*, 79
  attitude towards public affairs, 79
  emitting an opinion after the Shah's departure, 153
  monarchy and the Shah, 78, 149, 152
Britain (UK), viii, xiv, xv, 3, 9, 12–15, 20, 25, 28, 29–30, 37, 44, 46, 48, 50, 59–62, 66–7, 71, 73, 122, 124, 125, 131, 147, 155–62, 174
  and Azerbaijan crisis, 14–15
  and end of diplomatic relations with Iran, 69
  and operation Buccaneer 34, 65, 158
  and the Shah, 17, 89
  and Supplemental Oil Agreement, 22–3
  and TPAJAX, 84–7, *see also under* MI6
  early reaction to oil nationalisation, 33–5
  embassy reporting from Tehran, 64–5
  entrenched influence in Iran, 12–13
  lobbying the Shah, 24, 30, 52–4, 89, 90
  oil talks: Jackson mission, 40; Stokes, 42, Churchill Truman proposal, 59, 70, 72–3
  stereotyping Mosaddeq, 32, 34
  subversion, 65–7, 87, *see also* Boot, UK covert operation
  top secret evaluation report on the fall of Mosaddeq, 140–2
British Coal Industry Nationalisation Act (CBINA), 70–1
Bullard, Sir Reader, 17, 183n.31
Bushehri, Javad, 57, 198n.27
Butler, Baron Richard Austen (British Chancellor of Exchequer), 44
Byrnes, James Francis, 14, 180n.12, 182n.25

Cabell, General Charles P., 132
Carroll, George, 114–16, 119, 222n.66, 223n.74
Churchill, Winston, viii, 7, 12, 44, 49, 59, 60, 62, 86, 89, 94, 144, 161–3, 192n.19, 200n.48, 203n.74, 209n.55
CIA (Central Intelligence Agency):
  activities of agents in Tehran, 103–5, 123–5
  and money disbursed, 130, 136–8
  and official reaction to *coup* failure, 99, 121
  and release of Iran files, 8–10
  and the myth in Iran, 5–7
  assets in Iran, 85, 113, 125–7
  initial reaction to MI6 *coup* proposal, 69
  pressuring the Shah, 89–94
  scope of responsibilities in early years, 8, 178n.19

240 Index

CIA (Central Intelligence Agency) – *continued*
  taking credit (or disclaiming)
    Mosaddeq fall, 8, 120, 122, 131, 133, 145, 170
  the TPAJAX planning, 84–6
  see also vii–viii, xiv–xv, 1–5, 59, 97, 98, 103, 106, 108, 110, 113, 114–18, 120, 128–9, 133, 135, 140, 141, 144, 152–5, 160, 168, 170, 171, 173, 175, 176.n.3, 177nn.10–14, 178nn.18–20, 179n.24, 184n.33, 208nn.38–41, 209n.43, 210.nn.65–9, 211n.76, 213nn.99–100, 214n.102, 217nn.19–21, 218nn.26–32, 219n.45, 220nn.47–50, 221n.51, 222nn.59–65, 223n.67, 225nn.9–16, 226nn.23–6, 227nn.32–6, 228n.53, 229n.61–74, 232nn.15–28, 233n.31, 233n.2
Cottam, Professor Richard, 6, 106, 138, 154, 177nn.11–12, 206n.25, 230n.78, 233n.31, 234

Dād, newspaper, 218n.23, 226n.26
Daftari, General Mohammad, 108, 110, 117, 219n.46, 221n.56
D'Arcy, William Knox, 12, 191n.4
Darbyshire, Norman, 144, 212n.93
Davalu, Brig.Gen. 224n.3
De Golyer, Everett, 193n.34
Defence Materials procurement Agency (DMPA), 70
Demavand, Colonel, 220n.50
Democrat party of Azerbaijan, 13
Democrat party of Iran, 183n.29
Dixon, Pierson, 68–9, 203n.78
Dooher, Jerry, 24, 37, 188 nn.60–1
Dulles, Allen, 3, 71–2, 163
Dulles, John Foster, 3, 71–2, 87, 89, 97, 99, 124, 145, 163, 204n.88, 216n.7, 226n.21

Edālat Party, 13
Eden, Antony, 17, 45–8, 51, 59–60, 68, 72, 85, 126, 162, 183n.31, 195n.59, 196n.63, 200n.47, 203nn.74–8, 204nn.84–8, 209n.55
Eisenhower, Dwight D., xiii, 2, 3, 7, 62, 71, 73, 82, 86, 87, 89, 90, 94, 96, 97, 120, 121, 131–2, 136, 155, 161, 162, 170, 174, 178n.17, 209n.44–5, 211n.73, 212n.93, 223n.66, 228n.55, 234
Emami, Hassan (Emam'e Jom'eh), 53
Emami, Jamal, 29, 30, 191n.6
Entezam, Abdollah, 84
Eskandari, Abbas, 67
Eskandari Iraj, 228n.45
Etelā'āt (mass circulationTehran daily), 208n.36, 224n.76, 227n.32
Etelā'āt Māhineh, 217n.20, 227n.32
Etesami, Parviz, 209n.52

Fadā'iān Islam, 2, 21–2, 25, 39, 67, 77, 79, 152, 186nn.43–4, 187n.49, 202nn.29–31, 230n.81
Fakhrara'ei, Nasser, 21, 183n.30
Falle, Sir Samuel, xvi, 9, 65, 67, 69, 84, 202n.62, 234
Farahmand, Bashir, 96, 214n.106
Fardoust, General Hossein, 184n.31, 185n.35, 236
Faqihi Shirazi, 21
Farmān, newspaper, 226n.26
Farzanegan, Abbas, 85, 104–5, 113–16, 168, 225n.9
Fateh, Mostafa, 191n.4, 196n.71, 236
Fatemi Hossein, 25, 39, 44, 74, 76, 95, 99, 101, 103, 145, 150, 187n.49, 203n.80, 204n.1, 214n.106, 215.n.2, 209n.36, 230n.81
February 28, 1953 crisis (*noh'e Esfand* 1332), 72, 75–8, 80, 152, 163, 164, 173, 205n.1, 206nn.20–3, 209n.50, 232n.24
Firouz, Maryam, 182n.24
Firouz, Mozafar, 15, 182n.24
Firouz, Nosrat'dolleh, 182n.24
Forouhar, Daryoush, 127, 227n.34

Forouqi, Mohammad-Ali, 179n.4, 184n.31
Fouladvand, Brigadier-General, 112
Franks, Oliver S, 34, 36, 193nn.22, 35
Furlonge, Geoffrey, 192n.11

Garner, Robert, 48
Gasiorowski, Professor Mark, 129, 130, 210n.69 (plus extensive source references)
Gifford Walter, S., 47, 197n.12
Goiran, Roger, 125, 126
Goodwin, Joseph, 126
Grady, Ambassador Henry, x, 24, 26, 30, 37, 38 (fig. 7), 39, 50, 189n.63, 193n.33, 194n.41
Guilanshah, General Hedayatollah, x, 24, 26, 30, 37, 38 (fig. 7), 39, 50, 189nn.63–5, 193n.32, 194n.41, 195n.52
Gulf Oil, 7
Gutt, Camille, 198n.25

Haeri'zadeh, Abol'hassan, 192n.32, 201n.56
Haeri-Yazdi, Grand Ayatollah Haj Hossein, 78
Haj-Rezaie, Tayyeb, 231n.7
Hakim, Ayatollah Mohsen Tabataba'ei, 149
Hakimi, Ebrahim, 14, 179n.4
Hamidi, Colonel, 223n.70, 229n.61
Harkness, Richard and Galdyce, 6, 106, 137, 219n.40
Harriman, William Averell, x, 27, 34, 36, 41–2, 45, 49, 82, 192n.12, 193n.22, 194n.39, 196n.71, 198n.27, 208n.41
Hasibi, Kazem, 196n.71, 198n.15, 198n.26, 217nn.17–18
Hazhir, Abdol'hossein, 27, 179n.4
Hedayat, Sadegh, 189n.67
Hejazi, Gen. Abol'hossein, 203n.80
Helms, Richard, 8, 133, 178n.20
Henderson, Loy, viii, xi, 5, 6, 50–4, 56, 59–61, 69, 70, 71–2, 75, 77, 83, 85, 87, 89, 90, 96, 107, 118, 121, 131–6, 138, 141, 143, 145, 159, 164, 166–7, 170, 180n.11, 182n.20, 192n.10, 194n.41, 195n.49, 196n.68, 197nn.3, 6, 9, 11, 198n.24, 200n.48, 204n.87, 204n.92, 208n.33, 209n.45, 209n.48, 210n.58, 211n.73, 219nn.41–2, 221nn.54–5
Hezār'fāmil, 11
Hirad Rahim, 94, 213n.99
Houman, Ahmad, 53

Import-Export Bank (IMEXBANK), 24, 188n.55, 189n.64, 203n.75
International Court of Justice (ICJ), 33, 35, 41, 43, 44, 53, 56, 59, 60, 70–1, 158, 159, 160, 162, 195n.52, 200n.47, 204n.86
Iran party, 74, 219n.36
Islamic Revolution, 1, 2, 3, 22, 79, 150, 151, 175, 177, 183n.28, 185n.39, 186n.44, 187n.49, 231n.12

Jackson, Basil, 40, 41, 195n.50
Jafari, Sha'ban, 127, 205n.2, 206n.20, 206n.24, 230n.72
Jalali, Ali, 85, 119, 126–8, 170, 218n.26, 227n.32, 267n.35, 228n.47
Jasseb, Sheikh, 181n.17
Jeff, Sir Goldwyn, 43
Journal de Téhéran, newspaper, 212n.91, 226n.26
July 21, 1952 uprising, *see Siy'e Tyr* 1331

Kamal, Brig. Gen. Azizollah, 203n.80, 204n.1
Kashani, Ayatollah Seyyed Abol'qassem, vii, x, 2, 4
  and Ayatollah Khomeini, 22
  and Boroujerdi, 79–80, 164
  and *Fada'ian Islam*, 22
  and National Front, 39–40
  and *noh'e esfand* crisis, 76
  and Razmara, 25, 28, 29
  and *Siy'e Tyr* uprising, 55
  anti-Mosaddeq campaign, 83, 84, 87–8
  biographical sketch, 20–2

Kashani, Ayatollah Seyyed
    Abol'qassem – *continued*
  rift with Mosaddeq, 57–8, 59
  role in 19 August 1953, 137, 152–3
  see also 124, 130, 149, 150, 152, 157,
    163, 164, 165, 176n.1, 185n.41,
    186n.43, 186n.45, 187nn.47,
    49, 51, 189n.68, 198nn.26–7,
    199nn.28, 29, 30, 33, 40,
    201n.56, 202n.72, 205n.2,
    206n.20, 207n.31, 209n.53,
    211n.77, 212n.80, 214n.105,
    226n.23, 233n.32
Kashani, Seyyed Mahmoud, 233n.32
Kashani, Seyyed Mostafa, 185n.41
Kashanian, Hassan, 214n.105
Kasravi, Ahmad, 21, 25, 186n.43,
  208n.38
Kayvani, Farouq, 85, 119, 126–8, 170,
  218n.26, 267n.35
Keen, Major, 115
Keddie, Professor Nikkie, 180n.11
Kennedy administration, the,
  201n.59
Keshavarz, Fereydoun, 227n.45
Khajeh'nouri, Colonel, 215n.2,
  221n.51, 223n.68
Khajeh'nouri, Nazamul'molk, 215n.2
Khalatbari, Colonel Ziauddin, 111
Khameh'ei, Anvar, 181n.16
Khāndanī'hā, weekly magazine,
  208n.40, 220n.48, 230n.77
Khamenei, Ayatollah Seyyed Ali,
  187n.48
Khatibi, Hossein, 84
Khaz'al, Sheikh, 15, 81
Khiabani, Sheikh Mohammad,
  179n.6
Khosro-Panah, Lt. Colonel, 220n.50,
  223n.70
Khomeini, Ayatollah Rouhollah, 2, 21,
  22, 79, 88, 186n.43–4, 187n.49,
  199n.34, 207n29, 212n.80,
  231nn.7–12
Kianouri, Nour'uddin, xi, xvi, 95, 100,
  107, 108, 111, 127, 129 (fig. 29),
  135, 143, 151, 170, 174, 182n.24,
  183n.30, 186n.7, 186–7n.47,
  194n.42, 214n.102, 216nn.9–10,

218n.23, 220n.48, 227n.42–6,
  231n.4, 231n.12, 232nn.15–24
  see also Tudeh
Kinzer, Stephen, 114, 177n.4, 212n.94,
  213n.99, 222n.66, 229n.60
Komite'e Nejat'e Vatan (Committee for
  Salvation of the Fatherland),
  208n.42

Lambton, Dr Ann (Nancy), 66,
  202n.64
Langlie, Stephen, 148
Lavrentiev, Anatoly, 101, 166–7,
  216n.13
Levy, Walter, 196n.71
Lotfi, Abdol'ali, 192n.13
Louis, Professor William Roger, xiv,
  xv, 64
Love, Kennett, 74, 104, 106, 109, 138

Makin, Sir Roger, 68
Makki, Hossein, 28, 40, 58–9, 76, 87,
  189n.1, 199n.37, 201nn.55–6,
  205n.2, 298nn.39–40, 211n.77
Malaki, Khalil, 74, 295n.4, 219n.36
Mansour, Ali, 179n.4, 197n.6
Mansurpur, Colonel, 223n.70,
  230n.83
Mard'e Āsīā, newspaper, 226n.26
Masoudi, Abass, 227n.32
Mattison, Gordon, 227n.44, 229n.64,
  231n.3
Mazandi, Youssef, 218n.24
McGhee, George, 38–9, 45–6, 188n.57,
  188n.59, 190n.4, 192n.12,
  193n.29, 191n.1
McClure, General Robert, 114–15,
  222n.66, 225n.19
McNair, Sir Arnold, 56
McNair, William, 9
Meftah, Abdol'hossein, 101, 191n.10,
  230n.81
Melat'e Mā, newpaper, 226n.26
MI6 (External branch of SIS), xiv, 1, 2,
  4, 8, 9, 64–5, 67–9, 84–5, 86, 89,
  105, 113, 116, 119, 120, 124, 125,
  137, 140, 142, 144, 152, 155, 165,
  169, 178

Middleton, George, 52, 54, 59–61, 65, 67, 191, 198n.23
Mirlohi, Seyyed Mojtabla, 79
Mo'azzami, Abdollah, 87
Mo'azzami, Seyfollah, 222n.64
Modabber, General Nasrollah, 108, 142–3, 230n.82
Moharam-Ali Khan, 204n.1.
Momtaz, Colonel Ezatollah, 224n.78
Monshizadeh, Davoud, 227n.35
Montazeri, Ayatollah Hossein-Ali, 151, 153, 187n.49, 199n.30, 207n.28, 29, 31, 226n.24, 231n.12, 232n.15
Morrison, Herbert, 34, 68, 190n.3
Mosaddeq, Doctor Mohammad:
  and approach to Britain, 32–3, 64–8, 158
  and clerical establishment, 22, 25, 39, 77, 80, 83, 84, 87–8, 147, 150–4, 157, 163–4, 172–3
  and events on Wednesday 19 August, 106–9, 111–12
  and ICJ, 33–4, 53, 56
  and oil-less economy, 56
  and regime change, 56, 64, 100–3, 167
  and Security Council, 43–4
  and the Shah's dismissal order, 96
  and the US, 37–9, 87, 89, 96–7, 103, 131
  and World Bank oil proposal, 48–9
  appointment as prime minister, 29
  break-off of diplomatic relations with Britain, 69
  break-off of oil negotiations, 69, 72–3
  career background, 27–8, 30–1
  emergency powers, 57–8, 160, 200n.50, 202n.53, 206n.25
  handling of the oil crisis, 40–2, 44–50, 59–62, 70–1, 161–3
  last meeting with Henderson, 133–6
  legacy, xvi, 175
  Man of the Year, 52
  oil nationalisation, 28–9
  referendum, 75, 86, 88, 89, 91, 94, 103, 124, 165, 167
  reform of state institutions, 50, 62–4

  relations with the Shah, 17–18, 30, 40, 53–4, 75–7, 83, 88, 90, 91, 163–4 *see also under Siy'e Tyr and Noh'e esfand*)
  relations with the *Tudeh*, 38, 39, 74, 95, 107, 100, 111, 160
  rift among the allies of, 57–9
  surrender to new authorities, 112
  trip to US, 44–8
  see also vii–ix, x–xi, xii, xiv–xvi, 1–10, 12–13, 16–20, 22, 25, 27, 30, 32–3, 53, 56, 65, 66, 67–9, 82, 84–9, 91–2, 94–5, 98–100, 104–6, 113–17, 119, 121, 125–8, 130–3, 137–40, 146, 155–75
Mosaddeq, Doctor Qolam'hossein, 30, 38 (fig. 7), 42 (fig. 8), 44 (fig. 9)
Mostafa, Seyyed (Kashani's father), 185n.41
Movahed, Doctor Mohammad-Ali, 198n.15

Nader Shah (Afshar), 147
Naderi, Colonel, 201n.58, 210n.68
Nasiri, Colonel Nematollah, 95–6, 113 (fig. 25), 213n.100, 214nn.102–5, 222n.65
National Front, vii, 18, 22
  origins of, 27–8, 39
  rift within the ranks of, 57–9, 60–3
  seats won in the 17th legistaltive elections, 50, 55;
  the left wing of, 74, 82, 84, 97, 88, 100, 157–8, 160–1, 164, 189n.1, 193n.32, 197n.6, 199n.32, 201n.56, 208n.40, 209n.50, 201n.56, 208n.40, 209n.50
Navvabi, Colonel, 221n.51
Navvab, Hossein, 199n.28
Navvab-Safavi, Seyyed Mojtaba, x, 2, 21, 22 (fig. 3), 79, 152, 187n.48
NIOC, 6, 46, 71–2, 195n.50
Nitze, Paul, 204n.84
Nixon, Richard, 2, 133, 145, 176n.2
Noh'e esfand (28 February 1953 crisis), 72, 75–8, 80, 152, 163, 164, 173, 204n.1
Northcroft George, 28

Nouri, Sheikh Fazlollah, 185n.39
Nozari, Colonel, 108, 221n.51, 222n.65, 223n.70

Opposition, (Mosaddeq internal foes), 4, 62–4, 78, 160–1
Ordubadi, Colonel, 223n.70
Overthrow (the CIA internal history), 8–9, 85–6, 93, 98, 103–5, 108, 110–11, 114–16, 118–19, 121–5, 128, 130, 133–5, 138, 140, 143–5, 149, 151–2, 154, 168–71

Pahlavi, Prince Ali-Reza, 161, 198n.18
Pahlavi, Princess Ashraf, x, 63, 90, 91 (fig. 17), 140, 142, 161
Pahlavi, Mohammad-Reza Shah, vi, viii, x, xi, xv, 2–4, 7, 11, 13, 15–16, 25, 33, 47, 57–8, 89, 103–4, 124, 128–9, 161, 174
  accession to the throne, 16, 156, 183n.31
  and Ayatollah Boroujerdi, 78–9, 149, 151–4, 163–4, 172–3
  and Azerbaijan crisis, 15–17, 159
  and internal conspiracies, 83, 85, 164
  and Mosaddeq, 27, 29–30, 40, 52–6, 63–4, 90, 159, 163, 167, 174
  and Qavam, 14–15, 55–6
  and TPAJAX plot, 86, 89–90, 114, 114, 119–20, 123, 125, 133, 140, 164–6
  assassination attempt, 16, 183n.30, 18, 21, 25
  attitude towards oil nationalisation, 30, 40
  blackmailed by Roosevelt, 92–4
  character and style, 17–18, 184n.33
  constitutional prerogatives of, 18, 54–5, 88, 96, 116, 156, 160
  flight to Baghdad-Rome, 99–100 (fig. 21), 166, 172, 175
  pro-shah manifestations, 105–6, 108–10, 123, 125, 130, 132, 136, 139 (fig. 31), 147, 148 (fig. 32), 150, 154, 168

Pahlavi, Reza Shah, xi, 11, 12, 13, 16, 17, 43, 67, 81, 101, 102 (fig. 22), 128, 129, 147, 149, 157, 179
Pan-Iranist Party, 126–7, 129, 208n.41, 219n.36, 222nn.34, 36
Parcham'e Islam, newspaper, 21
Perron, Ernest, 64, 99, 185n.35, 205n.15
Pezeshkpour, Mohsen, 127, 227n.34
Pezeshkzad, Iraj, 233n.1
Pirnia, Hormoz, 76
Pishevari, Jaafar, 182n.24
Pravda, 5

Qajar, Ahmad Shah, 54, 212n.81
Qājār dynasty, 19, 31, 157, 183n.31, 183–4n.31
Qajar, Hamid Mirza, 183–4n.31
Qajar, Mozafar'uddin Shah, 12
Qajar, Nasser'uddin Shah, 19
Qajar, Sarem'odolleh, 183–4n.31
Qanatabadi, Shams, 199n.32, 201n.56
Qashqā'ei tribe, 14, 147
Qavam, Ahmad, viii, x
  and Azerbaijan crisis, 14–16, 159, 180n.11, 181nn.13, 19, 182nn.22–3, 183n.26
  and *noh'e esfand* (28 Feb. 53) crisis, 76, 163
  and *Siy'e Tyr* uprising, 54, 55 (fig. 13), 56, 159
  lobbying for premiership with Britain, 53, 67, 160
Qodveh, Mohammad-Reza, 219n.43
Qotb'zadeh, Sadeq, 177n.11
Queen Mother (Tajol'molouk Pahlavi), 53
Queen Soraya, x, 76, 94, 99, 100 (fig. 21), 205n.6

Rafi'ei, Qaem'maqam, 184n.33
Rafsanjani, Ali-Akbar Hashemi, 176n.1
Rahimi, colonel Azizollah, 206n.24
Ra'in, Parviz, 218n.24
Rashidian, Asadollah, 90, 94, 184n.33, 126 (fig. 27), 165

Rashidian brothers, 67–9, 77, 84–5, 87, 104–5, 117, 119, 121, 125–6, 130, 138, 141–2, 144
Rashidian, Qodratollah, 184n.33
Razmara, General Ali, vii, x, 22–3, 24 (fig. 4), 25–6, 28–30, 37, 40, 80, 161, 186n.45, 188n.61, 189n.67, 190n.4
Reza Khan, 13, 19, 31, 54, 67, 152
  see also Pahlavi, Reza Shah
Riahi, General Taqi, 63, 95–6, 112, 166
Rohani, Colonel, 223n.70
Rolin, Professor Henri, 53
Roosevelt, Kermit, x, xi, xv, 2
  and the CIA internal history *Overthrow*, 8, 106, 121(E), 170
  and TPAJAX assignment, 82, 92, 122
  blackmailing the Shah, 93–4, 165
  coaching Henderson, 133, 135, 167
  contradictions within or disclaimers by *Overthrow* (CIA internal history): 8–9, 106, 121(E), 124, 125, 128, 130, 133, 138, 143, 145, 154, 170
  debriefings in London and Washington, 7–8, 105, 132, 144, 172
  Eisenhower's view of, 7–8, 170, 178n.1
  family and career background 7, 123(26)
  interview with *World in Action*, 122(G), 130, 145, 225n.16
  managing a setback in Tehran, 105, 111, 118–19, 123–5, 128, 152
  obtaining Shah's clearance for publishing *Countercoup*, 7, 177n.14
  the issue of credibility of, xv, 4–5, 7–8, 114, 120–2, 138, 155, 168–9
  see also 93 (fig. 19), 97, 97, 140, 145, 151, 165
Roozbeh, Khosro, 189n.67
Ross, Thomas B., 7
Rougetel, le, Ambassador Sir John, 15, 186n.45, 188n.58, 202n.68
Rouhani, Fuad, 72–3

Sadiqi, Qolam'hossien, xi, xvi, 88, 106, 109 (fig. 23), 143, 217n.18, 220n.49, 222n.64
Sadr, Mohsen (Sadrol-Ashraf), 179n.4
Safavid dynasty, 18
Saleh, Ali-Pasha, 204n.92
Saleh, Allah'yar, 195n.47, 196n.71, 197n.6
Sanjabi, Karim, 88, 189–90n.1, 194n.38, 197n.4, 199n.33, 204n.92
Sanjābi, tribe, 147
Schwarzkopf, Norman, x, 5, 90–2 (fig. 18), 142, 212n.94
Schwind, Donald, 218n.24
Secret Intelligence Service (SIS)
  see MI6
Security Council, UN, vii, x, 16, 27, 35–6, 43, 44 (fig. 9), 45, 73, 145, 159
Seligson, Tom, 177n.5
Setāreh-Islam, newspaper, 226n.26
Shah, the, *see* Pahlavi, Mohammad Reza
Shā'hed, newspaper, 104, 125
Shahrestani, Ayatollah Kazem, 149
Shāhsavan, tribe, 147
Shayegan, Doctor Ali, 74
Shariat'madari, Ayatollah Kazem, 183n.28
Shinwell, Emanuel (Manny), 34, 158
Shepherd, Sir Francis, 26, 33, 40, 66
Shirazi, Ayatollah Mohammad-Taqi, 149
Shojā'at, newspaper, 231n.4
Shoja'eian, Lt. Ali-Ashraf, 214n.102
Sinclair, Major-General Sir Alexander, 8, 120, 178n.18
Siy'e Tyr (21 July 1952) uprising, viii, 54, 55, 57, 82, 87, 159, 160, 199n.28, 205n.3, 212n.82
Smith, General Walter Bedell, x, 84, 96, 97 (fig. 20), 121, 131, 134
Society of Retired Army Officers, 63
Sohayly, Ali, 179n.4
Stalin, Joseph, 14–16, 89, 159, 174
Stokes, Richard, 40, 42–3.
Sumkā, political party, 126

Supplemental Oil Agreement, 22–4, 28, 58, 61, 161
Sutten (US Consul-General in Tabriz 1946), 183n.27

Tabari Ehsan, 227n.45
Tabataba'ei, Ayatollah Mohsen Hakim, 149
Tabataba'ei, Seyyed Zia'undin, 13, 24, 30, 33, 39, 53, 66–7, 188n.61, 191n.6, 197n.7, 202n.68
Taleqani, Seyyed Mahmoud, 149
Tayyeb Haj-Rezaie, 231n.7
Tenet, George, 9
Tobacco boycott, 19, 185n.38
Towne, Gerald, 119
TPAJAX, viii, ix, xv, 1, 3, 4–8, 63
  alteration of, 91, 116
  bribing campaign, 87–8, 130, 137, 150, 165
  cause of failure, 95
  co-opting the Shah, 90–3
  cost of, 86, 122(F), 138, 170
  Eisenhower learning the failure of, 96–7
  failure of, 5, 94–6, 131, 133, 168
  grey and black propaganda, 98, 124, 128–9, 149, 151, 169
  Iranian assets, 85–6, 101, 125–30
  origins of, 68–9, 84–5
  planning, 86, 115, 144, 164–5
  planning errors, 86, 116, 171(14)
  structural link with the actual fall of Mosaddeq, 1, 113, 117, 130–1, 145–6, 155, 168(7), 171, 175
  see also 98, 104, 108, 113–14, 117–18, 120–4, 126, 130, 134, 137, 140–2, 144–6, 163, 167, 169, 171–3, 175
TPBEDAMN, 124, 126, 127, 160, 208n.41, 227n.36, 231n.12, 232n.14
Trott, A. C., 181n.14
Truman Library, 132–3, 167
Truman, President Harry, viii, x, xii, 23, 33–7, 40–1, 46, 47 (fig. 11), 50, 62, 68, 70–1, 97, 158
  Churchill-Truman joint oil proposal, 59–60, 161–2
Trygve Lie, 44 (fig. 9)
Tudeh Party, the, vii, xi, 3–5
  activities after the Shah's flight, 101, 107
  and assassination attempt against the Shah, 16, 21, 183n.30
  and Azerbaijan crisis, 15–16
  and Mosaddeq dispersal order, 107, 135–6, 167
  and Siy'e Tyr uprising, 55
  contacts with Mosaddeq on 19 August, 111
  early attitude towards Mosaddeq, 39, 161, 162
  fake Tudeh, 85,87, 124, 128, 129, 170
  growing strength of, 74, 205n.3, 84, 85, 87
  ideological drift after the Shah's flight, 99–100, 166, 175
  Mosaddeq's use of, 38, 74, 89, 103, 107, 111, 160
  origin and foundation of, 13–14, 157
  role played in unfolding the TPAJAX, 5, 95, 166
  see also 74–5, 82, 86, 105–6, 108, 113, 116, 119, 126, 127 (fig. 28), 133–5, 141, 143, 145, 147, 149, 150–1, 165, 167, 169, 173, 174
Tudeh Nafti (petro-Tudeh), 231n.12
Turkman, ethnic group, 147

United Kingdom (UK) see Britain
United Nations, x, 14, 33, 35, 43, 44, 56, 159
United States (US), the government of, viii, xiv, xv, 1–3, 5–7, 9
  and Azerbaijan crisis, 14–16
  and policy shift 'snuggling up' to Mosaddeq 96–7, 99
  and Razmara, 23–5
  and US embassy monitoring of 19 August developments, 110–11
  calling off TPAJAX, 121
  early attitude towards oil dispute, 35–8
  early efforts to resolve oil crisis, 40–1, 43, 46–50

final attempts to break oil deadlock, 71–2
Henderson meeting Mosaddeq, 133–5
plotting against Mosaddeq, 84–6, 89–90, 92–4
reaction in Washington to fall of Mosaddeq, 131–4
reporting TPAJAX *coup* failure to Eisenhower, 96
restraining British bellicosity towards Iran, 34
Truman-Churchill oil proposal, 59
see also 56, 61–2, 68–9, 74–5, 82, 103, 128, 141, 145, 160–4, 167, 175 (for CIA station activities in Tehran 16–19 August 1953, *see* CIA; and Roosevelt, Kermit)
Usoulīs, 18
USSR, 12, 14–16, 25, 33, 36, 82, 101, 174

Valatabar, Heshmattol'doleh, 163
Voshnouh village, 151, 153
Vosouq, General Ahmad, 199n.28
Vahedi, Seyyed Abdol'hossein, 79
Vakil, Mehdi, 44 (fig. 9)

Werbe, Susan, 177n.5
Wilber Donald, 8, 9, 21, 126, 128, 132, 137, 138, 151
Wisner, Frank, 84
Wise, David, 7
Woodhouse, Christopher, xvi, 8, 9, 65, 68–9, 84–5, 89–90, 106, 142, 146, 151, 191n.10, 192n.11, 193n.33, 202n.65, 203nn.78, 82, 209nn.52, 55, 220n.64, 212n.93, 219n.40, 230n.81
World Bank, vii, 48–9

Yazdanpanah, General Morteza, 63
Yazdi, Ibrahim, 177n.11
Yusefi, Lt. Colonel, 223n.70

Zaehner, Robin, 64–7, 85
Zahedi, Ardeshir, xvi, 76–7, 103–6, 117, 113 (fig. 25), 121, 123, 143, 154, 173, 201n.58, 206n.17, 208n.38, 210n.68, 213n.100, 214n.105, 217n.21, 218nn.23, 33, 222nn.59, 66, 224n.1, 225n.18
Zahedi, General Fazlollah:
and TPAJAX, 89, 91–2, 95–6
assuming power, 111, 145
biographical sketch, 81–2
cabinet minister in the Mosaddeq government, 31
changing plans, 106
emergence as opposition leader, 82, 83, 86
hideout, 121(E), 122(G), 222n.59
role in the 16th Majles elections, 28, 82
strategy following TPAJAX failure, 103–5
see also vii, x, xi, xvi, 4–6, 20, 28, 31 (fig. 5), 75–7, 81–7, 89, 91, 92, 95, 96, 99, 108, 113 (fig. 25), 114–25, 132, 136, 141–3, 154, 164, 165, 168, 171, 173, 203n.80, 208nn.38, 47, 209n.53, 211n.70, 213nn.99–100, 214n.105, 217nn.19, 21, 228nn.26, 32, 219n.46, 221n.56, 222n.59, 222n.64, 223nn.67–8, 224nn.1, 5
Zahmat'keshān Party (Toiler's Party), 58, 129 208n.41, 232n.28
Zand-Karimi, Colonel Mahmoud, 115–16, 222n.65, 223nn.67, 70
Zanjani, Ayatollah Reza, 149
Zarqami, Colonel Amir-Qoli, 105
Zirakzadeh, Ahmad, 190n.1
Zohari, Ali, 87, 199n.32
Zolfaqāri, tribe, 147